D0855549

Homosexuality

Homosexuality

RESEARCH IMPLICATIONS FOR PUBLIC POLICY

Edited by
John C. Gonsiorek
and
James D. Weinrich

Published in cooperation with the
Society for the Psychological Study of Social Issues

SAGE PUBLICATIONS
The International Professional Publishers
Newbury Park London New Delhi

Copyright © 1991 by Sage Publications, Inc.

All rights reserved. No part of this book may be reproduced or utilized in any form or by any means, electronic or mechanical, including photocopying, recording, or by any information storage and retrieval system, without permission in writing from the publisher.

For information address:

SAGE Publications, Inc.
2455 Teller Road
Newbury Park, California 91320

SAGE Publications Ltd.
6 Bonhill Street
London EC2A 4PU
United Kingdom

SAGE Publications India Pvt. Ltd.
M-32 Market
Greater Kailash I
New Delhi 110 048 India

HQ
76.3
.U5
H677
1991

Printed in the United States of America

Library of Congress Cataloging-in-Publication Data

Homosexuality: research implications for public policy / edited by John C. Gonsiorek and James D. Weinrich.
p. cm.
Includes bibliographical references and index.
ISBN 0-8039-4244-3. — ISBN 0-8039-3764-4 (pbk.)
1. Homosexuality—United States. 2. Homosexuality—Government policy—United States. 3. Gays—United States—Psychology. I. Gonsiorek, John C. II. Weinrich, James D.
HQ76.3.U5H677 1991 90-28341
CIP

93 94 15 14 13 12 11 10 9 8 7 6 5 4 3 2

Sage Production Editor: Michelle R. Starika

5

Contents

Preface
John C. Gonsiorek vii

Introduction
John C. Gonsiorek and *James D. Weinrich* xi

1. The Definition and Scope of Sexual Orientation
John C. Gonsiorek and *James D. Weinrich* 1

2. Homosexuality, Nature, and Biology: Is Homosexuality Natural? Does It Matter?
John A.W. Kirsch and *James D. Weinrich* 13

3. Masculinity and Femininity in Homosexuality: "Inversion" Revisited
Richard C. Pillard 32

4. Strange Customs, Familiar Lives: Homosexualities in Other Cultures
James D. Weinrich and *Walter L. Williams* 44

5. Stigma, Prejudice, and Violence Against Lesbians and Gay Men
Gregory M. Herek 60

6. Sexual Orientation and the Law
Rhonda R. Rivera 81

7. Psychological and Medical Treatments of Homosexuality
Charles Silverstein 101

8. The Empirical Basis for the Demise of the Illness Model of Homosexuality
John C. Gonsiorek 115

9. Constructionism and Morality in Therapy for Homosexuality
Gerald C. Davison 137

10. Sexual Orientation Conversion Therapy for Gay Men and Lesbians: A Scientific Examination
Douglas C. Haldeman 149

11. Homosexual Identity: Coming Out and Other Developmental Events
John C. Gonsiorek and *James R. Rudolph* 161

12. Lesbian and Gay Relationships
Letitia Anne Peplau 177

13. Lesbian Mothers and Gay Fathers
G. Dorsey Green and *Frederick W. Bozett* 197

14. Partner Notification as an Instrument for HIV Control
Edmund F. Dejowski, Lidia Dengelegi, Stephen Crystal, and *Pearl Beck* 215

15. AIDS Prevention and Public Policy: The Experience of Gay Males
John C. Gonsiorek and *Michael Shernoff* 230

Conclusion
John C. Gonsiorek 244

References 249

Index 286

About the Authors 291

Preface

John C. Gonsiorek

This volume began when two graduate students, dissatisfied with their disciplines' response to the public policy debates on homosexuality, decided to tackle the issue better than their more senior colleagues. They somehow succeeded. William Paul and James Weinrich, graduate students at Harvard in the mid-1970s, envisioned a pamphlet of one hundred pages or so, summarizing what science knew about homosexuality. As the project developed they involved me, then a graduate student in clinical psychology at the University of Minnesota, and Mary Hotvedt, in the process of completing her doctoral work in medical anthropology. As the four of us worked together, the scope enlarged and we became the Task Force on Sexual Orientation. It was clear that the project had become more than a pamphlet, and we began seeking sponsorship. The Society for the Psychological Study of Social Issues (SPSSI), Division 9 of the American Psychological Association, was the logical choice. SPSSI had developed and prospered since the 1930s as organized psychology's interface with social issues and public policy. Throughout SPSSI's history of careful objective analysis of social issues and courageous stands on their public policy implications, it has earned respect beyond the confines of academic psychology.

SPSSI's response was most generous. Under the leadership of two of the society's presidents, Lawrence Wrightsman and June Tapp, we were provided programming time at the American Psychological Association from 1978 to 1981 with which to hone our ideas, financial support, encouragement, critical feedback, and perhaps most important, mentorship. John Gagnon, Evelyn Hooker, and John De Cecco served as able advisers to the Task Force.

In 1982 the Task Force published its final report: *Homosexuality: Social, Psychological, and Biological Issues* (Sage Publications). Simultaneously, the mental health section of the Task Force report was published as a special issue of the journal *American Behavioral Scientist* in March 1982. The response to that first volume was positive. The Task Force disbanded, its mission successfully completed.

The decade of the 1980s, however, saw an intensification and polarization, not a resolution, of the public policy debates about homosexuality. The emergence of the religious right wing in the United States and its use of homosexuality as a scare tactic produced levels of distortion about what science knew concerning homosexuality that surpassed anything in the 1970s. The fear and panic that accompanied the AIDS (acquired immune deficiency syndrome) epidemic further impaired reasonable debate about the public policy aspects of homosexuality. On a positive note, the first waves of new information about homosexuality in the 1960s and 1970s attracted the interest of scientists and scholars from all disciplines. The 1980s witnessed an unprecedented development of knowledge and theory concerning sexual orientation. The four editors of the original 1982 volume had hoped the information would remain current for some decades, but that the need for it would lessen after the public policy debates had been resolved. The opposite occurred. There was more new information about homosexuality than anyone anticipated, rendering the volume dated, and the public policy debates became more acrimonious, making the need for an updated and more focused volume acute.

In 1987 William Paul and I began discussions with SPSSI to revise the volume for a paperback edition. William Paul's illness and eventual death from the complications of AIDS rendered him unable to participate in this revision. Jim Weinrich then took his place as coeditor. SPSSI, as before, provided the same catalytic environment of encouragement, critical feedback, and financial and technical support. This revision has also benefited from support and feedback from the Society for the Scientific Study of Lesbian and Gay Issues (Division 44 of the American Psychological Association), as well as from the Committee on Lesbian and Gay Concerns of the Board of Social and Ethical Responsibility of the American Psychological Association.

A multiauthored coedited volume results from the efforts of many more people than appear on the authors' list. Some individuals' contributions were especially noteworthy. Leonard Bickman, the chair of SPSSI's Publication Committee, was generous with his time and feedback. Terry Hendricks of Sage Publications is any editor's dream of managing editor and publisher. All of our authors were selfless in donating their time, energy, and labor, but three of them, Greg Herek, Letitia Anne Peplau, and Charles Silverstein, took a particular interest in the volume as a whole and provided meticulous and considered feedback. Clinton Anderson, Linda Garnets, Terry Gock, and Doug Kimmel also provided crucial assistance by reviewing the entire manuscript.

We dedicate this volume to our departed colleague, William Paul. We will long remember his ardent leadership of the Task Force on Sexual Orientation. We can think of no better memorial than to complete the project he twice spearheaded and attempt once again to provide a scientific base in understanding the public policy debates concerning homosexuality.

Introduction

John C. Gonsiorek
James D. Weinrich

This volume attempts to summarize what science knows about homosexuality and its relevance for public policy. Those for whom a survey is adequate will find the most relevant literature covered. Those who require greater depth can utilize the volume as a guide to more extensive sources.

The scholars who have contributed to this volume come from a variety of disciplines: social, clinical, and counseling psychology; law; psychiatry; social work; biology; nursing; and anthropology. This book does not attempt to address the complex range of concerns surrounding homosexuality as a social issue. Rather, it focuses on those issues that have been most central to current public policy debates about homosexuality. These include the nature and causes of sexual orientations; the reasons homosexuality is not a mental illness; the ethics of various mental health approaches to homosexuality; the effects of social and legal discrimination; newer biological and psychological understandings of homosexuality; homosexual people as couples and as parents; and the implications of the AIDS epidemic. The authors share a belief that scholarly explication of what science knows about these issues can clarify this controversial area in which discourse has typically been characterized by ignorance, distortion, and prejudice. The volume also shares a methodological perspective across many chapters, as a way to assist the reader to think critically about the material presented. In this manner, we hope to encourage readers to become discerning consumers of the scientific discourses on homosexuality, past, present, and future. The chapters are presented in a format accessible to the serious lay reader as well as professionals from various disciplines.

The past 25 years have seen intense, generally unresolved, and at times acrimonious debate about the meaning of homosexuality and the place of homosexual individuals in our society. Scientific information is often cited by proponents of all viewpoints to justify their positions.

Often, scientists and scholars have not spoken for themselves in these debates. Scientific and scholarly information abut homosexuality has been distorted and misused for political ends. Despite heterosexist bias having been thoroughly examined and critiqued (McDonald, 1981; Morin, 1977; Morin & Charles, 1981), it clearly persists.

The authors in this volume are unusual in their willingness to enter this debate. Their task has been a challenging one: To sift through the most important aspects of scientific knowledge on their topic and apply this to public policy debates in a manner that is objective, yet clear and uncompromising, when science does have something to say about homosexuality. To most Americans, homosexual activities and people have been mysterious. Since the mid-1950s when Evelyn Hooker did her pioneering work on psychological adjustment in homosexuals, there has been a steady accumulation of scientific information about homosexuality. To serious scientists and scholars, homosexuality and homosexual individuals are no longer mysterious.

Public policy debates about homosexuality include areas other than the biological and social sciences, such as moral values and religious concerns. This volume does not speak directly to those. We note, however, that proponents of all viewpoints have attempted to cloak themselves in the respectability of science. Not all religious and moral traditions are impervious to scientific understandings of human nature. For some traditions, science is important as a source of understanding, and we believe that this volume has much to offer those traditions that are receptive. We do not think it is too brash to say that those who call upon the biological, behavioral, or social sciences to support their points of view must seriously weigh the information contained in this volume if they are to retain credibility and integrity.

Selection of topics for this volume presented a challenge. We have often had to remind ourselves that issues that are settled for scientists and scholars (e.g., whether homosexuality is a biological aberration or an illness) are not settled for the public. Our perception of which topics are most crucial for the knowledge base of a general audience guided selection. We have also had to make some difficult decisions abut which areas have sufficient literature to warrant a summary of research findings relevant to public policy. Space constraints have been a consideration, as one of the purposes of this volume is to be accessible and affordable. Not everyone will agree with our choices, but we believe we have covered most, though certainly not all, topics germane to public policy debates. If limitations of space (and therefore, cost of this book) were not a factor, our next most logical choices would have been racial, ethnic, and cross-cultural diversity in depth; historical understandings; expanded legal coverage; the status of gay and lesbian youth; sexual orientation over the life span; and exploration of the relationships between homophobia, sexism, racism, and economic exploitation.

Like most scientific discourse, research on homosexuality has been filtered through societal biases. Among its other effects, this has meant that white, middle-class and above, adult, English-speaking males have been studied more than their numbers warrant. This situation showed some signs of improvement regarding women, who were more intensively studied in the 1970s and early 1980s than ever before. Ironically, the AIDS epidemic is again pushing research funding heavily in the direction of gay males to the exclusion of lesbians because of the vastly different HIV (human immunodeficiency virus) risk profiles of these two groups. (As a group, lesbians are probably at least risk based upon sexual orientation, while gay men are at greatest risk, based upon this variable.) The old sexist prejudices, though, have away of adapting themselves to new conditions, and much of the "new" male-oriented bias in research is simply that. Researchers have been considerably less sensitive to inclusion of nonadult and racial/ethnic minority populations in research, although a good deal of exciting work on identity development of this latter group is emerging. We have attempted to include information on women, non-middle-class samples, racial/ethnic minorities, and cultural diversity where it exists. We have been pleased to find this situation improved since we prepared the 1982 version of this book; we have been disappointed that so much distortion from equitable and representative sampling remains.

This volume begins with an exploration of the difficulties in defining and measuring sexual orientation and contains a brief introduction to the current debates about the "nature" of sexual orientation. Biological understandings of sexual orientation are then pursued from a variety of perspectives, including evolutionary and hormonal. Not only do these chapters by Pillard and by Kirsch and Weinrich provide a grounding; the ideas they elucidate are among the most misused in public policy debates. Weinrich and Williams introduce cross-cultural information, which develops another level of understanding sexual orientation.

Herek provides a thorough basis for understanding the social context of homosexuality as it affects both homosexual and nonhomosexual people. Rivera offers a similarly detailed review of the legal status of lesbian and gay citizens.

Silverstein initiates a series of chapters on traditional mental health concerns: diagnosis and treatment. He offers a historical perspective, critiques the intrusion of political agendas into mental health practice, and then reviews biologically based treatment modalities. The review by Gonsiorek follows, outlining the empirical reasons why the illness model of homosexuality was discarded. Davison then analyzes the ethical reasons why attempts to change sexual orientation are problematic, while Haldeman reviews the empirical literature on attempts to change sexual orientation, with special emphasis on the newer religiously oriented "conversion" treatments. In a sense, much of this section is "old hat" to those knowledgeable about mental health and sexual orientation. It is covered in such depth because the public policy debates about homosexuality continue to be cluttered with the discredited and obsolete belief that homosexuality is an illness, almost a decade and a half after it was depathologized. Further, in recent years, there has been an increase in religiously oriented conversion therapies. We judged this area to be one of the most persistently confusing for a lay readership, and so gave it considerable emphasis. For the professional reader, we believe our extensive coverage will provide a sound methodological understanding of these issues.

The next section samples what the newer lesbian and gay affirmative perspectives in psychology have to offer. Gonsiorek and Rudolph review identity development among lesbians and gay men, perhaps one of the issues most elaborated by this new perspective. The relationship of these ideas to racial/ethnic minority perspectives on identity development is briefly explored, and a proposed integration with self-psychology approaches is outlined. Peplau describes research on same-sex couples and places it in the context of understanding couples in general. Lesbians and gay men as parents may be one of the most common legal struggles pertaining to homosexuality today. Green and Bozett review what is known about homosexual people as parents.

No book written in the 1990s about homosexuality would be complete without discussion of the AIDS epidemic. Yet, in this area, it was hardest to decide which topics were most relevant. Where does scientific research have something to say abut public policy and AIDS, specific to homosexuality? Topics we considered had a tendency to mushroom, encompassing broad public policy dilemmas relating to health care resources, delivery systems, and other areas not specific to homosexuality. After some deliberation, we concluded that HIV infection prevention raised the greatest number of public policy issues specific to homosexuality. Dejowski and colleagues examine the empirical basis for the most commonly used prevention tool in public health, partner notification. Gonsiorek and Shernoff discuss what is known about HIV infection prevention strategies in gay men in the context of what is generally known about health behavior change.

A brief summary of the volume then follows. A master bibliography covers the entire volume, with one exception. The chapter on legal issues by Rivera retains its separate bibliography. A thorough bibliography is a useful tool for research and scholarship. The differences between legal and psychological citation systems are extensive. We decided it would be most useful for scholars in both areas to leave them separate.

This book has a narrow, almost unidimensional focus: What does science know about homosexuality and what does this mean for public policy? This focus is both an asset and a liability. We believe we have provided a sound introductory text, and a guide to further exploration of the literature to the serious student, both lay and professional. We are also aware of our own frustration in resisting opportunities to expand into related areas. We have opted, for better or worse, to do a limited task, hopefully well. The deciding factor was the lack of a focused comprehensive treatment of this area, except for our earlier 1982 version, which is outdated in part, and less focused than this volume. We hope others will use this volume to push the limits of scientific understanding of sexual orientation beyond the parameters in which this volume is contained.

1

The Definition and Scope of Sexual Orientation

John C. Gonsiorek
James D. Weinrich

The question of precisely who is and who is not homosexual is itself controversial. Various behaviors and individual life-styles have been confused with sexual orientation. Shively and De Cecco (1977) developed a useful distinction in dividing sexual identity into four parts. The first is *biological sex,* the genetic material encoded in chromosomes. The next is *gender identity,* the psychological sense of being male or female. *Social sex role* is adherence to the culturally created behaviors and attitudes that are deemed appropriate for males or females. Finally, *sexual orientation* is erotic and/or affectional disposition to the same and/or opposite sex.

It is important to note that the first three bear no necessary relationship to sexual orientation in any given individual. Each, however, has been confused with sexual orientation. Variations on these parameters (e.g., cross-dressing, sadomasochism, and fetishism) are not discussed here because they occur among both heterosexuals and homosexuals and are not specific to sexual orientation. *Gay* and *lesbian* are popular terms for people who define themselves as homosexual in contrast to the term *straight* used by gay people to describe heterosexuals, but also widely used by heterosexuals in other contexts. It is also important to note that a person's sexual behavior can be homosexual yet that person may not self-identify as gay.

The process of "coming out" and defining oneself as gay, together with the additional act of coming out publicly as gay, can create profound events in the lives of homosexual men and women living in a disparaging society, as described by Gonsiorek and Rudolph in this volume. Perhaps because of this, the term *sexual preference* is sometimes used. It might appear to outsiders that individuals going through this process have "chosen" their homosexuality. We suggest that the term *sexual preference* is misleading as it assumes conscious or deliberate choice and may trivialize the depth of the psychological processes involved. We recommend the term *sexual orientation* because most research findings indicate that homosexual feelings are a basic part of an individual's psyche and are established much earlier than conscious choice would indicate. Most experts in the area have concluded that sexual orientation is set by early childhood (Bell, Weinberg, & Hammersmith, 1981; Green, 1988; Money, 1988). The term *life-style* is also confusing because it suggests a unanimity in patterns of living that does not reflect the diversity within gay and lesbian populations. It also obscures many similarities between the lives of homosexuals and heterosexuals (see Peplau in this volume).

There is little unanimity about the use of the words *lesbian* and *gay* as opposed to *homosexual.* It can be argued that the word *homosexual* is problematic because it echoes with implications of diagnosis and pathology, it is archaic, and its root meanings are not entirely accurate. On the positive side, it has the benefit of having few implications for sense of identity and so can function in a more descriptive sense. It can be argued that the words *gay* and *lesbian* really describe a particular identity that goes beyond mere description, is not accurate for many homosexually behaving and desiring individuals and is primarily rooted in the sociopolitical context of the mid- and late-20th century Western world (although the use of both words to describe homosexuality has a venerable history). *Gay* may also connote frivolousness or triviality. *Lesbian,* however, lacks this connotation problem and may well be more precise and robust across time, at least in the Western world.

As editors, we have not attempted to impose any "politically correct" terminology upon the authors; some use one, the other, or both. The reader should be aware that all the words used can carry some excess meaning for someone, although *lesbian* comes closest to being ideal: nonclinical, nontrivializing, and few connotations other than a reasonably accurate historical one.

Bisexual experience is common both historically and currently, among individuals who self-identify as lesbian or gay. A cross-cultural study of male homosexuals in the United States, Holland, and Denmark (Weinberg & Williams, 1974) found that 36% to 59% of homosexual individuals studied (depending on the country) had had heterosexual intercourse. Yet these men thought of themselves as gay and were drawn from gay communities. The sexual experience of lesbians is at least as diverse, and probably more so (Bell & Weinberg, 1978; Reinisch, Sanders, & Ziemba-Davis, 1989), with estimates of 81% and 74%, respectively, of lesbian women who have engaged in heterosexual intercourse. The term *homosexual,* then, includes those who historically may have had heterosexual experiences. *Bisexual* is used only to indicate someone whose attractions are not *currently* confined to one sex.

Cultural factors are also relevant. Many societies do not conceptualize diversity in sexual behavior along dimensions of homosexual/heterosexual at all (Churchill, 1967; Ford & Beach, 1951). In some cultural/ethnic groups, both in and outside the Western world, same-sex *behavior* is not seen as homosexual *orientation,* which is defined instead by social sex role or participation in specific sexual acts. Finally, cultures, racial/ethnic groups within a culture, and social/educational classes in a culture vary in the existence and degree of negative sanctions associated with same-sex behavior or interest. (See also Weinrich & Williams, this volume.) These sanctions can affect the way sexual orientation is conceptualized, expressed, and reported in members of such groups.

In the remainder of this chapter we will summarize scientific research on the frequency of homosexuality in the general population and the difficulties in deriving these measurements. We will also discuss the way in which these scientific measurements are often abused politically.

THE INCIDENCE OF HOMOSEXUALITY

The scientific measurement of sexual behavior began with the work of Kinsey and his associates (1948, 1953). These were based on in-depth interviews, with approximately 20,000 subjects, covering a wide range of human sexual activities. Kinsey's data indicated an amount of homosexual activity greater than was previously acknowledged in U.S. society. The original findings have recently been updated, as Table 1.1 shows (Gebhard, 1972; Gebhard & Johnson, 1979).

These figures cannot be used uncritically. They describe a particular sample population at a particular time. Most of these statistics report behavior as opposed to inner orientation or fantasy, which will be discussed later. This fact alone should recommend caution to those who would conclude, for example, that many more men than women today are homosexual in orientation.

Other surveys (summarized by Gebhard, 1972) have tended to yield figures for exclusive homosexuals in the United States of about 2% to 5%. Meyer (1985), in a standard psychiatry text, estimated a prevalence of 4% to 6%. A telephone survey conducted for the *San Francisco Examiner* yielded 6.2% of national respondents and 10% of San Francisco respondents willing to identity themselves as lesbian, gay, or bisexual (Hatfield, 1989). In a cross-cultural study of same-sex behavior in men from France, the United Kingdom, and the United States, Sell, Wells, Valleron, Will, Cohen, & Umbel (1990) found that 11.6%, 7.8%, and 11.6%

Table 1.1
American Homosexuality According to Kinsey

	% Responding*	
	Men	*Women*
Had homosexual activity before puberty	47-57	30-43
Had more than "a little" homosexual fantasy during masturbation recently**	8-11	5-6
Had 5 or more partners or 21 or more orgasms from homosexual relations	10-17	3-5
Said he or she will probably have homosexual relations in the future	6-12	2-4
During most recent time period, had homosexual relations to orgasm and was		
never married	10-49	2-11
currently married	0-5	0-2
separated, widowed, or divorced	0-18	0-8

SOURCE: Adapted from Beghard and Johnson (1979). The authors warn that these figures underrepresent respondents with little education.
NOTE: Each range of percentages represents the second highest and second lowest figure for the various education/race/age breakdowns provided for that category.
*Respondents were of various races, educations, and ages over 16.
**Includes "present, but frequency unknown" category, the most common response.

of subjects, respectively, reported same-sex sexual behavior since age 15. Also, 10.8%, 4.7%, and 6.3%, respectively, reported same-sex sexual behavior within the last five years. This last is a powerful study, as it randomly surveyed large numbers of subjects (more than 5,700, roughly evenly divided among the three countries) and used well-trained field staff personally interviewing subjects. It can therefore stand as reasonably sound current national prevalence data.

A major problem facing such studies is the risk involved in self-disclosure, especially where the studies fail to ensure complete anonymity. It is possible, indeed quite likely, that these recurrent 2% to 6% figures represent an absolute minimum and that they represent homosexual individuals who are relatively open and who live within tolerant or cosmopolitan communities.

The work of Paul Cameron and associates (Cameron, 1986, 1988; Cameron, Proctor, Coburn, & Forde, 1985; Cameron, Proctor, Coburn, Forde, Larson, & Cameron, 1986) has received recent attention. Some of his statements appear scientific: "The only reports of reasonably randomly obtained, non-volunteer samples yielded estimates that about

98% of the general population is heterosexual" (Cameron et al., 1985), or "We found that about 2% of U.S. males claimed to be homosexual and about another 2% claimed to be bisexual in 1983" (Cameron, 1988). Cameron's work, however, is deeply flawed methodologically and contains misstatements even of his own previous results. For example, subjects in one of the two "randomly obtained" samples mentioned above (Cameron & Ross, 1981) answered a questionnaire whose first question was "When, in your opinion, does human life begin?" This and other political questions leading off the survey might have caused many respondents to decline to answer the questionnaire, but such bias was never considered. Likewise, Cameron's statement (quoted above) that approximately 4% of U.S. males were homosexual or bisexual is a misstatement of the data from his own survey; Cameron actually found that 5.8% of the men in his survey were homosexual or bisexual (Cameron et al., 1985). The 4% figure is the rounded version of a 4.45% *average* of the figures for men (5.8%) and for women (3.1%).

Scientists have a responsibility to be more accurate than this. Although the difference between 5.8% and 4% might not seem like much, the former is 45% higher than the latter (Weinrich, 1988a). Misstatements such as Cameron's do not represent scientific accuracy but rather are examples of right wing attempts to manipulate scientific data for political purposes. Cameron's intent appears to be to portray homosexuals as a rare minority and so inflate the incidence of HIV infection among homosexuals by reducing the absolute number of homosexuals estimated in the population. In a published letter (Cameron, 1986), Cameron attacked a previous author who was trying to estimate the proportions of homosexual men, drug abusers, and hemophiliacs with AIDS. To do so, one must divide the number of homosexuals with AIDS by the total number of homosexuals in the population under study, and so on with the other groups. As Cameron adjusted the absolute number of estimated homosexuals downward, the proportion affected by AIDS substantially increases—an attempt to make the rate of HIV infection appear higher among gay and bisexual men than it actually is.

WHAT DO THESE DATA MEASURE?

Most studies determine homosexual orientation by asking the individual, but few studies use objective observations to determine sexual orientation. The work of Kurt Freund and his associates is perhaps the most rigorous work in this area (Freund, 1974). Freund invented a device called a *plethysmograph* that fits over the penis and directly measures its blood volume; an analogous device can measure female genital blood flow. Sexual orientation—or, in Freund's terminology, "erotic orientation to body shape"—is observed by recording genital blood volume responses when the subject is shown photographs of naked people of various ages, appearances, and sexes.

Numerous studies have demonstrated the fundamental reliability and validity of this technique. (For a discussion of the ethics and limitations of plethysmography, see chapter 8 in Weinrich, 1987b, which also contains an extensive list of references.) Not surprisingly, plethysmography does not work well with involuntary subjects. It is therefore impractical to use it to determine the incidence of sexual orientations in the population at large. Nor can we assume a priori that erotic orientation to body shape correlates in any simple way with people's self-identification as homosexual or bisexual. The technique is scientifically useful, however, in demonstrating that sexual orientation (or erotic orientation) is not merely sexual behavior, nor is it just a behavioral choice (Freund, 1977; McConaghy, 1976). Freund has demonstrated that there are responses embedded in the nervous system that are related, however imperfectly, to what people term sexual or erotic orientation.

Those responses are distinct from actual sexual behavior. When an individual claims to be "cured" of homosexuality, for example, this usually means a cessation of homosexual *behavior.* Such individuals always or nearly always report that they are still responsive to same-sex desire, or feelings. Their behavior may have changed, but their orientation has not (see Haldeman's chapter in this volume for a further discussion).

By far the most common measurement has been verbal self-report. There are significant limitations to this method. First, individuals must accurately appraise their own degree of same-sex interests. As described in the chapter by Gonsiorek and Rudolph, individuals prior to the coming out process (and at times during and after this process) often distort their degree of same-sex interests as a way to defend against this realization. Therefore *when* one asks an individual (during adult development) about same-sex interests is crucial. Further, given the social condemnation of homosexuality, there are constraints on verbal self-report. Research subjects who have reasons to doubt the confidentiality or anonymity of the data or who are simply frightened of negative repercussions, regardless of guarantees of safety, are likely to underreport same-sex orientation. For example, as Ross (1985) noted in a cross-cultural sample of men from Ireland, Finland, Australia, and Sweden, individuals expecting the most negative reaction from others to their homosexuality are less likely to report homosexual activity in themselves. Similarly, Craig (1987) estimated prevalence of homosexuality among male drug abuse patients in treatment, and derived an 11%

figure. This was higher than expected, but he nevertheless concluded it was an underestimate because sexual orientation is easy to disguise. It is likely that self-report measures represent an underestimate, to an unknown degree, of homosexual orientation.

There are other problems with self-report, focused on how the data are conceptualized. Kinsey's group conceptualized sexual behavior as falling on a 7-point continuum from exclusively heterosexual (score of 0) to exclusively homosexual (score of 6). A person in the middle of the scale (score of 3) would be more or less equally bisexual, for example. Kinsey's work was revolutionary at the time because it suggested more same-sex behavior than was previously anticipated and also more clearly developed the notion of bisexuality. Kinsey's notion of a heterosexual/homosexual continuum challenged the dichotomous, either/or, view of sexual orientation.

There may be significant problems, however, with a single continuous scale. Shively and De Cecco (1977) expanded the Kinseyan continuum concept, adapting Bem's (1974) revisions of the concepts of masculinity and femininity. Shively and De Cecco suggested that a single continuous scale like Kinsey's might be insufficient to explain sexual behavior and orientation. They suggested that sexual orientation can be better conceptualized with two continuous scales. Separate ratings for homosexual and heterosexual behavior can then be made, and the ratings then graphed on "Homosexuality" and "Heterosexuality" axes that are perpendicular to each other. Their proposed scheme would eliminate a restrictive implication of the Kinsey scale, namely that the bisexual positions can appear to be watered down mixtures of the two dichotomized components and that one form of sexual expression is at the expense of the other. For example, in their scheme it would be possible to differentiate an individual who has a high degree of homosexual interests and no degree of heterosexual interest from an individual who has a high degree of homosexual interest and simultaneously a moderate or high degree of heterosexual interests. Such a differentiation is not possible with the simple Kinsey scale.

There are other considerations in the definition of homosexuality. The original Kinsey continuum readings used composite scores of sexual behaviors and fantasy to arrive at the ratings. It may be the case that a third aspect is also important: affectional, as opposed to sexual, orientation. This aspect refers to the sex with whom an individual prefers to relate on an affectional, intimate, or friendship-based level as opposed to sexual behavior or sexual fantasy level. As these three aspects may not be congruent, it may be useful to rate individuals separately on the three aspects of sexual behavior, sexual fantasy, and affectional orientation, which Klein, Sepekoff, and Wolf (1985) attempt to do with their Sexual

Orientation Grid. Berkey, Perelman-Hall, and Kurdek (1990) have recently described a similarly complex multidimensional scale for sexual orientation. Weinrich (1988b) has examined the eroticization of friendship as opposed to body shape in some detail.

As noted earlier, psychological processes, whether part of the coming out process or others, may intervene to restrict the accuracy of this information. Many individuals deny their same-sex feelings, and for other individuals self-identity and behavior are not necessarily congruent. For example, an individual may call herself lesbian and by that mean any complex arrangement of sexual, affectional, or political variables at a point in time. Gay men and lesbians may, at times, differ in the bases for self-definition, perhaps related to differences as males and females. For example, Golden (1990) describes how many lesbian women, and some heterosexual women as well, perceive choice as an important element in their sexual orientations. Lesbians appear to perceive affectional orientation and political perspectives as central to self-definition, while gay males appear to view sexual behavior and sexual fantasy as central. Since the organized lesbian and gay communities are nascent, the bases for self-definition can change over time as these communities evolve. It can safely be assumed that there is no necessary relationship between a person's sexual behavior and self-identity unless both are individually assessed.

Perhaps the most dramatic limitation of current conceptualizations is change over time. There is essentially no research on the longitudinal stability of sexual orientation over the adult life span. In other words, even if one could satisfactorily measure the complex components of sexual orientation as differentiated from other aspects of sexual identity at one time, it is still an unanswered question whether this measure will predict future behavior or orientation. Certainly, it is not a good predictor of past behavior and self-identity, given the developmental process common to most gay men and lesbians; i.e., denial of homosexual interests and heterosexual experimentation prior to the coming out process.

Recently, there was an attempt to overcome the inaccuracies of verbal self-report in a national sample survey (Fay, Turner, Klassen, & Gagnon, 1989). In this study, a substantial number of subjects skipped over or refused to answer questions about homosexuality—at least 223 out of 1,450 in this case, or 15.4%. This refusal rate makes it difficult to estimate the percentage of individuals with various degrees of homosexual experience, since the percentage of reported homosexuality may be less than 15%.

Some data from the Fay et al. (1989) study are presented in Table 1.2. The top half of Table 1.2 represents the percentages of men who reported particular levels of homosexual behavior at particular ages; the bottom

Table 1.2
Reported and Imputed Male Homosexual Behavior in a Random U.S. Probability Sample in 1970

Percent who reported homosexual contact to orgasm (of self or partner):

Age at last contact	*Once or twice*	*Rarely or occasionally*	*Fairly often*	*Total*
< 15	2.6	2.3	0.3	**5.2**
15-19	1.0	1.4	0.5	**3.0**
> 19	0.8	1.7	0.6	**3.1**
Total	**4.4**	**5.4**	**1.4**	**11.3**

Percentage who reported homosexual contact to orgasm, or to whom it was statistically imputed:

Age at last contact	*Once or twice*	*Rarely or occasionally*	*Fairly often*	*Total*
< 15	4.1	3.7	0.6	8.4
15-19	1.8	2.5	0.9	5.2
> 19	1.7	3.7	1.4	6.7
Total	**7.6**	**9.9**	**2.9**	**20.3**

SOURCE: Calculated from Fay, Turner, Klassen, and Gagnen, (1989), Table 2.
NOTE: Percentages are of the entire sample of 1,450 men (21 years old or older), not of particular rows or columns. Percentages might not appear to add correctly due to rounding error.

half represents the higher proportions to which the scientists *imputed* probable homosexual behavior. The process of imputation was statistical. The statisticians examined associations between those respondents who reported homosexual experience and those respondents' answers to certain other questions. They then extrapolated from such answers, and from demographic data such as age and marital status, to statistically guess the rate of homosexual behavior among the nonresponders. As is evident in Table 1.2, this imputation process roughly doubles the amount of probable homosexual behavior in all categories.

Such statistical guessing is a controversial but informative exercise. It suggests that those who refuse to respond to questions about homosexual behavior may be disproportionately likely to have homosexual experience. The imputed figures themselves might be underestimates, since homosexual contacts without orgasm in either partner were not included, and individuals who consider themselves to have a homosexual orientation but were celibate would not have been counted.

Given such significant measurement problems, one could conclude there is serious doubt whether sexual orientation is a valid concept at all. Indeed, there has been such debate, in the form of theories and reactions to them. *Social constructionism* suggests that there is nothing "real" about sexual orientation except a society's construction of it (see the works of Ettore, 1980; Kitzinger, 1987; Plummer, 1975; Weeks, 1985; and Weinberg, 1984 for various social construction approaches). Social constructionists conclude it is a fundamental logical error to look for "sexual orientation" in other cultures or in premodern times. There may have been same- or opposite-sex erotic behavior, but other cultures construct such behavior so differently from our own that it is useless to try to understand it in current Western terms. (This school of thought is discussed in more detail in the chapter by Weinrich and Williams in this volume.)

Essentialism suggests that homosexual desire, identity, and persons exist as real in some form, in different cultures and historical eras (see the works of Bell, Weinberg, & Hammersmith, 1981; Boswell, 1980; and Bullough, 1976 for different essentialist perspectives). Not surprisingly, social constructionists generally reject the possibility of biological factors in sexual orientation, while essentialists can accept (but do not necessarily require) biological factors. As with many dichotomous understandings of human behavior, interactionist or blended positions are the most likely to have empirical validity and heuristic value. For example, Williams (1986, p. 274) notes: "If behavior is socially constructed, of what is it constructed? What is the substructure on which a culture inscribes its variations?" (see also Epstein, 1987, for an overview of this debate). Our own position is an interactionist one. Within a more traditional psychological framework, this uncertainty about the nature and validity of the concept of sexual orientation can be viewed as a problem of *construct validity* (see Cronbach & Meehl, 1955).

Regardless of these philosophical debates, most present-day North Americans tend to label themselves homosexual, heterosexual, or bisexual despite the fact that these labels do not capture the full range of complexity of sexual orientation and sexual identity. This debate does, however, instruct us that cultural constructs about sexual orientation can have powerful effects on shaping self-concept and identity (for example, Schippers, 1990, p. 6, states: "What we are interested in in psychotherapy is the client's interpretation or reconstruction of his or her personal sexual history") as well as scientific discourse (for example Cass, 1983-1984, p. 121, notes that identity as a homosexual "can only arise in those societies where homosexual categorization is acknowledged").

THE POLITICIZATION OF DEFINITIONS OF SEXUAL ORIENTATION

The incidence of homosexuality raises problems in measurement that are interesting and important scientific problems. The public discourse on the incidence of homosexuality, however, often takes a more adversarial course. Arguments are sometimes made, for example, that the numbers of gay men and lesbians are "swelling," with the implication that this represents some sort of threat, recruitment, or plot. On the other hand, there are some attempts (e.g., Cameron's work, discussed above) to revise downward the number of gay men with the implication that this especially small group is particularly AIDS-infested or undeserving of civil rights because of their small numbers. We offer the following perspectives on this issue.

First, it is important to note that definitional problems are common in the social sciences. For example, in the 1960s and 1970s there was a vigorous debate between personality and social psychologists about whether personality variables exist at all. This is no trivial matter, as the description and measurement of personality was and is a core feature of certain aspects of research and applied psychology. The debate quieted down *without* being particularly resolved, and with both personality and social psychological theories enriched by the challenges. We are also reminded of the ferment in the 1960s and 1970s on the purported relationship between IQ and race. This is an instructive example of how certain data, contaminated by socioeconomic variables, could be manipulated and construed by scientists with racist or bigoted attitudes into a full blown "theory" that nonwhites had a genetic disposition to inferior IQ. Methodological and definitional problems in science are standard; indeed they are indications of vigorous scientific thinking. They are, however, easily abused for political purposes.

As the chapters by Silverstein, Davison, and Haldeman in this volume describe, scientists and health care practitioners have been as guilty of this bigotry as the general public. It is important to realize that whether the topic be race, sexual orientation, ethnicity, or others, scientists suffer from societal biases and bigotry no less than the general population. Given, however, the ethical and professional obligations of scientists and health care practitioners to operate without such bias, these examples raise a pointed ethical and moral challenge to the health care professions and the behavioral sciences about the professionally appropriate responses to individuals who encourage bias out of bigotry, ignorance, or both. Paul Cameron was, in fact, expelled from the American Psychological Association for violating the Preamble of the APA's "Ethical Principles for Psychologists." Generally, however, behavioral scientists are reluctant to censure colleagues for fear of inhibiting free exchange of ideas, unless the behavior is clearly egregious.

SUMMARY

The available research suggests that the incidence of homosexuality in the United States is currently in a range from 4% to 17%. Despite considerable definitional problems and difficulties in measurement, these figures appear to be sound or at least workable approximations. The definitional problems in the measurement of sexual orientation are no worse than others endemic in the social and behavioral sciences. They suffer, however, from the tendency for social science information to be misused by bigoted or ill-informed scientists and practitioners as well as the media and general public. The proper scientific and professional response involves both holding accountable those members who act unprofessionally and developing more rigorous models to address the real definitional problems involved.

Be that as it may, homosexuals as a group are the first, second, or third most numerous minority in the United States—depending on which variation of the estimates is used. There are significant definitional problems, the solutions to which will illuminate the nature of human sexuality. There is no serious doubt, however, that there is a very large group of people who consistently have same-sex behavior and interests throughout most of their lives.

2

Homosexuality, Nature, and Biology: Is Homosexuality Natural? Does It Matter?

John A.W. Kirsch
James D. Weinrich

> 1 For this cause God gave them up into vile affections: for even their women did change their natural use into that which is against nature: And likewise also the men, leaving the natural use of the woman, burned in their lust one toward another, men with men working that which is unseemly [Romans 1: 26-27].

One of the lessons of the history of science is that getting the Right Answer is, as often as not, a matter of asking the Right Question—or posing it in a scientifically testable way. As the quotation above suggests, people have for a long time wondered whether homosexuality is "natural" or "unnatural." They have also asked what causes homosexuality: for example, by wondering what went wrong in the childhoods of homosexuals to make them homosexual. But are these the Right Questions to ask?

Much of the controversy about such questions results from asking wrong questions, and then from attempting to answer them in a manner that ignores biology. In this chapter we will first explain why "Is homosexuality biologically natural?" is a Wrong Question. Then we will discuss how evolutionary theory and methodology provide a better framework for understanding homosexuality than most people realize—in particular, we will explain how it is that something might indeed have "gone right" in the development of homosexuality instead of having "gone wrong." And finally, we will discuss what consequences,

AUTHORS' NOTE: Besides those thanked in the versions of this chapter published in the first edition, J.D.W. acknowledges NIMH grants #43298 and 45294 for support.

if any, this knowledge has for the social debate on the acceptability of homosexuality.

IS HOMOSEXUALITY BIOLOGICALLY NATURAL?

Many people believe that what animals do is important in deciding whether homosexuality is biologically natural, so it is to the animal world that we will first turn, by summarizing some of the most recent information gathered by modern biologists on homosexual behavior in animals. But there is more to biological definitions of "natural" than animal behavior, so we will next discuss such evidence. (We will not discuss theories of naturalness in which biology does not play an explicit role, because Boswell [1980, especially chap. 11] has written the definitive discussion on this topic.) Finally, we will discuss why the question of naturalness is a Wrong Question to ask. Indeed, people often talk as if the connection between a scientific finding and its social consequence is obvious—but in this case it is not.

Homosexual Behavior in Animals

2 PLAYBOY: How do you explain homosexuality to a nine-year-old?

BRYANT: I explained in simple terms to the little ones that some men try to do with other men what men and women do to produce babies; and that homosexuality is a perversion of a very natural thing that God said was good, and that it is a sin and very unnatural. I explained to the children that even barnyard animals don't do what homosexuals do.

PLAYBOY: That's simply untrue. There is a lot of evidence proving not only that barnyard animals do engage in homosexuality but that . . . many primitive cultures [do too]. . . .

BRYANT: That still doesn't make it right (Kelley, 1978, p. 82).

In quotation 2, Anita Bryant asserts that barnyard animals don't perform homosexual acts. But consult the footnotes in Chapter 11 of the Kinsey reports (Kinsey, Pomeroy, Martin, & Gebbhard, 1953) and you will discover that homosexual behavior in the barnyard has been observed in bulls, cows, stallions, donkeys, cats, rams, goats, and pigs, and has been observed outside the barnyard in antelope, elephants, hyenas, monkeys, apes, rabbits, lions, porcupines, hamsters, mice, and porpoises. Churchill (1967, chap. 3) contains a compilation of other examples of homosexuality in animals. Interestingly, one of the first catalogues of examples of homosexuality among nonhuman animals, covering an extraordinary range of phyla, was published outside the usual scientific literature: it was André Gide's platonic dialogue, *Corydon*, published in 1926.

The problem with most such observations made through the 1950s and early 1960s is that they came from watching animals living in captivity—zoos or cages. Even though a behavior seen in captivity is almost always seen in the wild, it is often seen at an atypical frequency or in an atypical context. So it is very difficult to use these observations to reach conclusions about a behavior's evolution or function. This distinction can be crucial in certain definitions of "natural."

To answer these objections, let us discuss a few instances of homosexual behavior in the animal kingdom, considering only observations that could clearly be related to free-ranging populations living with little human interference (Weinrich, 1980a). We will start with the examples from "low" on the evolutionary ladder (although, as biologists, we do not enjoy using adjectives that are so judgmental), and move to those animals more closely related to humans.

Male-male sexual behavior as an expression of dominance. For the two examples we are about to discuss—lizards and sheep—we find male-male sexual acts performed as an expression of the dominance (superior strength, access to food or mates, and so on) of one animal over another. It would be hotly debated whether such acts are similar to anything at all in human homosexuality. These patterns are not consensual, and when they involve humans the men involved (prisoners) typically prefer heterosexual acts with women once they are released from prison. Accordingly, these men are not considered to be homosexually oriented. This implies that at best one might consider such behaviors in animals and humans to be part of the spectrum of male-male sexual behavior, but not part of what is ordinarily termed "homosexuality." With that qualification, let us proceed.

In a species of lizard (*Anolis garmani;* see Trivers, 1976), females maintain small territories in trees, several females per tree. Mature males maintain large territories (one to two trees), enclosing those of several females. Each male mates with females within his own territory. But sometimes there lives within a male's territory another male—one who is sexually mature but not yet grown large enough to be clearly distinguishable from females. (Males grow larger than females in this species.) Until such a male grows too large to look female-sized, he can copulate with females nearby. However, such a small male also acts like a female in copulation when the larger male comes around. Indeed, two such homosexual copulations between males in a wild population were recorded by Trivers (1976, p. 266).

In mountain sheep (*Ovis dalli stonei;* see Geist, 1975), male-male battles end with the losing ram being mounted (with an erection) by the winning ram. Intromission is suspected (Geist, personal communication), but is hard to document because of the coyness of other authors and because these observations were made at a distance. Another author (Denniston, 1980, p. 34) stated that feral male goats have been observed ejaculating in homosexual encounters.

As mentioned above, although these animal patterns involve sexual behavior between males, they are not of a homosexual orientation in the human sense. But there is a human analogy: In men's prisons, heterosexual men stronger or more dominant than others often force those weaker or less dominant to undergo anal intercourse. It is interesting to see that even when we look for examples not only of homosexual orientation but more generally of any sexual behavior between men, we can find examples in animals that share some similarities with human behavior (albeit atypical in this case).

> **3** Homosexual behavior has never been the main choice, or even a customary minor part of the sexual pattern, of any mammal living in the free state. The occasional mounting of male animals by other males—apes in particular—is not true homosexuality but is in part playful and learning behavior in the immature, and in part a way of avoiding violent fighting between two males [dominant bouts] (Hunt, 1974, p. 299).

Homosexual pair bonds. The vast majority of mammal species are not at all monogamous. However, a few mammals—and over 90% of bird species—are at least as monogamous as humans are. Biologists call the relationship between members of a monogamous, mated pair a *pair bond.* Since heterosexual pair bonds are most common in birds, it is in that group of animals that we might expect most easily to find examples of homosexual pair bonds.

In western gulls (*Larus occidentalis;* see Hunt & Hunt, 1977), most pairs are heterosexual: one male and one female. But in the population studied, 8% to 14% of the mated pairs cooperating in incubating the eggs laid in a given nest were female-female. These pairs engaged in most of the courtship and territorial behaviors shown by male-female pairs, and a few performed mounting and attempted copulation. In the best-studied case (Hunt & Hunt, 1977), seven of eight female-female pairs stayed together over more than one breeding season. Evidently, in some of these pairs a male must have at least every now and then been involved, because some of the eggs were fertile. There are now reports from two other species that show similar patterns in wild populations (ring-billed gulls and California gulls; see Ryder & Somppi, 1979; Conover, Miller, & Hunt, 1979).

Homosexuality as affection or practice. Field biologists studying the behavior of wild primates (monkeys and apes) have occasionally reported observing homosexual interactions in the wild, but virtually none of them has pursued or published these findings. Often, as in quotation 3, the homosexual behavior observed has been dismissed as mere dominance assertion (like that in lizards or sheep mentioned above). Sometimes such a dismissal is legitimate, for primates often do exhibit routine dominance mounts.

But other kinds of homosexual mounts also take place. Wild langurs (*Presbytis entellus,* a kind of monkey) of both sexes have been observed performing homosexual behaviors. Sarah Hrdy (personal communication) sometimes observed male-male mounts when an all-male group encountered a "harem group" of females whose male leader (and sex partner) was looking for food elsewhere. Hrdy said that this male-male mounting often involved high levels of excitement, frequent hugs, and other reciprocal acts unrelated to mere dominance interactions. Apparently, this is a means for members of an all-male group to enlist cooperation for an attempt to "steal" copulations from the harem male. It is as if the males were trying to show off to the females what good copulators they were. James J. Moore (personal communication) has confirmed these observations, having seen well over 40 male-male interactions in three months of field work.

Homosexual behavior between primate females has also been observed, and (in the reports we have been able to gather) assumes a remarkably consistent form. Typically, one female mounts another in a way that stimulates her own and/or her partner's genitals. Sexual excitation ensues, and sometimes orgasm is reached. Often, a female's estrous state correlates with her role in the activity. And less clearly sexual interactions (like "hide-and-seek " games) often invite or follow sex. (These generalizations were made from the following sources: langurs, Srivastava, Borries, & Sommer, in press; Hrdy, 1975, p. 237, and Hrdy, personal communication; rhesus monkeys, Akers & Conaway, 1979; stumptail macaques, Chevalier-Skolnikoff, 1974, 1976; and Goldfoot, Westerborg-van Loon, Groeneveld, & Slob, 1980.)

These homosexual patterns do not duplicate human homosexuality but do resemble certain aspects of human homosexual behavior. Most or all of females engaging in homosexual relationships also engage in heterosexual ones—although it would be hard to demonstrate which

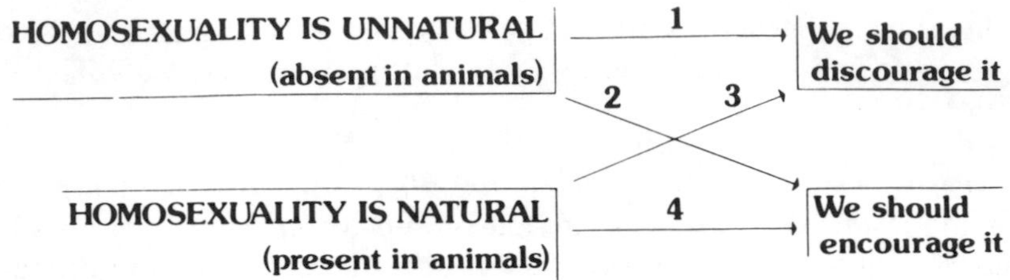

Figure 2.1. The Four Possible Relationships Between Facts of Nature and Attitudes Toward Homosexuality

NOTE: American society adopts argument #1: that homosexuality is unnatural, and that it should thus be discouraged. A quotation attributed to Lucian adopts argument #2: that homosexuality's very unnaturalness means it is a higher human trait and should be encouraged. Had the facts been considered different (lower left box), one would still be able to arrive at whichever conclusion one wished (arguments #3 and #4): see text. Most discussions implicitly assume that naturalness is directly related to presence in nonhuman animals. For the consequences of assuming this is not the case, see text. Diagram © 1977 by James D. Weinrich.

they prefer. Individual females certainly do have preferences, and pursue them, among both males and females. A situational bisexuality is one human parallel, as are certain forms of homosexual love.

What Does Homosexual Behavior in Animals Mean?

From the above discussion, it should be clear that animal homosexuality covers a wide range of behaviors, just as human homosexuality does. There is scarcely any aspect of human same-sex sexual behavior that does not have at least a moderately close parallel in some animal species (for more detail, see Weinrich, 1980). But what consequences does this evidence have for humans, as we address the question of what society should do about homosexual behavior?

First, certain statements about homosexuality in animals have to be changed. For example, views expressed in quotations 2 and 3 are no longer tenable.

But this does not necessarily mean that society will be forced to change its conclusions. This is clear from examining Figure 2.1 together with quotation 2. Bryant begins by asserting that homosexuality is unnatural because it does not occur in animals (upper left box), and concludes that homosexuality should be discouraged in humans (upper right box). The logic used (arrow #1) for a moment seems unassailable: for if homosexuality is unnatural, wouldn't it make sense to discourage it in humans?

The problem with this logic (or lack thereof) is this: If the facts about animal sexuality are different, would it not follow that homosexuality should be encouraged in humans? Bryant didn't think so; after being challenged, she changed her argument to arrow #3, concluding that even if homosexuality does occur in animals, "that still doesn't make it right."

This same game can be played on the other side, too, of course: Since every variation of human homosexuality takes place in some animal species, then homosexuality must be natural in humans—and, according to the logic of the upper half of the figure, should be allowed or encouraged. Once again, the logic presented (arrow #4) sounds fine until the alternative possible fact and argument (arrow #2) is considered. Just this was done in a fictional debate from ancient Greece as to whether homosexual love or heterosexual love is better (see pseudo-Lucian, 1967). In this debate, the advocate for the homosexual side argued that homosexuality does not exist in animals and heterosexuality does—and hence that nonprocreative homosexuality is superior to base, procreative, heterosexual lust. Clearly, even arrow #2 has had its supporters.

In fact, the whole enterprise—as symbolized in Figure 2.1—is bogus. When one rises above the *scientific* level of truth or falsity of any one "fact," or the appropriateness of any one arrow, we have to ask whether *any* of these arguments are valid. We take a jaded view and answer in the negative. When animals do something that people like, they call it "natural." When animals do something people do not like, they call it "animalistic." Likes and dislikes have been decided by a process outside the boundaries of Figure 2.1.

In short, it is a Right Question to ask whether homosexual behavior occurs widely in our species and in other species, and the answer to this question is yes. But to ask what this means for humans is a Wrong Question, or at least an oversimplified one.

Other Arguments That Homosexuality Is Unnatural

If asking about the implications of animal sexuality is a Wrong Question, then what about other ways of judging whether homosexuality is natural from a biological point of view?

> **4** Biologically, moreover, homosexuality is abnormal in the sense that no children can be born of it. It is true, of course, that even contraception is abnormal in this sense, but the heterosexual couple using contraception has it within their power to be fertile or not, as they choose, and even when they choose not to, they are still employing the neural, hormonal and muscular responses of sexuality in the fashion which evolution, with the goal of reproduction, cunningly designed to provide maximum reward (Hunt, 1974, p. 29).

Unfortunately for quotation 4, this is also a Wrong way to make an argument. A diagram similar to Figure 2.1 is easy to construct here, too. This quotation equates normality or naturalness with reproduction, and this is, to put it charitably, weak. In a later section of this chapter, we will discuss this in more detail. But even assuming that naturalness is equivalent to reproductiveness, this does not mean that heterosexuality is much better. For what of celibate priests and nuns? Or contraception? Wouldn't all these be condemned? Few systems of belief of which we are aware oppose both of these nonreproductive choices.

Quotation 4 also cites choice as the essential component of naturalness, but this is equally problematic. Consider heterosexual cases where choice is absent: coitus after sterilization, coitus by postmenopausal women, and attempts at coitus by physiologically impotent men. Or a case where choice is present but homosexuality is not involved: masturbation by heterosexuals after marriage. Quotation 4 would have to judge all these phenomena unnatural, too.

> 5 Homosexuality is biologically absurd and anatomically ridiculous (Swanson, 1974, p. 108).

In quotations 4 and 5, teleology enters the debate. Teleology is the notion that things are directed toward an end or shaped by a purpose. In quotation 4, "evolution" by natural selection is stated to have "the goal of reproduction," and has "designed" sexual processes to feel the best when used for reproductive ends. Teleology's presence in quotation 5 is signaled by the words "absurd" and "ridiculous," which require some system to make sense of or give a goal to sexual acts.

The ultimately sensible system referred to implicitly or explicitly in these two quotations is evolutionary biology. The essence of evolutionary biology is comparison—of individuals within a species, of different species, of communities of species. If a structure, function, or behavior occurs in a number of individuals or species, and if it persists through several generations, then that feature can be presumed to serve some evolutionarily advantageous function. That is, it must contribute to the persistence of the species by giving an advantage (or at least no reproductive disadvantage) to the individuals possessing that feature. Thus, when teleology is invoked for a particular characteristic, one must form a hypothesis about its value to the organism and test this notion against what is known of the natural history of the animals or plants that have it—and of those that do not. That is, if heterosexuality is a persistent feature of a species, it must have an evolutionary purpose or function; the same is true of homosexuality.

> **6** There is also recent evidence that homosexuality may be related to certain biological pathologies: Research on animals and human beings . . . has shown that virilizing hormonal imbalances in the mother during gestation lay down important male patterns of reactivity in the developing neural structure of a female fetus, who later on, in childhood and beyond, exhibits classically male patterns of play and aggressiveness. Comparable congenital "errors," it is thought, may underlie some or much of the classically female behavior of some male homosexuals (Hunt, 1974, pp. 299-300).

The evidence referred to in quotation 6 is reviewed in Chapter 3. Most of it has been disproved; although the part relating to neural patterns laid down in the fetus is not disproved, it is not yet widely accepted. Even if it turns out to be true, on what grounds are the prenatal hormones judged to be "imbalances" and "errors"? It is not much help to define the precursors to be imbalanced and in error just because the results produce (in theory) homosexuality; that would be circular. How do we know that homosexuality is something having gone wrong, rather than a normal variation in which something went right?

> **7** Heterosexual object choice is determined from birth due to cultural and environmental indoctrination. It is supported by universal human concepts of mating and the family unit with the complementariness and contrast between the two sexes (Socarides, 1970, p. 1201).

There are several variations of the argument in quotation 7, all of them assuming in common that homosexuality must be unnatural because there is no conceivable socialization mechanism by which it could occur—only a pathological version could have produced it. This argument falls on the border between biology and psychology, and is a perfect example of the problems faced by the standard psychoanalytic view of homosexuality, which has only very recently begun to diversify—notably with the publication of two books (Friedman, 1988, and Isay, 1989), which are the first psychoanalytic publications taking the view that homosexual and heterosexual orientations are a pair of normal variations in human development.

The biological assumption in quotation 7 is that we know how the central nervous system learns sexual preferences—by "cultural and environmental indoctrination" in this case. That is, a person acted upon by these socializing agents in these ways turns out not to exhibit homosexuality under normal conditions. If homosexuality results, then something must have gone wrong.

But such a theory of human learning is incorrect. Biologically based predispositions in learning patterns do exist, and cannot be understood without references to evolution and biology (Seligman, 1970, and Lockard, 1971, provide reviews). There is considerable evidence that humans *often* fail to be influenced by even the most stringent cultural and environmental indoctrination, as anyone who has struggled for freedom in an oppressive regime knows. Normal human behavior is more complicated than stimulus and response.

Conclusions

There is a long and sordid history of statements about human uniqueness. Over the years, we have read that humans are the only creatures that laugh, that kill other members of their own species, that kill without need for food, that have continuous female sexual receptivity, that lie, that exhibit female orgasm, or that kill their own young. Every one of these fanciful statements is now known to be false. To this list must now be added the statement that humans are the only species that exhibit "true" homosexuality. Does anyone ever state that we alone exhibit true heterosexuality? Yet we take a skeptical view of efforts to make some kind of simple connection between facts about nature and conclusions about social policy. Figure 2.1 is far too applicable to far too many situations to be ignored.

DOES HOMOSEXUALITY SERVE AN EVOLUTIONARY PURPOSE?

In the first half of this chapter, we argued against the misuse of teleology in debates about whether homosexuality is biologically natural. But some Right Questions ask about teleology in sexual behavior, and it is to these questions that we now turn.

We start with a paradox. The criterion of evolutionary success is number of offspring (reproductive fitness) and consequently the continued (and sometimes increasing) representation of genetically determined traits in succeeding generations. How can homosexual behavior persist if exclusive homosexuals do not reproduce as frequently as heterosexuals? And if, as is certainly true, natural selection can (and has) over the millennia acted upon genes that influence the sexual object choices of individual animals and humans? By definition, natural selection ought to eliminate any gene predisposing toward or even permitting the expression of homosexual behavior extensive enough to interfere with or reduce reproduction.

Three mechanisms, to our knowledge, have been advanced whereby the paradox is resolved: (1) density-dependent population control, (2) balanced polymorphism, and (3) kin selection for a type of altruistic behavior associated with homosexuality. We will discuss each in turn.

Density-Dependent Maintenance of Homosexuality

It has been suggested that homosexual behavior is useful (and therefore selected for in humans) precisely because homosexuals leave fewer offspring—that homosexuality is a natural population control measure that comes into operation when numbers become too great (that is, its frequency depends on the population density). The idea that homosexuality can provide a mechanism to limit population size may be traced back at least to Aristotle. In his comments on the Cretan constitution in *Politics* (1272a, 23-26), Aristotle states that "companionship" or "intercourse with males" was encouraged among Cretan men in order to reduce population pressure on the food supply. And in our era, the science fiction author Arthur C. Clarke (1958) suggested the same.

Superficially, this is an attractive hypothesis, but its chief difficulty is that under conditions of high density the frequency of any gene disposing toward homosexuality would be drastically reduced, since individuals would not breed. Consequently, the representation of such a gene would decline in subsequent generations; eventually homosexuality would disappear. Moreover, biologists now regularly reject such "group selection" hypotheses, or accord them a minor role in facilitating evolution.

Additionally, the problems of overpopulation seem to be relatively new for humans—many if not most hunter-gatherer bands are not now (and apparently rarely were) on the brink of starvation (Yellen, 1990), and we are not aware of any evidence that homosexuality was less common in uncrowded societies than it is in ours. One would expect more homosexuality where there is more overcrowding, but Kinsey was fond of pointing out that some of the most uncrowded areas of the world (northern Africa, for example) had some of the longest-lasting homosexual traditions. Furthermore, this explanation ignores comparative information from other species, which in most cases do not face the problem of keeping populations down, yet often display homosexuality.

Balanced Polymorphism

A more plausible hypothesis has been advanced by G. E. Hutchinson (1959), one of evolutionary biology's most respected practitioners, who was the first biologist to attempt to place homosexuality in an evolutionary context. His important paper has been strangely neglected, especially in view of the fact that it occurs in the same volume as one of Hutchinson's most famous essays.

Hutchinson suggested that the persistence of a gene for homosexuality might be explained by positing some special advantage for *heterozygotes.* Readers who already know what heterozygotes are may skip to the next paragraph, but for those who are rusty on genetics, let us explain. Every genetically determined characteristic has its ultimate physical basis in a particular fragment of the long, twisty molecule known as DNA. Each such fragment is located on the chromosomes that are found in the nuclei of living cells. Each individual has two rather similar sets of chromosomes in each cell, except in the eggs or sperm, which have half the number of chromosomes, or one representative of each pair. At fertilization the normal double number is reestablished: One set is contributed by the father's sperm and one by the mother's egg. Since every person has two of each kind of chromosome, he or she also has two "doses" of each gene, which may be exactly alike or somewhat different. Alternative forms of the same gene are known as *alleles,* and are the reasons for variation in some traits, such as eye color. If the alleles received from mother and father are the same, an individual is said to be *homozygous;* for an eye color gene there are two kinds of homozygotes: double-blue or double-brown. But if the contributions of the parents are unlike, the offspring is said to be *heterozygous.* For many familiar traits, including eye color, one allele is *dominant*—that is, it is expressed at the expense of the other. For example, a person heterozygous for eye color has brown eyes—not blue, and usually not something in between. However, for other features, a heterozygous combination (like the blood type AB) might result in both traits being expressed. Of course, in any given instance there may be many more than just two different alleles in the population at large (although no *particular* person can inherit more than two kinds of alleles).

Establishing a possible genetic basis for behavioral traits such as sexual orientation is enormously more complex than doing so for eye color or blood type, and if there is such a basis, almost certainly many different genes play a role in determining the trait. Nevertheless, the simple genetic model involving a few basic kinds of response and their genetic causes provides at least a starting point for discussion.

The presumption is that there is a gene determining sexual preference or orientation and that there are two alleles of that gene that determine, in one case, a disposition toward heterosexuality and, in the other, toward homosexuality. Exclusive homosexuals or heterosexuals would carry a double dose of the corresponding allele; such uniform individuals are termed "homozygotes." If the heterozygotes (individuals with both kinds of allele) had increased fitness (that is, left more offspring than did homozygotes), it would explain why the allele for homosexuality is maintained even though homozygous homosexuals do not have offspring.

This selection for heterozygosity is the essence of *balanced polymorphism,* where an allele that would be deleterious in the homozygous state is maintained in a population due to the advantage it confers when in combination with the alternate allele. In humans, as every high school biology student learns, the allele causing sickle-cell anemia is lethal in homozygotes, but in heterozygous combination with the "normal" allele confers resistance to malaria, thus explaining the high incidence of sickle-cell anemia in populations exposed to malaria. Such heterozygous advantage is the least we must demand from a "homosexual gene" in Hutchinson's theory if it is to be maintained in a population, for it is surely too much to expect that repeated mutation maintains the conspicuous incidence of homosexuality.

Unfortunately, there has been no test of Hutchinson's hypothesis, and it would be difficult to construct a crucial experiment. For one thing, and as noted, it hardly seems likely that only a single gene is involved in determining sexual orientation. Nevertheless, one of us (Weinrich, 1987a, 1987b) has proposed a theory in which bisexuals would have higher reproductive success than either exclusively homosexual or exclusively heterosexual individuals in societies in which everyone is forced or expected to marry. We will leave the details of this theory in the original references for interested readers, but the main tenet is that married individuals who fall in love only with members of their own sex are much less likely than heterosexuals to have illegitimate children.

This is not at all a forced example. Historical study (Boswell, 1980) demonstrates that homosexuality in association with heterosexuality may have been common in certain societies; consequently, homosexuality in these contexts may not have reduced individual fitness. In the oft-cited example of ancient Greece, men were ordinarily expected to marry and breed as well as take male lovers. As for the United States, the well-known studies of Kinsey and his associates (1948) showed that only 4% of American males were *exclusive* homosexuals for a period of three years prior to being interviewed, whereas a much higher percentage had had both homosexual and heterosexual experience.

We can also think of another test that focuses on the use of homosexual behavior in a nonsexual context—that is, a behavior that superficially involves sexual arousal and sometimes even orgasm but that is not primarily or originally engaged in for sexual pleasure or for love. This explanation assumes that such an indirect usage of sexual responses might contribute to social—and hence ultimately reproductive—success, but not directly by way of the sexual acts performed. For example, a large percentage of observations of homosexuality in animals does involve the transfer of superficially sexual behavior to situations involving territory maintenance or dominance displays (for example, the mounting behavior in lizards and mountain sheep mentioned earlier in this chapter). If there is any heterozygous advantage, it might well be connected with the ability of those individuals (heterozygotes) who are capable of homosexual behavior, as well as inclined to reproduction, to secure a dominant position in the social hierarchy, maintain a territory, and secure mates.

Ritual mountings of subordinates by dominant males are common in mammals, although as always we must make sure that no one mistakes this kind of behavior for the loving or entirely lustful sexual behavior that goes on between consenting adult *Homo sapiens.* That said, heterozygous advantage of a roughly similar type could account for some homosexual behavior in human societies. For example, a good deal of such behavior in prisons, fraternities, and the military is really about territory and dominance, and not primarily for sexual gratification or for love. It is therefore performed, for the most part, by people who think of themselves as heterosexual, not homosexual, and in a very real sense these self-identifications are correct. It ought to be possible to collect data to see whether such bisexually behaving heterosexuals indeed have higher than expected reproductive success by virtue of their increased interest in dominance or other manipulative behaviors. We suspect that such information might already be available for animal and even human societies. If a gene promotes reproductive success through homosexual acts, it will spread under the action of natural selection just as genes for heterosexual behavior have.

Altruism and Kin Selection

But of course, these interactions are not what most people think of when they think of homosexuality. Although sex and dominance are not exactly strangers in human sexual behavior, everyone would agree that they are two distinct concepts, and that most people's sexual interactions are not as inseparably dominance-oriented as they so often are in animals. Accordingly, let us try to understand, particularly among humans, those instances of homosexual relationships that must be considered simply loving and erotic.

If there are fewer examples of these in animals, it is probably because ethologists have traditionally avoided imputing emotions to other organisms. (This may be changing. The usefulness of ascribing emotions and consciousness to animals is argued positively by Griffin, 1976.) Purely loving homosexual relationships between individuals are harder to explain genetically, yet we think this can be done if the question of selective advantage is not posed so simply. The context of evolutionary argument has, until recently, been one in which only sexual behaviors leading directly to reproductive fitness of the individual were considered subject to natural selection. In fact, natural selection often operates more subtly than this.

As with many issues in evolutionary biology, we may profitably return to Darwin's work for insight. He recognized a class of hereditary behaviors that, benefiting other individuals, apparently *reduce* the behaving organism's own reproductive output. Such individuals appear to be acting altruistically—that is, performing actions that are of benefit to other members of the same species but seem to detract from the altruist's own reproductive fitness. But examples of such "reproductive altruism" are numerous. For example, one individual may utter an alarm call that alerts its fellows to the approach of a predator, while endangering the signaler itself. Or young may be cared for cooperatively (seemingly regardless of which individuals are the genetic parents of the young). Food sharing is known in some species of insects and mammals, and certain insect castes (for example, worker bees) will commit suicide (as a result of stinging) in defense of the colony. (A thorough treatment of reproductive altruism, with numerous examples, is found in Wilson, 1975a.) Once again, it would seem likely that genes predisposing toward such behavior ought to be speedily eliminated by natural selection.

Yet altruism is common in many species; it must be the case that altruistic behavior is genetically determined and is therefore favored by natural selection. Of necessity, altruism is correlated with being social, and understanding how altruism can evolve and be maintained depends on appreciating this fact, its connection with sexuality, and the importance of mating between genetically different individuals.

Recall that every member of a sexually reproducing species carries two alleles representative of each gene, derived from each of its two parents (for example, two brown-eyed alleles, or one for brown eyes and one for blue eyes). There is a sense in which the members of a population may be said to share these genes in their various forms. During each episode of reproduction the members of the interbreeding group "pool" their alleles, from which the next generation's individuals, with their allele combinations, are constructed.

The hypothesis of *kin selection* introduced by W. D. Hamilton accounts for reproductive altruism by showing that if the recipients of altruistic acts are close relatives of the altruist, the altruist is in effect favoring its own success because its kin will very likely share many of the altruist's alleles (drawn from the common and limited gene pool). Thus, if an altruistic act increases the recipient's likelihood of leaving or raising offspring, then the chances of multiplying the representation of "altruism genes" is also increased—because, in the terminology of kin selection, the *inclusive fitness* of the group has been raised. In acting altruistically, the individual is really serving its own interests (or, more precisely, those of its genes).

For readers interested in the details of the kin selection theory, there is a variety of sources. A superb popular account is Dawkins (1976). The mathematics and many of the deeper insights were developed by Hamilton in a series of papers starting in 1964, of which the last is an excellent review (Hamilton, 1972). A mid-level account can be found in Wilson (1975a) or Trivers (1985).

As Wilson points out, such analysis "has taken most of the good will out of altruism" (Wilson, 1975a, p. 120). Humanists will argue that there is a residuum of altruism not covered by the kin-selectionist's austere definition, including acts performed without any conscious thought or apparent possibility of reproductive gain. We remain uncommitted on this point, since Trivers (1971; see below) is extremely clever in attempting to account for even these, but henceforth we use the more restricted phrase "reproductive altruism" to emphasize that we are talking about a special biological definition. In reproductive altruism, within species as well as between them, nobody seems to be doing anything for nothing!

Wilson has suggested (1975a, chap. 27; 1975b; 1978) that homosexuality might be one expression of reproductive altruism in humans: In primitive societies, he argues, homosexuals, freed from the need to direct energy toward raising their own offspring, may have given a special advantage to their kin by providing various forms of help that would not have been available in kin groups lacking homosexuals (since all members would be competing to raise their own offspring). Increase in the fitness of the homosexuals' near relatives would have favored the continued representation of helpful individuals whose helpfulness was correlated with possession of "homosexual genes." Of course, there is a trade-off of advantages and disadvantages here, since too many individuals with such genes means no reproduction at all, but a balance between heterosexuals and homosexuals would have been struck by natural selection.

There is a string of "ifs" in Wilson's argument, but it is worth noting that in primitive societies homosexuality is often valued in the sense that shamanism is frequently associated with homosexual behavior (see Churchill, 1967; Weinrich, 1977; and the chapter by Weinrich and Williams in this book). Moreover, Wilson's idea is scientifically sound in that it predicts certain consequences of the hypothesis under changed environmental conditions. One is that with the trend away from close kin groups consequent on modern transportation, human beings will become even more mixed genetically as they tend to live more distantly from near relatives. Selection for altruistic acts then can no longer operate according to a model requiring close relatedness of altruist and recipient. Thus, the number of homosexuals should decrease gradually as the conditions favoring selection for homosexuality become rarer. Although in theory this suggestion should give heart to the conservative politicians who seem apoplectic in the face of the advances made by gay liberation, somehow we suspect that a new Figure 2.1 will come into play, and this suggestion will end up being used and abused by all sides in the debate. Actually, any observation of a diminution in genetically based homosexuality will be difficult to disentangle from the presumably opposite effects of sexual liberation, since such cultural changes are so much more rapid than those alterations that occur on an evolutionary time scale. And in the short run, AIDS is devastating homosexual male communities (while leaving lesbians even less affected than heterosexuals) far more quickly than any possible adverse natural selection can. Of course, since most of the gay men lost to AIDS would not have had children anyway, there is little or no direct effect on the numbers of gay men to be expected in the future.

Trivers (1974) also accounts for homosexuality in the context of kin selection, but by suggesting that it is an outcome of the clash of interests between parents and their offspring. He shows that there are situations in which it will be to parents' advantage not to allow their young to reproduce; evolution may have selected for the ability of young to become homosexual in such circumstances. Although Trivers's explanation bears a formal resemblance to psychoanalytic ones accounting for homosexuality as a result of early experiences, the environmental situation that a psychiatrist would interpret as pathological is, in Trivers's interpretation, a necessary outcome of the maximization of inclusive fitness. That is, it is an attempt to understand what went right, not what went wrong.

Finally, there is another theory that suggests that homosexuality's evolution may be closely connected to our species' unique properties: namely, the theory of "reciprocal altruism" (Trivers, 1971). Trivers argues that unrelated humans (and members of other species), with their long memories and persistent relationships, perform reproductively altruistic acts with the expectation that sometime in the future those acts will be reciprocated, and in the knowledge that the possible consequences of not acting altruistically may be disagreeable. While reciprocal altruism must have evolved in a situation where the participants were closely related, such behavior need not be limited to kin groups, and has now become characteristic for our species. The key to the theory is to explore biologically the fact that *everyone gains fitness if they cooperate.* The biological aspects of this insight are so important, according to some scientists, that the consequences are found throughout the sciences (a good example of a book applying these sociobiological insights to psychology is Glantz & Pearce, 1989).

CONCLUSIONS: BEYOND BIOLOGY

Let us now return to the questions posed in the title of this chapter. Is homosexuality natural? If so or if not, does it matter?

Of the 7 quotations listed in the first half of this chapter, we have discussed only 6 in detail. Quotation 1, from the King James translation of the Bible, has until now escaped our scrutiny. Note that this quotation doesn't really present an argument, but merely the opinion that homosexual acts are "against nature," "vile," and "unseemly." Frankly, we believe that many arguments against homosexuality are mere opinion, like this one. Although people are entitled to their own opinions, we believe it can be of value to consider where those opinions come from, and to try to evaluate them scientifically.

We have stressed evolutionary theories so strongly in this chapter because, despite all the opinions that biological facts cannot be permitted to directly influence moral choices, many people still believe that evolution cannot possibly explain a nonreproductive behavior. That belief is incorrect. Despite the difficulties of testing evolutionary explanations, they are appealing because they go a long way toward explaining the cross-cultural occurrence of homosexuality, the failure of classic psychoanalytic explanations, and the lack of clear-cut physical determinants of sexual orientation and preferences. In suggesting how homosexual behavior may have contributed to the real evolutionary success and unique adaptations of human beings, they make homosexuality a very natural thing—regardless of whether its occurrence in animals is "natural" or not.

Human homosexuality is as biologically natural as human heterosexuality. This is a carefully worded statement. Its only social consequence is that biological arguments cannot be used to distinguish morally between homosexuality and heterosexuality. Like left- and right-handedness, the two are expressions of a single human nature that can be expressed differently in different individuals.

If homosexuality is therefore part of the range of behavior that has molded *Homo sapiens,* then it is clear that homosexuality is not a disease, and certainly the general object should not be to "cure" it. At the same time, should the hypothesis of reproductive altruism be shown to have factual support, we would hope that its acceptance would not lead to a narrow expectation of how homosexuals should behave (e.g., by decreeing that homosexuals must act altruistically in return for being allowed to indulge in formerly prohibited acts). To do so would be to fall prey to the *naturalistic fallacy:* that what is, is right. There are plenty of morally wrong things that are perfectly natural in the evolutionary sense. If the biologically natural is used to support ethical decisions, it is important that the facts be correct. But the illogical arguments of Figure 2.1 lurk everywhere. Thus, our aim in this chapter has not been to justify homosexual behavior on biological grounds, but rather to show that the frequent condemnation of gay people because homosexual behavior is unnatural must be rejected because the premise of unnaturalness is false.

The fundamental and profound paradox of human biology is that it frees us to act sometimes unbiologically. With due respect for the environment and for each other, that ought to be possible: Part of the joy of being human often lies in transcending the biological constraints that have, nevertheless, shaped us. We should not fear learning what made us the way we are, for by doing so we can understand our future. Is homosexuality natural? Yes, as natural as heterosexuality is. Does it matter? Society says it does, and if we understand what made us the way we are, we can reach our own decision.

3

Masculinity and Femininity in Homosexuality: "Inversion" Revisited

Richard C. Pillard

Students of human sexuality have observed, rightly or wrongly, that homosexual (HS) men often appear more "feminine" than heterosexual (HT) men and HS women seem more "masculine" than their HT counterparts. The assertion that HS individuals often exhibit behavioral traits more or less characteristic of the opposite sex appears in writings of the pioneers of sex research. Richard Krafft-Ebing, author of the influential 19th-century text *Psychopathia Sexualis,* classified his male HS cases according to the associated loss of masculine personality characteristics ("eviration") or the acquisition of feminine ones ("effemination"). (Some of these we would now recognize as transsexuals, e.g., cases #108 and #109.) Of HS women he observed, "the sexual anomaly often manifests itself by strongly marked characteristics of male sexuality" (Krafft-Ebing, 1901, p. 392). British sexologist Havelock Ellis noted, "there is a distinctly general, though not universal, tendency for [male] sexual inverts to approach the feminine type, either in psychic disposition or physical constitution or both. . . . In inverted women some degree of masculinity or boyishness is equally present . . . " (Ellis, 1922, pp. 287-288).

These observations led some early sex researchers to regard homosexuals as a transitional or intermediate stage between male and female (Hirschfeld, 1936; Ulrichs cited in Kennedy, 1980/1981). They were, of course, aware that many HS men were entirely masculine in temperament and behavior and many HS women entirely feminine; but they did not recognize the contemporary distinction between homosexuality and transsexuality. Thus, a relationship between homosexuality per se and atypical gender behavior might have seemed stronger than it is if some gender atypical individuals like transsexuals were wrongly included as homosexual, and if a substantial number of gender *typical* individuals leading covert HS lives managed to escape notice. (I adopt "atypical gender behavior" as a descriptively neutral term to avoid prejudging whether the behaviors in question are either etiologically or phenomenologically "masculine" or "feminine.") Indeed, the frequency of homosexuality was greatly underestimated by sex researchers until the Kinsey surveys of 1948 and 1953. The first question asked in this review, therefore, is how persuasively the association between homosexuality and atypical gender behavior is supported by current research.

A more subtle question is to what extent atypical gender behaviors in fact resemble characteristics of the opposite sex. When gay liberation pioneer Harry Hay was teased, as a boy, by other boys for throwing a baseball "like a girl," he was surprised to find the girls telling him otherwise. "You don't throw like a girl, you throw like a sissy," they said. So if these atypical gender behaviors do indeed resemble the opposite sex on initial impression, do they also exhibit similar manifestations and derive from similar biological and psychosocial precursors (insofar as these are known)?

To some observers, the resemblance is striking. They point to the early onset of these behaviors (sometimes commencing in the third year of life), to their pervasiveness, and to a seeming "innate" quality—all of which resemble the typical development sequence of gender characteristics of the opposite sex and could suggest common causal factors, possibly in the prenatal hormonal environment (Dörner, Rohde, Stahl, Krell, & Masius, 1975; Ward, 1974).

On the other hand, some psychoanalysts suggest that the seeming femininity of HS men (little is written about women) derives from factors in the child's family milieu, for example, a weak, passive father, and represents an unconscious effort to avoid the dangers of maleness or to caricature or mock the female role (Bieber et al., 1962; Gadpaille, 1972; Ovesey & Woods, 1980; Stoller, 1968). Some authors use the adjective "effeminate" instead of "feminine" to signal this distinction. As Stoller says, "the connotation of 'effeminate' is that one is mimicking and therefore that there is hostility in what is clearly an acted role" (Stoller, 1967, p. 314). For recent critiques of analytic theory see Friedman (1988) and Isay (1989).

Still others, especially sociologists, see the atypical gender behavior of HS men (and presumably of HS women) as an attempt to adopt or conform to a socially prescribed role. They suggest that for young men, "feminine" or "camp" mannerisms may be acquired or become temporarily exaggerated to serve as symbols of membership in the gay subculture (Goode, 1981; Omark, 1978; Simon & Gagnon, 1967). According to Goode, "In early stages of exploring the possibility that they 'are' gay, a high proportion of young men adopt the effeminate mannerisms of the homosexual stereotype (or 'role'). It is not until they are more thoroughly socialized . . . that they realize that there is no necessary connection between homosexual behavior and effeminacy . . . " (Goode, 1981, pp. 57-58; see also the comments following that article by Whitam, Omark, & Goode.)

The terms in Table 3.1 permit us to be more specific about the intent of this chapter. Individuals of different sexual orientation are to be compared on measures of sex-dimorphic characteristics and of gender role. If HS men differ significantly from HT men in the direction of the average score earned by women, they may be considered more "feminine" on the measured trait. This concept is presented schematically in Figure 3.1. A similar logic applies to assessing the "masculinity" of HS women. However, because of an unfortunate bias in research, most of the existing studies have been done only on men. Indeed, the literature on women is so meager that reviewing it may be useful chiefly to point out how androcentric the field has been (Katchadourian, 1979, especially discussions by Katchadourian and Maccoby; Money, 1980; Money & Ehrhardt, 1972; Stoller, 1968).

PSYCHOLOGICAL STUDIES

Sex-dimorphic traits in HS individuals have been assessed by three complementary strategies: (1) prospective studies of behaviorally feminine boys and "tomboy" girls, (2) retrospective studies of childhood atypical gender behavior in adult men and women, and (3) studies employing psychological and other measures to compare HS and HT adults on traits known to be gender dimorphic.

Prospective studies. Behaviorally feminine boys (sometimes called sissy boys) are often seen in early childhood but few have been followed through the development span until they acquire a stable adult sexual orientation. For those who have been followed, the evidence is striking and consistent across studies: HS (and possibly transsexual) men are greatly overrepresented (Bakwin, 1968; Green, 1976, 1979, 1985, 1987; Green, Roberts, Williams, Goodman, & Mixon, 1987; Lebovitz, 1972; Money & Russo, 1979; Zuger, 1966, 1978b, 1984, 1988).

Green emphasized the variability of outcomes; some feminine boys do seem to make a completely HT adjustment (though few of these have been followed beyond age 25) and many nonfeminine boys appear to develop an HS orientation. Also, boys in the summarized studies were referred for evaluation because of concern about their feminine behavior (in only a few cases because of other symptoms). We do not know what happens to feminine boys who are not referred, whose behavior may have been better received by the family, or what fraction of the population they comprise.

Table 3.1

Term	*Definition*	*Measure*
Atypical gender behavior	Behaviors that do not conform to the gender norm.	See Table 3.2
Gender identity or Core gender identity	The individual's primary identification as male or female, usually a permanent trait determined in childhood.	Clinical interview or Self-report
Gender role	A set of expectations (roles) about how men and women ought to behave in a given culture at a particular time in history.	Bem Sex Role Inventory or Personal Attributes Questionnaire
Sex-dimorphic or sex-typical characteristics	Those traits, behaviors, cognitive abilities, etc., on which men and women in a given culture reliably differ.	Fe scale of the California Psychological Inventory or M scale of the Guilford-Zimmerman Temperament Survey
Sexual orientation	The erotic attraction to one sex or the other; homosexual, bisexual, or heterosexual partner choice.	Kinsey Heterosexual-Homosexual Continuum (7-point scale)

NOTE: "Sexual orientation" is a standard term, but several writers emphasize the heterogeneity among individuals with similar orientation (Bell & Weinberg, 1978; De Cecco, 1981). Some also caution against assuming that bisexuals invariably stand in the middle of a continuum between HS and HT (MacDonald, 1983).

Variants of "gender identity" include male-to-female and female-to-male transsexuals and some transvestites. It is now recognized that transsexual and transvestic individuals are not necessarily HS in their orientation and that whatever atypical gender behaviors they may show are not necessarily relevant to those of HSs (Freund, Steiner, & Chan, 1982; Green & Money, 1969; Stoller, 1968).

Some writers use "gender role" to encompass "sex-dimorphic characteristics," but useful distinctions may be made between these concepts (Maccoby, 1979). In particular, different instruments are used to measure them; also, gender roles are specifically human attributes while sex-dimorphic characteristics may be examined in animals as well. It should be clear that these definitions are purely phenomenologic and imply no assumption about mechanisms or causes.

Retrospective studies. These have examined whether HS adults recall atypical gender behaviors in childhood more often than do their HT counterparts. In these studies, subjects were usually asked about preference for doll play, domestic activities and dressing up, preference for playmates of the opposite sex, preference for (or avoidance of) rough-and-tumble games, being regarded by peers as a "sissy" or a "tomboy," and the wish to become a member of the other sex.

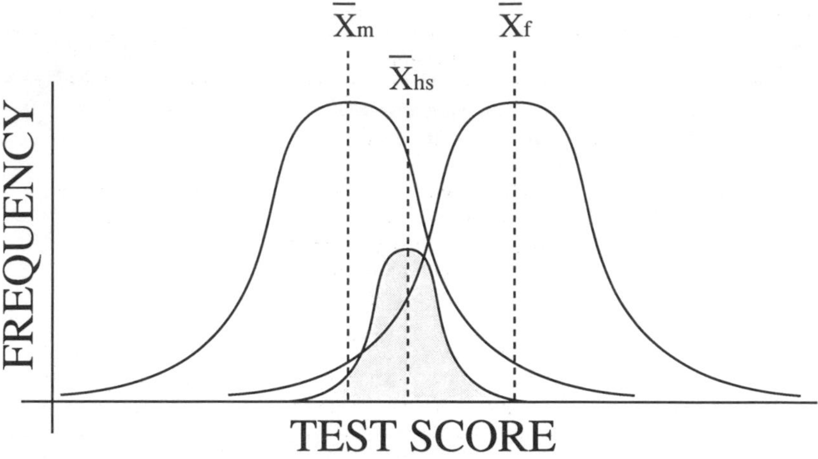

Figure 3.1.

Despite variation in subject selection and item administration, all studies reviewed found that both HS men and women scored very significantly higher than HTs on the atypical gender items (Bell, Weinberg, & Hammersmith, 1981; Bieber et al., 1962; Evans, 1969; Friedman & Stern, 1980; Grellert, Newcomb, & Bentler, 1982; Harry, 1983c; Henry, 1948, cited by Zuger, 1978a; Holeman & Winokur, 1965; Poole, 1972; Saghir & Robins, 1973; Thompson, Schwartz, McCandless, & Edwards, 1973; Whitam, 1977b; Hockenberry & Billingham, 1987).

Caution is in order about the accuracy of recollections of childhood behavior. Carrier (1986) has called attention to possible sources of distortion in data such as those reported. However, these reports are so consistent with direct observations of gender-atypical children and seem to have such culturally invariant properties (Whitam, 1980, 1983) that it is hard to wholly discount their credibility. Indeed, Zuger (1988) argues that childhood gender-atypical behavior is not simply a marker of adult homosexuality but the beginning of homosexuality itself. For a review of this topic, see Zucker (1985).

HS and HT adults compared. Masculinity-femininity (MF) testing was originated in the 1930s by two of the pioneers of personality testing, Lewis Terman and Catherine Miles, as a spin-off of their study of intelligent children. Terman and Miles noticed that their boy and girl subjects gave consistently different responses to a number of test items. They did not insist that these differences ought to be encouraged, nor that they formed any kind of "objective" standard against which boys and girls ought to be measured. Rather, they used a rationale called "criterion validity," which means that differences were demonstrated to exist between women and men in a particular culture (ours) at a particular time (the 1930s), but without reference to any underlying theory. The result was the Terman and Miles MF scale (Terman & Miles, 1936).

Although this scale was developed to be able to "tell the boys from the girls," Terman and Miles decided to try to use it *within* a single sex (males), and accordingly administered the scale to 123 HS men. They found this group to be "by far the most feminine-testing group encountered in our investigations."

Currently, a widely used test containing an MF scale is the Minnesota Multiphasic Personality Inventory (Dahlstrom, Welsh, & Dahlstrom, 1975). However, use of this scale is controversial, because of the inclusion of such items as #69, "I am very strongly attracted by members of my own sex," and #179, "I am worried about sex matters." Obviously, if these items figure into an MF scale, they will confound the issues of sexual orientation (to whom are you attracted) and MF (do you answer other items in ways that are psychologically similar to your own sex or the other sex). This diminishes the validity of the MMPI MF scale as a pure measure of sex-dimorphic traits.

Other scales do better. Several standard psychological tests, such as the California Psychological Inventory (CPI) and the Guilford-Zimmerman Temperament Survey (1978), include MF scales composed purely of criterion-validated, sex-dimorphic items (some of which are listed in Table 3.2). The CPI femininity scale has even been validated cross-culturally (Gough, 1966; Levin & Karni, 1971; Nishiyama, 1975).

Several other adjective checklists plus the Goodenough Draw-A-Person test and others have also been used with HS adults to measure the MF dimension.

As suggested above, some workers are not sure that when a man shows "feminine" behavior it is the same femininity seen in women. Kurt Freund and colleagues have accordingly put together a scale (the Feminine Gender Identity scale, or FGI) that measures feminine wishes and recollections in men. Responses to its items are almost certainly sex dimorphic, even though not everyone agrees with Freund's methods of constructing the scale (Blanchard & Freund, 1983; Freund, Langevin, Satterberg, & Steiner, 1977; Freund, Nagler, Langevin, Zajac, & Steiner, 1974).

Table 3.3 list studies in which HS and HT individuals were compared on one or another psychological measure of characteristics presumed (or demonstrated) to be sex-dimorphic. Most of these studies can be faulted, because the measures were not validated carefully enough, or because the HS sample was small, atypical (patients, prisoners, members of gay groups, and so on), or not well matched with HT controls.

Table 3.2
Sample Items From Three Self-Administered Psychological Questionnaires

Measure	*Sample items*	*Scored for*
Fy scale from the California Psychological Inventory	A windstorm terrifies me.	Femininity
	At times I feel like picking a fight with someone.	Masculinity
	I would like to be a nurse.	Femininity
M scale of the Guilford-Zimmerman Temperament Survey	You would rather go to an athletic event than a dance.	Masculinity
	You cry rather easily.	Femininity
	You are willing to take a chance alone in a situation where the outcome is doubtful.	Masculinity
Bem Sex Role Inventory		
Masculinity scale	Self-reliant	Masculinity
	Defends own beliefs	Masculinity
	Strong personality	Masculinity
Femininity scale	Yielding	Femininity
	Flatterable	Femininity
	Eager to soothe hurt feelings	Femininity

NOTE: The Fy and M scales have items that are scored one-dimensionally: that is, masculinity and femininity are viewed as two ends of a single continuum. The Bem is scored two-dimensionally: that is, masculinity and femininity are viewed as two independent dimensions.

Nevertheless, in virtually all of them, HS men achieved significantly more feminine scores and HS women significantly more masculine scores than their HT controls. In many cases, this was the largest and in some cases the *only* difference noted on the tests administered. (This outcome cannot be accounted for by nonspecifically greater psychopathology in HS subjects: see Gonsiorek, 1982a, and Gonsiorek's chapter in this volume.)

Sex role inventories developed by Bem (1974, 1978, 1979, 1981) and by Spence and Helmreich (1978) are different from the gender-dimorphic scales cited above in two important ways. First, these inventories were constructed by asking judges to select items representing *desirable* attributes for each of the sexes. Thus, they explicitly reflect social judgments of the stereotypic female or male sex role. Interestingly enough, when groups of female and male subjects rate themselves on these inventories, some of the items prove to be sex dimorphic, but many are not. The second important difference is that masculinity and femininity are treated as separate and potentially *independent* (orthogonal) traits. That is, a subject can be rated as "masculine," as "feminine," as both ("androgynous"), or as neither ("undifferentiated"); see Figure 3.2.

Table 3.3
Summary of Studies in Which Psychological Tests Measuring Putatively Sex-Dimorphic Traits Were Administered to HS and HT Subjects

Study Authors[a]	*Tests*[b]	*Subject sex*[c]	*Cross-gender response?*[d]
1. Aaronson & Grumpelt (1961)	MMPI	M	Yes
2. Adelman (1977)	MMPI	F	Yes
3. Berdie (1959)	ACL	M	Yes
4. Bernard & Epstein (1978a, 1978b)	ACL	M	Yes
5. Braaten & Darling (1965)	MMPI	M	Yes
6. Buhrich & McConaghy (1979)	DAP, CPI	M	CPI Yes; DAP No
7. Burton (1947)	MMPI	M	Yes
8. Clarke (1965)	ACL	M	No
9. Clingman & Fowler (1976)	ACL	M	Yes
10. Cubitt & Gendreau (1972)	MMPI	M	Yes
11. Darke & Geil (1948)	MMPI	M	Yes
12. Dean & Richardson[e] (1966)	MMPI	M	Yes
13. Doidge & Holtzman (1960)	MMPI	M	Yes
14. Evans (1972)	ACL	M	Yes
15. Fromhart (1971)	MMPI	M	Yes
16. Gough (1952, 1966)	CPI	M	Yes
17. Heilbrun (1976)	ACL	M and F	Yes
18. Horstman (1972, 1975)	MMPI	M	Yes
19. Krippner (1964)	MMPI	M	Yes
20. Langevin, Paitich, Freeman, Hardy, & Mann (1978)	MMPI	M	Yes
21. Manosevitz (1970a, 1970b)	MMPI	M	Yes
22. Money & Wang (1966)	DAP	Boys	Yes
23. Ohlson & Wilson (1974)	MMPI	F	No
24. Panton (1960)	MMPI	M	Yes
25. Pierce (1973)	MMPI	M	Yes
26. Singer (1970)	MMPI	M	Yes
27. Stringer & Grygier (1976)	DPI	M	Mixed[f]
28. Terman & Miles (1936)	MF	M	Yes
29. Whitaker (1961)	DAP	M	Yes
30. Williams (1981)	MMPI	M	Yes
31. Wilson & Greene (1971)	CPI	F	Yes

NOTES: a. These studies represent all the articles located by a Medline search of *Index Medicus* and *Psychological Abstracts* through January 1990, plus references cited therein.
b. Key to studies listed:
MMPI Minnesota Multiphasic Personality Inventory Mf or Hsx scale
ACL An adjective checklist of adjectives differentially endorsed by women and men
DAP Draw-A-Person test
CPI California Psychological Inventory Fe or Fy scale
DPI Dynamic Personality Inventory
MF Masculinity-Femininity Scale
c. Gender of subjects: F = Female; M = Male
d. "Yes" means that HS subjects scored significantly in the direction of the other sex for the scale cited. For the DAP, "Yes" is recorded if HS subjects drew opposite-sex figures significantly more often than HT subjects.
e. For a critical comment, see Zucker and Manosevitz (1966).
f. Of 16 sex-differentiating scales, 8 distinguished HS from HT men in the feminine direction, 6 showed no significant difference, and 2 distinguished HS men in the masculine direction.

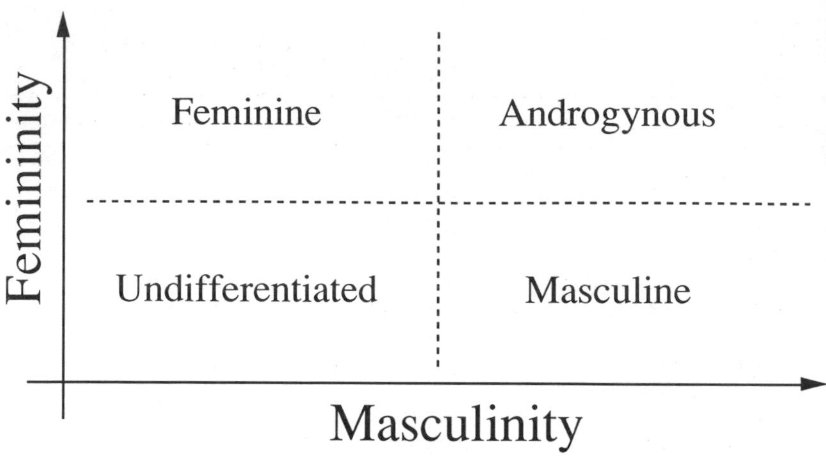

Figure 3.2. Masculinity and Femininity in the Bem Sex Role Inventory

Sample adjectives from the Bem Sex Role Inventory are included in Table 3.2. In four studies using these questionnaires, HS men scored more feminine and HS women more masculine than HT controls (Bernard & Epstein, 1978a, 1978b; Hooberman, 1979; Oldham, Farnill, & Ball, 1982; Spence & Helmreich, 1978). However—and this is important—very often HS men scored *just as masculine* as HT men and HS women scored *just as feminine* as HT women. This is not a contradiction, because these scales are specifically set up to make possible such an outcome.

OTHER STUDIES

It is now time to turn to variables that are not so dependent on pencil-and-paper reports: variables such as body build, motor behavior, cognitive abilities, and verbal interaction patterns. The data available here are from scattered and generally small-scale studies, so the review will be brief.

Several investigators have collected anthropometric data on HS men and found that they had narrower shoulders in relation to pelvic width and less muscle strength (Coppen, 1959; Evans, 1972). One sample of HS women were reported to be taller (Griffiths et al., 1974); another sample of 123 HS women had larger busts and waists but were not taller (Kenyon, 1968). In one study of several hundred HS women, the "dominant" women were taller, broader across the shoulders, and more muscular with bigger arms and legs than the "passive" partners (Perkins, 1981) (with apologies for the quaint terminology). Since all but one of these studies are at least 15 years old, one wonders if they would stand up to modern research standards. Surely some attempt at replication is needed before they can be accepted as established findings.

When it comes to cognitive abilities such as performance on IQ tests, truly unbiased studies have only very recently begun. In the first half of this century there was a great deal of interest in this question, presumably because it was assumed that HS individuals would score lower than HTs on these tests. In fact, results suggested no differences or perhaps that HSs scored higher (Weinrich, 1978, 1980)! There are, however, reliable sex differences in IQ test subscores, women excelling at verbal fluency and sustained attention, while men tend to be better at mathematical and spatial tasks. The hypothesis, then, is that HS and HT individuals might differ from each other in these subscores, in ways that parallel these male-female differences.

Several research teams have compared HS and HT individuals on tests of cognitive abilities. One study (Wilmott & Brierly, 1984) suggested that HS men were better on verbal but not on spatial tasks as compared with HT men (a confirmation of the "femininity" hypothesis) but the other studies came up with completely different results (Gladue, Beatty, Larson, & Staton, 1990; Sanders & Ross-Field, 1986, 1987). Still other researchers show little or no evidence of any differences at all (Baker & Ehrhardt, 1974; Dalton, 1979; Finegan, Zucker, Bradley, & Doering, 1982; McCauley & Ehrhardt, 1977; Meyer-Bahlburg, 1979).

The question of hormonal differences is extremely controversial, and has been extensively studied in two domains: prenatal sex hormones (i.e., those influencing the fetus during gestation to develop along masculine or feminine paths), and adult sex hormones (i.e., those involved in the expression of adult sexual patterns).

Meyer-Bahlburg (1977, 1979, 1980) reviewed this literature extensively. For men, Meyer-Bahlburg found few if any differences in the levels of sex hormone levels circulating in the blood of adults, but there were consistent if patchy results suggesting that some (not all) HS women had higher levels of so-called "masculine" hormones.

There has been a recent spate of interest in the finding by Gladue, Green, and Hellmann (1984) that HS men appear to have a luteinizing hormone surge after receiving a small dose of female sex hormone (estrogen). This hormone surge is typical of women and unlike that of HT men. This finding has not always been replicated by other researchers and a spirited controversy is now underway (Baum, Carroll, Erskine, & Tobet, 1985).

The question of prenatal hormonal differences is far more difficult to study, because even if one could measure hormone levels directly in human fetuses we would still have to wait 20 or more years for the children to reach adulthood to assess their sexual orientation with any degree of certainty. Nevertheless, a few studies suggest prenatal hormones can affect sexual orientation (Meyer-Bahlburg, 1984; Money, Schwartz, & Lewis, 1984; for childhood gender nonconformity, see Meyer-Bahlburg, Feldman, Cohen, & Ehrhardt, 1988), although suggesting that such hormonal variation accounts for all or even most homosexuality would exceed the optimism of even the most ardent proponents of these theories.

CONCLUSIONS

Are HS and HT individuals alike, or are they different? Do most HS individuals psychologically resemble their own sex or do they resemble the other sex? In the most extensively studied area—pencil-and-paper questionnaires of psychological interests and feelings—substantial numbers of HS men respond in ways that are intermediate between the modal patterns for HT men and HT women (see Figure 3.1). Although there is much less evidence for HS women, a similar statement about them is probably correct.

In another well-studied area—adult hormones—the evidence is that HS men and women have generally normal levels of circulating sex hormones. In the other domains reviewed—prenatal hormone levels, cognitive abilities, observable physical and behavioral characteristics—the evidence is not conclusive.

One point that seems certain is that there is no single "type" or "style" of homosexuality but rather many styles with many origins and outcomes. Homosexual behavior is simply too varied in its expression, too widely occurring in nature, to be the result of any simple, single "cause." That said, it does seem possible that sexual orientation in some individuals—heterosexual as well as homosexual—is a response to some profound biological prompting, as yet poorly understood. James Weinrich and I have proposed (1987) a theory suggesting that some gay men and lesbian women are more androgynous than HT individuals—not just androgynous in the kinds of psychological characteristics measured by Bem and Spence and Helmreich, but also androgynous in some sexual behavior patterns (preference for monogamy, certain sex roles, and so forth) that may be related to brain architecture. That is, HS men's sexual behavior patterns may indeed be more "feminine" *but no less masculine* than their HT counterparts; likewise, certain HS women may be psychosexually more "masculine" *but no less feminine* than HT women. To speculate further, this gender-role flexibility might operate not as a deficit or a handicap, but on the contrary as a way of increasing the diversity of temperaments and behaviors available within our species. Insofar as this diversity is genetically determined and acts to benefit those who share the individual's genes, the trait could be favorably selected in the course of evolution (Kirsch & Rodman, 1977; Weinrich, 1987a, 1987b). In a society so deeply committed to the notion that homosexuality is a mistake or aberration, it is important to consider a hypothesis that perhaps it is part of a completely natural way of being, sometimes better than, sometimes worse than, and usually not much different from any other part of nature's plan.

4

Strange Customs, Familiar Lives: Homosexualities in Other Cultures

James D. Weinrich
Walter L. Williams

Studies of other cultures offer an impressive contrast to the American notion that homosexuals are always scorned, abnormal, acting like the opposite sex, dangerous, likely to molest innocent children, and easily distinguishable from normal heterosexuals. Yet since American popular culture is for the most part ethnocentric, when it interprets sexuality in other cultures the result has often been disastrously inaccurate. Typical heterosexual American tourists who see two Italian men or two Greek women walking down the street arm in arm or holding hands might get upset, since they know how to interpret such behaviors only in terms of homosexuality. When typical homosexual American tourists visit gay bars in countries like Japan or Mexico, they are often surprised to discover that most if not all of the patrons are married or plan to marry and have children—and so they wonder why so many homosexuals in those countries are still "in the closet" and not facing up to what is supposed to be their true nature.

In the context of this ethnocentrism, it is not surprising that early cross-cultural research on homosexuality emphasized the differences that are apparent when other cultures are described in their own terms. Intellectually, this point of view culminated in the *social constructionist* school, which, when applied to homosexuality research, views the nature of sexual orientation as constructed within a particular society as opposed to reflecting a fixed, underlying essence. Social constructionists have pointed to bisexuality, historical variation, and cross-cultural differences to support the notion that homosexuality is not merely an objectively observed trait. Instead, they claim that in an important sense

---

AUTHORS' NOTE: We thank John Boswell, John Gonsiorek, Ralph Hexter, and Richard Pillard for comments on early versions of the manuscript.

the concept of a person "being a homosexual" does not really exist as an independent, fixed entity. It "exists" only in the minds of Westerners.

There is now a growing literature on homosexual behavior in other cultures, both modern ones and those that existed in past eras. Most important, several societies have been investigated in far more detail concerning their attitudes toward "homosexuality," whatever that is, than typically was reported in the early cross-cultural studies. We can now begin to compare the *diversity* of homosexual behavior patterns in different studies and see if the range of behaviors falling into these categories is similar or different across cultures and across time.

The result is surprising: the more a culture is studied, the more different patterns of homosexuality or homosexual behavior turn up in it, and the more this range of behavior seems similar to the range (if not the proportions) observed in other cultures, including Western culture. Yet each culture maintains its own way of interpreting this range of behavior, plucking out certain patterns as modal or "normal," ignoring but not denying the existence of others, and stigmatizing or trying to wish away the existence of yet other patterns. In doing so, most cultures subject their members to a unique combination of pressures, and construct concepts and terminologies that tend to make their members unaware of certain patterns and unable or unlikely to understand patterns that fall outside of the socially recognized ones.

In contrast, we believe that in order to arrive at a more complete understanding of human sexuality, including what our culture calls homosexuality, we need not only to include a social constructionist approach but also to go further. In particular, we have the following goals in this chapter:

- To help readers steeped in our own culture's view of homosexuality to realize that this point of view is a distorted one in many ways, and to describe the positive contributions of the social constructionist movement.
- To show how social constructionism is inadequate as a model to describe the full diversity of findings now emerging from detailed investigations of same-sex eroticism in other cultures and at other times.
- Finally, to draw conclusions about how to use these insights in understanding "the modern homosexual identity" in America today.

HOMOSEXUALITY AS A SOCIAL CONSTRUCTION

The *social constructionist* view was first applied to the study of homosexuality by Mary McIntosh, when she wrote:

> The current conceptualization of homosexuality as a condition is a false one, resulting from ethnocentric bias. Homosexuality should be seen rather

as a social role. Anthropological evidence shows that the role does not exist in all societies, and where it does it is not always the same as in modern western societies. Historical evidence shows that the role did not emerge in England until towards the end of the seventeenth century. Evidence from the "Kinsey Reports" shows that . . . the polarization between the heterosexual man and the homosexual man is far from complete. (McIntosh, 1968, p. 182)

Asserting that social constructionism is the *only* valid tool for this area of analysis, McIntosh's paper has been enormously influential. Note that it explicitly cites cross-cultural evidence, cross-historical evidence, and the existence of bisexuality in its support. A milder social constructionist view was defended by anthropologist Joseph Carrier, who did fieldwork in Mexico:

What is considered homosexuality in one culture may be considered appropriate behavior within prescribed gender roles in another, a homosexual act only on the part of one participant in another, or a ritual act involving growth and masculinity in still another. Care must therefore be taken when judging sexual behavior cross-culturally with such culture-bound labels as "homosexual" and "homosexuality" . . . . From whatever causes that homosexual impulses originate, whether they be biological or psychological, culture provides an additional dimension that cannot be ignored. (Carrier, 1980, p. 120)

Though Carrier alleges that cultural factors are important, he stops short of saying that other factors (such as biological ones) are not. Another position was defended by Erich Goode, who buttressed McIntosh's position with facts about ancient Greece:

By focusing on same-gender sexual preference exclusively we may fail to notice differences that may be far more remarkable. . . . For instance, in ancient Greece, men who preferred the sexual company of other men . . . were of a type quite unlike our contemporary versions: most were married, had at least occasional sex with their wives, and they sired children. (Goode, 1981, p. 62)

And finally, Jonathan Katz, who used to talk about "gay people" in history (a nonconstructionist usage), has with his most recent book given up the term and adopted an openly hostile attitude toward it:

In recent years, it has become common . . . to speak of "homosexual behavior" as universal. As allegedly universal, this "homosexual behavior" was the same, for example, in the American colonies in the 1680s as it is in Greenwich Village in the 1980s. I don't think so. It is only the most one-

> dimensional, mechanical "behaviorism" that suggests that that act of male with male called "sodomy" in the early colonies was identical to that behavior of males called "homosexual" in the 1980s. (Katz, 1983, pp. 17-18)

The notion common to all these social constructionist views is that sexual orientation cannot be properly or completely understood apart from the social milieu in which it is embedded. The most extreme proponents of this point of view claim that "homosexuality" did not really exist until the term was coined in the modern West (by a German sexual reformer, Károly Kertbeny, in 1869): that the construction of sexuality is so important that it is improper to talk about "gay people in the Middle Ages," for example, or about "lesbians in ancient Greece."

It is important to realize that this point of view is far stronger than just pointing out how wrong it would be to assume that the "ancient French," for example, spoke "French." Social constructionists claim that the very term *homosexuality* skews the discussion in a Western direction in ways that we Westerners have trouble comprehending. Imagine, for example, a hypothetical society that attached a great deal of importance to the question of whether its citizens were dog lovers or cat lovers. Imagine that scientists constructed complicated psychological questionnaires to determine whether someone was a "feliphile" or a "caniphile," scored people on scales of "petual orientation," and received or were denied tenure on the basis of whether they could prove the existence of "bipetuality." Those allegedly scientific terms have a bizarre ring to us, in a society that cares little about whether someone prefers to spend time with dogs, cats, both, or neither. But someone raised in such a society might very well come into ours and make gross misinterpretations of our social patterns.

This is, according to the social constructionists, exactly the point. "Homosexuality" has no more of a real existence than "caniphilia" does. Our society makes the definition and shows concern only because it wants to differentiate and thereby control people who display variation in that trait. These are terms, they say, no more applicable outside their time and place than "French culture" is.

HOMOSEXUALITY IN OTHER CULTURES

Let us now discuss some specific examples of the variations we see around the world and throughout history in people's constructions of and attitudes toward sexual behavior between males or between females. For reasons of space, we will focus on only two categories of variation, exemplified by ancient Greece and by various mixed-gender institutions in a variety of societies.

In ancient Greece, attitudes toward what we now call "homosexuality" varied from time to time and from place to place. It would be inaccurate to write as if these attitudes were uniform, just as it would be incorrect to talk about "the American view of sex" as if this view were uniform from coast to coast and from 1776 to 1999! Nevertheless, many Greek writers in ancient times wrote as if they considered the pleasures of one sex as opposed to the other to be morally equivalent, and as if a particular person could find pleasure in one sex one day and the other sex the next. Plutarch, for example wrote:

> The noble lover of beauty engages in love wherever he sees excellence and splendid natural endowment without regard for any difference in physiological detail. The lover of human beauty [will] be fairly and equably disposed toward both sexes, instead of supposing that males and females are as different in the matter of love as they are in their clothes. (Translation from Boswell, 1982)

As it happens, the Greeks had a word for each of several specific sexual tastes, but no word at all for what might be called today's generic "homosexual." Plutarch saw sexual orientation in terms that would please the social constructionists. Indeed, Goode (quoted above) made nearly this point.

Moreover, the ancient Greeks often had attitudes toward same-sex sexual relations that were stunningly different from those even imagined today. In Plato's *Symposium,* for example, the dinner guests are each asked to give a brief speech about love. Amazingly to modern observers, each guest talks about love *between men;* not only is this form of love taken in stride, it seems to be the unspoken basis of discussion. This attitude is not anomalous; various city-states in ancient Greece had rules and regulations about how a male should go about courting another male, specified particular gifts that ought to be given at particular stages of the relationship, and so on.

In ancient Greece, homosexuality was not at all associated with an identification with the opposite sex. In fact, quite the opposite was true; it seemed logical, for example, for them to assume that the most masculine men would want to associate with and have sex with other males. Sappho, whose famous poetry expressed her love for young women, was not considered anything but feminine, as her society defined femininity. In contrast, in today's society it is a stereotype that lesbians are masculine (some excessively so), and that gay men are effeminate (some to the point of parody or pity). Gay civil rights groups often point out that most homosexuals today do not cross-dress, that many transvestites are heterosexual, and so on.

What is sometimes hard to convey to Western citizens, however, is the fact that in some cultures cross-dressing and androgynous gender behavior were or are indeed statistically correlated with homosexual behavior, but *in a way that was appropriate or even approved for the culture* in which they took place. This is difficult because Westerners usually cannot imagine how ordinary heterosexuals could take such behaviors in stride. After all, isn't such gender-nonconformist behavior inherently upsetting to the heterosexual majority?

Not necessarily. In Thailand, for example, there is the institution of the effeminate *kathoey* (Jackson, 1989). It is their gender role that sets them apart from ordinary men (they enjoy dressing in women's clothes), as well as their sexual orientation (they like having sex with heterosexual men).

It is important to realize that *kathoey* are accepted in Thai culture. Nearly every town has its annual *kathoey* beauty pageant, for example, which townspeople of all ages attend approvingly. And every town has many heterosexual men who have sex with *kathoey* and report enjoying it. Perhaps most important of all, these sex partners of *kathoey* are not considered unusual or deviant in any way.

In fact, there are many cultures today, and there have been many others in the past, in which some people of one sex dress as or, to a greater or lesser extent, take the role of members of the other sex, and with which homosexuality is often involved.

Among certain Eskimo and American Indian tribes, this type of person is called a berdache by anthropologists. Among the Chukchee in Siberia (Bogoras, 1904-1909), berdache males acquired magical or shamanistic gifts as the result of their transformation. Among the Chukchee, there were three levels of transformed shamans. Those at the lowest level just arranged their hair as women did, sometimes only every now and then. Those at the middle level dressed as women at the commands of the spirits, and for longer periods of time. And those at the highest level had the greatest powers, dressed as women full-time, spoke using the female linguistic forms, and formally got married to men—unlike the other two types, who married women.

Many North American Indian tribes had similar institutions, although the exact details differed from tribe to tribe (see Williams, 1986). Each tribe had its own name for berdaches. For example, the Sioux term is *winkte.* The Sioux traditional medicine man, Lame Deer, said:

> We think that if a woman has two little ones growing inside her, if she is going to have twins, sometimes instead of giving birth to two babies they have formed up in her womb into just one, into a half man-half woman kind of being. We call such a person a winkte. . . . In the old days a winkte

> dressed like a woman, cooked and did beadwork. He behaved like a squaw and did not go to war. . . . There are good men among the winktes and they have been given certain powers. . . . [one] winkte . . . told me that if nature puts a burden on a man by making him different, it also gives him a power. He told me that a winkte has a gift of prophecy. (Lame Deer & Erdoes, 1972, pp. 149-150)

Among most American Indian tribes, as hinted in the passage above, being a berdache was not just a sexual matter: it has an important spiritual component. A berdache had a spiritual personality, and this spirituality was reflected in the roles his society assigned to him. Rather than being seen as a *cross*-dresser—namely, someone who dresses convincingly in the clothes of the opposite sex—berdaches are usually more accurately viewed as *gender mixers,* or people who combine aspects of both masculine and feminine styles in a single person, or who even have personality traits or behaviors that are associated with neither the masculine nor feminine averages. Often, this gave berdaches the right to arrange marriages, or made them especially useful to the rest of society by acting as go-betweens in gender matters or affairs of the heart.

In parallel fashion, many Native American cultures also gave social recognition to the fact that some females were inclined toward activities usually performed by men. They might mix these occupations with some traditional feminine pursuits, while other females made a nearly complete social transformation to masculine activities. For example, in 1576 the Portuguese explorer Pedro de Magalhaes de Gandavo wrote about a remarkable group of female warriors when he visited the Tupinamba Indians of northeastern Brazil:

> There are some Indian women who determine to remain chaste: these have no [sexual] commerce with men in any manner, nor would they consent to it even if refusal meant death. They give up all the duties of women and imitate men, and follow men's pursuits as if they were not women. They wear the hair cut in the same way as the men, and go to war with bows and arrows and pursue game, always in company with men; each has a woman to serve her, to whom she says she is married, and they treat each other and speak with each other as man and wife. (quoted in Williams, 1986, p. 233)

With such a person it is usually a mistake to assume that "he" "really" "is" a man or a woman. Usually the members of the tribe viewed a berdache, in a way that seems very strange to Westerners, as both masculine and feminine, and neither! There is no better illustration of this than the following quote about berdaches in the Tewa tribe, who are called *quethos* (Jacobs, 1983):

> Although the Tewa elders with whom I have spoken would not assign a male or female sex to quetho, I pushed the point further on a number of occasions, asking if women were ever quethos. The answer was no. Then I asked if men were the only ones who were quethos. Again, the answer was no[!]. In trying to force a categorization of quethos as women or men. . . , I only exasperated my Tewa friends.

In the Arabic culture of Oman, it is hard to imagine an environment more hostile to "homosexuality" as the West sees it. Islam prescribes the death penalty for homosexual behavior, and many aspects of one's life are completely determined just by one's sex. For example, the sexes are rigidly separated. Men are not permitted to be in the presence of a woman for even a moment unless a man related to the woman—preferably her husband—is present as a chaperone. There are, however, exceptions. The anthropologist Unni Wikan reported about her fieldwork in Oman:

> I had completed four months of fieldwork when one day a friend of mine asked me to go visiting with her. Observing the rules of decency, we made our way through the back streets away from the market, where we met a man, dressed in a pink dishdasha, with whom my friend stopped to talk. I was highly astonished, as no decent woman stops to talk with a man in the street. So I reasoned he must be her very close male relative. But their interaction was too intimate. I began to suspect my friend's virtue. Could the man be her secret lover? No sooner had we left him than she identified him. "That one is a *xanith,*" she said. In the twenty-minute walk that followed, she pointed out four more. (Wikan, 1982, p. 169)

In Oman, men wear white dishdashas, women wear something else entirely, and *xaniths* wear a pastel-colored dishdasha. *Xaniths* do not in this sense "cross-dress," even though many of them take up stereotypically feminine occupations. In a sense, men and women in Oman are not each others' "opposite sex," but are instead "the other sex" (or perhaps even "another sex"). It is difficult to explain this to Westerners, whose conceptions of manhood and womanhood are so closely tied to the genitals, and are seen as two, and only two, "opposite sexes."

In Hinduism, there is the *hijra* caste, made up of genetic males who worship a female goddess, and who wish to change their sex to female (Nanda, 1984, 1990). When hijras are ready they undergo a castration and penectomy (penis-removing) operation that finalizes their status in the caste. Many *hijras* earn their living performing songs and dances at marriages and other heterosexual rites, and by performing free-lance shows in various places, such as college campuses. Their welcome at the locations where they entertain is sometimes ambivalent; *hijras* who have not been paid (or paid well enough) after their sometimes uninvited performances have been known to lift their skirts and show off to the crowd what they have underneath. Since one of the rules of the sect forbids underwear, this is a display most hosts want to avoid! In Indian culture, *hijras* are considered among the outcastes, yet even so they have managed to work their way into a begrudging acknowledgment by society.

All these examples of intermediate-gender status show, according to the social constructionists, that culture is an overwhelmingly important force in determining the different forms that homosexual behavior takes in society. We agree that merely to describe this variability in cross-cultural terms overlooks the importance of the social construction of the very terms used in categorizing same-sex eroticism. On the other hand, it is a mistake to assert that these enormous differences are the end of the matter or the only important matter. Let us now turn to some similarities across cultures.

CROSS-CULTURAL SIMILARITIES

The ancient Greeks had no single word for what we now call "homosexuality"—a fact that is interpreted by the social constructionists as evidence that "homosexuality" did not then exist. They do not claim that same-sex acts did not take place; just that it is nonsensical to apply our 20th-century term to a pattern of behavior that is constructed under completely different conditions.

However that may be, consider the following creation myth recounted in Plato's *Symposium:*

> Formerly the natural state of man was not what it is now, but quite different. For at first there were three sexes, not two as at present, male and female, but also a third having a male-female sex . . . , [All these humans] had four arms and an equal number of legs, and two faces [and twice the usual number of the various parts of the body], and two privy members. . . . They had terrible strength and force, and great were their ambitions; they attacked the gods. . . .
>
> So Zeus and the other gods held council what they should do. . . . "I will tell you what I'll do now," says [Zeus], "I will slice each of them down through the middle!" . . . and then he sliced men though the middle. . . . So when the original body was cut through, each half wanted the other. . . .
>
> Then each of us is [half] of a man; he is sliced like a flatfish, and two made of one. So each one seeks his other [half]. Then all men who are a cutting of

> the old common sex which was called manwoman are [erotically] fond of women. . . . The women who are a cutting of the ancient [double] women do not care much about men, but are more attracted to women. . . . But those which are a cutting of the [double] male pursue the male. . . . So when one of these meets his own [matching] half, . . . then they are wonderfully overwhelmed by affection and intimacy and love, and . . . never wish to be apart for a moment. (Plato, reprinted 1956, pp. 86-88)

There are several striking things about this creation myth—things that are just as striking even if we take account of the possibility that Plato was joking instead of seriously recounting a myth already familiar to his listeners and readers. First, the myth suggests that the speaker believes that there are three kinds of people: females who are attracted to females, males who are attracted to males, and people who are attracted to the other sex. This is inconsistent with the notion, so popular among social constructionists, that these categories were literally unrecognizable and unknown before the 17th or the 19th century. Second, the myth completely turns on its head the Western stereotype that homosexuals resemble the opposite sex; it attributes heterosexuality, not homosexuality, to a kind of hermaphroditism! Third, the ancient Greek pattern is commonly interpreted as one in which there was always, or ideally, a significant age difference between sex partners (i.e., that men courted youths, who in turn courted boys)—yet if one is yearning, according to this myth, for one's matching twin, it follows that one is yearning for someone of exactly the same age! And fourth, notice how all the really "positive" words—like "wonderfully," "affection," and "love"—are reserved for the men who pursue men. This is quite the opposite of the mainstream view in modern Western society, where some critics of homosexual relationships can actually get away with claiming that the love that homosexuals feel for each other is not "real" love.

In fact, ancient Greek society did recognize differences between people who were attracted to their own sex, people who were attracted to the other sex, and people who were attracted to both. But they didn't make a big deal about these differences. In fact, they probably made about as much of them as we nowadays make about the differences between introverts and extroverts, or between dog lovers and cat lovers. We have humorous books and monologues (e.g., Dizick & Bly, 1985) in which dog lovers and cat lovers cast aspersions on each other's personalities. But no one makes any particular "petual orientation" illegal! It is likely that Plato would not comprehend how some Americans could believe that certain kinds of homosexual sex are crimes worse than murder.

Now let us move on to the mixed-gender institutions like the *kathoey*, the amazon, the berdache, the *xanith*, and the *hijra*. Here, anthropologists point out how much cross-cultural variation has been revealed by their studies of these kinds of people, and emphasize all the differences between these institutions and our own society. Berdaches, for example, had a specifically spiritual vocation, and often had a respected place in their tribes. The *kathoey* in Thailand are well respected for their particular talents, and are taken so much in stride by the common people that there is an Ann Landers-style advice column written for them that is published in a major national newspaper (the columnist's name translates as "Uncle Go"). *Hijras* are only grudgingly respected, if at all, hold very particular religious beliefs, and cannot return to the male sex after their castration operation. *Xaniths* were neither revered nor reviled, were trusted to be around women, and occasionally were known to switch back to the ordinary man's role later in life. In all four cultures, males in these mixed-gender categories have sex almost exclusively with ordinary "heterosexual" men in their tribes or villages, and those other men are not regarded as deviant or special. Similarly, American Indian amazons married women, and those women were seen as ordinary wives. How could these institutions be more different from each other? And just think of the enormous differences separating these kinds of social constructs from the ancient Greek pattern. What could be more ridiculous than to claim that all these diverse kinds of people could be called "homosexual"? The term seems enormously inappropriate.

To arrive at a more complete explanation of the world, however, we must allow ourselves to be dazzled not only by differences, but also by subtle similarities. Both diamonds and coal are made of carbon, and because of that fact, if you heat them they will burn. Although coal and diamonds are extremely dissimilar substances, they are also alike in a subtle and interesting way.

The better we get to know ancient Greece, and the more we learn about same-sex erotic behavior patterns in other cultures, the more we are discovering that the *range* of these patterns is far more similar from culture to culture than it might at first seem. In ancient Greece, there were effeminate men, but homosexuality in such men was not the common pattern of homosexuality seen in that culture, and so it is usually not the first or most often described pattern in the literature. In modern Thailand, terms are emerging to describe types of homosexual that are more familiar to modern Westerners, but it would be a mistake (and an insult to the intelligence of Thais) to claim that Thais were unaware of these kinds of people before Western culture provided them with a vocabulary to describe them. In Mexico, where for reasons of machismo it is extremely important to declare oneself in the male world as either "butch" (inserting) or "fem" (inserted into), a considerable proportion of homosexual men actually take both roles (the butch role with someone who is more fem than they are, and the fem role with someone more butch). This makes their pattern a lot more similar than it would otherwise appear to American gay men, who typically play down butch-fem distinctions and are flexible in their insertor/insertee patterns. One of us (Williams, 1986, pp. 99-100) reports that particular berdaches were known to prefer partners much older than themselves, much younger, or about their same age. And Jacobs claims that the *quethos* among the Tewa resembled "contemporary gay males" to her in important respects (Jacobs, 1983, p. 460).

What may have appeared to be cross-cultural variation is in part variation in anthropologists, not variation in the cultures the anthropologists are describing. We expand upon this idea in Figure 4.1. This is not to deny that there is actual underlying variation in the cultures themselves, nor is it to deny that there are significant variations in the social constructions of those underlying patterns (obviously, such variation is enormous). Nor do we wish to propose that one particular culture's point of view is the "real" or "correct" or "best" way of interpreting observations. After all, from a chemist's point of view the most important fact about coal and diamonds is that they are both made of carbon; from the jeweler's point of view it is that one sparkles and the other does not. Neither viewpoint invalidates the other.

We believe, therefore, that there is a need to go beyond a social constructionist view. We suggest that an *interactionist* view can contribute even more to the study of human sexuality, by emphasizing the interaction of numerous factors in producing human eroticism. There is no need to deny similarities across cultures any more than there is a need to deny individual variation within a single culture.

DISCUSSION AND CONCLUSIONS

The terms *sexual orientation* and *sexual preference* are sometimes used interchangeably and at other times hotly debated. When debated, it is usually over the issue of choice. *Orientation* is used more often by those who think there is little choice involved, and *preference* is used by those who think choice is important. This element of choice can be highlighted by comparing it with religion.

At some level, people can choose to be Catholic, say, or Anglican, or Islamic, and a society can choose to make Catholicism or Anglicanism or Islam a state religion. Of course, most people choose to believe what the state has mandated. Of course, there is social value in announcing one's conformity in such a society, and in some sense there is a de facto enshrining of heterosexuality in modern Western societies as if it were

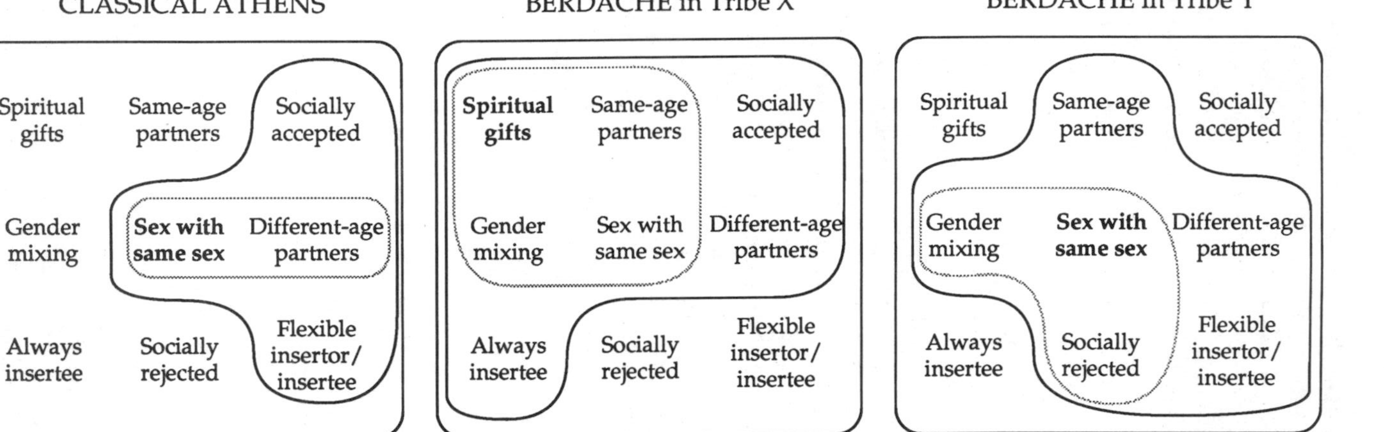

Figure 4.1. Can Cultural Variation Coexist With Underlying Uniformity?

NOTE: Recent anthropological work suggests that there is more underlying uniformity from culture to culture than had previously been thought. In classical Athens, it is documented that some people who had sex with other members of their sex preferred partners of the same age as themselves, and others preferred people of more different ages. Likewise, some of these liaisons were culturally accepted, and others rejected; some had strong preferences for insertor/insertee roles, others did not; and some cross-dressed or otherwise blurred stereotypical gender distinctions. Although we are not aware of any attribution of special spiritual gifts to these people, let us assume for the sake of argument that some homosexually behaving individuals were so regarded. The solid line enclosing four of the nine attributes reflects the fact that only this combination was widely recorded in the literature of the time, and the dotted line encircles the two attributes that survive modern Western censorship.

Native American berdaches varied individually and from tribe to tribe, and the set of traits reported by hypothetical observers varied even more. Whereas Tribe #1 would have listed one set of traits exhibited by their berdaches, Tribe #2 would think of the role as encompassing a different set (solid lines), and they could have given different weights to the centrality of same-sex affection (boldface). Different anthropologists might have reported different aspects of the socially designated role (dotted lines), thus creating the impression that entirely different "types" of individuals "existed" in different societies, whereas in fact the underlying distribution of different kinds of people was far more similar (albeit not identical). Finally, if special rewards or disapproval are attached to particular roles or for failing to fit into specified roles, people reflecting "the same" set of traits in two different cultures might have strikingly different feelings about their inclinations.

the state sexual preference. Thomas Szasz (1970, chap. 13), for example, compares homosexuality and heresy, homosexuals in his view having the role of sexual heretics dissenting from the heterosexuality mandated by the state.

This is an argument that helps fight antigay prejudice in a culture that takes religious pluralism seriously. In present-day Iran, in contrast, Szasz's argument would probably be just as applicable, logically speaking, but would promote the execution of homosexuals, not their liberation. As we scholars debate such matters, we must be careful not to overlook how societies will try to apply our findings in political debates. On the other hand, we should not become overly concerned when someone points out how some extremist government might use a scholarly or scientific finding in support of its oppressive policies; it is usually the tail that wags the dog in such instances. Although an oppressive power will often look to the ivory tower for intellectual justification for its oppression, residents in the tower (and their critics!) should not fool themselves into thinking that their ideas are causally involved in creating the oppression in the first place. They should only feel guilty if they have encouraged or helped along the oppression or the misuse of their ideas.

Most people are trained in childhood for the religion that they will come to believe in as adults, just as most children in our society are trained for the heterosexuality they will ultimately find stimulating. But think also of the people who convert to a religion other than the one they were raised in, or those who adopt a sexual orientation label for themselves different from the heterosexual one. In both these situations, the adult identity label is taken on as a result of deep thought (or even inner conflict) over a long period of time. The label results from deep inner emotions—emotions that in many people are susceptible to socialization, but not always in a simple way. (This is one reason why Szasz's (1970) insights about homosexuality and heresy make sense.)

In fact, people can "be" Catholic even if they don't go to Mass or practice Catholic rituals, or even if they know logically that this or that story about this or that saint is false. People can "be" defined as Catholics if they believe in their deepest feelings that certain statements about Christ and God are true. If they don't believe those statements in their heart of hearts, then they are not really Catholic, no matter how often they go to Mass or how hard they consciously try to pretend they believe them.

Likewise, people can be defined as "homosexual" even if they do not perform any homosexual acts, or even if they despise the gay world or their homosexual feelings. People are homosexual if they experience romantic and/or sexual arousal repeatedly and consistently in the presence of some members of their own sex, but not with members of the other sex. A homosexual person can exist in a society that has no name for the trait. In a society that does not categorize individuals according to their sexual inclinations, homosexually inclined persons are unlikely to set themselves apart by choosing distinctive social arrangements or by calling themselves distinctive names. But the more perceptive people in such a society will, if the occasion arises, be able to discern the existence of these different patterns and comment upon them. This is, indeed, exactly what happened in certain medieval and ancient Greek debates about whether same-sex or other-sex love was better. Some people like Plato understood that different people have different sexual orientations, but because their society did not attach as much significance to these traits, they could be discussed in an offhanded way.

Just as psychologists can go to other cultures and, presumably, classify individuals as "introverts" or "extroverts," even if the cultures themselves have no names for those traits, so can sexologists go to other cultures and pick out individuals as "homosexual," "heterosexual," "bisexual," or "asexual." It is important to note that this does *not* imply that our Western sexual taxonomy is the best one, or that all persons in such a society will fit into our molds. Perhaps a majority will not. Yet it is quite misleading for us to declare, as some social constructionists have done, that there is no such thing as homosexuality or homosexuals in such cultures.

When different cultures give different reasons for an apple falling to earth, that does not demonstrate that gravity works differently in different societies. A culture that says the fall was "because of gravity" is not necessarily more right than one that says it fell "because it was ripe." In fact, we would be at least as intrigued if we could resurrect Plato or Sappho and have them classify members of our society in ancient Greek terms, or have a Native American berdache or Thai *kathoey* classify our friends using their native taxonomies. This cultural exploration becomes culturally imperialistic only if someone insists that our point of view is the best way, the only way, or the only interesting or intellectually respectable way, of classifying people.

If we were to do this exercise, we would discover some fascinating and subtle similarities in the ways that different societies have divided the sexual spectrum. For example, in the societies we have discussed so far, each culture considers the origins of the alternative gender trait to be important enough to merit an explanation. In each case it is alleged that the origins are beyond the control of the individual exhibiting the trait. Plato's myth alleges that we were ripped apart from our other halves against our will. Amazons were often believed to be masculine as a result of a dream instruction from the spirit world. The Sioux medicine man Lame Deer said that *winktes* were twins merged prenatally into psychic hermaphrodites. *Quethos* were alleged to have had their genitals exposed to the moon during infancy. The Chukchee *berdache* went on a vision quest and had dreams revealing his status to him. In most gender-mixing institutions, the trait could be recognized in children, even when the children themselves might be unaware of it.

We conclude that the spectrum of gender-role variability in other cultures is not too different from the spectrum in our own, even though there are different emphases in each society. Indeed, the younger generation of anthropologists, less worried about asking sexual questions than their predecessors and more knowledgeable about the various sexual predilections known (or unknown) to science, will more likely manage to ask the right questions of the younger generation of native informants, who may well be less worried about answering them. As a result, variability in anthropologists may decrease, and we might get a better estimate of the true amount of variability among cultures.

The homosexualities we see in the modern West bear some striking resemblances to the homosexualities we see everywhere else on the globe, and saw throughout history. There are similarities running through them, and there are also important differences. In ancient Greece, and in parts of the Middle Ages, there were societies that paid relatively little attention to the question of whether it was men or women people found themselves falling in love with. Even so, from both time periods debates have survived—fictional works, and presumably entertaining ones—in which someone saying homosexual love was better debated someone who said heterosexual love was better (for example, pseudo-Lucian, 1967). As Boswell (1982) points out, those differences were recognized at those times; they were not invented in the 17th (according to McIntosh) or 19th (according to Katz) century.[1]

At the same time, society's attitudes toward those (real) traits were very different from those of our own society, and this had enormously important consequences. Our society has taken a natural kind of sexuality and made it taboo, in a way that is completely unnecessary for its stability or its values. It is time for us to learn from other cultures that uniform sameness is not a desirable goal for society. We can learn to appreciate and value diversity, and realize that with work and good will, we can love our homosexual and bisexual members, our *quethos,* our *xaniths* and *hijras,* our butches and our fems, as we love all the other members of our human family.

NOTE

1. In fairness to these authors, we should point out that McIntosh was talking about England, and Katz was talking about the British North American colonies.

5

Stigma, Prejudice, and Violence Against Lesbians and Gay Men

Gregory M. Herek

Institutional and personal hostility toward lesbians and gay men is a fact of life in the United States today. At the cultural level, homosexuality remains stigmatized through institutional policies. Statutes prohibiting antigay discrimination in employment, housing, and services are in force in only two states (Wisconsin and Massachusetts), the District of Columbia, and a few dozen municipalities and local jurisdictions (for example, San Francisco, New York, Chicago). Lesbian and gay military personnel are subject to discharge if their sexual orientation is discovered, no matter how exemplary their service records. Gay civilians routinely are denied government security clearances, or are subjected to more intensive investigation than are heterosexual applicants. Lesbian and gay relationships generally are not legally recognized and, in 24 states and the District of Columbia, the partners in same-sex relationships are forbidden by law from private sexual contact (see, for example, Herek, 1989, 1990a; Melton, 1989; Rivera, this volume).

Many individual heterosexuals' attitudes toward gay men and women are consistent with this institutional hostility. Roughly two-thirds of Americans[1] condemn homosexuality or homosexual behavior as morally wrong or a sin (polls by *ABC*, 8/87; *Los Angeles Times*, 8/87; *Roper*, 9/85); this pattern appears not to have changed significantly from the late 1970s (polls by *Yankelovich*, 3/78; *Gallup*, 11/78).[2] According to Gallup polls (Colasanto, 1989), only a plurality of Americans feel that homosexual relations between consenting adults should be legal (47% versus 36% who say they should not be legal).

AUTHOR'S NOTE: I wish to thank Mark Snyder for his valued advice on this chapter, as well as Clinton Anderson and Bill Bailey for their comments on an early draft. I also extend special thanks to John Gonsiorek for his encouragement, assistance, and patience throughout the preparation of this chapter.

Many heterosexual Americans also reject gay people at the personal level. In 1987, a *Roper* poll found that 25% of the respondents to a national survey would strongly object to working around people who are homosexual, and another 27% would prefer not to do so; only 45% "wouldn't mind." In a 1985 *Los Angeles Times* poll, 50% of respondents reported that they did *not* feel *un*comfortable around homosexual men and women, while 35% reported discomfort around gay men or lesbians. This was a change from a 1983 poll, in which 40% reported not feeling discomfort, and 38% reported some discomfort.

Negative attitudes often are expressed behaviorally. Of 113 lesbians and 287 gay men in a national telephone survey, for example, 5% of the men and 10% of the women reported having been physically abused or assaulted in the previous year because they were gay. Nearly half (47%) reported experiencing some form of discrimination (job, housing, health care, or social) at some time in their life based on their sexual orientation ("Results of poll," 1989).[3] Other research similarly has found that significant numbers of gay men and lesbians have been the targets of verbal abuse, discrimination, or physical assault because of their sexual orientation (Berrill, 1990; Herek, 1989; Levine, 1979a; Levine & Leonard, 1984; Paul, 1982).

Despite widespread antipathy toward gay Americans, however, national surveys during the last two decades indicate a growing willingness to grant basic civil rights to gay people: Americans are increasingly reluctant to condone discrimination on the basis of sexual orientation (for example, Colasanto, 1989; McClosky & Brill, 1983; Schneider & Lewis, 1984; see Rayside & Bowler, 1988, for evidence of a similar trend in Canada). The proportion of American adults surveyed by the Gallup organization who say that homosexual men and women should have equal rights in terms of job opportunities increased from 56% in 1977 to 59% in 1982, and to 71% in 1989; the proportion opposing such rights declined from 33% to 28% to 18%, respectively (Colasanto, 1989). Similarly, *Roper* surveys found that the proportion of Americans agreeing that "homosexuals should be guaranteed equal treatment under the law in jobs and housing" rose from 60% in 1977 to 66% in 1985, while the proportion supporting legalized discrimination declined from 28% to 22%. When asked about specific occupations, respondents sometimes are more willing to discriminate but still show a steady trend toward supporting gay rights. In Gallup polls (Colasanto, 1989), the proportion stating that gay people should be hired as doctors increased from 44% in 1977 to 56% in 1989; similar increases were observed for salespersons (from 68% to 79%), members of the armed forces (51% to 60%), clergy (36% to 44%), and elementary school teachers (27% to 42%).

Data collected by the *National Opinion Research Center* (NORC) show increasing support for free speech rights for gay Americans during the last two decades. When asked in 1973 whether a person who "admits he is a homosexual" should be able to teach in a college or university, 47% would have allowed him to teach whereas 48% would not, a virtual tie. By 1980, the balance had shifted in favor of allowing him to teach, 55% to 42%. By 1988, the gap had widened from 57% to 39%. Similarly, the proportion who would allow the hypothetical homosexual man to make a speech in their community increased from 61% in 1973 to 66% in 1980 to 70% in 1988; the proportion who would *not* allow him to speak decreased in those years from 35% to 31% to 26%, respectively. Asked whether a book in favor of homosexuality, written by the same man, should be removed from the local public library, the proportion responding affirmatively dropped from 44% (1973) to 40% (1980) to 36% (1988).

In summary, although they show increasing willingness to extend basic civil liberties to gay men and lesbians, most heterosexual Americans continue to condemn homosexuality morally and to reject or feel uncomfortable about gay people personally. This chapter uses social science theory and empirical research to describe and explain these negative attitudes, with special emphasis on research findings relevant to policymakers. The chapter begins with a discussion of gay people as a stigmatized minority group. Next, it reviews social psychological data on antigay prejudice and discusses the characteristics shared by antigay attitudes and stereotypes on the one hand, and those directed at other minorities on the other. Next, consequences of prejudice are described. Finally, after a brief discussion of the linkage between antigay attitudes and public reactions to AIDS, suggestions are offered for eradicating antigay prejudice.[4]

At the outset, a note about terminology is necessary. Hostility toward gay people has been labeled variously as *homoerotophobia* (Churchill, 1967), *heterosexism* (Morin & Garfinkle, 1978), *homosexphobia* (Levitt & Klassen, 1974), *homosexism* (Lehne, 1976), *homonegativism* (Hudson & Ricketts, 1980), *antihomosexualism* (Hacker, 1971) and *antihomosexuality* (Klassen, Williams, & Levitt, 1989). The most widely used summary label for these attitudes is *homophobia* (Smith, 1971; Weinberg, 1972). Aside from its linguistic awkwardness (its literal meaning is "fear of sameness"), the term "homophobia" reflects at least three assumptions: that antigay prejudice is primarily a fear response; that it is irrational and dysfunctional for individuals who manifest it; and that it is primarily an individual aberration rather than a reflection of cultural values. Empirical data do not support these assumptions (Fyfe, 1983; Herek, 1986c; Nungesser, 1983). This chapter, therefore, uses social psychological terminology to describe hostility toward gay people. Such hostility at the cultural level is labeled *stigma* (e.g., Goffman, 1963). Individual intolerance is considered here to be a particular *attitude,* defined as an evaluation of persons, issues, or objects on such dimensions as good-bad, like-dislike, or favorable-unfavorable (e.g., McGuire, 1985). *Prejudice* and *bigotry* here refer to a strongly negative or hostile attitude toward a social group or its individual members (e.g., Allport, 1954; Stephan, 1985). For lack of better terms, *tolerance* and *acceptance* are used to describe the opposite of prejudice, that is, positive or favorable attitudes.

GAY PEOPLE, MINORITY GROUPS, AND PREJUDICE

Gay People as a Minority Group

Although the notion that gay people compose a minority group comparable to racial, ethnic, and religious minorities was articulated 40 years ago (Cory, 1951), it only recently has begun to enjoy a degree of acceptance in American society (see also Kameny, 1971). Lesbians and gay men differ from other minorities in important respects (Paul, 1982). Nevertheless, they can reasonably be viewed as a minority group because they manifest four important characteristics by which minority groups are defined (e.g., Seeman, 1981; Tajfel, 1981). First, gay people are a subordinate segment within a larger complex state society. Second, they manifest characteristics that are held in low esteem by the dominant segments of society (support for these two points can be found throughout this volume, as well as in Paul, Weinrich, Gonsiorek, & Hotvedt, 1982). Third, they are self-consciously bound together as a community by virtue of these characteristics (e.g., Altman, 1982; D'Emilio, 1983; Levine, 1979b).[5]

Finally, they receive differential treatment based upon these characteristics, ranging from discrimination (Gross, Aurand, & Addessa, 1988; Levine, 1979a; Levine & Leonard, 1984; "Results of poll," 1989; Rivera, this volume) to assault and victimization (Herek, 1989; Herek & Berrill, 1990; Paul, 1982; "Results of poll," 1989). Although the existence of such differential treatment usually is not disputed, its justification often is (Hacker, 1971). Public figures generally are unwilling to endorse outright violence against gay people, although Sen. Jesse Helms [R-NC] and other elected officials attempted to block passage of the Hate Crimes Statistics Act because it included antigay violence among the "hate crimes" to be monitored by law enforcement personnel (Cohen, 1989). Discrimination in employment, housing, and services, in contrast, frequently is justified on the basis of beliefs that gay people possess various undesirable characteristics, for example, that they are mentally ill and dangerous to children. These unfounded stereotypes are discussed later in this chapter.

A principal justification for discrimination and hostility toward gay people appeals to religious morality. Because homosexuality is condemned by several major religions, it is argued, laws prohibiting discrimination would require heterosexual individuals to violate their personal moral standards. In this context, gay people can be viewed as a religious minority group: Although they do not manifest a unified religious ideology, they often are persecuted on the basis of the dominant majority's religious beliefs (Herek, 1990a; Paul, 1982). Opposition to civil rights for gay people is perceived by some Americans as a litmus test of religious commitment (the correlation between religiosity and antigay prejudice is well documented; see Bierly, 1985; Gentry, 1987; Herek, 1984a; 1987a; Klassen, Williams, & Levitt, 1989; Maret, 1984; Schneider & Lewis, 1984). Many Roman Catholics, fundamentalist Christians, and Orthodox Jews have used religious teachings to justify their active opposition to enactment of statutes or policies designed to protect gay people from discrimination (for statements of the argument, see Bryant, 1977; Congregation for the Doctrine of the Faith, 1986; LaHaye, 1978; for descriptions of antigay activism by church officials, see chapter 7 of Rueda, 1982). Although moralistic arguments are no longer widely accepted to excuse racial or religious intolerance, they still carry sufficient weight when applied to homosexuality that religious institutions often are exempted from antidiscrimination statutes, as in the 1989 Massachusetts law. Indeed, Supreme Court Justices White and Burger both cited Judeo-Christian teachings in their written opinions upholding the constitutionality of state sodomy statutes (*Bowers v. Hardwick*, 1986).

Finally, gay people can be viewed also as members of a political minority. The relatively recent flourishing of visible gay communities is largely a result of political and legal struggles against prejudice and discrimination that have spanned four decades (Adam, 1987; Bérubé, 1990; D'Emilio, 1983). These communities constitute a political force for gay concerns, especially in cities like San Francisco (Altman, 1982; Shilts, 1982). Acknowledging one's membership in the community through coming out to others can itself be defined as a political act (Kitzinger, 1987) or can be motivated by the desire to challenge antigay policies or attitudes (Brown, 1976; Hippler, 1989). The political minority status of gay people was recognized by the California Supreme Court in 1979 (*Gay Law Students Association v. Pacific Telephone and Telegraph*, 1979). Noting that the civil rights struggle of the gay community "must be recognized as political activity" (p. 32) and that publicly acknowledging one's own homosexual orientation is an important aspect of this struggle, the court ruled that discrimination against openly gay individuals constitutes illegal discrimination on the basis of political activity.

THE SOCIAL PSYCHOLOGY OF ANTIGAY PREJUDICE

Although each form of bigotry has its own unique history and content, antigay prejudice manifests the same general psychological structure and dynamics as racism, anti-Semitism, and other prejudices against stigmatized groups. Each can be understood by the same social scientific theories and measured by the same methodologies (e.g., Bierly, 1985; Gergen & Gergen, 1981; Herek, 1984a, 1987b, 1988).

Correlates of Antigay Prejudice

Empirical research has demonstrated that heterosexuals' attitudes toward gay people are consistently correlated with various psychological, social, and demographic variables. In contrast to heterosexuals with favorable attitudes toward gay people, those with negative attitudes are (1) more likely to express traditional, restrictive attitudes about gender roles; (2) less likely to report having themselves engaged in homosexual behaviors or to self-identify as lesbian or gay; (3) more likely to perceive their peers as manifesting negative attitudes; (4) less likely to have had personal contact with gay men or lesbians; (5) likely to be older and less well educated; (6) more likely to have resided in areas where negative attitudes represent the norm (e.g., rural areas; the midwestern and southern United States); and (7) more likely to be strongly religious and to subscribe to a conservative religious ideology (Herek, 1984a).

Additionally, heterosexual males tend to manifest higher levels of prejudice than do heterosexual females, especially toward gay men (Herek, 1984a, 1988; Kite, 1984). This sex difference may result from the strong linkage of masculinity with heterosexuality in American culture, which creates considerable pressures (both social and psychological) for males to affirm their masculinity through rejection of that which is not culturally defined as masculine (male homosexuality) and that which is perceived as negating the importance of males (lesbianism). Because heterosexual women are less likely to perceive rejection of homosexuality as integral to their own gender identity, they may experience fewer pressures to be prejudiced and consequently have more opportunities for personal contact with gay people, which, in turn, tends to foster positive attitudes (Herek, 1986b, 1987b, 1988).

Some individuals display a personality pattern of general intolerance for stigmatized groups, often subsumed under the label *authoritarianism* (e.g., Adorno, Frenkel-Brunswik, Levinson, & Sanford, 1950; Altemeyer, 1988). A significant correlation has been consistently observed between antigay attitudes and high scores on measures of authoritarianism (Altemeyer, 1988; Herek, 1988; Hood, 1973; Karr, 1978; Larsen, Reed, & Hoffman, 1980; MacDonald and Games, 1974; Smith, 1971; Sobel, 1976). Given this propensity for some individuals to express intolerant attitudes toward a variety of out-groups, it is not surprising that antigay prejudice has been found to correlate with racism (Bierly, 1985; Henley & Pincus, 1978).[6] Herek (1987a) demonstrated that this correlation is affected by religious orientation. White heterosexual college students tended to score high on both antiblack racism and antigay prejudice if their religious beliefs were extrinsically motivated (i.e., if their religion functioned primarily as a means for fitting in with a social group). In contrast, those with intrinsically motivated religious beliefs (i.e., beliefs that provide an overarching framework by which all life is understood) tended to score low on racism and high on antigay attitudes. Herek (1987a) explained this pattern as reflecting the norms and values associated with each orientation: Intrinsics conformed to religious ideals (which condemn racism but not antigay prejudice), while extrinsics conformed to community norms (which fostered both racism and antigay prejudice).

Stereotypes and Cultural Ideologies

Strongly correlated with negative attitudes toward lesbians and gay men is acceptance of negative stereotypes—exaggerated and fixed beliefs—about them (e.g., Allport, 1954). Because stereotypes and prejudice both involve reactions to individuals in terms of their group membership, and because beliefs about the characteristics of a group often include an evaluative component, the two concepts often are equated (Ashmore & DelBoca, 1981). Some researchers, however, have found it useful to distinguish between them and have begun to study the cognitive processes through which stereotyping occurs (e.g., Brewer & Kramer, 1985). Insights from this approach are described in the next section.

Stereotyping: Belief creates reality. The continually changing world constantly bombards us with an overwhelming amount of sensory stimulation. Interpreting and responding to each separate item of information is beyond human mental capabilities. Yet individual survival requires that we be able to detect important occurrences in the environment, make reasonably accurate predictions about how they will affect us, and behave accordingly. Consequently, we use a variety of strategies for judging the importance of information and for integrating it with our past experiences. These strategies enable us to perceive the world as reasonably stable, fairly predictable, and generally manageable (e.g., Snyder, 1981).

One such strategy is categorization, a mental process whereby we associate or "clump" different objects (including people) according to some characteristic that they all share. Once an object is grouped with others, we have available a considerable amount of information about it by simply recalling the defining features of the category. For example, trying to remember the individual characteristics of 25 different objects in a room is impossible for most people; but if 20 of those objects fit the category of "chair" and the remaining five fit the category of "table," the memory task suddenly becomes fairly simple.

When categorization is applied to people, the consequence often is a stereotype (e.g., Hamilton, 1981). Stereotypes result when we (1) categorize people into groups on the basis of some characteristic; (2) attribute additional characteristics to that category; (3) then attribute those other characteristics individually to all of the group's members (e.g., Snyder, 1981). Whereas a categorization is based on features that actually define the group (for example, belief that all gay people have a primary sexual or romantic attraction to others of their own sex), a stereotype involves characteristics that are unrelated to the criteria for group membership (for example, the belief that all gay men are effeminate or that all lesbians hate men). Heterosexuals often notice only those characteristics that are congruent with their stereotypes about gay people (*selective perception*), fail to recall incongruent characteristics retrospectively (*selective recall*), and use the content of stereotypes as the basis for *illusory correlations.* Each of these phenomena is discussed here briefly.

People often perceive the world selectively, attending to information that supports their stereotypes and ignoring information that contradicts them. This process of selective perception influences heterosexuals' responses to gay men and lesbians. For example, Alan Gross and his colleagues (Gross, Green, Storck, & Vanyur, 1980) found that students at their university believed gay men generally to be theatrical, gentle, and liberated, whereas heterosexual men were thought to be more aggressive, dominant, competitive, strong, and stable; the same students believed lesbians generally to be dominant, direct, forceful, strong, liberated, and nonconforming, whereas heterosexual women were perceived as more likely to be conservative and stable. The researchers asked a separate sample of students to describe a woman or man in terms of these characteristics after watching a brief videotaped interview with her or him. Students who were told that the person was gay rated her or him higher on "gay traits" and lower on "heterosexual traits" than those who received no information about the interviewee's sexual orientation. Using only a gay male stimulus person, Gurwitz and Marcus (1978) found the same effect at a different university.

Stereotypical beliefs not only distort perceptions of current interactions; they also can affect an individual's memory for past events. Snyder and Uranowitz (1978), for example, provided undergraduates with a 750-word life history of a woman named "Betty K." After reading the file, some students were told that Betty later became involved in a lesbian relationship and went on to a satisfying career as a physician living with her female lover. Other students learned that Betty married and went on to a satisfying career as a physician living with her (male) husband. On subsequent factual questions, students tended to remember events that fit with their subsequent knowledge about Betty's sexual orientation. Those who learned that Betty became a lesbian tended to remember that she did not have a steady boyfriend in high school, for example, whereas students who learned that she married heterosexually recalled that she dated boys (see also Snyder, 1981).

Heterosexuals' observations of gay people as a group are likely to be distorted by illusory correlations, i.e., the erroneous perception that a particular characteristic occurs with disproportionate frequency among gay men and lesbians. In their classic studies, Chapman and Chapman (1969) found that illusory correlations influenced perceptions of homosexuality among clinicians and lay people alike. In one study, clinicians responding to a survey were asked to describe their own observations of the kinds of responses "prominent in the Rorschach protocols of men with problems concerning homosexual impulses" (Chapman & Chapman, 1969, p. 273).[7] The responses that the clinicians reported they had observed more frequently with homosexual respondents (for example, human/animal anal content, feminine clothing, humans with sex confused) had in fact been found in separate empirical studies *not* to be unusually prevalent among homosexual respondents. The clinicians' associations of certain signs with homosexuality, in other words, were not accurate. The Chapmans found, however, that the signs listed by the clinicians closely matched those that members of the lay public associated with homosexuality. The clinicians' impressions thus appeared to have been shaped by cultural ideologies about homosexuality rather than by their own unbiased observations.

In a subsequent experimental study, the Chapmans presented college students with various types of responses to a series of Rorschach cards, each response attributed to a person manifesting particular "symptoms." For example, the response of "a woman's buttocks" on Card IX might have been attributed to a man who "has sexual feelings toward other men" or, alternatively, to a man who "feels sad and depressed much of the time." Although each kind of response was paired with each symptom exactly the same number of times, the students perceived that particular responses were given more frequently by homosexual men. These were the *same* responses that clinicians in the first study had believed to be associated with homosexuality. The Chapmans concluded that the students' observations, like those of the clinicians, had been influenced by their preexisting ideas about homosexuality; they erroneously remembered "seeing" certain Rorschach signs more frequently because those signs fit with their preconceptions.

Because of illusory correlations, and the selective perception and recall of stereotype-confirming information, antigay stereotypes are very resistant to change, even when reality contradicts them. Thus, many heterosexuals erroneously "see" (or remember seeing) a disproportionate number of gay men and women who are maladjusted, obsessed with sex, and incapable of committed relationships. They fail to notice gay people who violate these stereotypes or heterosexuals who fulfill them.

The content of antigay stereotypes. Negative stereotypes about lesbians and gay men, like those about other minority groups, do not result from cognitive processes that occur in a social vacuum. Rather, they are shaped by historically evolved cultural ideologies that justify the subjugation of minorities. Because these ideologies are ubiquitous in popular discourse (for example, through mass media), individual stereotypes are continually reinforced. Some stereotypes reflect ideologies that are specific to a particular out-group. Gay men, for example, are presumed to manifest characteristics that are culturally defined as "feminine," and lesbians are widely believed to manifest "masculine" characteristics (e.g., Herek, 1984a; Kite & Deaux, 1986, 1987).[8] This belief is sufficiently strong that men and women who manifest characteristics inconsistent with those culturally prescribed for their gender are more likely than others to be labeled homosexual (Deaux & Lewis, 1984; Storms, Stivers, Lambers, & Hill, 1981). Lesbians and gay men who violate stereotypical expectations, as many do, may actually be disliked (Laner & Laner, 1979; Storms, 1978), and an individual who is perceived as being able to label a nonobvious homosexual may subsequently be better liked by others (Karr, 1978).

Other stereotypes reflect cultural ideologies about out-groups in general, usually portraying out-group members as simultaneously threatening and inferior to members of the dominant in-group. Adam (1978) has documented some themes common to cultural images of gay people, blacks, and Jews alike: All are perceived as animalistic, hypersexual, overvisible, heretical, and conspiratorial (see also Gilman, 1985). Yet another ideology ascribes disease (physical and mental) to all three groups. As Szasz (1970) noted, for example, Benjamin Rush (considered by many to be the father of American psychiatry) proposed that being black was itself an illness, a form of congenital leprosy. Being black also was equated by many 19th century white Americans with being insane; further, free blacks were alleged to be substantially more prone to mental illness than were black slaves (Gilman, 1985). In 1851, Samuel Cartwright even identified a form of psychopathology unique to blacks: *drapetomania,* a disease that caused black slaves to run away from their owners (quoted in Gilman, 1985, p. 138). Jews also have been regarded as mentally ill (Gilman, 1985) and as carriers of disease, for example, plague in the 14th century (W. McNeill, 1976) and venereal disease in Nazi Germany (see Erikson, 1963, for an account of the Nazi stereotype of Jews). Similarly, homosexuality was officially labeled a mental illness by the American Psychiatric Association in the 1952 and 1968 editions of the *Diagnostic and Statistical Manual of Psychiatric Disorders* (Bayer, 1987). This classification, which was eliminated in 1973 (leaving only the diagnosis of "ego-dystonic homosexuality," which was dropped in 1986), originally was urged by mental health professionals who considered it preferable to the then-prevalent view of homosexuality as criminal (see Bérubé, 1990). Empirical evidence, however, overwhelmingly showed no correlation between sexual orientation and psychopathology (see Gonsiorek, this volume).

Case study of a stereotype: Homosexuals and children. A particularly powerful cultural image of out-groups portrays them as threats to the in-group's most vulnerable members (for example, children, women). Anita Bryant, who campaigned successfully in 1977 to repeal a Dade County, Florida, ordinance prohibiting antigay discrimination, frequently appealed to stereotypes based on this image. For example, she named her organization "Save Our Children." She summarized the dual focus of this cultural ideology in her comments about homosexual teachers: "First, public approval of admitted homosexual teachers could encourage more homosexuality by inducing pupils into looking upon it as an acceptable life-style. And second, a particularly deviant-minded teacher could sexually molest children" (Bryant, 1977, p. 114).

Although both statements are wrong, this chapter will focus only on the second of Bryant's assertions (for data that the presence of a gay role model does not encourage otherwise heterosexual children to adopt a homosexual orientation, see Falk, 1989, and Green, Mandel, Hotvedt, Gray, & Smith, 1986). Newton (1978) concluded from his review of the literature that gay men are no more likely than heterosexual men to molest children (although sexual abuse by women occurs [Johnson & Shrier, 1987] it appears to be rare). In perhaps the most sophisticated study of its kind, Groth and Birnbaum (1978) found that, in their sample of 175 adult males who were convicted in Massachusetts of sexual assault against a child, *none* had an exclusively homosexual adult sexual orientation. Most of the men (83, or 47%) were classified as "fixated," meaning that they had never developed an adult sexual orientation; 70 others (40%) were classified as adult heterosexuals; the remaining 22 (13%) were classified as adult bisexuals, meaning that "in their adult relationships they engaged in sex on occasion with men as well as with women. However, in no case did this attraction to men *exceed* their preference for women. . . . There were no men who were primarily sexually attracted to other adult males . . . " (p. 180). Since 1978, no credible new data have been published that contradict the conclusions of Newton (1978) or Groth and Birnbaum (1978).

Why do many lay people continue to believe this stereotype? One reason is that understanding the data concerning child molestation requires sufficient knowledge and sophistication to distinguish male-male sexual molestation from adult homosexuality, and to understand that male-male molestations are perpetrated by men who are heterosexuals or who lack any adult sexual orientation (Groth & Birnbaum, 1978). Once parents have perceived a threat to their children, however, their level of emotional arousal typically is too high to permit easy assimilation of such complex concepts. Instead, they are prone to overly simplistic thinking, errors of reasoning, and faulty decision-making processes (Janis & Mann, 1977; Kahneman, Slovic, & Tversky, 1982).

The highly emotional reaction evoked by the topic of child sexual abuse undoubtedly is a major reason why antigay activists promulgate the stereotype. A notable example is a pamphlet titled *Child Molestation and Homosexuality,* distributed in 1985 by the Institute for the Scientific Investigation of Sexuality (ISIS) whose chairperson was listed as Paul Cameron, Ph.D.[9] The pamphlet cover features a photograph of a young boy being pulled by a male arm into a men's restroom along with the caption, "Homosexuality is a crime against humanity." Among its many questionable conclusions, the pamphlet states, "Gays perpetrated between a third and a half of all recorded [child] molestations" and "Gays are thus at least 12 times more apt to molest children than heterosexuals are. . . . " These assertions are based on the author's untenable "assumption that all molestations of boys were by homosexuals." The same erroneous assumption is the basis for a paper published by the same author, provocatively titled "Child Molestation and Homosexuality" (Cameron et al., 1986). Drawing data from a door-to-door survey in seven U.S. cities and towns, Cameron refers to male-to-male sexual assaults as "homosexual" molestations (e.g., p. 327), despite his lack of data about the sexual orientation of perpetrators.[10]

Falsely accusing minority group members of child molestation is not a strategy unique to antigay activists. Historically, disliked minority groups have often been portrayed as preying upon the vulnerable, especially young children. Oberman (1984), for example, quotes a 16th century German account of how a group of Jews "purchased seven Christian children" whom they subsequently "pierced with needles and knives, tortured, and finally killed," and then "prepared the blood with pomegranates and served it for dinner" (p. 99). As noted by Adam (1978), lynchings of American blacks were traditionally justified with the contention that "many Negroes were literally wild beasts with uncontrollable sexual passions" (p. 45); black males were portrayed as a threat to white women. Today, a decreasing number of Americans believe the accusation that gay people are child molesters, as evidenced in the Gallup poll data that 42% of respondents would allow gay people to be elementary school teachers (Colasanto, 1989). Nevertheless, many of the remaining 58% undoubtedly continue to accept the stereotype.

The Psychological Functions of Antigay Prejudice

National surveys reveal that heterosexual Americans show considerable variability in their attitudes toward lesbians and gay men. This raises the question of why some heterosexuals are strongly hostile toward gay people while others are tolerant or accepting in their attitudes. This question has been addressed by Herek (1984a, 1986a, 1987b), using a perspective that other researchers earlier applied to whites' attitudes toward blacks (Katz, Sarnoff, & McClintock, 1956; McClintock, 1958) and Americans' attitudes toward Russians (Smith, Bruner, & White, 1956). Within this *functional* approach, attitudes are understood according to the psychological needs they meet.

From a content analysis of essays about homosexuality written by 205 heterosexual college students, Herek (1987b) detected three principal functions. Attitudes serving an *Experiential-Schematic* function assisted the respondent in making sense of her or his previous interactions with gay people and provided a guide for future behavior. Those who had experienced pleasant interactions with a gay man or lesbian, for example, generalized from that experience and accepted gay people in general. A total of 14% of the respondents had attitudes serving an exclusively Experiential-Schematic function; another 9% manifested the Experiential-Schematic function along with one or more others.

In contrast to the Experiential-Schematic function, the other attitude functions were not based on actual experiences with gay people. Rather, they were beneficial to the respondent in that they permitted expression of important aspects of the self. Attitudes serving a *Self-Expressive* function increased the respondent's feelings of self-esteem in either of two ways: (1) by expressing values of central importance to her or his self-concept (for example, a fundamentalist Christian condemning homosexuality as a way of affirming her or his religious identity) and (2) by expressing opinions supported by friends or family (for example, telling a "fag joke" in order to gain others' friendship). A plurality of the respondents (40%) had attitudes serving an exclusively Self-Expressive function; another 43% manifested this function along with others. In a second study, Herek (1987b) found that the Self-Expressive function can be further broken down into *Value-Expressive* and *Social-Expressive* functions.

Finally, some respondents' attitudes served a *Defensive* function: They reduced anxiety associated with an unconscious psychological conflict, such as personal conflicts about sexuality or gender. With Defensive attitudes, an unacceptable part of the self is projected onto gay people; by rejecting (or even attacking) gay people, individuals are able symbolically to attack that unacceptable aspect of themselves. A total of 11% of the respondents manifested a Defensive function, and another 24% manifested Defensive attitudes in conjunction with one or more other functions.

The functional approach is important not only because it explains the motivations for antigay prejudice in individuals, but also because it suggests a strategy for changing attitudes. Prejudice can be eradicated most effectively by appealing to the primary psychological functions that it serves. This means that different strategies will be necessary for changing the antigay attitudes held by different individuals. For example, creating social norms that support acceptance of gay people will be an effective strategy for reducing prejudice among heterosexuals whose hostile attitudes derive from their need to be accepted by others. Presenting alternative, noncondemnatory religious perspectives on homosexuality (e.g., Boswell, 1980; J. McNeill, 1976) will be most likely to have a positive effect on individuals whose prejudice results from their need to perceive themselves as a religious person. The effectiveness of this strategy will be increased when respected religious leaders publicly support acceptance of gay women and men (see Herek, 1984a, 1986a, 1987b for further discussion).

THE CONSEQUENCES OF ANTIGAY PREJUDICE

Like members of other stigmatized groups, gay people face numerous psychological challenges as a result of society's hostility toward them. In addition to the psychological consequences of antigay prejudice detailed by Gonsiorek and Rudolph in this volume, three topics warrant brief elaboration in this chapter: consequences of hiding one's sexual orientation, consequences of overt victimization, and consequences of antigay prejudice for heterosexuals (see also Garnets, Herek, & Levy, 1990).

As a result of antigay prejudice, many individuals feel compelled to hide their homosexuality or "pass" as heterosexual (e.g., Humphreys, 1972; see also Goffman, 1963). Respondents to the Teichner national survey of lesbians and gay men, for example, waited an average of 4.6 years after knowing they were gay until they came out (which presumably involved disclosing their homosexual orientation to another person). Depending on the area of the country, between 23% and 40% had *not* told their families that they were gay; between 37% and 59% had *not* disclosed their sexual orientation to coworkers ("Results of poll," 1989). Hiding one's sexual orientation creates a painful discrepancy between public and private identities. Because they face unwitting acceptance of themselves by prejudiced heterosexuals, gay people who are passing may feel inauthentic, that they are living a lie, and that others would not accept them if they knew the truth (Goffman, 1963; Jones et al., 1984). The need to pass is likely to disrupt longstanding family relationships and friendships as lesbians and gay men create distance from others in order to avoid revealing their sexual orientation. When contact cannot be avoided, they may keep their interactions at a superficial level as a self-protective strategy. Passing also creates considerable strain for gay relationships. Even openly gay people are deprived of institutional support for their long-term relationships (for example, insurance benefits). Those who are passing additionally must actively hide or deny their relationship to family and friends; consequently, the problems and stresses common to any relationship must be faced without the social supports typically available to heterosexual lovers or spouses.

Once they come out, lesbians and gay men risk rejection by others, discrimination, and even violence, all experiences with psychological consequences that can endure long after their immediate physical effects have dissipated (Garnets, Herek, & Levy, 1990). Being the target of discrimination, for example, often leads to feelings of sadness and anxiety (Dion, 1986); it also can lead to an increased sense that life is difficult and unfair, and dissatisfaction with one's larger community (Birt & Dion, 1987). Suffering assault or other overt victimization can create considerable psychological distress. As for any crime victim, consequences typically include immediate feelings of disbelief, denial, and fear; this initial reaction often is followed by alternations from fear to anger, sadness to elation, self-pity to guilt, self-confidence to inadequacy. Feelings of personal loss, rejection, humiliation, and depression are common. Behavioral and somatic reactions include sleep disturbances and nightmares, headaches, diarrhea, uncontrollable crying and restlessness, increased use of drugs, and deterioration in personal relationships (e.g., Bard & Sangrey, 1979; Frieze, Hymer, & Greenberg, 1984; Janoff-Bulman & Frieze, 1983). Additionally, antigay attacks may be interpreted as violations of oneself as a gay person and may revive earlier feelings of "internalized homophobia" (Malyon, 1982b, 1982c). Attempts to make sense of the attack, coupled with the common need to perceive the world as a just place, may lead to feelings of being punished for being gay (Bard & Sangrey, 1979; Lerner, 1970). This type of self-blame can lead to feelings of depression and helplessness (Janoff-Bulman, 1979), even in individuals who are comfortable with their sexual orientation. Those who are still coming to terms with their gay identity may experience added psychological distress, both because they lack a strongly developed gay identity that would increase their psychological resilience and coping skills, and because they lack adequate social support from others who can affirm their gay identity (Anderson, 1982; Garnets et al., 1990).

Although not often discussed, antigay prejudice also has negative consequences for heterosexuals. Because of the stigma attached to homosexuality, many heterosexuals restrict their own behavior in order to avoid being labeled gay; this pattern appears to be especially strong among American males (e.g., Herek, 1986b; Lehne, 1976; Pleck, 1981). For example, many men avoid clothing, hobbies, and mannerisms that might be labeled "effeminate." Antigay prejudice also interferes with same-sex friendships. Males with strongly antigay attitudes appear to have less intimate nonsexual friendships with other men than do males with tolerant attitudes (Devlin & Cowan, 1985).

AIDS AND ANTIGAY PREJUDICE

Much as the 19th century cholera epidemics were popularly portrayed as visitations (either divine or natural) upon Catholics, blacks, and other disliked American minorities (Rosenberg, 1987), the 20th century AIDS epidemic has been interpreted by some as God's punishment for male homosexuality (Blendon & Donelan, 1988; Herek, 1990b; Herek & Glunt, 1988). In a *CBS/New York Times* poll (September 1988), the proportion of respondents with "a lot" of sympathy for people with AIDS was 46%; when asked specifically about sympathy for "people who get AIDS from homosexual activity," however, the proportion dropped to 17%. Sixty percent replied "not much" or volunteered that they felt no sympathy at all for people who get AIDS from homosexual activity, in contrast to only 20% who did so when homosexuality was not mentioned in the question. Hostility toward gay people is correlated with overestimating the risks of HIV transmission through casual contact and with endorsement of punitive and restrictive AIDS-related policies (Herek & Glunt, 1990; Pleck, O'Donnell, O'Donnell, & Snarey, 1988; Pryor, Reeder, & Vinacco, 1989; Stipp & Kerr, 1989). About one-tenth of the respondents to *Gallup* polls indicated that they had begun to avoid homosexuals as a way to avoid getting AIDS or that they planned to do so (12% in 1987, 11% in 1988).

Despite these examples of the connection between AIDS-related stigma and antigay prejudice, however, the exact nature of the relationship is not yet clear. Most heterosexuals probably developed their attitudes toward gay people before the AIDS epidemic; AIDS thus may simply have provided a convenient hook upon which to hang preexisting prejudice (Herek & Glunt, 1988). Many groups monitoring antigay violence reported an upsurge in incidents when public awareness about AIDS increased during the mid-1980s (Berrill, 1990; Herek, 1989). Although this increase may partly reflect improved reporting, many of the assailants in the attacks made verbal references to AIDS. Of the 7,248 incidents of antigay harassment and victimization reported to the National Gay and Lesbian Task Force in 1988, 1,259 (17%) were AIDS-related; in 1986 and 1987, the percentages were 14% and 15%, respectively (Berrill, 1989). As more heterosexuals have become better informed about AIDS, however, the apparent rise in antigay prejudice may have reversed, with support now increasing for legalizing homosexual relations and for equal employment opportunities (Colasanto, 1989; Schneider 1986).

ELIMINATING ANTIGAY PREJUDICE

Because antigay attitudes have complex cultural roots, are affected by many other social and psychological variables, and serve a variety of psychological functions, they cannot be eradicated through any one approach. Nevertheless, two clear conclusions can be drawn from empirical research. First, heterosexuals with openly gay friends or acquaintances are more likely than others to hold accepting attitudes toward gay people in general (see, e.g., Gentry, 1987; Herek, 1984a, 1988; Schneider & Lewis, 1984). This pattern may result partly from a preference among gay people for disclosing their sexual orientation to others perceived as likely to be already supportive (Schneider, 1986; Weinberg, 1983; Wells & Kline, 1987). Nevertheless, knowing an openly gay person is predictive of supportive attitudes even in demographic groups where hostility is the norm, for example, among the highly religious and the uneducated (Schneider & Lewis, 1984).

Second, heterosexuals' attitudes tend to become more favorable after they are exposed to an educational program about gay people and homosexuality (Stevenson, 1988). Attitude change has been documented after general human sexuality courses (Cerny & Polyson, 1984), courses and workshops on homosexuality (Anderson, 1981; Morin, 1974), lectures about homosexuality (Goldberg, 1982), lectures by openly gay people (Lance, 1987; Pagtolun-An & Clair, 1986), video presentations featuring gay people (Goldberg, 1982), videos ridiculing prejudice against other (nongay) minority groups (Goldberg, 1982), and exercises in which participants role-played a gay person coming out to others (Serdaheley & Ziemba, 1984). The only strategy demonstrated to be counterproductive is exposing heterosexuals to explicitly sexual films or videos about homosexuality (Goldberg, 1982; Nevid, 1983), which may evoke discomfort, anxiety, and other negative feelings among heterosexual viewers (Mosher & O'Grady, 1979). Even this effect appears to be diminished by combining presentation of the sexually explicit material with one or more other attitude-change strategies (Anderson, 1981; Cerny & Polyson, 1984).

Several possible reasons can be suggested for why educational programs and courses change attitudes. They may serve principally to provide factual information and refute stereotypes about gay people. Or they may provide an opportunity for developing positive feelings toward a specific gay person. Alternatively, they may create social norms that promote tolerance and discourage antigay prejudice, or they may simply cue participants to provide "correct" (i.e., unprejudiced) responses to attitude measures regardless of their own true attitudes. Because the studies conducted to date have not investigated the social psychological variables involved in their "treatment" conditions, we do not know which of these factors played a role in fostering attitude change.

The research described in this chapter offers additional ideas for combating prejudice against lesbians and gay men. Recognizing the cognitive processes that underlie prejudice, for example, reveals the limitations inherent in attitude-change strategies that simply provide heterosexuals with "the facts" about gay people. Such strategies are likely to be undermined by selective perception, selective recall, and illusory correlation; the "facts" are perceived through the lens of individuals' preconceptions. Informational strategies must directly confront these cognitive processes, for example, by providing memorable examples of gay people that contradict existing stereotypes.

The motivations for antigay prejudice are broader than a simple desire to possess accurate information about the world. The functional approach to attitudes suggests that antigay stereotypes and prejudices often reflect needs for self-esteem or social support. It highlights the importance of understanding how heterosexuals benefit from expressing antigay attitudes, and provides a general strategy for changing negative attitudes by making them dysfunctional. Further, this approach reminds us that any effective program of attitude change must not only provide information about gay people (preferably through personal contact), but also confront religious values, social norms, and personal anxieties.

Antigay prejudice cannot be eradicated among individuals without simultaneously attacking its institutional roots (Berrill & Herek, 1990; Herek, 1990a). Institutional changes such as enactment of antidiscrimination statutes and policies have at least two effects on individual attitudes. First, they identify antigay discrimination and prejudice as unacceptable and require that people modify their behavior accordingly. One likely consequence of such behavior change is attitude change: People who are required to act in a nonprejudiced manner may subsequently change their attitudes as well. Second, institutional change permits and encourages lesbians and gay men to disclose their sexual orientation to coworkers, neighbors, and others. Coming out to heterosexuals is perhaps the most powerful strategy lesbians and gay men have available for attacking prejudice. Empirical research with other minority groups has shown that intergroup contact often reduces prejudice in the majority group when the contact meets several conditions: when it makes shared goals salient, when intergroup cooperation is encouraged, when the contact is ongoing and intimate rather than brief and superficial, when representatives of the two groups are of equal status, and when they share important values (Allport, 1954; Amir, 1969). These conditions are most fully met when lesbians and gay men disclose their sexual orientation to their relatives, friends, neighbors, and coworkers. By coming out to their loved one, gay people can refute myths and stereotypes, change social norms, and challenge traditional moral values concerning sexuality by juxtaposing them against values of caring for a loved one.

As the decade of the 1990s begins, prejudice against lesbians and gay men appears finally to be facing serious challenges throughout American society. Some aspects of heterosexuals' attitudes are changing, albeit slowly. Lesbians and gay men now are widely perceived as a minority group entitled to at least some of the legal protections accorded other minorities. In contrast to the situation only 20 years ago, Americans now appear to think differently about homosexuality depending upon the context in which it is raised: Many still consider homosexual behavior to be immoral from a religious perspective, yet within a legal context, they consider gay people to be entitled to freedom from discrimination. This change offers optimism for future prospects of eliminating prejudice against lesbians and gay men.

Joining the chorus of outcry against this long-entrenched form of bigotry are social and behavioral scientists, who have recognized it as a serious societal problem. They have created an impressive body of scientific theory and empirical research on the social and psychological bases of hostility toward lesbians and gay men. This ever-expanding knowledge base offers tools for formulating and implementing social policy that will hasten the elimination of antigay prejudice.

NOTES

1. Following popular usage, the word *American* is used in this chapter to describe residents of the United States of America.

2. Much of the national survey data described in this chapter were obtained through the Roper Center, University of Connecticut at Storrs. To assist the reader in distinguishing Roper Center data from data obtained through published reports, I have italicized the names of the polling organizations for the former. I am grateful to Professor Bliss Siman of Baruch College, City University of New York, for her assistance in securing these data.

3. In March-April of 1989, the *San Francisco Examiner* commissioned Teichner Associates to conduct telephone interviews with a gay and lesbian national sample (n=400) as well as a sample of gay residents of the San Francisco Bay area (n=400). Approximately 27,000 calls were made to obtain 800 responses; 6.2% of the national respondents and 10% of the Bay area respondents identified themselves as lesbian, gay, or bisexual to the interviewers (Hatfield, 1989). Although the sample is biased by the willingness of respondents to identify themselves as gay to a telephone interviewer, the poll represents the first published study of its kind in the United States.

4. This chapter is not intended to be a complete literature review; for additional references, see Dynes (1987), Herek (1984a), Morin and Garfinkle (1978), Plummer (1975), and Warren (1980).

5. Not all people who are homosexual necessarily identify with the gay community or participate in it. The same can be said for African-Americans, Jews, and other minority groups.

6. Verbal reports of racial attitudes (and correlation coefficients based on those reports) are affected considerably by social norms discouraging expression of racism (Crosby, Bromley, & Saxe, 1980). In the author's personal research experience, such norms do not appear to operate to a significant degree with verbal expressions of antigay prejudice, especially with nonstudent samples.

7. Note that this study was conducted before the 1973 decision by the American Psychiatric Association to remove homosexuality as a diagnosis from the Diagnostic and Statistical Manual.

8. As with popular images of gay sexuality, this stereotype reflects, in part, differences between the gay community and the dominant heterosexual culture in norms concerning gender roles. Lesbian and gay communities are considerably more accepting of behaviors that would be perceived by the larger society as violations of gender roles, and many gay

men and lesbians choose to violate gender norms for political reasons (e.g., D'Emilio, 1983; Vance, 1984). Sexual orientation is not inherently related to gender role conformity or nonconformity, as evidenced by similarities between gay and heterosexual samples in studies of gender role orientation (e.g., Stokes, Kilmann, & Wanlass, 1983).

9. Paul Cameron has been labeled in the gay press as "the most dangerous antigay voice in the United States today" (Walter, 1985, p. 28; see also Fettner, 1985). In 1984, all members of the American Psychological Association received official written notice that "Paul Cameron (Nebraska) was dropped from membership for a violation of the Preamble to the *Ethical Principles of Psychologists.*" At its membership meeting on October 19, 1984, the Nebraska Psychological Association adopted a resolution stating that it "formally disassociates itself from the representations and interpretations of scientific literature offered by Dr. Paul Cameron in his writings and public statements on sexuality." In 1985, the American Sociological Association adopted a resolution that included the assertion that "Dr. Paul Cameron has consistently misinterpreted and misrepresented sociological research on sexuality, homosexuality, and lesbianism" ("Sociology group criticizes work of Paul Cameron," 1985). Cameron's credibility has also been questioned outside of academia. In his written opinion in *Baker v. Wade* (1985), Judge Buchmeyer of the U.S. District Court in Dallas referred to "Cameron's sworn statement that 'homosexuals abuse children at a proportionately greater incident than do heterosexuals,'" and concluded that "Dr. Paul Cameron . . . has himself made misrepresentations to this Court" and that "there has been no fraud or misrepresentations except by Dr. Cameron" (p. 536).

10. Brown and Cole (1985) criticized the sampling methods of Cameron et al. (1985, 1986) for several reasons: The representativeness of their sample is highly doubtful. The locations for data collection (Omaha [NE], Los Angeles [CA], Denver [CO], Washington [DC], Louisville [KY], Bennett [NE], and Rochester [NY]) appear to have been selected solely on the basis of convenience, and the sampling methods are not adequately described in their published reports. Additionally, the response rate appears to have been unacceptably low. Cameron et al. (1985, 1986) report their "compliance rate" to be 43.5%. Based on the figures and calculation methods provided in the published papers, this rate should actually be 47.5%. Even this corrected percentage, however, is not the appropriate one for assessing the adequacy of the sample. Instead, a *response rate* (R) should be calculated as:

$$R = C/T$$

where C = the number of completed interviews and T = the total number of eligible elements, i.e., the sum of completed interviews and mail-ins *plus* mail-ins not returned *plus* refusals *plus* "not homes." Unfortunately, Cameron et al. (1985, 1986) report the number of "not homes" in combination with vacant units; the former should be included in the response rate calculation, but the latter should not. Thus, only a lower limit for their true response rate can be computed from their published data; this lower limit is $R = 4340/(4340 + 1426 + 3363 + 9289) = 24\%$. Whether the true response rate is closer to 47% or 24%, we must conclude that the Cameron et al. sample does not permit generalizations from the data to any larger population.

6

Sexual Orientation and the Law

Rhonda R. Rivera

Throughout the other chapters of this book, reputable social scientists discuss their research into the essence of the sexual orientation of a minority of the earth's people, i.e., an orientation toward the same gender. These social scientists dedicated to the scientific method for "truth finding" attempt to be, for the most part, judgment free. To enter the area of laws, one leaves the arena of scientific method for the highly political and hence judgmental arena of the legislature and the courts. The laws enacted (or not enacted) in the United States are often the product of majoritarian popular consensus. The content of majoritarian popular consensus is seldom based on the scientific method. Rather, legislation often reflects half-truths, prejudice, popular myth, and "common sense." The courts, in a sense, temper the severity of such popular judgment by applying and construing the law with some deference to reason. Yet in the United States, "judge-made" law is not necessarily based on reason either. The judge's influence is often the result of the socioeconomic class of the judges, e.g., male, over 50, white, upper-middle-class, mostly Christian, and, of course, outwardly heterosexual. What informs the judge's decisions are the morals and mores of his class. Therefore, the law dealing with persons whose sexual orientation is toward the same gender is not often based on a search for truth, reason, or justice but often tends to reflect the limited knowledge and homophobic biases of legislators and judges.

THE CRIMINALIZATION OF HOMOSEXUALITY

Until approximately 1962, the sexual conduct of most Americans (gay and nongay) was criminalized.[1] In 1948, Kinsey pointed out that 95% of all American men were committing sexual acts that were considered criminal;[2] presumably, if the laws had been enforced, 95% of all American men would have been in jail. Starting with Illinois in 1962, many states in the 1970s adopted the Model Penal Code, which decriminalized private, adult, consensual sex regardless of the gender of the partners. In the 1970s and 1980s, other states decriminalized most sexual conduct, including same-sex conduct, by action of their highest state courts, which found such laws to be unconstitutional under the privacy rights granted by the particular state's constitution.[3] By this writing, same-gender sexual conduct is not criminal in 26 states. Yet in 24 states, same-gender sexual conduct—private, adult, and consensual—is a crime.[4] Such conduct, in many cases, is a felony with severe penalties ranging in some cases as high as 20 years in jail.[5] In fact, in some of the 24 states where same-gender sexual conduct is still criminally prohibited, the Model Penal Code has been enacted, decriminalizing adult private consensual sex regardless of the gender of the participants, but subsequently the legislature turned around and recriminalized solely same-gender sexual conduct.[6]

For those legal activists who held that private, adult, sexual conduct, regardless of the gender of the participants, was protected by a fundamental right of privacy belonging to all Americans, the state by state approach was unsatisfactory. Legal scholars who held the "privacy" position were convinced that persons' sexual lives were protected by the Constitution of the United States under a "fundamental" right of privacy.[7] These scholars and litigators believed that a solid line of cases would lead the Supreme Court of the United States to a "privacy" conclusion.

In 1968, the Supreme Court in *Griswold v. Connecticut* found a fundamental right of privacy in the married sexual union.[8] Subsequently, in *Eisenstadt v. Baird,* which followed in 1972, Justice Brennan clearly centered the right to privacy in the "individual," each person having a privacy right in how he or she conducted procreative or nonprocreative sexual conduct.[9] Other Supreme Court cases followed that, in many legal scholars' minds, laid a clear track of precedent to adult, private, consensual sex as a fundamental right of all American citizens. In 1973, the Court found a privacy right in *Roe v. Wade,* holding that a woman had a fundamental right to decide to carry a fetus to term or to abort.[10] In *Stanley v. Georgia,* the court held that a person could possess and read what some considered pornography, as long as the reading occurred in his or her own home.[11] In *Carey v. Population Services,* the Court reinforced privacy rights with regard to birth control devices and birth control information.[12] A footnote in the *Carey* decision was interpreted by many lawyers to mean that the Supreme Court was getting ready to tackle the issue of private, adult, consensual sexual conduct within the privacy arena.[13]

A setback occurred when, in 1975, a federal three-judge panel upheld the Virginia sodomy law. In *Doe v. Commonwealth's Attorney,*[14] the court in a perfunctory opinion upheld the Virginia criminalization of sodomy. The arguments were four in number: (1) a secular argument grounded in the Judeo-Christian religious beliefs about same-gender sexual conduct as sin,[15] (2) a historical argument that since such laws had been on the books for a long, long time, they were, by their very longevity, valid,[16] (3) an argument that same-gender sexual conduct undermined the American "family" and that gay Americans were "no portion of marriage, home or family life,"[17] and (4) a circular argument that since the Virginia legislature had long criminalized such conduct, such conduct was properly criminal![18] The United States Supreme Court summarily affirmed the case without opinion, although three justices voted to set oral argument and hear the case.[19] Antigay activists hailed this decision as a federal constitutional imprimatur on sodomy laws. Meanwhile, gay legal activists sought the "perfect" case to bring to the Supreme Court. Simultaneously, the *Doe* case cast a chill over other cases where same-gender activity was an issue. For example, in cases where gay parents were seeking visitation or custody of their children, judges often relied on the proposition that gay people were (under *Doe*) criminals, were thus inherently immoral, and therefore were presumptively *unfit* to visit or have custody of their own children.[20]

In 1985, gay legal activists seeking to overturn sodomy laws believed they had the perfect case to take to the Supreme Court. In Georgia, Michael Hardwick was arrested in his own bedroom within a private home while having sex with another adult male. The sexual conduct was private, adult, and consensual. Michael Hardwick was a young man who had no prior criminal record, nor was he a gay activist—just a private man. The decision of the Supreme Court in 1986 in *Bowers v. Hardwick*[21] stunned both gay and nongay legal activists. The Court, in upholding Georgia's right to criminalize adult, consensual, private sex between two persons of the same gender, two men in this case, selectively ignored prior privacy precedent, in particular the *Eisenstadt* decision. Moreover, the *Bowers* decision, like *Doe* had a perfunctory air. Again, the Court relied on Judeo-Christian literature and history;[22] again, gay people were perceived as a threat to the American family and as no part of American family life.[23] Justice Blackmun, on the other hand, wrote a thorough and precedent-following dissent.[24] Surprisingly, a firestorm of criticism of the decision occurred in major newspapers and among prominent legal scholars.[25] The country apparently was more progressive than the Court. In fact, opinion polls in the 1980s showed that most Americans believed all Americans (gay and nongay) had a fundamental right of privacy for adult, consensual, sex.[26] In *Plessy v. Ferguson*,[27] Afro-Americans were denied equal rights, and those Americans had to wait 58 years until 1954 when *Brown v. Board of Education*[28] recognized that racial discrimination fundamentally violated the equal protection clause of the Constitution. How long will gay citizens wait for *Bowers* to be overruled?

Three legal trends subsequently emerged. (1) Courts at all levels cited the *Bowers* case as justification for permitting discrimination against gay persons in other legal arenas. For example, in Missouri, the *Bowers* case was cited to deny custody to a gay father.[29] (2) Many legal activists of gay causes turned to the state courts and sought to have sodomy laws overturned on the basis of a privacy right found in state constitutions.[30] (3) Last, some legal activists planned to find another "perfect" case to challenge sodomy laws before the Supreme Court, this time using an equal protection strategy. These strategists sought a case to present gay issues within the context of a "suspect classification."

A suspect classification has three criteria:

1. subjection to a long history of persecution for irrational stereotypes,
2. inability to obtain relief from nonjudicial branches of government, and
3. immutability of the trait, which makes it impossible or highly unlikely for its members to escape from the class.[31]

For example, race has been held to be a suspect class.[32] Once a group falls under this rubric, any legislation that uses this classification to treat citizens differently is *presumed* by the Court to be invidious, discriminatory, and constitutionally prohibited. The state must overcome this burden and show the law to be constitutional. Laws directed at suspect classes seldom stand up under such judicial scrutiny and hence often are held to be unconstitutional. Gay legal strategists seek to have the court find gay men and lesbians to constitute a "suspect class." Criteria (1) and (2) pose little problem. The issue centers on the "immutability" characteristic. Some persons believe that any gay person can "change" if he or she really wants to, while many others, including reputable social scientists and medical personnel, hold that sexual orientation is basically immutable.[33] This latter position is well articulated in Richard Green's recent article, *The Immutability of (Homo)sexual Orientation: Behavioral Science Implications for a Constitutional (Legal) Analysis.*[34] Green, a noted psychiatrist in the gender field as well as a lawyer and law professor, argues that sexual orientation is legally immutable. Green and other noted medical doctors and psychiatrists have determined that sexual orientation is fixed by the age of two.[35] Many experts now state that sexual orientation is determined *before birth* and that only a very rare person can truly "change" his or her sexual orientation.[36] Moreover, any "change" is only in conduct, not in basic orientation, which then must be suppressed.

"Gayness" as an immutable characteristic, and hence a suspect class, has been found in a few lower federal courts and in some state courts.[37] On appeal, these findings have been either reversed or obscured by a different holding.

A number of legal scholars hold that an immutability argument, while attractive pragmatically, is morally and constitutionally unprincipled: All Americans acting privately must have a fundamental right of privacy under the Constitution, and this right must include the right for adults to *choose* same-gender conduct or opposite-gender sexual conduct when acting privately and with consent.[38]

Arguing either approach has some strong obstacles within both the American judiciary and American legislatures. In dealing with same-gender conduct, both institutions are mired in prior actions based on ignorance, homophobia, mythology, stereotypes, and unproven assumptions as discussed in Chapter 5 of this volume. A close reading of court opinions also reveals that the ideas on which these opinions are based are often inconsistent both internally and among decisions and courts. How these attitudes play out is best shown by turning to various areas of the law and exploring in those areas the treatment of persons alleged to be gay.

THE MILITARY

In no other area of American life is discrimination against gay men and women so clearly stated and institutionally supported.[39] Prior to 1944, whatever discrimination existed was based on the medical model. In theory, at induction, doctors were relied upon to diagnose "homosexuals" and exclude them from the service. In fact, few gay men and women were "diagnosed," and the great majority, thousands and thousands, served their country admirably for long periods and were honorably discharged. In 1944, as the war was ending and the need for unlimited manpower no longer existed, the U.S. military instituted formal rules prohibiting gay men and women from serving their country.[40] Some military personnel were excluded or removed under these regulations with dishonorable discharges and often after harsh interrogations. Again, however, the greater part of gay military personnel remained relatively closeted and served their tours of duty honorably and were discharged honorably or retired under the military retirement system.[41] Most gay military cases prior to the 1970s concerned persons caught in the midst of a forbidden act.[42] The Stonewall riot in 1969 created a different atmosphere,[43] and in 1976 Leonard Matlovich, a decorated Vietnam war hero and airman, directly challenged the system by announcing his sexual orientation to the Secretary of the Air Force, his military unit. He was immediately dishonorably discharged.[44]

The Matlovich case ended after many years when the military gave him an honorable discharge and a monetary settlement.[45] The military was forced to settle with Matlovich because of a loophole[46] in the military regulation. So as not to face similar situations, in 1981 the military issued new regulations prohibiting gay personnel.[47] The basic premise of the regulations is that "homosexuality is incompatible with military service."[48]

> The presence in the military environment of persons who engage in homosexual conduct or who, by their statements, demonstrate a propensity to engage in homosexual conduct, seriously impairs the accomplishment of the military mission. The presence of such members adversely affects the ability of the Military Services to maintain discipline, good order, and morale; to foster mutual trust and confidence among servicemembers; to ensure the integrity of the system of rank and command; to facilitate assignment and worldwide deployment of servicemembers who frequently must live and work under close conditions affording minimal privacy; to recruit and retain members of the Military Services; to maintain the public acceptability of military service; and to prevent breaches of security.[49]

Who are the persons prohibited? Under the new regulations not only are "homosexuals" prohibited but so are "bisexuals." Moreover, one becomes a class member not solely by conduct, but by desires and/or speech as well.[50] Military personnel who have self-identified as gay or lesbian have been discharged with no proof of any conduct or overt behavior (beyond their "speech").[51] Arguably, these persons are being penalized for their "status" and not their conduct. Note that "status" crimes were found unconstitutional by the Supreme Court in 1962 in *Robinson v. California*.[52]

Gay military personnel have constantly challenged the military regulations in American courts. The case closest to success was *Watkins v. United States*, in which a three-judge panel of the 9th Circuit held, two to one, that the military regulations were unconstitutional because gays and lesbians constituted a "suspect class."[53] While overturned by the 9th Circuit sitting en banc,[54] the *Watkins* decision is a landmark opinion coming from a federal court. Shortly after the *Watkins* decision, the Supreme Court refused to hear two other gay military cases, one of which—*Ben-Shalom*—raised First Amendment issues.[55] Ben-Shalom was a self-identified lesbian whose case was not burdened either by proof or admission of prohibited conduct.[56] The speech issue will not go away: in the military's most embarrassing case yet, the Naval Academy dismissed in 1989 a 4th-year midshipman, top in his class, after he told his commander he believed that he was gay.[57]

The federal courts have a long history of deference to military decisions on the basis of national security, and the courts treat the military legally as "a separate society"[58] with its own law: the Uniform Military Code of Justice.[59] Yet, in 1989, the military was forced by representatives Gerry Studds and Patricia Schroeder to release to the public two studies commissioned by the Pentagon. These studies concluded that discrimination in the military against gay men and women had no rational basis and that a study of the service records of gay military personnel showed them to be superior on the average to comparable records of nongay military personnel.[60] Congressional inquiry has also revealed that weeding gay personnel out of the military costs the American taxpayers $23 million a year.[61]

Will this bastion of homophobia fall? The answer to this question is important. The U.S. military changed American society with its successful integration of blacks; moreover, the integration of women is also causing significant social change. The similar acceptance of gay men and lesbians in the military is crucial, as crucial as the reversal of *Bowers*, to the equal protection of gay people in the United States.

STUDENTS AND UNIVERSITIES

While military personnel's speech on gay issues is not legally protected, the Supreme Court and numerous federal appeals courts and state supreme courts have reached the opposite conclusion as to the free speech rights of gay college students[62] and to a lesser extent, gay high school students.[63] Both federal and state courts have held that meeting, forming formal student groups, advocating, even socializing together are constitutionally protected as free speech and free association. Courts have forced state universities and colleges to provide equal space and equal funding to gay student groups.[64] Lest one become too sanguine, the attitude of the current chief justice of the Supreme Court, William Rehnquist, is clearly revealed in one of these student cases. When the Supreme Court declined to hear an appeal of *Gay Lib v. University of Missouri*,[65] Rehnquist dissented, saying that letting homosexual students congregate to advocate the repeal of sodomy laws is similar to letting persons with measles congregate with persons without measles to advocate the repeal of quarantine laws.[66] While perhaps a ludicrous remark on its face, the content of this dicta reveals a basic ignorance by a Supreme Court justice about same-gender sexual orientation. If Chief

Justice Rehnquist truly believes that a same-gender sexual orientation is communicable (a variation of the argument that "gays do not reproduce, so they must recruit"), the immutability argument will certainly fail to move him.

IMMIGRATION

While the legal rights of gay students are relatively well settled, the area of gay immigration is in legal chaos. In *Boutilier v. Immigration and Naturalization Service* in 1967, the Supreme Court upheld a prohibition against gay and lesbian immigration because the immigration law forbade the entrance of "psychopathic personalities."[67] Gay men and women, according to the Court, fell under that diagnosis. The diagnosis of "psychopathic personality" had to be certified by a federal public health doctor.[68] In 1979, the Public Health Service, through the Surgeon General of the United States, announced that public health doctors would no longer certify gay people as "psychopathic personalities" because new studies clearly indicated that a same-gender sexual orientation was not a diagnosable mental illness.[69] Following this policy change, the Court of Appeals for the 9th Circuit in *Hill v. United States Immigration and Naturalization Service* said that without such certification, gay and lesbian immigrants had to be admitted.[70] Meantime, in 1983, the 5th Circuit in *In re Longstaff* upheld the deportation of a gay male immigrant without the certification.[71] Thus, the federal appellate courts remain split on the issue. The Supreme Court has refused consistently to grant certiorari on the issue, permitting the two conflicting decisions to stand.[72]

The immigration issue was resolved in 1990 by the passage of a new federal immigration law that removed the prohibition on gay and lesbian immigration based on sexual orientation.[73]

EMPLOYMENT

Criminalization, the military, student rights, and immigration are all important legal issues for gay men and lesbians. However, for many gay citizens, these issues are not daily ones. The one legal issue that presses on the daily existence of almost all gay citizens is employment discrimination. Gay employees wonder whether, in order to pursue a career and have a stable livelihood, they must be closeted and live in constant fear of being found out.

Most Americans believe at the gut level that everyone has a "constitutional right" to hold a job as long as he or she is doing the job. To most Americans, working has a built-in "just cause" constitutional criterion. The reality of American employment law often comes as a shock to the average working person. First, most employment law is state idiosyncratic. Even so, the basic legal principle underlying all state employment law is "employment at will."[74] The employment at will doctrine holds that employer and employee are in equal positions: the employee can quit "at will," and the employer can fire "at will." At its broadest, "at will" can encompass whimsical, capricious, and arbitrary decisions. Three significant limitations exist. First, federal law supersedes state law and prohibits employment discrimination on the basis of certain enumerated classifications: gender, race, nationality, age, and handicap.[75] If the worker can prove that he or she was discriminated against under one of these enumerated classifications, federal law, in theory, will protect him or her. The second major limitation on the at will doctrine is where a union contract protects the worker. In such a case, a contractual "just cause" requirement for discharge exists for all workers protected by the union-employer contract.[76] The third significant limitation exists where the employee as an individual has an express or implied contract with the employer. Such contracts are rare; however, in modifying the employment at will doctrine, state courts are now more willing to find implied contracts. While the employment at will doctrine is under strong attack,[77] in most states it remains a serious obstacle to worker protection from arbitrary and capricious job actions.

For gay and lesbian employees who work for private employers, protections are virtually nonexistent. Federal laws provide no protection. Legal strategists have sought to include sexual orientation within the protected "gender" classification of Title VII but have been unsuccessful.[78] As previously indicated, individual express or implied employment contracts are rare. Union workers who are gay or lesbian are protected, at least in theory. Every labor union has a federally mandated duty to "fairly represent" any aggrieved union worker.[79] Labor unions, until very recently, have been less than proactive in their attitude toward gay and lesbian union members. Union attitudes, at least on the national level, have changed dramatically. Almost all national unions have policies supporting and protecting the rights of gay and lesbian members.[80] Follow-through on the level of the local union is more problematic.

Two states, Wisconsin[81] and Massachusetts,[82] have state statutes that prohibit discrimination based on sexual orientation for both private and public employment within the state. California protects the employment rights of openly gay persons through the combined authority of the California Labor Code and a California Supreme Court case.[83] Under the California Labor Code, one cannot be fired for "political activity."[84] In 1979, the California court held that openly gay citizens are engaged in "political activity."[85] Ironically, closeted gays and lesbians would not be similarly protected.

A small number of cities and counties in the United States have employment laws that protect employees on the basis of their sexual orientation.[86] However, by far the majority of these statutes apply to public but not private employers.

The progress in protecting gay employees in public employment has been quite dramatic since 1968. In the late 1960s, gay and lesbian federal employees began challenging the government's right to fire them arbitrarily.[87] They began to assert their due process rights. The federal Constitution prohibits both federal and state governmental action unless due process is followed and equal treatment occurs. Gay federal employees insisted on "due process" hearings, and consequently the government was held to the standard of showing a "rational nexus" between its actions (firing) and the reason (sexual orientation).[88] During the early 1970s, the federal government was unable to prove to the satisfaction of federal courts that any rational nexus existed between a person's sexual orientation and his or her job performance. Thus in 1976, the Carter administration issued a new standard for federal employment through the Office of Personnel Management.[89] This policy stated that the private lives of federal employees were not relevant to personnel decisions.

All state governments are also held to the due process standard because the Fourteenth Amendment to the Constitution applies the due process requirements of the Fifth Amendment to state action. State court decisions have been fewer and more often find against the gay employee. Many courts seem to find an apparent rational nexus between sexual orientation and police and fire work.[90] Perhaps, analogously, those state functions parallel the federal military in the minds of judges. Yet to the contrary, some major cities actively recruit gay and lesbian police and fire officers.[91]

In at least nine states, governors have issued executive orders prohibiting discrimination in state government positions on the basis of sexual orientation.[92] The president of the United States has *not* issued such an order nationally.

Protecting one's self from the homophobic actions of employers is still difficult, especially in private employment. However, for both state and local government employees, prospects of a harassment free and firing free workplace are much better than 10 years ago. A federal bill adding "sexual orientation" to the list of federally protected categories of Title

VII has perennially languished in the House and Senate since its first introduction in 1981.[93] The bright side is that each year more and more legislators courageously sign on to sponsor the "gay rights" bill.[94]

CHILD CUSTODY

Second to employment problems for gay and lesbian citizens are the obstacles and inequities imposed on gay family life. In both *Doe v. Commonwealth's Attorney*[95] and *Bowers v. Hardwick*,[96] the Supreme Court apparently took judicial notice of the erroneous idea that gay people are not within families. Such a view is ludicrous on its face because at a minimum all gay persons have mothers and fathers, not to mention grandparents, uncles and aunts, and siblings. However, a large number of gay persons are also parents, and many have primary or sole care of their offspring. Moreover, many gay and lesbian individuals form family units by committing themselves to a relationship with a second individual. Nongay married couples without children are considered a family unit by the law;[97] gay men and lesbians are fighting for a similar status.

After divorce, gay parents usually seek custody or reasonable visitation of their children who were born of the heterosexual union. This context often creates the most homophobic and vitriolic reactions by courts.

Custody matters are state issues, so rarely does the Supreme Court hear such issues. Moreover, custody issues are decided by judges rather than jurors. Custody decisions are very difficult to challenge at the appellate level. The cases are "fact intensive"; appeals as of right are only on matters of law. Finally, the standard by which judges are guided to assess the facts is vague and broad. The judge in theory chooses what is in the "best interest of the child," an inherently subjective standard.[98] Some states have sought to limit judicial decision making in this area by setting guidelines more precisely defining the best interests of the child.[99] However, even in those cases, the intensely subjective nature of the decisions remains.

Gay parents seeking custody or reasonable visitation are beset by four myths:

1. Gays and lesbians are child molesters. This myth has been repeatedly disproven in scientific literature[100] but many judges tenaciously cling to it. For example, in a Missouri case, a psychologist testified extensively on this issue, explaining that pedophilia is a sexual disturbance not tied to sexual orientation.[101] He further testified that 95% of all reported child molesting is done by men and within that male group, their sexual orientations conform to the percentages of the population

of nongay and gay men.[102] In the face of overwhelming evidence, the Missouri judge found the testimony "suspect" because "every trial judge . . . knows that the molestation of minor boys by adult males is not as uncommon as the psychological expert's testimony indicated."[103]

2. The gay parent will change the child's sexual orientation. Social scientists have shown that sexual orientation most likely is fixed by biology early in life.[104] No evidence exists that a gay parent could convert a child even if he or she so chose. One New Jersey judge stated that the only effect he could predict would be that children of gay parents would grow up to be more tolerant people.[105]

3. Children of gay parents will be teased and stigmatized. Perhaps they will. Increasingly, gay litigators have relied on Chief Justice Burger's holding in *Palmore v. Sudoti,*[106] a rare family law case decided by the Supreme Court. The *Palmore* case involved a Caucasian child of a divorced white couple. The wife remarried an Afro-American. The biological father claimed that "it was not in the best interests of a white child to live in a "[racially] mixed marriage" home. In finding for the mother and her new husband, Chief Justice Burger said:

> There is a risk that a child living with a step parent of a different race may be subject to a variety of pressures and stresses not present if the child were living with parents of the same racial or ethnic origin.
>
> The question, however, is whether the reality of private biases and the possible injury they might inflict are permissible considerations for removal of an infant child from the custody of its natural mother. We have little difficulty concluding that they are not. The Constitution cannot control such prejudices but neither can it tolerate them. Private biases may be outside the reach of the law, but the law cannot, directly or indirectly, give them effect.[107]

4. Same-gender sex is per se immoral, and hence gay parents are per se immoral and therefore unfit as parents. Since this argument is basically a religiously and morally based conclusion, one cannot rationally disprove such an accusation. If the trier of fact holds to that persuasion, the search for best interests of the child is unlikely to be objective. In the latter situation, the custody trial becomes a trial of the gay parent's sexuality and conduct.[108]

Notwithstanding the problems, gay parents have become increasingly successful in their suits. A number of state courts hold that sexual orientation is irrelevant to the determination of custody.[109] However, in other states gay custody battles are arduous; the parent expends a lot of money (experts are expensive), waits a cruel time (the wheels of justice grind slowly), and is often emotionally devastated.

A perusal of the case law in this area indicates that especially on the east and west coasts of the United States, courts are finding more and more for the gay parents based on factors external to sexual orientation.[110]

Gay persons who were not heterosexually married previously still have child custody problems where the child was technically illegitimate, where the child was conceived by artificial insemination by donor, or where the child is a foster child or potential adoptee.[111] Some of the issues are the same regardless of how the child was conceived; however, keeping custody is much easier when the father's whereabouts are unknown because no legally cognizable adversary remains.

GAY FAMILY ISSUES

Gay family issues are more complex than just custody fights. The common mythology is that gay men and lesbians (especially the men) are promiscuous and do not form lasting relationships. In *Homosexualities,* Bell and Weinberg showed that viewing all gay people in such a monolithic way was inaccurate and misleading. He found that gay couples form relationships in much the same way and of the same length as nongay couples.[112] Gay relationships are as varied and complex as nongay relationships.

Increasingly, gay couples have become aware of the economic discrimination practiced against them in a society that uses heterosexual married units as the standard of "family." The vast majority of gay couples cannot obtain employment health benefits for their significant others, and the sickness or death of one's primary partner does not count toward sick leave or bereavement leave.[113] Gay couples cannot file joint income tax returns even when such a joint filing might be monetarily advantageous.[114]

Gay legal activists are pushing increasingly on these issues, seeking the equalization of economic benefits between gay and nongay couples.[115] Other activists would go farther and seek the right to marry. In Denmark, quite recently, marriage has been expanded to cover gay couples,[116] and in Sweden, Swedish law guarantees equal economic rights to gay couples without legalizing gay marriage.[117]

In some American cases, the concept of "family" has been broadened to encompass gay couples. The most striking case is *Braschi v. State Associates Co.,*[118] where the highest New York court held that a life partner of a man who died from AIDS was his "family" and hence entitled to keep their apartment.

Another famous case has brought to light another gay "family" problem. In 1983, Sharon Kowalski was seriously injured on the way home from work. Her life partner, Karen Thompson, was denied both entrance to her partner's room and participation in the decisions about her care because Karen was *not* a member of Sharon's family (*legal* family—blood or marriage). Sharon and Karen had lived together for seven years and purchased a home together, but Sharon had never come out to her parents. The parents proceeded to shut Karen out of Sharon's life and denied the validity of their relationship.[119] In response to such situations, lawyers for gay and lesbian clients attempt to create some protection for the life partner by use of common law doctrines. Such a legal package usually consists of wills, medical powers of attorney, housing agreements, and so forth.[120] While much legal progress has been made in protecting gay and lesbian couples as couples, the fight over family status for gays is now reaching the courts and legislatures. In 1989, San Francisco passed a domestic partnership act that allowed gay couples "to register."[121] However, a referendum repealed that ordinance, although a milder version has been passed as this book went to press.[122] Many union contracts in Ohio provide that the state as an employer cannot discriminate on the basis of sexual orientation.[123] However, the fight for benefits for life partners has met numerous obstacles, a few rational.[124]

SUMMARY

The legal status of gay men and lesbians in 1990 is a mixed bag. Much progress toward equal treatment under the law has been made. However, as long as *Bowers* is still precedent, the stigma of criminalization hangs over all American gay men and lesbians.

NOTES

1. On January 1, 1962, Illinois became the first state to decriminalize adult, consensual, private sexual conduct. 1961 I11. Laws p. 1983, § 11-2. All the sexual acts penalized when committed between persons of the same gender can be performed by persons of the opposite gender. Laws that forbade certain sexual acts often did not differentiate as to married or unmarried persons, gay or nongay persons.

2. A. Kinsey, W. Pomeroy, & C. Martin, *Sexual Behavior in the Human Male* 389-393 (1948).

3. People v. Onofre, 51 N.Y.2d 476, 415 N.E.2d 936, 434 N.Y.S.2d 947 (1980), *cert. denied*, 451 U.S. 987 (1981); Commonwealth v. Bonadio, 490 Pa. 91, 415 A. 2d 47 (1980); Commonwealth v. Sefranka, 382 Mass. 108, 414 N.E.2d 602 (1980).

4. Ala. Code § 13A-6-65(a)(3) (1988); Ariz. Rev. Stat. Ann. §§ 13-1411, -1412 (1989); Ark. Code § 5-14-122 (1987); D.C. Code Ann. § 22-3502 (1989); Fla. Stat.§ 800.02 (1988); Ga. Code Ann. § 16-6-2 (1988); Idaho Code § 18-6605 (1988); Kan. Stat. Ann. § 31-3505 (1988); Ky. Rev. Stat. Ann. § 510.100 (Michie/Bobbs-Merrill, 1989); La. Rev. Stat. Ann. § 14.89 (West 1986); Md. Crimes and Punish. Ann. Code § 554 (1987); Mich. Comp. Laws §§ 750.158, .338a, .338b (1979); Minn. Stat. § 609.923 (1988); Miss. Code Ann. § 97-29-59 (1972); Mo. Rev. Stat. § 566.090 (1988); Mont. Code Ann. § 45-5-505 (1989); Nev. Rev. Stat. § 201.190 (1988); N.C. Gen. Stat. § 14-177 (1989); Okla. Stat. tit. 21, § 886 (1988); R.I. Gen. Laws § 11-10-1 (1981); S.C. Code Ann. § 16-15-120 (Law. Co-op. 1985); Tenn. Code Ann. § 39-2-612 (1982); Tex. Penal Code Ann. § 21.06 (Vernon 1989); Utah Code Ann. § 76-5-403 (Supp. 1989); Va. Code Ann. § 18.2-361 (1989); *see also Developments in the Law—Sexual Orientation and the Law*, 102 Harv. L. Rev. 1508, 1519-1521 (1989).

5. *See, e.g.*, Ark. Code § 5-4-401 (1987) (1 year); Ga. Code Ann. § 16-6-2(b) (1988) (20 years); Idaho Code § 18-6605 (1988) (not less than 5 years); Mich. Comp. Laws § 750.158 (1968) (15 years or indeterminate sentence if individual is a "sexually delinquent person"); N.C. Gen. Stat. §§ 14-1.1, -177 (1989) (10 years); S.C. Code Ann. § 16-15-120 (Law Co-op. 1985) (5 years).

6. 1977 Ark. Acts 2118 (No. 828 § 1); 1989 Tenn. Pub. Acts 1169, 1206 (Ch. 591, enacting Tenn. Code Ann. § 39-13-510 [criminalizing "homosexual acts"] to replace Tenn. Code Ann. § 39-2-612 [crimes against nature]).

7. *See, e.g.*, Karst, *The Freedom of Intimate Association*, 89 Yale L.J. 624 (1980); Richards, *Sexual Autonomy and the Constitutional Right to Privacy*, 30 Hastings L.J. 957 (1979); Richards, *Unnatural Acts and the Constitutional Right to Privacy: A Moral Theory*, 45 Fordham L. Rev. 1281 (1977).

8. Griswold v. Connecticut, 381 U.S. 479 (1965).

9. Eisenstadt v. Baird, 405 U.S. 438 (1972).

10. Roe v. Wade, 410 U.S. 959 (1973).

11. Stanley v. Georgia, 394 U.S. 557 (1969).

12. Carey v. Population Services, 431 U.S. 678 (1977).

13. *Id.* at 688 n.5, 694 n.17. The Court observed that it had "not definitely answered the difficult question whether and to what extent the Constitution prohibits state statutes regulating [private consensual sexual] behavior among adults." *Id.* at 694 n.17.

14. Doe v. Commonwealth's Attorney, 403 F. Supp. 1199 (1975), *aff'd mem.*, 425 U.S. 901, *reh'g denied*, 425 U.S. 985 (1976).

15. *Id.* at 1202.

16. *Id.* at 1202-1203.

17. *Id.* at 1202.

18. *Id.*

19. Doe v. Commonwealth's Attorney, 425 U.S. 901 (1976), *aff'g* 403 F. Supp. 1199 (1975) (Justices Brennan, Marshall, and Stevens would note probable jurisdiction and set oral argument).

20. *See* Dailey v. Dailey, 635 S.W.2d 391 (Tenn. Ct. App. 1981). In this case, the attorney for the ex-husband argued, "But Your Honor, this is the Bible Belt. This [a lesbian raising her children] might be okay in New York or California, but this is the Bible Belt." The lesbian mother's attorney attempted to educate the court with expert testimony about homosexuality; the opposing attorney argued that in Tennessee the mother was a criminal for engaging in lesbian sexual activity. The mother lost custody of her child, and visitation was severely restricted. *See also Gay and Lesbian Parents* 199-215 (F. Bozett ed. 1987); Clark, *Lesbian Mothers Lose Custody*, Gay Community News, May 16, 1981, at 1; Roe v. Roe, 228 Va. 722, 324 S.E.2d 691 (1985).

21. Bowers v. Hardwick, 478 U.S. 186 (1986).

22. *Id.* at 196.

23. *Id.* at 191.

24. *Id.* at 199 (Blackmun, J., dissenting).

25. *See, e.g.*, Coleman, *Disordered Liberty: Judicial Restrictions on the Rights to Privacy and Equality in* Bowers v. Hardwick *and* Baker v. Wade, 12 Thurgood Marshall L. Rev. 81 (1986); Goldstein, *History, Homosexuality, and Political Values: Searching for the Hidden Determinants of* Bowers v. Hardwick, 97 Yale L.J. 1073 (1988); Stoddard, Bowers v. Hardwick: *Precedent by Personal Predilection*, 54 U. Chi. L.R. 648 (1987); Note, *An Imposition of the Justices' Own Moral Choices*, 9 Whittier L. Rev. 115 (1987); *Crime in the Bedroom*, N.Y. Times, July 2, 1986, at 26 (editorial); *A Government in the Bedroom*, Newsweek, July 14, 1986, at 36.

26. *See, e.g.*, *A Government in the Bedroom*, *supra* note 25, at 36.

27. Plessy v. Ferguson, 163 U.S. 537 (1896).

28. Brown v. Bd. of Educ., 347 U.S. 483 (1954).

29. J.P. v. P.W., 772 S.W.2d 786 (1989).

30. *See, e.g.*, Michigan Org. Human Rights v. Michigan, No. 88-815820 CZ (Cir. Ct. Wayne Cty., filed June 29, 1989).

31. Plyler v. Doe, 457 U.S. 202, 216 n.14 (1982); Frontiero v. Richardson, 411 U.S. 677 (1973).

32. Korematsu v. United States, 323 U.S. 214, 216 (1944).

33. *See* J. Money, *Gay, Straight, and In-Between* (1988); A. Bell, M. Weinberg, & S. Hammersmith, *Sexual Preference* (1981); *Homosexual Behavior* (J. Marmor, ed.) (1980); A. Bell & M. Weinberg, *Homosexualities* (1978).

34. J. Psychiatry & Law 537 (Winter 1988).

35. *Id.* at 539-554.

36. *Id.* at 555-568.

37. *See, e.g.*, Watkins v. U.S. Army, 847 F.2d 1329, 1349, *reh'g en banc ordered*, 847 F.2d 1362 (9th Cir. 1988); High Tech Gays v. Defense Indus. Sec. Clearance Office, 668 F. Supp. 1361 (N.D. Cal. 1987), *rev'd*, _F.2d_ (9th Cir. 1990) (1990 U.S. App. LEXIS 1329).

38. Dunlap, *Toward Recognition of "A Right to be Sexual", 7 Women's Rights L. Rptr. 245, 247 (1982).*

39. Rivera, *Our Straight-Laced Judges: The Legal Position of Homosexual Persons in the United States*, 30 Hastings L. J. 799, 837-855 (1979).

40. *Homosexuals in the Military*, 37 Fordham L. Rev. 465, 465-466 (1969); C. Williams & M. Weinberg, *Homosexuals and the Military* 27-29 (1971). For an excellent history of gay men and lesbians in World War II, see A. Berube, *Coming Out Under Fire* (1990).

41. C. Williams & M. Weinberg, *supra* note 40, at 60.

42. Rivera, *Queer Law: Sexual Orientation Law in the Mid-Eighties, Part II*, 11 U. Dayton L. Rev. 275, 287-288 (1986).

43. Rivera, Book Review, 132 U. Pa. L. Rev. 391, 397 (1984).

44. Matlovich v. Secretary of the Air Force, 414 F. Supp. 690 (D.D.C. 1976), *vacated*, 591 F.2d 852 (D.C. Cir., 1978). For a biography of Matlovich see M. Hippler, *Matlovich, The Good Soldier* (1989).

45. Matlovich v. Secretary of the Air Force, 414 F. Supp. 690 (D.D.C. 1976), *vacated*, 591 F.2d 852 (D.C. Cir., 1978).

46. *Matlovich*, 591 F.2d at 855-857.

47. Dept. Def. Directive No. 1332.14 (1981) revised (1982) (Enlisted Administrative Separations).

48. Dept. Def. Directive No. 1332.14, encl. 3, § H.1.a (1982) (Enlisted Administrative Separations).

49. *Id.*

50. Dept. Def. Directive No. 1332.14, encl. 3, § H.1.b.1 (1982).

51. Ben-Shalom v. Secretary of the Army, 489 F. Supp. 964 (E.D. Wis. 1980), *aff'd on other grounds*, Ben-Shalom v. Marsh, 703 F. Supp. 1372 (E.D. Wis. 1989); Pruitt v. Weinberger, 659 F. Supp. 625 (C.D. Cal. 1987); Matthews v. Marsh, No. 82-0216 P, slip. op. (D. Me. Apr. 3, 1984), *vacated* 755 F.2d 182 (1985); Steffan v. Cheney, No. 88-3669-OG slip. op. (D.D.C. Nov. 15, 1989) (1989 U.S. Dist. LEXIS 13640) (dismissed for failure to comply with discovery).

52. Robinson v. California, 370 U.S. 660 (1962).

53. Watkins v. U.S. Army, 847 F.2d 1329 (9th Cir. 1988), *reh'g granted*, 847 F.2d 1362 (1988) (en banc), *aff'd. on other grounds*, 875 F.2d 699 (1989).

54. Watkins v. United States, 875 F.2d 699 (9th Cir. 1989) (en banc).

55. Ben-Shalom v. Stone, 110 S. Ct. 1296 (1990), *denying cert. to* Ben-Shalom v. Marsh, 881 F.2d 454 (7th Cir. 1989); Woodward v. United States, 110 S. Ct. 1295 (1990), *denying cert. to* 871 F.2d 1068 (1989).

56. Ben-Shalom v. Secretary of the Army, 484 F. Supp. 964, 973 (1980).

57. Steffan v. Cheney, No. 88-3669-OG, Slip. op. (D.D.C. Nov. 15, 1989) (1989 U.S. Dist. LEXIS 13640) (dismissed for failure to comply with discovery).

58. Parker v. Levy, 417 U.S. 733, 743 (1974).

59. The Uniform Code of Military Justice, 10 U.S.C. §§ 801-940, is the direct descendant of the Articles of War approved by the Continental Congress on September 20, 1776. The Uniform Code, passed May 5, 1950, and in full force and effect by May 31, 1951, superseded the Articles of War and replaced separate disciplinary laws of each branch with a single statute encompassing both substantive and procedural law for all the armed services. The UCMJ, amended by the Military Justice Act of 1968, expanded the right of the accused to the services of a certified military lawyer, and expanded the role of the military judge. Some offenses punishable under the UCMJ are peculiar to the military, for example, "Conduct Unbecoming an Officer and a Gentleman."

60. M.A. McDaniel, *Preservice Adjustment of Homosexual and Heterosexual Military Accessions: Implications for Security Clearance Suitability*, Defense Personnel Security Research and Education Center, PERS-TR-89-04 (1989) at 21; T.R. Sarkn, & K.E. Karols, *Nonconforming Sexual Orientations and Military Suitability*, Defense Personnel Security Research and Education Center, PERS-TR-89-002 (December 1988) at 33.

61. *See* National Gay Rights Association Newsletter, Spring 1985, at 1; *For the Record: A Review of Gay and Lesbian News for the Period Ending Nov. 2, 1984*, The Advocate, Nov. 27, 1984, at 3.

62. *See* Stanley, *The Rights of Gay Student Organizations*, 10 J.C. & Univ. L. 397 (1983-84).

63. Fricke v. Lynch, 491 F. Supp. 381 (D.R.I. 1980).

64. Gay Student Services v. Texas A&M Univ., 737 F.2d 1317 (1984), *appeal dismissed*, 471 U.S. 1001 (1985).

65. Ratchford v. Gay Lib., 434 U.S. 1080 (1978), *denying cert. to* Gay Lib v. University of Mo., 558 F.2d 848 (1977).

66. *Id.* at 1080, 1084.

67. 363 F.2d 488 (2d Cir. 1966), *aff'd*, 387 U.S. 118 (1967).

68. Section 212(a) (4) provides that aliens "afflicted with psychopathic personality or sexual deviation" shall be excluded from admission into the United States. 8 U.S.C. § 1182(a)(4) (1976).

69. Memorandum from Julius Richmond, assistant secretary for Health, United States Department of Health, Education and Welfare, and surgeon general, to William Foege and George Lythcott (Aug. 2, 1979), *reprinted in* 56 Interpreter Releases 398-399 (1979).

70. 714 F.2d 1470 (9th Cir. 1983).

71. 716 F.2d 1439 (5th Cir. 1983), *cert. denied*, 467 U.S. 1219 (1984).

72. *See, e.g.*, Nat. L.J., Oct. 17, 1983, at 3, col. 2.

73. H.R. 1280, 101st Cong., 1st sess. (1989).

74. An early characterization of the employment at will doctrine recognized the employer's traditional right to discharge an employee "for good cause, for no cause or even for cause morally wrong." Payne v. Western & Atl. R.R., 81 Tenn. 507, 519-520 (1884), *rev'd on other grounds sub nom.*, Hutton v. Watters, 132 Tenn. 527, 179 S.W. 134 (1915).

75. Title VII of the 1964 Civil Rts. Act, 42 U.S.C. § 2000e-2000e-17 (1982), Age Discrimination in Employment Act, 29 U.S.C. §§ 701-960 (1982), Rehabilitation Act of 1973, 29 U.S.C. §§ 701-960 (1982).

76. F. Elkouri & E. Elkouri, *How Arbitration Works* 652-654 (4th ed. 1985).

77. *See* Leonard, *A New Common Law of Employment Termination*, 66 N.C.L. Rev. 637 (1988).

78. De Santis v. Pacific Tel. & Tel. Co., 608 F.2d 327 (9th Cir. 1979); Smith v. Liberty Mut. Ins. Co., 569 F.2d 325 (5th Cir. 1978); Holloway v. Arthur Anderson & Co., 566 F.2d 659 (9th Cir. 1977).

79. Under § 9(a) of the National Labor Relations Act, the representative selected by the majority of the employees in an appropriate bargaining unit is the exclusive representative of all unit employees. National Labor Relations (Taft-Hartley) act § 9(a), 29 U.S.C. § 159(a) (1982). The union's right of exclusivity has been judicially determined to carry with it a correlative duty to fairly represent all unit employees. For more information on the duty of fair representation, see L. Modjeska, *Handling Employment Discrimination Cases* § 7.5 (1980).

80. *See* The AFL-CIO and Civil Rights: Report of the AFL-CIO Executive Council and Resolutions Adopted by the Fifteenth Constitutional Convention of the AFL-CIO (Oct. 6, 1983) (unpublished manuscript).

The ILGWU adopted its resolution without controversy at its 38th convention held May 30, 1983. The Advocate, Aug. 4, 1983, at 12. The AFSCME resolution was adopted at its convention on June 23, 1982. Gay Community News, Apr. 30, 1983, at 2. The SEIU accepted a unit of employees of the Gay and Lesbian Community Services Center on January 31, 1984. *Id.*, Feb. 11, 1984, at 1. The CWA attempted to negotiate a sexual preference nondiscrimination clause in its contract with the state of New Jersey, but was unsuccessful. *Id.*, June 25, 1983, at 2. The Newspaper Guild, the nation's largest union of editorial employees, passed a resolution in support of nondiscrimination on the basis of sexual orientation at its convention in Cleveland, Ohio, on June 27, 1983. *Id.*, July 23, 1983, at 1.

Other unions who support gay rights include the American Postal Workers Union, the International Longshoreman's and Warehousemen's Union, the Screen Actors Guild, the United Auto and Aerospace Workers Union of California (AFL-CIO), the Department Store Employees Union of California, Local 715 of the SEIU, the Chicago Teachers Union, the Union of Boston Public School Teachers, the Massachusetts Restaurant and Hotel Workers Union, the Joint Council of Teamsters No. 28 of Washington, the Black Coalition of Building Trades of Rhode Island, the Central Labor Council of Santa Clara County, California, the Massachusetts Amalgamated Meatcutters Union, and the AFSCME Locals 22, 1164, 1902 & 2083. The Advocate, June 26, 1984, at 42.

81. 1981 Wis. Laws ch. 112 (primary employment provisions codified at Wis. Stat. Ann. §§ 16.765, 111.31-.32, .70, .85, 230.01(2) (West 1988).

82. 1989 Mass. Adv. Legis. Serv. ch. 516 (Law. Co-op.).

83. Gay Law Students Ass'n v. Pacific Tel. and Tel. Co., 24 Cal. 3d 458, 595 P.2d 592, 156 Cal. Rptr. 14 (1979).

84. Cal. Labor Code §§ 1101-1102 (West 1989).

85. *Gay Law Students*, 24 Cal. 3d at 485, 595 P.2d at 610, 156 Cal. Rptr. at 32.

86. *See* National Gay Task Force, *Gay Rights Protections in the U.S. and Canada* (July 1984) (survey of jurisdictions protecting gay and lesbian civil rights, listing 44 U.S. cities and 12 counties).

87. Dew v. Halaby, 317 F.2d 582 (D.C. Cir. 1963), *cert. dismissed per stipulation*, 379 U.S. 951 (1964).

88. *Norton v. Macy*, 417 F.2d 1161 (D.C. Cir. 1969).

89. Memorandum, Policy Statement on Discrimination on the Basis of Conduct Which Does Not Adversely Affect the Performance of Employees or Applicants for Employment (OPM May 12, 1980).

90. *See, e.g.*, Childers v. Dallas Police Dep't, 513 F. Supp. 134 (N.D. Tex. 1981), *aff'd mem.*, 669 F.2d 732 (5th Cir. 1982).

91. *See, e.g.*, Peterson, *Los Angeles County to Recruit Gay Deputies*, The Advocate, March 28, 1989, at 15; Purdum, *Homosexuals Assist Police Recruiting Drive*, N.Y. Times, May 16, 1987, at 11 (National ed.) (New York City); De Luca, *Boston Police Discuss Recruiting Gay Officers*, Gay Community News, April 5-11, 1987, at 3; *Officer Almsteld—On the Force and Openly Gay*, The Advocate, Sept. 17, 1984, at 19 (San Francisco).

92. *E.g.*, Exec. Order No. B-54-79 (Cal. 1979); Exec. Order No. 86-14 (Minn.); Exec. Order No. 85-15 (N.M.); Exec. Order No. 28 (N.Y. 1983); Exec. Order No. 83-64 (Ohio); Exec. Order No. 87-20 (Or.); Exec. Order No. 1975-5 (Pa.); Exec. Order No. 85-11 (R.I.) Exec. Order No. 85-09 (Wash.).

93. *See, e.g.*, H.R. 655, 101st Cong., 1st Sess., 135 Cong. Rec. H96-97 (daily ed. Jan. 24, 1989); S. 47, 101st Cong., 1st Sess., 135 Cong. Rec. S340 (daily ed. Jan. 25, 1989); *Civil Rights Act Amendments of 1981: Hearings on H.R. 1454 Before the Subcomm. on Employment Opportunities of the House Comm. on Education and Labor*, 97th Cong., 2d Sess. (1982); *Civil Rights Amendments Act of 1979: Hearings on H.R. 2074 Before the Subcomm. on Employment Opportunities of the House Comm. on Education and Labor*, 96th Cong., 2d Sess. 1980).

94. *See Majority Whip Signs On*, Wash. Blade, Mar. 30, 1990, at 19 (74 cosponsors in the House, 8 in the Senate, for Civil Rights Amendments Act of 1989).

95. 403 F. Supp. 1199 (1975), *aff'd mem.*, 425 U.S. 901, *reh'g denied*, 425 U.S. 985 (1976).

96. 478 U.S. 186 (1986).

97. Married couples, for example, can file joint income tax returns and are eligible for increased Social Security benefits.

98. Finlay v. Finlay, 240 N.Y. 429, 433, 148 N.E. 624, 626, 211 N.Y.S. 429, 434 (1925).

99. *E.g.*, Mich. Comp. Laws § 722.23 (Supp. 1989).

100. Pedophilia, a sexual preference for children, is distinct from homosexuality. *See* D. J. West, *Homosexuality Re-Examined* 212-217 (1977); D. J. West, *Homosexuality 118-119 (1967); Comment, Private Consensual Homosexual Behavior: The Crime and Its Enforcement*, 70 Yale L.J. 623, 629 (1961). Homosexual men primarily prefer men of their own age rather than children. Institute for Sex Research, *Sex Offenders* 639 (1965); M. Schofield, *Sociological Aspects of Homosexuality* 147-155 (1965), *cited in* W. Barnett, *Sexual Freedom and the Constitution* 129-130 n.51 (1973). In fact, child molesters tend to be heterosexual in orientation. Schofield, *supra* at 115; Institute for Sex Research, *supra* at 9.

101. J.L.P. (H) v. D.J.P., 643 S.W.2d 865, 866-867 (Mo. Ct. App. 1982).

102. *Id.*

103. *Id.* at 869.

104. *See* A. Bell, M. Weinberg, & S. Hammersmith, *supra* note 33, at 183-187, 221-222.

105. M.P. v. S.P., 169 N.J. Super 425, 438, 404 A.2d 1256, 1263 (App. Div. 1979).

106. 466 U.S. 429 (1984).

107. *Palmore*, 466 U.S. at 433. For an application of *Palmore* in a lesbian mother case *see* S.N.E. v. R.L.B., 699 P.2d 875 (Alaska 1985).

108. *E.g.*, Roe v. Roe, 228 Va. 722, 324 S.E.2d 691 (1985); Townend v. Townend, No. 639, slip op. (Ohio Ct. App. Sept. 30, 1976).

109. *E.g.*, S.N.E. v. R.L.B., 699 P.2d 875 (Alaska 1985); Bezio v. Patenaude, 381 Mass. 563, 410 N.E.2d 1207 (1980); Gottlieb v. Gottlieb, 108 A.D.2d 120, 488 N.Y.S.2d 180 (N.Y. App. Div. 1985).

110. *See* Rivera, *supra* note 43, at 406; Rivera, *supra* note 42, at 369-371.

111. *E.g., In re* Charles B., No. 88-2163, slip. op. (Ohio Mar. 28, 1990) (1990 Ohio LEXIS 133), *rev'g* No. CA-3382, slip. op. (Ohio Ct. App. Oct. 28, 1988) (1988 Ohio App. LEXIS 4435).

112. A. Bell & M. Weinberg, *supra* note 33, at 129-138, 217-228.

113. For a discussion of those employers who *do* provide benefits to gay significant others, see Freudenheim, *Rising Worry on 'Partner' Benefits* N.Y. Times, Aug. 16, 1989, at D1; Gorney, *Making It Official: The Law and Live-Ins,* Wash. Post, July 5, 1989, at C1; R. Eblin, *Domestic Partnership Recognition in the Workplace* (Feb. 28, 1990) (tentative title; publication anticipated in 51 Ohio St. L.J.).

114. The Internal Revenue Code limits the filing of a joint return to "[a] husband and wife." I.R.C. § 6013(a) (West Supp. 1990).

115. *See, e.g.,* Cox, *Alternative Families: Obtaining Traditional Family Benefits Through Litigation, Legislation and Collective Bargaining,* 2 Wis. Women's L.J. 1 (1986); R. Eblin, *supra* note 113.

116. *See, e.g.,* Isherwood, *Denmark Legalises Homosexual Marriages,* Daily Telegraph, May 27, 1989, at 11.

117. *See, e.g.,* Ahlberg, *Live-In Lovers in Sweden, Including Gays, Given Same Rights as Married Couples,* L.A. Times, Mar. 27, 1988, pt. 1, at 15.

118. 74 N.Y.2d 201, 544 N.Y.S.2d 784 (Ct. App. 1989).

119. *See In re* Guardianship of Kowalski, 382 N.W.2d 861 (Minn. Ct. App. 1986); *In re* Guardianship of Kowalski, 392 N.W.2d 310 (Minn. Ct. App. 1986); K. Thompson & J. Andrzejewski, *Why Can't Sharon Kowalski Come Home?* (1988).

120. *See generally Sexual Orientation and the Law* §§ 1.01-4.12 (R. Achtenberg ed. 1989).

121. San Francisco, Cal., Ordinance 176-189 (June 5, 1989); *see* Gorney, *Making It Official: The Law and Live-Ins,* Wash. Post, July 5, 1989, at C1.

122. *Final Election Results: San Francisco,* San Francisco Chronicle, Nov. 10, 1989, at B7.

123. *E.g.,* Contract between the State of Ohio and Ohio Civil Service Employees Assn., Local 11, 1986-1989 art. 2, § 2.01.

124. *E.g.,* I.R.C. § 89 (West Supp. 1989) (taxing employer-paid health insurance benefits for life partners who were not legal dependents). Section 89, which was complex and potentially affected the tax status of many employee benefit plans, has been repealed. Act of November 8, 1989, Pub. L. No. 101-140, § 202, 103 Stat. 830.

7

Psychological and Medical Treatments of Homosexuality

Charles Silverstein

This chapter examines two moments in time, separated by centuries of social change. The first occurred in 1641 in Boston. According to the records, William Hackett was hanged in the public square for the crime of sodomy. Because of the nature of the crime, we know almost exactly what this unfortunate man did to bring himself to the attention of the city fathers and to end with his public execution. He had sex with a cow, probably anal intercourse (Bullough, 1976). We know this because the city fathers executed the cow as well!

The second event took place on December 15, 1973, when the American Psychiatric Association announced that homosexuality per se was no longer on their list of mental disorders. This event, also a public one, was announced at a news conference, rather than by the town crier. It caused a stir around the world that affected the lives of millions of people, rather than that of one man (and cow) in the first event. Seventeen years have passed since the APA made the brave decision to reverse their long-standing judgment that homosexuality is a mental illness. It may be enough time to stand back from the controversy, to consider its meaning as a social event, and to examine the ways in which it has resolved some social problems, while at the same time has created new ones.

The events cited above might seem to have little in common, but, in fact, they have a number of shared features. Both represent a social judgment about the behavior of citizens. In the sodomy case, the social judgment was that a man may not have intercourse with a cow. In the APA decision men and women who chose to engage in intimate relations with a member of the same sex were freed from the label "mentally ill." Punishment for violating the moral code is the second similarity. Boston's civil authorities decreed sodomy a capital crime. While some may object, I suggest that psychiatric diagnosis of deviant sexuality is also a form of punishment, and that punishment for violating social rules is one of psychiatry's major purposes.

A third similarity is the belief in a higher authority, in the form of a revered book upon which to judge social behavior. In the first case the Bible is the authority. In the second, it is the *Diagnostic and Statistical Manual* of the American Psychiatric Association. Drawing a parallel between these two books may seem unfair. On one hand, the Bible is said to be the word of God and therefore unchangeable; on the other hand, the psychiatric diagnostic system is said to be based upon empirical science, and changeable through knowledge. Neither is quite true. While God's words may remain the same, they are constantly reinterpreted. The APA diagnostic system changes over time, but does so almost exclusively by searching out new forms of mental illness. At least the Bible, unlike the statistical manual, does not get heavier with each succeeding edition.

It is noteworthy that the most heated responses to the removal of homosexuality from the diagnostic system came from orthodox religious groups and orthodox psychoanalysts (Socarides, 1975). The reason is that they share the same philosophical system, one rooted in Judeo-Christian morality. The essential point is that psychiatry and therefore psychiatric diagnosis is the child of Western religion.

MEDICAL DIAGNOSIS AND SOCIETY

The Western world is replete with examples of diagnosis used to enforce correct social behavior. The witch hunts of the 16th and 17th centuries are a good example. Most of the ostensible witches who were burned, stoned, and drowned were old, ignorant, and poor women who were considered unusual (Rosen, 1969). There are, however, lessons to be learned from this period. Women confessed to being recruited by the Devil and to participating in witches' sabbaths. Were they demented? Were they lying? No doubt some confessed only to reduce the level of torture applied to them, but others probably succumbed to the intense social pressures and believed they were deviant.

In 1924 the Congress of the United States passed an immigration act excluding or severely limiting immigration from many Eastern European countries. Most historians interpret this law as racist and nativist (Snyderman & Hernstein, 1983). The work of Goddard (1917) (of the Kallikack family studies) was often cited as scientific evidence for the inferior genetic intellectual endowment of certain national groups. Testing 178 steerage passengers with his new IQ test, Goddard found feeblemindedness in:

83% of Jews
80% of Hungarians
79% of Italians
87% of Russians

> Researchers recall with sad smiles the miraculous finding, some years after the Ellis Island test, that Jews and Italians improved dramatically in intelligence after they had lived in this country for awhile, and that their children, raised as English speakers, seemed somehow to have been spared their parents' feebleminded genes. (Fallows quoted in Snyderman & Hernstein, 1983, p. 986)

The greatest confusion between social order and scientific judgment is found in perceptions of sexual behavior. Masturbation was socially acceptable until the end of the 18th century, when it suddenly became a medical concern (Shorter, 1975). It was believed that excessive self-indulgence would lead to neurological damage and eventual insanity. John Kellogg developed corn flakes (Carson, 1957) with the intention of producing a food that would reduce libidinous feelings and he hoped, eliminate masturbation in children. Nowadays, masturbation is considered a healthy expression of one's sexuality and is even used as a therapeutic technique. Homosexuality was considered another sexual deviation. It traveled from sin to sickness and has been illegal and immoral almost everywhere in the United States until recent years.

How then does society decide what behaviors to diagnose? Psychotherapy has offered a facile answer. Those who suffer are treated. This is a circular solution. We now understand that, as a society, we train people to suffer. We decide which behaviors are acceptable, we tell people they are deviant, we stigmatize and oppress them, and when they come to us unhappy about themselves, we tell them to get treatment. Witches did not invent themselves, their society did. Goddard's steerage passengers knew they were poor, but they did not know they were also feebleminded until they were turned away from our shores. Women who masturbated were forced to undergo clitoridectomies (Barker-Benfield, 1975). Homosexuals, doomed to a life of depression and misery, committed suicide. All of these people suffered because they were taught to suffer, first by their society at large, and then by the "scientific" community that confirmed the societal condemnation by inventing a medical illness to explain their "immoral" behavior. A primary purpose of psychiatric diagnosis, therefore, is an attempt by society to control those people whom it fears.

THE TREATMENT OF HOMOSEXUALITY AS A DISEASE

Perceptions of the ostensible causes of homosexuality reflected the fears of society, and the treatments offered reflected the strength of these fears. This is as true today as it was in the 1641 sodomy case. The psychiatric/psychological establishment had previously invented many theories to explain the genesis of homosexual behavior. Freud (1922, 1923) believed it resulted from a faulty resolution of the Oedipus complex. Stekel (1933), who like Freud, subscribed to 19th century notions of bisexuality (Sulloway, 1979), believed that homosexuality occurred because of the forces of repression. Rado (1940), objecting to Freud's acceptance of bisexuality, developed the "phobic theory" of homosexuality and from his work the adaptation school of psychoanalysis was born (Rado, 1949). Although Freund, Nagler, Langevin, Zajac, and Steiner (1974) discredited this phobic theory by empirical research, it remains a popular one. Main subscribers of Rado's work include Bieber et al. (1962), Socarides (1978), and Hatterer (1970).

The behaviorist school in psychology also attempted to change gay people into heterosexuals by employing techniques that were often caustic. Haleman, in this volume, details these approaches and other change attempts. Masters and Johnson (1979), though not strict behaviorists, described attempts to change sexual orientation of gay people. Paradoxically, they also describe homosexuals as better lovers than heterosexuals in another section of their study. Gonsiorek (1981) and Silverstein (1980) have argued that their work lacks scientific credibility and theoretical consistency.

Modern psychotherapists have developed an extremely controversial form of treatment. It is like an Alcoholics Anonymous twelve-step program and uses drug addiction as the paradigm to treat "sexual addiction" (Carnes, 1983) and "sexual compulsion" (Mattison, 1985; Quadland, 1985). The conceptual soundness and therapeutic rationale for this treatment program has been questioned by Wedin (1984) and Levine and Troiden (1988). Their patients are encouraged to seek treatment for compulsive masturbation, frequent sex, failure of monogamy, and guilt over sexual acts. Needless to say, advocates of this approach have applied it to gay men, lesbians, women in general, prostitutes, and other suppressed groups. Critics find the conceptual framework elusive, the treatment puritanical, and the judgment of the therapists suspect. It seems as if the advocates of treatment for sexual compulsions are influenced as much by the moral code as by concern for their patients. The claim that patients request this help is reminiscent of the claim of patients who requested clitoridectomies for their masturbation, and of women who admitted to being witches.

Underlying these attempts by psychiatry and psychology to change sexual orientation is a basic philosophical belief concerning the nature of humankind. One must make some kind of assumption about the potential malleability of human behavior. Are people like wet clay that can be molded at will? Is a therapist a potter at the wheel, changing and remaking the patient according to the aesthetics of the day, or, once fired, will the pot be impenetrable and brittle? It would have been enough for the psychotherapeutic community to have taught gay people to suffer and to believe that they were deficient members of their society. On top of that, as attempts to change sexual orientation reliably failed (see Coleman, 1978; Martin, 1984; and Haldeman in this volume), homosexuals were judged failures even in the attempt to change their sexual orientation! Alternatively, researchers suggested improvements in the therapeutic approaches. Never did they seriously consider the possibility that sexual orientation cannot be molded like wet clay.

THE REMOVAL OF HOMOSEXUALITY AS A MENTAL ILLNESS

How, then, was it possible for the American Psychiatric Association to remove homosexuality from their list of mental disorders, when they knew their decision would meet the rage of those members who had made their reputations by treating it (Socarides, 1978; Voth 1977)? The battle began in 1972, when the annual meeting of the Association for the Advancement of Behavior Therapy was held at the Hilton Hotel in New York. The Gay Activist Alliance decided to stage a demonstration against one of the presenters known for his work in the use of aversion therapy. This demonstration led to an invitation to make a presentation before the American Psychiatric Association Nomenclature Committee. There was wide disagreement over the APA's decision (Barr & Catts, 1974; "Sexual survey #4," 1977).

Bayer (1981) has provided a fascinating historical record of the political wrangling that went on behind the scenes. Many people believe that social science research changed the minds of committee members. It seems more plausible that the committee responded to new social values, just as an earlier committee voted to define homosexuality as psychopathic behavior because it was congruent with the social values of its day (American Psychiatric Association, 1942). The APA decision came during a period of egalitarianism in our society, as gay liberation followed on the heels of the black civil rights movement and the women's liberation movement.

Some critics, appalled by the removal of homosexuality from the list of mental disorders, have argued that a vote of hands (referring to the committee vote) is not science. They forget that it was another vote of hands that placed homosexuality on the list in the first place. For the record, it should also be noted that the first statistical table of mental illnesses in America (Association of Medical Superintendents, 1871) did not list homosexuality on its list of causes of disease.

Socarides (1975), a longtime proponent of the illness theory of homosexuality based on the empirically discredited (Freund et al., 1974) phobic theory of homosexuality (Rado, 1940, 1949) fought a vociferous battle against recognition of the APA nomenclature change. Socarides (1980) cites a March 12, 1973, letter from Abram Kardiner, a well-known Columbia psychoanalyst. In the letter Kardiner states that gay organizations pressured the APA to remove homosexuality. "This is only one facet of the tidal wave of *egalitarianism* and divisiveness that is sweeping the country" (emphasis added). He goes on to say:

> By supporting the claims of the homosexuals, and to regard it as a natural variant of sexual activity, is to deny *the social significance of homosexuality.* Above all it mitigates against *the family and destroys the function of the latter* as the last place in our society where affectivity can be cultivated (emphasis added).

Kardiner's objections to homosexuals achieving a level of equality are analogous to the male doctors of the 19th century who felt women who wanted to be physicians were blurring the distinction between male and female sex roles. Women now join occupations traditionally considered masculine. Perhaps because the role of women is no longer devalued, the homosexual role, previously identified as identical to that of women (Kiernan, 1884) loses much of its feared status. In any case it is social judgment and values that have shifted here; an empirical basis for viewing homosexuality as a disease remained nonexistent before, during, and after the 1973 decision (see Chapter 8 in this volume).

BIOMEDICAL TREATMENTS OF HOMOSEXUALITY

It would seem that the battle over the diagnostic status of homosexuality has ended. However, while some forms of social control masquerading as science, such as psychoanalysis, have fallen out of favor, others have emerged to take their place. The latest is the work of biomedical researchers in the United States and East Germany. Three techniques have been developed that attempt to prevent the development of homosexuality: surgery, hormone treatment, and prenatal treatments. These techniques are built on the belief that biology is destiny.

Surgical Techniques

Steinach, in 1917, was the first to use a surgical technique to "cure" homosexuality (Schmidt, 1984; Wolff, 1986). He performed a unilateral castration on a homosexual man, and then transplanted testicular tissue from a heterosexual man into the castrated patient, in the hope that he would be cured. According to Schmidt (1984), at least 11 men were operated on from 1916 to 1921. The experiments were not successful.

In 1962 a new surgical technique was introduced by Roeder. Since then 75 men considered sexually abnormal have been subjected to hypothalamotomies (Schmidt & Schorsch, 1981; Rieber & Sigusch, 1979). Most of these men had either been imprisoned or involuntarily committed to mental institutions. There is disagreement over the effects of the surgery. The surgeons make no clear claims for success, and there is no evidence that sexual orientation was changed. A three-year follow-up on 10 of the patients showed that three refused to participate in the evaluation, one died, and three had "examination findings normal in every respect" (Müller quoted in Schmidt & Schorsch, 1981, p. 319)—whatever that means. The last two patients were found not to have changed their sexual behavior adequately; both were surgically castrated. Sex researchers in Germany were able to create enough publicity about this surgery that a moratorium was placed on the use of these surgical techniques (Sigusch, Schorsch, Dannecker, & Schmidt, 1982).

Peripheral Hormone Treatment

To many people, homosexuality has meant inadequately masculine men and hypermasculine women. Consequently, there have been attempts to cure a gay man of his homosexuality by injecting him with androgens; he would thus be restored to a proper androgen/estrogen balance. Meyer-Bahlburg (1977, 1979, 1984) recently concluded:

> In summary, the available endocrine data on male homosexuals vs. heterosexuals make it seem highly unlikely that deviations in peripheral hormone levels or hormone production *after puberty* can be held responsible for the development of male homosexual orientation in general. (Meyer-Bahlburg, 1984, p. 379, emphasis added)

Downey et al. (1982) confirmed the same findings with respect to women. Pillard, this volume, discusses these studies in more detail. To our knowledge, no sex researcher in the United States now advocates the use of hormone treatment after puberty to change sexual orientation.

Prenatal Hormone Treatment

Biomedical researchers are now concentrating their studies on the influence of hormones during fetal development. The most prominent researchers in this field are Dörner et al. in Germany and Meyer-Bahlburg in the United States. The work of their two groups has caused great controversy. Dörner (1976, 1980) and Dörner et al. (1975) conducted a series of animal studies investigating the influence of prenatal hormones upon adult rat sexual behavior. Dörner believes he has identified an area of the brain that he named the "dual mating center." One part of the hypothalamus is said to control male sexual behavior, mounting, intromission, and ejaculation. A different section controls female sexual behavior or lordosis, a posture that allows a male to mount a female. Dörner states that if perinatal androgens are high, the male center of the brain will predominate, but if androgens are low, the female center predominates. Dörner also attempted to influence adult sexual behavior in the rat through the perinatal administration of sex hormones. He claims that male rats experimentally deficient in androgens showed lordosis, and that female rats treated with androgens soon after birth demonstrated mounting behavior.

In a giant step from rat studies, Dörner then claimed that the same prenatal theory would explain adult sexual orientation in humans (Dörner, et al., 1980, 1983, 1987). If the "female" center develops in the brain of a genetic and somatic male, a homosexual orientation results. If the "male" center develops in the brain of a genetic and somatic female, lesbianism will occur. A bisexual orientation, therefore, is explained as the effects of an intermediate level of androgens. He believes that in humans, sexual dimorphism of the brain occurs during the fourth to seventh month. He further states that he has found proof of his theory in a study of positive estrogen feedback in gay men (Dörner, 1976), and in the effects of maternal stress, which, during fetal development, is said to cause homosexuality (Dörner et al., 1980, 1983). Dörner's most recent work has been to use the drug lisuride to "cure" homosexuality in rats(!) (Dörner, Gotz, Rohde, Stahl, & Tonjes, 1987). Dörner states both implicitly and explicitly that he is attempting to eradicate homosexuality.

> It was concluded from these data that . . . it might become possible in the future—at least in some cases—to correct *abnormal sex hormone levels* during brain differentiation in order *to prevent the development of homosexuality.* However, this should be done, if at all only if it is *urgently desired by the pregnant mother* (Dörner, 1983, p. 577, emphasis added).

At this point we should discuss both the conceptual and social problems raised by Dörner's work.

The analogy between rat studies and human behavior is obviously the first conceptual problem (Meyer-Bahlburg, 1984). Mounting behavior in the rat is assumed to be analogous to human sexual behavior. This follows from the assumption that the "mating center" found in the rat is a homology to a human sexual behavior center. The question "Can a rat be a homosexual?" sounds absurd. While an adult rat can perform sexual behaviors, one would be hard pressed to claim that a rat has a sexual identity, a gender identity, or romantic attachments. One also could not claim that rat sexual behavior is influenced by the moral and social standards of the time. The question therefore forces us to look at behavior that is socially, rather than biologically, controlled.

The second conceptual problem is Dörner's definition of abnormality. Upon what criteria does he decide what endocrinological events are normal or abnormal, and upon what criteria is behavior in the adult classified as normal or pathological? None of his research addresses these questions. For the moment let us be generous and assume that his prenatal hormonal differences exist. Since they do not lead to abnormal physical problems, his criteria for abnormality can only be that they create a homosexual adult. This end result is abnormal only in the sense that he, like the society in which he lives, disapproves of homosexuality. Without this opprobrium, the development of "male and female centers" of the brain become nothing more than variations in normal development of brain differentiation.

Another problem rests with Dörner's assumption of a one to one correlation between sexual orientation and gender behavior. From his point of view, homosexuality in men is represented by feminine behavior, and in lesbians by masculine behavior. It is the scientific equivalent of the social opinion that gay men are really women, and lesbians are "butch." It serves to reinforce sex role stereotypes that historically have been used to keep both sexes in their proper social roles.

Meyer-Bahlburg and his colleagues at Psychiatric Institute in New York have also worked toward identifying the prenatal hormonal influences on sexual orientation and gender behavior (Downey et al., 1982; Ehrhardt et al., 1985; Meyer-Bahlburg, 1977, 1979, 1982, 1984). Unlike Dörner, however, he understands that social learning has an effect upon adult sexual performance. With respect to sexual orientation, he says that "in all likelihood, a comprehensive theory combining endocrine and social factors will turn out to best reflect the empirical data" (Meyer-Bahlburg, 1984, p. 390).

Meyer-Bahlburg's work is criticized by De Cecco (1987) and Gagnon (1987), who claim that his work is designed to investigate the effects of prenatal hormones on sexual orientation. He has been criticized for repathologizing homosexuality. While denying it, Meyer-Bahlburg acknowledges that he looks for *endocrine abnormalities* that may lead to the development of homosexuality.

Perhaps Ruse (1984) stated the question in the hearts of critics of Meyer-Bahlburg (and certainly Dörner): "Can it really be that one who takes a biological approach to human social behavior, and in particular to human homosexual inclinations and behaviors, has no moral axe to grind?" (p. 148).

It is the concern for the moral and social conditions under which gay people live that is left out of Meyer-Bahlburg's work. He has stated: "Even if hormonal abnormalities were found to play an etiological role, this would not automatically qualify homosexuality for the categorization as a mental disorder" (Meyer-Bahlburg, 1988, p. 117).

This statement avoids the essential question. What would he do if he found hormonal "abnormalities" played an etiological role in the development of homosexuality? His critics appear to believe that his next avenue of research would be to find a way of changing the "abnormal" prenatal hormonal environment to prevent the development of homosexuality. He has not responded to this criticism, and his motivation will remain suspect until he does.

The implications of biomedical research are awesome, and the ethical problems monumental. If these efforts should succeed in unlocking the biological component of human sexuality, would parents be given the right to influence the fetal development of their children? Would such scientific knowledge advance society, or would it only pander to its fears? We have no right to expect the general population to avoid influencing the development of their children given the opportunity. We must expect that parents will want children who have socially desirable characteristics, including physical type, intelligence, coloring—and sexual orientation.

Of course, biomedical research may fail to prevent the development of homosexuality. Even so, prenatal treatment may still be offered. This chapter argues that therapeutic treatment represents punishment inflicted on people who have transgressed the sexual rules of our society. The purpose of that punishment is twofold: first to punish the transgressor, and second to prevent others from participating in nonconformist sexual activities. *The efficacy of the treatment has rarely been the criteria governing its use.* When breakfast cereals did not prevent children from masturbating, torturous devices were invented to prevent it from happening. Steinach tried to cure homosexuality through surgery in 1917, and in the 1970s and 1980s other surgeons performed brain surgery until stopped for moral and ethical reasons, not because their experiments were a failure.

Psychologists and psychiatrists attempted to cure homosexuals of their sexual affliction by various means. Aversion therapy ended only because it was no longer fashionable in the egalitarian 1970s, not because it did not work. Psychoanalysis has had an even longer life, and after years of failing to "cure" homosexuality, most psychoanalysts still maintain that homosexuality is a pathology that is curable with years of "treatment." Since our society has laid a veneer of guilt over one's sexual desires, any form of treatment will find a willing supply of volunteers. The problem with biomedical research is that it has eschewed moral and ethical considerations and thereby reinforced society's fear of uncontrolled sexual desire.

THE POSITIVE APPROACH TO PSYCHOTHERAPY FOR GAY PEOPLE

It is difficult to point to the first instance of a therapy not based upon the belief that homosexuality is a pathology. That history has not yet been written. However, one can point to the formation of gay counseling centers as the most significant step toward providing an alternative form of therapy for gay people. In the early 1970s, gay counseling centers were formed in New York, Philadelphia, Pittsburgh, Boston, Seattle, and Minneapolis. Some were staffed only by peer counselors, while others were staffed by both peers and professionals. All provided low-cost service to gay people who were experiencing emotional distress but did not want to change their sexual orientation. Previously, the professional community had been obsessed with the causes of and cures for homosexuality. Instead, the gay counseling centers affirmed the homosexuality and then proceeded to treat the person. These centers provided a setting where gay professionals could gather together and exchange information and ideas. Much of the literature on homosexuality is a direct result of these centers.

Kinsey (1948, 1953) provided the first unbiased scientific information on the sexual behaviors of men and women in the United States. Out of Kinsey's institute came other sex researchers, such as Simon and Gagnon (1967b). Later, Sonenschein (1966, 1968) began writing about an ethnographic approach to homosexuality, by which he meant a description and functional analysis of the gay community. The work of Bell, another Kinsey colleague (1972, 1978, 1981), followed. Most of these early sex researchers acknowledged the contribution of Hooker (1957), who was the first to establish that under blind analysis, no difference could be found in mental health status between homosexual and heterosexual men. Not as well recognized is Gundlach's (1967) early research on lesbians. From the psychiatric ranks came the work of Szasz (1970, 1977) and Halleck (1971).

The concept of sex research unfettered by psychoanalytic theory became a new discipline, and two new journals were published, the *Journal of Sex Research* and *Archives of Sexual Behavior.* Both were multidisciplinary and published statistical and clinical papers about all facets of human sexuality. Then, in 1976, the first issue of the *Journal of Homosexuality* was published. *JH* gave rise to the largest collection of published papers on psychotherapy with gay people (Coleman, 1987; Gonsiorek, 1982b; Ross, 1988). The original edition of this book (Paul, Weinrich, Gonsiorek & Hotvedt, 1982), Hetrick and Stein (1984) and Stein and Cohen (1986) rounded out the list of resources available for professionals who rejected the medical model of homosexuality. A practical and theoretical book about psychotherapy for gay people by Gonsiorek and Brown and a book of clinical case histories edited by Silverstein are now in progress.

The publication of papers and books demonstrating an alternative approach to treating gay men and women was decisive in teaching professionals about the therapeutic needs of the gay community. Gay professionals began using the term "gay affirmative psychotherapy." This suggested that homosexuality was an acceptable life-style, and that therapists should attempt "to provide corrective experiences to ameliorate the consequences of biased socialization" (Malyon, 1982c, p. 62).

Mosher (1989) had similar thoughts in mind when he wrote, "To understand what it is like to make homosexual choices in American society, you need to be able to see with gay eyes, to hear with gay eyes, to feel with a gay heart—you need empathy for the gay perspective" (p. 506).

The published literature on psychotherapy since the nomenclature change can be divided into three areas. The first is the effect of external stressors upon the behavior of the gay person. These stressors would include homophobia (Herek, 1984a, 1989), relationship to the family (Myers, 1982; Silverstein, 1977a), parenting children (Kirkpatrick, 1987a; Loulan, 1986; Martin, 1989), civil and legal rights (Knutson, 1979/1980), "coming out" (Coleman, 1982), problems of adolescents (Hetrick & Martin, 1987a, 1987b; Martin & Hetrick, 1988; Gonsiorek, 1988), impediments to successful love relationships (Burch, 1986; Peplau & Amaro, 1982; Silverstein, 1981), discrimination (Herek, 1984b), and the recent epidemic of AIDS (Nichols, 1986; Shernoff, 1988). In these topical areas one can find the greatest amount of published material, because gay people continue to suffer the effects of discrimination. The published material attempts to define the sources of stress and to suggest ways to alleviate it. Presumably, if the external stressors were eliminated, psychotherapy for those problems would also be eradicated. Coping with a discriminatory world is the central theme in all of the papers cited above.

The second type of literature attempts to define internal psychological processes that cause emotional pain for gay people. The majority of these papers discusses the effect of low self-esteem and self-hate, or "internalized homophobia" (Herek, 1984a, 1984b; Smith, 1988). Other topics include affective disorders, sexual problems (Hall, 1987; Reece, 1987), merger in lesbian relationships (Burch, 1986), identity formation (De Cecco, 1981, De Cecco & Shively, 1983/1984), and borderline conditions (Silverstein, 1988). The chapter by Gonsiorek and Rudolph in this volume explores a number of the same themes.

A few writers have tried to bridge the gap between a gay affirmative model and traditional psychoanalytic therapy (Hencken, 1982) suggesting that one can use the techniques of analytic therapy while rejecting analytic beliefs about normal, i.e. heterosexual, development. Isay (1985), writing in traditional psychoanalytic organs, discusses heterosexual bias in the treatment of gay people, and recently suggested that psychoanalysis ignored the special relationship between gay sons and their fathers (Isay, 1987). Silverstein (1981) came to similar conclusions in his research. Lewes (1988) attempts to demonstrate, within the psychoanalytic framework, that a homosexual orientation can be a normal outcome of the Oedipus complex. Mainstream psychoanalysis is not sympathetic to these ideas.

This literature is distinctly different from the old psychoanalytic theories in one important way. Psychoanalysis was obsessively concerned with the cause of homosexuality and with its cure. The new forms of treatment reject concepts of etiology because it assumes a condition of abnormality. New therapeutic techniques assume that same-sex preferences are an acceptable variation of human sexuality. This is why gay affirmative therapy is a directive form of treatment as opposed to earlier techniques that maintain a guise of neutrality while drawing out the societally induced self-hate in their gay patients.

But what have we learned about the needs of gay men and women by the use of affirmative forms of therapy? Do they carry into the consulting room dreams of a life free from discrimination and internal conflict? As gay therapists look back at their years of experience, and as the published papers suggest, gay women and men are trapped by subscribing to generally accepted middle-class values. They have been banging on the door of American society in the hope of fading into the mainstream of social life. Gay people are having children, buying houses, striving for success, and in general, maintaining households that are indistinguishable from those of married heterosexuals.

The mystique of gay life was abandoned with the APA nomenclature change, and even more so in light of the AIDS epidemic. The theories about the genesis of homosexuality suggested that gay people suffered degenerative brain diseases, were sexually promiscuous, and were sinful and harmful to the family structure. Although homosexuality was rejected by society, these epitaphs created an aura of uniqueness surrounding gay people. They were members of a subculture and were feared almost as much as they were despised.

Ironically, in their attempts to "cure" homosexuality psychoanalysts provided the very atmosphere that maintained its uniqueness. Instead of remolding gay people into a heterosexual form, they perpetuated an underground society whose insularity was strengthened by the fear of a common enemy.

PROSPECTS FOR THE FUTURE

How has treatment changed since the 1973 APA decision? Before the 1970s, homosexuality was classified as a mental disorder and all treatments were designed to change it to heterosexuality. The APA decision clarified the *mental status* of homosexuality. It is not a mental pathology. With this decision came a wave of new therapies whose goal was to treat the societally induced ills of gay people and to assist in their integration. These have been successful. Gay people now participate in all levels of our society, and when conditions are right, do so openly as gay people.

At the same time, biomedical researchers in Europe and the United States have attempted to demonstrate that homosexuality has its first cause in "abnormal" prenatal hormone activity. They have therefore shifted the focus from a psychological pathology to a physical one. Dörner states explicitly that this knowledge should be used to change homosexuals into heterosexuals, and that parents and physicians should jointly decide on the future sexual orientation of the child. There are therefore two treatment fronts since the APA change, and not a little animosity between them.

Psychotherapists can now be a positive force in the lives of gay people, and loving relationships between gay men and between lesbians are reinforced by affirmative therapists. At the same time some biomedical researchers seek techniques to prevent the birth of children who might ultimately be gay.

This chapter began by noting two moments in time, one in 1641 with the hanging of William Hackett for sodomy, the second the APA nomenclature change normalizing homosexuality. Unfortunately, the issue has not yet been fully resolved. There is a third "moment" yet to come. It will arrive when more publicity surrounds the work of biomedical researchers on sexual orientation, and their potential claim to reverse a homosexual orientation. Other "moments" will come, too, whenever mental health professionals and researchers are irresponsible, blind, and arrogant enough to convince themselves and society that the social control of disenfranchised groups constitutes good science.

8

The Empirical Basis for the Demise of the Illness Model of Homosexuality

John C. Gonsiorek

In Charles Silverstein's chapter, he describes how diagnostic "fashion" changes over time, especially in the manner in which psychiatric diagnosis is used as an agent of social control and conformity. One might conclude from Silverstein's argument that diagnosis is hopelessly contaminated by psychiatry's function as an agent of social control. If one accepts this point of view, then the diagnosis of homosexuality as a disease or illness can be seen as simply another example of social control by mental health professionals of socially and politically unpopular groups.

This idea has its proponents and, indeed, this criticism has been leveled at psychiatry on general grounds not specific to the study of homosexuality (Szasz, 1961, 1970). This chapter, however, pursues a different point of view. How can one understand the pathology or nonpathology of homosexuality if one *does* believe in the reasonableness of psychiatric diagnosis? My own position as a clinical psychologist trained in the medical model is as follows. I would maintain that the diagnostic enterprise has vigor and validity when applied to serious forms of mental illness. For example, the evidence for the existence and universality of schizophrenia and most mood disorders is strong. Like Silverstein, however, I believe that psychiatric diagnosis is frequently abused when it labels and pathologizes unpopular or different groups of people. My perspective is that psychiatric diagnosis is legitimate, but its application to homosexuality is erroneous and invalid because there is no empirical justification for it. In other words, the diagnosis of homosexuality as an illness is bad science. Therefore, whether one accepts or rejects the plausibility of the diagnostic enterprise in psychiatry, there is no basis for viewing homosexuality as a disease or as indicative of psychological disturbance.

This is an important distinction. Silverstein suggests that the initial creation of the illness of homosexuality, its later removal, and the unsuccessful attempts to reinstate it are essentially political acts. I propose a somewhat different conclusion, namely, that although psychiatric diagnosis can often be characterized as a political act, doing so is an abuse of a reasonable and potentially proper diagnostic function. From this perspective, then, the political pressure placed on the American Psychiatric Association in the early 1970s was a necessary but not sufficient condition for the depathologizing of homosexuality. The other condition that was also necessary but not sufficient was an empirical basis for discarding the illness model of homosexuality—which is the focus of this chapter. Given my view that psychiatric diagnosis represents a peculiar amalgam of reasonable science mixed with inappropriate political and social control agendas, change in psychiatric diagnosis requires both political will and empirical justification, both of which are necessary but neither of which alone is a sufficient condition for change.

From a historical perspective, homosexuality first evolved into a medical "illness" in the late 19th century or early 20th century depending on the country (see Bérubé, 1990, for a discussion of the initial medicalization of homosexuality in the United States). In 1973, the American Psychiatric Association removed homosexuality as an illness, replacing it with ego-dystonic homosexuality, a vague and problematic concept that attempted to label dissatisfaction with same-sex orientation as an illness. In 1986, ego-dystonic homosexuality was itself removed, probably because it created more confusion than illumination. Bayer (1987) presents background on these changes.

It is noteworthy that those who have attempted since the 1973 depathologizing of homosexuality to maintain the position that homosexuality is an illness have consistently and systematically ignored the empirical basis for the change, treating it instead as a purely political act. As an example, Jones and Workman (1989) in their review focus on tangential issues such as AIDS, monogamy, the number of individuals who may be homosexual, theories of a causation of homosexuality, whether sexual orientation can be changed, and others. They do not discuss the empirical data base on whether homosexuality is an illness. They eventually conclude that the illness status of homosexuality is unresolved. By focusing on emotional but irrelevant issues, these authors, operating from a so-called "Christian" psychological perspective, provide misinformation and confusion.

In a similar manner, some psychoanalytic theorists (e.g., Socarides, 1978) continue to develop increasingly complex and arcane theoretical structures to "prove" the inherent psychopathology of homosexuality, again ignoring the evidence against such an illness perspective.

Such developments since 1973 are almost solely the province of conservative psychoanalytic theorists and so-called "Christian" psychotherapists. A reader of their works can note a virtually complete absence of any reference to the literature that will be cited in this chapter. It is my view that this continuing attempt to pathologize homosexuality in the face of strong and consistent disconfirming evidence is unprofessional, irresponsible, and scientifically invalid. It is based on beliefs that have nothing to do with science, specifically dogmatic beliefs about religious, philosophical, and social concerns. Readers, however, can judge for themselves after reviewing the contents of this chapter.

METHODOLOGICAL PROBLEMS

A careful examination of research data can not only answer the important question of whether homosexuality per se is a sign of mental illness or psychological disturbance, but also clarify a number of methodological issues that tend to become confused in the study of homosexuality.

For example, much of the psychoanalytic theorizing about the causes of homosexuality focuses on certain family patterns that are alleged to predispose a child toward homosexuality. Whether or not one believes these theories of causality of homosexuality (the evidence generally does *not* support these theories—see Bell, Weinberg, & Hammersmith, 1981), there is an implication in this research that since a pattern is alleged to be more frequent in the families of homosexuals, this is evidence that homosexuality per se is disturbed because such family patterns are indicative of psychological disturbance. On the face of it, this reasoning may sound plausible. In reality, it is circular. The veracity of theories holding that certain family patterns are pathological is very much in question. When "differences" are found, they are alleged to be evidence in favor of the theory. But the existence of difference does not explain what those differences mean.

Careful examination of an example can help clarify this point. Suppose one divides subjects into two groups on the basis of a variable of interest: heterosexual versus homosexual (forgetting for a moment the difficulties in determining sexual orientation as discussed in the chapter on definition problems), low average versus high average IQ, or introverted versus extroverted personalities. One may then study a number of variables in the two groups to determine if they differ on these. Suppose further that one finding is that the two groups differ on a family variable that one's favorite theory says is a sign of psychological disturbance. Can one then conclude that the group with more of this variable is more disturbed?

No. Even if the research design is strong, and the results are replicated in other independent research, the problem of determining the meaning of such findings remains. It is not reasonable to assert that because one's favorite theory would lead to a conclusion that family pattern X means disturbance, therefore individuals with family pattern X are more disturbed. What would be required for proof of greater disturbance are reliable, valid, and well-established measures of disturbance. Then, if the group with the allegedly disturbed family pattern *also* scored in a disturbed range on the measures, there would be strong evidence for both a conclusion of greater disturbance and for one's favorite theory. If the well-established measure of disturbance does not show disturbance in the group, then one's favorite theory—or other research design factors—may be at fault. But certainly a conclusion that the group with family pattern X is more disturbed is unwarranted.

Homosexuals and heterosexuals may differ from each other in many ways; indeed, it would be curious if they did not. However, the answer to whether these differences indicate disturbance can be found in the results of the most reliable and well-validated indices of disturbance in the mental health armamentarium: psychological testing. To anticipate the conclusion of this chapter, these testing results overwhelmingly suggest that there are few, if any, consistent, measurable differences between heterosexual and homosexual populations, and these are not in the range of scores indicative of greater disturbance in the homosexual groups.

It is important to understand some other concepts before proceeding. One is the notion of normal range differences. Normality, whether defined as day-to-day adjustment in life, scores on various psychological tests, or the absence or presence of certain signs and symptoms, is not a unitary phenomenon. Normal, if it is to have any meaning at all, refers to a *range* of behavior, characteristics, test scores, or whatever, and it is this *normal range* that is the meaningful and workable concept of normality. It is possible, then, for two groups of subjects to have different average, or mean, scores and both be normal—that is, within the normal range. For example, individuals or groups of differing heights, or degrees of social introversion or extroversion, can all be in the normal range. Further, the normal range is often redefined for different populations. For example, certain well-constructed psychological tests such as the MMPI can be used in different cultures and countries if the normal range and deviance from the normal range are redefined by thorough research. Even variables less dramatic than major cultural differences, such as education level and social class, can sometimes warrant this renorming of the normal range on a test.

Differences can be statistically significant and still be in the normal range. In some circumstances, it is possible to create statistical significance by using large samples or repeated independent measures. The existence of statistical significance indicates that the differences meet certain mathematical criteria for being assigned a probability of occurrence. Differences that are real mathematically may or may not be important or meaningful in a psychological or clinical sense, or in the context of what is known about normal ranges of difference. Finally, the existence of statistical significance provides no necessary justification for the manner in which such differences are interpreted. A useful feature of a well-constructed psychological test is that the limits of the normal range for different populations are determined by independent research evidence, not by theory alone or by the comparative characteristics of the groups used in a given study.

Another concept is important: the notion of base rates. Does the statement that homosexuality per se is not a sign of psychological disturbance mean that there are no disturbed homosexuals? No. It means that the proportion, or base rate, of disturbed individuals in homosexual and heterosexual populations is roughly equivalent. Using the following figures solely for illustrative purposes, if 5% of the general population is seriously disturbed psychologically, 10% moderately disturbed, 15% slightly disturbed and 70% within the normal range, then the statement that homosexuality is not in itself indicative of disturbance may mean that roughly the same proportions also hold in homosexual populations; i.e. that many disturbed homosexuals can be found.

Further, there are some reasons (one being increased levels of external stress) to believe that certain measures of disturbance may be higher in some homosexual populations, as well as in other disparaged groups. This also can be congruent with a conclusion that homosexuality in itself is not an indicator of psychological disturbance. If homosexuals as a group are subject to more external stress, then a proper comparison group may not be heterosexuals in general, but heterosexuals with roughly equivalent external stress. Use of improper comparison groups is confusing and often invalid because one then compares groups with inherently different base rates.

The illness model of homosexuality maintains that the existence of persistent homosexual feelings in an individual is *in and of itself* absolutely predictive of psychological disturbance. It is important to note that findings supportive of the existence of *any* group of homosexual individuals who are not psychologically disturbed refutes this model. One could even push the argument, then, that the comparative rates of psychological disturbance in homosexual and heterosexual populations are irrelevant to the question of whether homosexuality is an illness. The only relevant issue is whether any well-adjusted homosexual individuals exist at all. Differences in base rates of mental health problems between homosexuals and heterosexuals do require an explanation, however, but that explanation is not central to the question of whether homosexuality per se is an illness.

SAMPLING PROBLEMS

The largest methodological problem in the scientific study of homosexuality is how to define and obtain a representative—or even useful—homosexual sample. Few research endeavors to date have used a representative homosexual sample. Demographic research has consistently concluded that homosexual behavior cuts across social, economic, educational, ethnic, racial, religious, regional, and other sociological variables (see Gebhard, 1972). For a phenomenon so frequently studied, homosexual behavior remains strikingly uncorrelated with most of the major groupings into which social scientists assign subjects. The homosexual population does not differ from the general U.S. adult population, except that the homosexual population tends to be disproportionately unmarried and childless. The knowledge that a given individual is homosexual is relatively uninformative. Yet, every study in this area has sampled from particular, and sometimes unusual, segments of the homosexual population.

In earlier studies, samples were often drawn from legally or psychiatrically involved homosexuals. These samples are unacceptable for a variety of reasons. Any comparison between homosexual patient groups and heterosexual nonpatient groups is specious: the patient versus nonpatient dimension is overriding, regardless of sexual orientation. Comparisons between homosexual and heterosexual patients in many settings are difficult to untangle. Where there are psychiatric problems in addition to the issue of sexual orientation, one is hard pressed to determine where the psychiatric problem ends and the sexual orientation concern begins. The use of a heterosexual patient control group does not remedy this.

There have been and still remain mental health professionals who are intolerant of homosexuality. If a researcher is sufficiently aware of a patient's homosexuality to include that person in a homosexual sample, the possibility exists that the subject may experience distress merely as a result of that knowledge, contributing further to whatever stresses previously existed.

A homosexual patient sample, by definition, consists of nonadjusted homosexuals. While findings based on such samples may be illuminating in discovering things about nonadjusted homosexuals, these findings are not applicable to nonpatient homosexuals.

A study by Turner, Pielmaier, James, and Orwin (1974) illustrates this. Male homosexuals who sought aversion therapy treatment for their homosexuality were compared with a sample of male nonpatient homosexuals from homophile organizations who had never sought psychiatric treatment. The Eysenck Personality Inventory (EPI) and the Sixteen Personality Factor Questionnaire (16PF) were given to both groups. The patient group scored significantly higher on measures of neuroticism and were more aggressive, tense, conservative, and group dependent than the nonpatient group. Simply stated, homosexual patient samples are not representative of nonpatient homosexuals.

Samples of homosexuals in psychoanalysis present an added complication. Given the requirements of such treatment—that is, intensive, expensive, often upsetting, and of extremely long duration—it is likely persons who willingly undergo this regime are exceptionally motivated, exceptionally troubled, or both. Further, psychoanalytic patients are notoriously atypical in that they are often better educated, more intelligent, and of higher socioeconomic status. Involuntary patient samples have all the shortcomings of psychiatrically involved samples and also some of the difficulties of legally involved samples, described below.

Legally involved samples are inappropriate, as are samples from institutions such as the armed forces. The salient feature about such samples is that their homosexual behavior has come to the attention of law enforcement agencies. Given that most homosexuals do not become legally involved on account of homosexual behavior, this sample probably includes a good proportion of homosexuals whose reality testing or behavioral controls are tenuous. Consenting adult sodomy statutes are difficult to enforce. With few exceptions, homosexuals who are legally involved become so not because of private sexual relations with a consenting adult but because sexual relations are either not in private, not consenting, or not with an adult; or because of other unusual circumstances, such as police entrapment or harassment. Such samples are unusual and atypical.

Samples of prisoners whose crimes are nonsexual but who are known to prison authorities, and samples from the armed forces or similar institutions, all suffer from the problem of the "known homosexual." Given the aversive and perhaps dangerous consequences of being known as homosexual in such environments, these individuals are an unusually stressed group. In addition, homosexuality in prison must be viewed with caution, as it probably reflects more about the social hierarchy among prisoners than it does their sexual orientation (see Money, 1972a, pp. 73-74; Scacco, 1982).

The unsuitability of psychiatrically and legally involved samples has come to be accepted by most researchers in recent years. Most current studies utilize homosexual samples obtained through gay and lesbian bars, social and friendship networks, organizations, and clubs. While these samples are interesting in their own right, they do not constitute a representative sample of homosexuals.

Gay or lesbian bar samples heavily tap individuals who use alcohol. Bar samples are also skewed toward those who are urban, young, extroverted, and lacking a consistent sexual partner. Further, sources in the gay and lesbian communities estimate that the percentage of homosexuals who go to gay and lesbian bars with any frequency may be as low as 10 to 25%. Homosexual organizations are likely to be skewed toward persons who are open about being homosexual and probably more politically active or conscious. This quality alone places these individuals in a minority and makes them unusual. Samples using friends of the experimenter and derived contacts are likely to be biased in the direction of being like the experimenter: well educated, middle-class, and so on. Samples from social networks will tend to be homogeneous and contain consistent biases, as friendship networks by their nature contain like individuals. Further, researchers have almost exclusively utilized North American, white, middle-class, English-speaking samples. This particular bias in the research is so problematic that it is unclear if the knowledge base on homosexuality is applicable at all beyond these limited populations.

Finally, it must be remembered that in many places homosexuals remain potential and even likely targets for embarrassment and harassment. Some homosexuals, particularly those who are successful and established professionally, may be unwilling to take the risks involved in being subjects of research. Furthermore, this may tell us something about those homosexuals who are willing to be researched.

Burdick and Stewart (1974) studied male homosexual undergraduates from a university homosexual organization. In the first part of the study, all subjects were administered the EPI, a psychological test. All were asked to return in a few days to complete a second part, which they were told was a battery of physiological measurements. This second part was a deception; the experimenters simply listed which subjects returned (25 out of 67 did). Those individuals who returned had significantly higher mean scores on both the neuroticism and extroversion scores of the EPI. Burdick and Stewart theorized that there is a tendency for homosexuals who readily volunteer for psychological research to be less well adjusted than those who do not. While this conclusion requires more research, it does suggest that homosexual volunteers for research may be an unusual group. The assumption that research volunteers are likely to be representative of homosexuals is not justified.

Note that our discussion of sampling so far has not referred to the issues and complexities in defining who is homosexual, discussed in the chapter on definitional problems. The reason is that most researchers have not attended to these complexities. The level of sophistication used in most studies is an assumption that individuals who are in homosexual organizations, bars, and the like, or who say they are homosexual, are in fact homosexual. There is a further assumption that control groups are entirely heterosexual—despite the fact that incidence data would suggest otherwise. More astute researchers asked their heterosexual samples if they were heterosexual, and the most astute have asked both their samples for a self-rated Kinsey score. However, researchers have varied as to what Kinsey scores constitute a homosexual sample; some have used exclusive homosexuals (Kinsey 6), while others have included a mix of bisexuals and homosexuals, including some predominant heterosexuals (Kinsey 1 through 6), as well as other combinations.

Research on homosexuality has been characterized by poor and biased sampling procedures and vague, erroneous, or simplistic assumptions abut the definition of homosexuality. That raises two question: Can adequate sampling and definition be accomplished? Can the literature tell us anything valid about homosexuals? The answer to both is a cautious and qualified yes.

While it is impossible to obtain a completely representative sample of homosexuals, workable approximations can be achieved. There is nothing to suggest an important relationship between homosexuality and most major demographic variables. Therefore any homosexual sample should mimic the major demographic characteristics of the locality from which the sample is taken. The other principle is that sampling should be diverse. As any subgroup in the general homosexual population is bound to be skewed in some fashion, homosexual subjects should be drawn from as wide a variety of sources as possible. These sources and the demographic characteristics of the samples should then be described in considerable detail. While these procedures will not eliminate sampling problems, they should reduce them, and a clear and detailed description of procedures will make any sampling limitations apparent.

As for the second question, it is not possible to make statements about all homosexuals. Certain questions about homosexuality, however, can be answered. For example, whether homosexuality per se is or is not pathological and indicative of psychological disturbance is easily answered. As I will discuss later, studies on a variety of samples have consistently concluded that there is no difference in psychological adjustment between homosexuals and heterosexuals. Therefore, even if other studies find that some homosexuals are disturbed, it cannot be maintained that sexual orientation per se and psychological adjustment are related.

Further, it is possible to make statements about those homosexual samples that have been adequately researched. These samples tend to be white, English-speaking, young, North American, middle-class, and educated. This bias plagues much research in the behavioral sciences. Therefore, while generalizations beyond the samples studied should be avoided and conclusions reserved and cautious, some things have been learned about some homosexuals.

SOME EXAMPLES OF METHODOLOGICAL AND SAMPLING PROBLEMS

A number of studies will be discussed to illustrate problems of sampling, definition, and faulty assumptions. A concern for elucidating underlying theoretical problems and methodological issues permeates many parts of this book. This emphasis is a deliberate attempt to educate the reader in a long-range fashion so that as new theories and data develop, a reader can be equipped with conceptual tools to evaluate and understand new ideas. One of the purposes of this volume is to train the reader to be a skeptical and discerning consumer of the past, current, and future scientific literature on homosexuality.

Oliver and Mosher (1968) conducted a study using a prison sample, and their work is a good example of the difficulties with legally involved samples. Based on guard reports, they identified three groups that they termed heterosexual, homosexual insertee, and homosexual insertor. Using the MMPI, they found that the homosexual insertee group had significantly higher scores on a number of scales than the heterosexual group, but that the homosexual insertor group had even greater elevations, and on more of the scales. While this study may be an interesting examination of psychological characteristics of various prisoners, it is difficult to see what bearing this study has on homosexuality. Using prison guard reports is highly suspect; the insertee group is probably best characterized by their role as victims and as a group are likely to be vulnerable and less powerful for a variety of reasons, only one of which might be homosexuality. This critique is one that Mosher (in press) now accepts as valid.

Doidge and Holtzman (1960) looked at four groups of Air Force trainees. One group was suspected of homosexual offenses and judged predominantly homosexual; another was suspected of homosexual offenses and judged "accessory." Both groups had been interrogated. A heterosexual group, suspected of other kinds of offenses, had also been interrogated and constituted the third group. A final group consisted of heterosexual normals, neither suspected of offenses nor interrogated. MMPI profiles of the homosexual accessory, heterosexual disciplinary, and heterosexual normal groups were very similar. The homosexual predominant group had a markedly different profile, with extreme elevations on many MMPI scales. Doidge and Holtzman concluded that homosexuality per se was indicative of psychopathology.

This study illustrates a number of severe methodological errors and also the social context of research. Doidge and Holtzman's description of the advantages of studying male homosexuals in the Air Force sounds more like a case against such a study:

> The almost complete lack of privacy and the barracks-type of living are likely to stimulate sexual drives in male homosexuals. Prevailing cultural attitudes and stringent military policy heighten the conflict, precipitating contact with the psychiatric clinic. In the Air Force, all homosexual suspects are subjected to exhaustive interrogations by special investigators. [1960, p. 9]

It is apparent that homosexuals in such a setting are subjected to extreme levels of harassment and stress, to the point of "precipitating contact with the psychiatric clinic," and the control groups they used were inadequate.

Further, the authors provide no clear and replicable explanation of how they determined which persons were accessory or predominant homosexuals. As one group is indistinguishable from normals and the other is severely disturbed, this distinction and the mechanism by which it was made are crucial. This study is an example of the inadequacy of legally and psychiatrically involved samples, of how certain social contexts are inappropriate for research efforts, and of how research may create the problem it seeks to investigate.

Similar issues are demonstrated in Cattell and Morony's (1962) study of Australian males. One group consisted of prisoners convicted of homosexual acts; another, of prisoners convicted of general non-homosexual crimes; a third group, of unconvicted homosexuals obtained through social worker contacts; and a fourth group, of (presumably) heterosexual normals who were employed as clerical workers. Using the 16PF, Cattell and Morony claimed that the profiles of the two homosexual groups were highly similar and could, for all practical purposes, be taken as representing a homosexual-type profile. They stated that this homosexual-type profile was significantly different on many scales from both the Australian general criminal and American normal profiles, using a complicated statistical procedure to make this comparison. They concluded that homosexuality, per se, was neurotic and pathological.

It would appear that Cattell and Morony's unconvicted homosexual sample was meant to be a counterpart to the heterosexual normal group in the same way that the homosexual prisoner group was a counterpart to the heterosexual prisoner group. However, it seems that this unconvicted homosexual sample is psychiatrically involved, or somehow involved with agents of society. Their description of this sample is as follows: "Through discreet social worker contacts, and discreet infiltration of the communication channels of homosexuals, it was possible to get measures of 33 uncharged male homosexuals." This poorly described sample does not appear to be a functioning homosexual group; the reason these individuals are known to social workers is not explained. What Cattell and Morony appear to have obtained are two highly particular samples of homosexuals: one from prisons and the other through social worker contacts.

Their combining of the two homosexual groups into a type is suspect. While there were similarities in scores between the homosexual groups, there were also differences, and combining these groups is more confusing than informative. Further, Cattell and Morony then argued that while there were differences between the American normative sample on which the test was standardized and the Australian heterosexual normal group, these were not statistically significant. Based on this argument, they then compared the composite Australian homosexual-type group with the American normative sample. This comparison is invalid. The fact that the American normative and Australian heterosexual normal groups were not statistically significant does not preclude the possibility that there were enough differences to bias the data analysis; especially when using a questionably derived composite homosexual-type group and also when using, as Cattell and Morony did, a statistical technique (multivariate data analysis) that is very sensitive to chance variation in the data. This technique is properly used with larger samples and requires replication before firm conclusions can be drawn. Any comparisons made should have been with Australian samples only, for the reasons above and also to avoid an invalidating cross-cultural biasing effect. Evans (1970) has criticized this study on other grounds, stating that the authors' interpretation of the data was questionable.

The Cattell and Morony study is a good example of how combining samples in inappropriate ways, using improper comparison groups, questionable sampling procedures, as well as the more technical problems with statistical analysis and interpretation of data, can work together to make a potentially interesting study misleading.

One final example, the study by Bieber et al. (1962), will focus more on social contextual factors—specifically researcher bias—although this study too is riddled with major problems in sampling and interpretation of results, as discussed by Gonsiorek (1977, pp. 12-13). This study is an excellent example of researcher bias. It compared male heterosexual and homosexual patients in psychoanalysis. This sample, as discussed above, is problematic in its own right. More importantly, the same group of psychoanalysts developed a theory about homosexuality; developed the questionnaire to test their theory; designed the research study; served as analysts for the patient subjects; served as raters in the research project on their own patients; interpreted the results; and finally concluded that their theory had been verified. There are too many sources of potential researcher bias in this research. In fact, it would be difficult to build more potential for researcher bias into experimental procedures than the Bieber group did.

The Psychological Test Research

One line of psychological test research has attempted to create special scales, signs, or scoring patterns to differentiate homosexuals from heterosexuals. Two tests, the Minnesota Multiphasic Personality Inventory (MMPI) and the Rorschach, attracted most of these attempts.

The original Masculinity-Femininity (MF) scale of the MMPI was an attempt to differentiate homosexuals from heterosexuals. The inability of this scale to do this without an intolerably high inaccuracy rate (particularly in the direction of calling many more people homosexual than actually exist in the groups; termed a "false positive" rate) was so striking that early proponents of the MMPI issued caveats about the scale's ineffectiveness at making this differentiation (see Dahlstrom, Welsh, & Dahlstrom, 1973). This scale more accurately measures adherence to social sex role norms, and is so strongly influenced by variables such as educational levels and occupational interests that the most likely interpretation of a moderately elevated MF score in males is that the individual is well educated. The scale's ability to differentiate women is seriously attenuated overall, because of inadequate sampling of women during original development of the scale.

Other researchers attempted to create new MMPI scales to differentiate homosexuals from heterosexuals. These included attempts with a homosexuality scale (HSX) (Friberg, 1967; Manosevitz, 1971; Panton, 1960; Pierce, 1973); a sexual deviate (SD) scale (Hartman, 1967); as well as others. The results of this research activity were disappointing. Panton's (1960) HSX scale may have some utility in differentiating men who engage in homosexual activity while in prison from those who do not, but this research was not able to effect the desired differentiation outside prison samples. Attempts to use other MMPI scales fared no better (see Gonsiorek, 1977, pp. 11-20).

Using the Rorschach, a number of attempts were made to discover signs that could predict homosexuality. Wheeler's (1949) 20 signs for male homosexuality attracted most of the efforts. However, when Goldfried, Stricker, and Weiner (1971) reviewed the literature on Wheeler's signs, they concluded that only 6 of the 10 could probably discriminate homosexual tendencies. This is a much more vague and less useful concept than homosexual behavior. In addition, these studies depended heavily on patient samples, making them of little value beyond these samples.

Another kind of study has directly addressed whether homosexuality per se is pathological. For convenience, these studies will be reviewed by psychological tests used. The studies discussed below have sampling problems to varying degrees, and a handful were so strikingly flawed to warrant discussion earlier in this chapter as prototypes of poor design. However, some information can be gleaned from these works.

Using the MMPI, a number of researchers found that male homosexuals as a group did not score in the disturbed or pathological ranges of the various clinical scales (Braaten & Darling, 1965; Dean & Richardson, 1964; Horstman, 1972; Manosevitz, 1970b, 1971; Panton, 1960; Pierce, 1973).

The Dean and Richardson (1964) study sparked an instructive debate that illustrates some of the issues outlined earlier. In this study, homosexual subjects scored significantly higher than heterosexuals on three clinical scales. However, as the scores of both homosexual and heterosexual groups were both within the normal range, the authors concluded that the homosexual group was not more disturbed than the heterosexual group. However, Zucker and Manosevitz (1966) proposed that Dean and Richardson had "explained away" important differences, and proposed a diagnostic scheme based on these three scales. Dean and Richardson (1966) countered that significant differences may be interesting, but they are not indicative of disturbance unless the scores of one group are in a pathological range. As the scores of both groups were within the normal range, Dean and Richardson again concluded that the homosexual group was not more disturbed.

On MMPI studies with homosexual women, both Miller (1963) and Ohlson and Wilson (1974) found no indication of greater disturbance in either homosexual or heterosexual groups. Interestingly enough, there were significant but normal range differences in both these studies, with the heterosexual groups scoring higher on a number of clinical scales. As both groups in each study were within the normal range, the authors correctly concluded as they did. However, at least one writer (Freedman, 1975) has erroneously concluded on the basis of significant but normal range differences that some homosexual samples may be better adjusted psychologically. This illustrates the same specious reasoning that Zucker and Manosevitz utilized, but with the conclusion reversed.

Other studies (Doidge & Holtzman, 1960; Oliver & Mosher, 1968) were reviewed earlier as examples of particularly poor research design. While they did find significant differences suggestive of greater psychological disturbance in their homosexual samples, these findings are by-products of the faulty sampling and poor design.

Other tests frequently utilized in this line of research are Cattell's 16 Personality Factor Questionnaire (16PF) and Eysenck's Personality Inventory (EPI), as well as different versions and subsections of these tests. A study by Cattell and Morony (1962) conducted in Australia and using the 16PF concluded that homosexuality per se was neurotic and indicative of psychopathology. However, as was discussed earlier in this chapter, this study is seriously flawed. Evans (1970) also criticized this study and conducted his own study on American male homosexuals. While he did find differences between his homosexual and heterosexual groups, he concluded that these differences were of sufficiently small magnitude to support a conclusion that homosexuality per se was not an indication of psychological disturbance. Turner, Pielmaier, James, and Orwin (1974), using the 16PF and the EPI, also concluded that homosexuality is not pathological. Siegelman (1972b), using a derivation of the 16PF, studied male homosexuals and heterosexuals. He found some normal range differences and concluded that there was no difference in psychological adjustment between his heterosexual and homosexual groups.

A number of studies were conducted comparing homosexual and heterosexual women, using the 16PF, California Personality Inventory (CPI), and/or Edwards Personal Preference Schedules (EPPS). The bulk of these studies (Freedman, 1971; Hopkins, 1969; Siegelman, 1972a; Wilson & Green, 1971) concluded that there is no evidence to support differences in psychological adjustment between homosexual and heterosexual women. Two other studies (Eisinger, 1972; Kenyon, 1968) concluded that their homosexual samples were psychologically disturbed; however, these two studies have research design problems that make their interpretation difficult. Eisinger did not compare homosexual and heterosexual groups, but rather compared scores from a homosexual sample with normative data for the EPI. As Eisinger gave no information on demographic characteristics of her sample, it is difficult to determine if this comparison was appropriate. Kenyon used Kinsey ratings of 0 to define the heterosexual sample and ratings of 1 through 6 to define the homosexual sample. As the reader will recall from the chapter on definitional problems, this means that some predominantly heterosexual and bisexual individuals were mixed together in the "homosexual" sample. Kenyon's data are therefore difficult to interpret unless they can be broken down by Kinsey ratings in a more meaningful fashion.

A number of researchers utilized the Adjective Check List (ACL). Chang and Block (1960), using this test, found no differences in general adjustment between homosexual and heterosexual males. Evans (1971), using the same test, found that male homosexuals appeared to have more problems with self-acceptance than heterosexual males, but that only a small minority of the homosexuals could be considered maladjusted. Thompson, McCandless, and Strickland (1971) used the ACL to study psychological adjustment of both male and female homosexuals and heterosexuals, concluding that sexual orientation was not related to personal adjustment in either sex. Hassell and Smith (1975) used the ACL to compare homosexual and heterosexual women, and found a mixed pattern of normal range differences that might suggest poorer adjustment in the homosexual sample.

Other psychological measures have also been used. Ohlson (1974), using the Jourard and Laskow Self Disclosure Questionnaire, found no significant differences between male homosexuals and heterosexuals, and concluded that homosexuality is nonpsychopathological. Christie and Young (1986), using the Tennessee Self Concept Scale (TSCS) with homosexual and heterosexual women, found no evidence that self-conduct markedly differs between the two groups. Clark (1975), using the TSCS, found no differences between groups of males along the Kinsey Scale. Carlson & Steuer (1985), in a study on aging, found that age did not have a more negative impact on homosexual men. They utilized measures of self-esteem and depression. Using both male and female samples in Ireland, Carlson and Baxter (1984) found no differences between homosexual and heterosexual individuals on measures of depression or self-esteem. Using a variety of questionnaires and measures, LaTorre and Wendenburg (1983) found that homosexual, bisexual, and heterosexual women did not differ in psychological characteristics. Nurius (1983), using a large student sample of men and women, found significant differences between homosexual, heterosexual, and bisexual groups, but not to a level that would suggest psychopathology. Measures of depression, self-esteem, relationship discord, and sexual discord were utilized. Harry (1983a) in a study primarily focusing on gender roles, found no differences between homosexual and heterosexual males on a self-esteem measure.

All the studies reviewed so far have utilized objective personality measures, which use an objectively scored, usually true-false format and have a considerable body of empirical research to guide interpretation of the tests. Projective tests use a more freestyle response format; their scoring, while structured, often requires some degree of subjective judgment. A number of studies using such tests have focused on homosexual-heterosexual group comparisons.

Some of the unsuccessful attempts at differentiating homosexuals and heterosexuals using the Rorschach were discussed earlier in this chapter. A famous study using projective testing was conducted in the late 1950s by Evelyn Hooker (1957). This study is also noteworthy because it was early, and one of the most serious challenges to the belief that homosexuality per se indicated psychological disturbance. Hooker administered a battery of projective tests—Rorschach, Thematic Apperception Test (TAT), and Make-A-Picture-Story Test (MAPSI)—to 30 homosexual and 30 heterosexual males, all recruited from community organizations and none with legal or psychiatric involvement. The projective test protocols were given to a panel of projective test experts. These raters were given no information on which protocols were from heterosexual or homosexual subjects. The raters were unable to differentiate the homosexual from heterosexual subjects. Hooker concluded that homosexuality as a clinical entity does not exist and that homosexuality per se is not pathological.

This review of the psychometric studies on homosexuality is not complete, but it does include the better-known and better-designed studies in this area. The general conclusion is clear: These studies overwhelmingly suggest that homosexuality per se is not related to psychopathology or psychological adjustment. Reviews by Gonsiorek (1977); Hart et al. (1978); Meredith and Reister (1980); Reiss (1980); and Reiss, Safer, and Yotive (1974) reached the same conclusion and can be consulted for greater detail. The few studies that suggest the contrary are typically among the weakest methodologically, and some of these are so flawed as to be uninterpretable. Differences between homosexual and heterosexual groups are typically found, and these tend to be within the normal range. The pattern of these differences, however, is not sufficiently consistent to describe a typical homosexual personality or adjustment style. These differences may reflect idiosyncrasies in the samples used. They may reflect the generally increased level of stress experienced by many homosexuals in a society that is generally intolerant of homosexuality, or the development of an increased variety of coping mechanisms to deal with these stresses. Some of the processes theorized to mediate this relationship between homosexuals and a rejecting society are discussed in the chapter by Gonsiorek and Rudolph.

The meticulous reader will note that much of the research reviewed here occurred in the 1960s and 1970s. There is a historical reason for this. Most of the research cited here was sparked by Evelyn Hooker's seminal study, which elicited a line of research for about 25 years. This research was so consistent in its lack of findings suggesting inherent psychopathology in homosexuality that researchers began moving on to other projects by the 1980s. Recent research has dropped off because the question of inherent pathology in homosexuality has been answered from a scientific point of view and has not been seen as requiring more research.

RESEARCH ON RATES OF PSYCHIATRIC PROBLEMS

Another line of research examines data from psychiatric interviews concerning symptoms and life history events. Two of the earliest large-scale studies were done by Saghir, Robins, Walbran, and Gentry, comparing male homosexuals and heterosexuals (1970a) and female homosexuals and heterosexuals (1970b). In the study of men, Saghir's group found that there were no differences between groups on interview questions pertaining to drug abuse, antisocial features, mood disorders, anxiety, or phobias. However, the homosexual group had a history of more suicide attempts, more excessive drinking, and greater utilization of psychotherapy services. In their matching research on women, they found no differences between homosexuals and heterosexuals in the number of individuals seeking psychotherapy services or having mood disorders, anxiety, phobias, or antisocial personality features. However, the female homosexual groups more often reported mental health difficulties and a history of drug use.

Saghir and Robins (1973), in a single study, compared psychiatric and personal history information on groups of males and females, both homosexual and heterosexual. They found virtually no differences in signs of psychiatric symptomatology between homosexual and heterosexual samples with the exception of greater alcohol abuse in the female homosexual sample as combined with the female heterosexual sample. Weinberg and Williams (1974), in a large study comparing homosexual and heterosexual men in the United States, Denmark, and Holland, also looked at items related to psychiatric history and found no differences in degree of psychological problems between homosexual and heterosexual groups. Prytula, Wellford, and Demonbreun (1979) administered a self-report inventory concerning adolescence to homosexual and heterosexual college students. Their study suggested more psychological problems during adolescence for young homosexual men. Pillard (1988), using a psychiatric questionnaire, attempted to estimate lifetime episodes of mental disorder in homosexual versus heterosexual men and found no differences.

Bell and Weinberg (1978) reported higher rates of loneliness and depression in homosexual as opposed to heterosexual samples and also a higher rate of attempted suicide. Roesler and Deisher (1972) suggest a high rate of adolescent suicide attempts in gay men and lesbians, and Gibson (1986) speculated that gay and lesbian adolescents may account for 30% of adolescent suicides. In their review of the literature, however, Buhrich and Loke (1988) concluded that systematic studies did not show a greater rate of *completed* suicide among homosexual as opposed to heterosexual populations. They did conclude, however, that suicide *attempts* appeared to be higher among homosexual as compared with heterosexual groups. They speculated that a higher incidence of alcoholism among homosexual populations, greater stressors on homosexual populations, and greater instability of homosexual relationships may be the cause of this difference.

Kourany (1987), in a survey of psychiatrists who work with adolescents, reported that those who treat homosexual adolescents consider them at higher risk for suicide and also reported the impression that their suicide attempts were more severe. In a review of the literature on suicide risk among gay men and lesbians, Saunders and Valente (1987) found that homosexuals attempt suicide more frequently than heterosexuals and implicated higher rates of risk factors such as alcohol abuse and interrupted social ties as predisposing factors. Rich, Fowler, Young, and Blenkush (1986) found little difference between homosexual and heterosexual male populations who actually completed suicide. Harry (1983b) suggested that a possible link was that those gay men who were gender nonconforming during childhood experienced increased social isolation that led to a higher risk of later suicide.

There have been attempts to systematically ignore the problem of suicide in gay and lesbian youth. Secretary of Health and Human Services (HHS) Louis Sullivan's rejection of portions of an HHS report on youth suicide relating to gay and lesbian youth is only the most recent example of this (American Psychological Association, 1990). Obviously such politically based censorship does not help to answer the research subtleties involved here.

With regard to rates of alcoholism, Mosbacher (1988) reviewed the literature on alcohol and substance abuse rates in homosexual and heterosexual women and concluded that lesbians appear to be at greater risk for alcohol abuse than heterosexual women. Similarly, Anderson and Henderson (1985), in their review, concluded that there was an increased risk of alcoholism among lesbian populations and theorized that it is due to heightened stress resulting from societal oppression. Kus (1988) concluded that there is a higher instance of alcoholism among gay men and theorized that this is related to lack of self-acceptance concerning homosexuality. Herek (1990c, p. 1040) raised questions about the nonrepresentative samples used in some of this research, and concluded that truly empirical support for a higher incidence of alcoholism among homosexuals is lacking.

In recent years, the United States armed services have been looking into the suitability of gay men and lesbians as members of the armed forces. Rivera, in this volume, describes the legal situation of gay men and lesbians in the military. In an internal study, McDaniel (1989) posed the question whether homosexuals would be suitable for national security clearances. He collected information about educational experience, alcohol and drug use, criminal activities, and other factors on a self-report inventory and compared individuals who were discharged from the armed services for homosexuality versus other groups. McDaniel found that homosexuals showed better preservice adjustment than heterosexuals in areas relating to school behavior; that homosexuals displayed greater levels of cognitive ability than heterosexuals; and that homosexuals had greater problems with alcohol and drug abuse than heterosexuals. With that latter exception, homosexuals resembled those who had successfully adjusted to military life more than those who were discharged for being unsuitable. The study concluded that the adjustment of male homosexuals tended to be better or equal to that of male heterosexuals and that female homosexuals tended to score somewhat lower on preservice adjustment compared with female heterosexuals. McDaniels noted, however, that females as a whole tended to show better preservice adjustment than males as a whole and noted that female homosexuals, while having poorer adjustment than female heterosexuals, had better adjustment than male heterosexuals.

In their summary of the military suitability of homosexuals, Sarbin and Carols (1988) concluded that homosexual orientation is unrelated to military job performance and that the main problem facing integration of homosexual individuals into the military is primarily a problem of maintaining group cohesion within the general military structure when an unpopular minority group is absorbed. Recent historical research (Bérubé, 1990) documents that many gay men and lesbians served in the armed forces during World War II without any particular problem. When personnel needs declined after the war, harassment of lesbian and gay military personnel began in earnest. Bérubé notes that similar rationales were used by the military at a different time to screen out blacks—until they, too, were needed.

Herek (1990c), in his review of the social science data, concluded that the denial or restriction of government security clearances for gay people had no rational or empirical justification. In addition to the lack of psychopathology discussed above, he also concluded that lesbians and gay men are no more likely than heterosexuals to be subject to blackmail or coercion, nor unreliable or untrustworthy, nor likely to disrespect or fail to uphold laws.

In summary, this line of research suggests that there are few differences between homosexual and heterosexual individuals related to psychiatric symptomatology and essentially no differences in areas related to performance in key areas of life functioning in the real world. A few differences are suggested: higher rates of attempted but not completed suicide, and alcohol or drug abuse possibly higher among homosexual individuals. In both there appears to be a linkage with higher rates of external stress.

CONCLUSIONS

It is my conclusion that the issue of whether homosexuality per se is a sign of psychopathology, psychological maladjustment, or disturbance has been answered, and the answer is that it is not. The studies reviewed and the findings in this chapter ought to be the touchstone of further theory and research in the study of homosexuality, because they represent the most carefully designed, reliable, valid, and objective measures of adjustment in the armamentarium of the behavioral sciences. Again, this is not to say that psychologically disturbed homosexuals do not exist; nor does it mean that no homosexuals are disturbed because of their sexuality. Rather, the conclusion is that homosexuality in and of itself bears no necessary relationship to psychological adjustment. This should not be surprising; heterosexuals disturbed because of their sexuality fill many therapists' caseloads. Because sexual expression is one of the most intimate, psychologically rich, and complex of all human interactions, it is not surprising that individuals who are troubled or disturbed will likely manifest problems in their sexual relationships, regardless of sexual orientation.

Until the findings cited here are overturned by psychological test data of equal or better research design, breadth, and numbers, theories contending that the existence of differences between homosexuals and heterosexuals implies maladjustment are irresponsible, uninformed, or both.

Although it is clear that homosexuality is not in and of itself related to psychopathology, there are persistent suggestions that the particular stresses endured by gay men and lesbians, especially in adolescence and young adulthood, may cause an upsurge in attempted suicide and perhaps chemical abuse, perhaps temporary or perhaps in a segment of homosexuals. These do not suggest the inherent psychopathology of homosexuality; rather they suggest additional especially stressful developmental events in the lives of some gay men and lesbians that require theoretical explication. The elucidation of these events is the focus of the chapter by Gonsiorek and Rudolph.

9

Constructionism and Morality in Therapy for Homosexuality

Gerald C. Davison

Imagine for a moment that you are an anxious person and that being anxious is against the law. You must try to hide your fears from others. Your own home may be a safe place to feel anxious, but a public display of apprehension can lead to arrest or at least to social ostracism. At work one day an associate looks at you suspiciously and says, "That's funny. For a crazy moment there I thought you were anxious." "Heck no," you exclaim a bit too loudly, "not me!" You begin to wonder if your fellow worker will report his suspicions to your boss. If he does, your boss may inform the police, or will at least change your job to one that requires less contact with customers, especially with those who have children.

There are many parallels between the way an anxious person is treated in this seemingly improbable fantasy and the recent (if still not current) plight of homosexuals. Sexual attraction among members of the same sex has been amply documented throughout recorded history in many different cultures. In many societies homosexual practices have been suppressed by harsh laws; indeed in some states of contemporary America laws exist by which homosexuals can be arrested and imprisoned, although not all these statutes are rigidly enforced. Never have societal sanctions eliminated homosexuality, nor does it seem likely that they could. The widespread prevalence of homosexuality, even though such practices are often threatened by punishment, has led some workers to believe that this aspect of sexuality is, in some important way, part of human nature.

AUTHOR'S NOTE: Some of the material in this chapter is drawn from previous publications: G. C. Davison and J. M. Neale (1978). *Abnormal psychology: An experimental clinical approach.* Second edition. New York: John Wiley, by permission; G. C. Davison (1976). Homosexuality: The ethical challenge. *Journal of Consulting and Clinical Psychology, 44,* 157-162; and G. C. Davison (1978). Not can but ought: The treatment of homosexuality. *Journal of Consulting and Clinical Psychology, 46,* 170-172, copyright by the American Psychological Association, portions reprinted by permission.

Recent years have seen a growing liberalization of views on adult human sexual conduct. One of the earliest progressive statements was issued in 1974 by the Association for Advancement of Behavior Therapy on my initiative while I was president of the group.

> The AABT believes that homosexuality is in itself not a sign of behavioral pathology. The Association urges all mental health professionals to take the lead in removing the stigma of mental illness that has long been attributed to these patterns of emotion and behavior. While we recognize that this long-standing prejudice will not be easily changed, there is no justification for a delay in formally according these people the basic civil and human rights that other citizens enjoy.

Several other professional groups, including the American Psychological Association and the American Psychiatric Association, also moved away from an illness view of homosexuality. Indeed the third edition of the American Psychiatric Association's official nomenclature, DSM-III (American Psychiatric Association, 1980), included homosexuality only under a special rubric, "ego-dystonic homosexuality," a diagnosis to be applied when a person was troubled by his or her homosexual inclination (note that DSM-III belied its continuing bias by not having an ego-dystonic *hetero*sexuality category). And the current version, DSM-IIIR, dropped even this residual diagnosis, adding a category that is nonspecific with respect to the gender of the person one is sexually attracted to, namely, Sexually Disorder Not Otherwise Specified, defined by the presence of "persistent and marked distress about one's sexual orientation" (American Psychiatric Association, 1987, p. 296, revised from 1980). Silverstein, in this volume, describes the historical, social, and political context of diagnosis.

As encouraging as these developments have been to those committed to removing the stigma of homosexuality, a less obvious but perhaps even more important political and ethical issue must be addressed, namely, the availability of therapeutic regimens for shifting sexual orientation from same-sex to opposite-sex partners. The following may illustrate this predicament:

> *API (Apocryphal Press International).* The governor recently signed into law a bill prohibiting discrimination in housing and job opportunities on the basis of membership in a Protestant church. This new law is the result of efforts by militant Protestants, who have lobbied extensively during the past ten years for relief from institutionalized discrimination. In an unusual statement accompanying the signing of the bill, the governor expressed the hope that this legislation would contribute to greater social acceptance of Protestantism as a legitimate, albeit unconventional, religion.

At the same time, the governor authorized funding in the amount of two million dollars for the coming fiscal year to be used to set up within existing mental health centers special units devoted to research into the most effective and humane procedures for helping Protestants convert to Catholicism or Judaism. The governor was quick to point out, however, that these efforts, and the therapy services that will accompany and derive from them, are not to be imposed on Protestants, rather are only to be made available to those who express the voluntary wish to change. "We are not in the business of forcing anything on these people. We want only to help," he said.

THE MYTH OF THERAPEUTIC NEUTRALITY

My basic premise is, to paraphrase Halleck (1971), that therapists never make ethically or politically neutral decisions: "Any type of psychiatric intervention, even when treating a voluntary patient, will have an impact upon the distribution of power within the various social systems in which the patient moves. The radical therapists are absolutely right when they insist that psychiatric neutrality is a myth" (1971, p. 13).

The very naturalness of what therapists agree to do with particular kinds of cases tends to blind them to their prejudices and biases. Surely no ethical issues are worth discussing when one helps a severely disturbed child to stop banging his head against the wall. But this is an extreme case, and I suggest that most of what therapists deal with falls into that important gray area in which biases play a controlling role in what is done. This seems to be particularly the case in the approach to those people who have homosexual behavior or feelings. In spite of the apparent decline in requests for change of sexual orientation (Rosen & Beck, 1988), I would suggest that most therapists by and large still regard homosexual behavior and attitudes to be undesirable, sometimes pathological, and at any rate generally in need of change toward a heterosexual orientation. Indeed, homophobia continues to be prevalent among both lay and professional people (Forstein, 1988). If therapists are less busy trying to discourage people from homosexual practices than they were twenty years ago, I would argue that this is due to fewer people seeking such alteration. Thus, while much has changed since I first set forth these arguments in an address to the Association for Advancement of Behavior Therapy (Davison, 1974), there are issues, some of them not specific to homosexuality, that merit review and analysis.

SOME RELEVANT AND IRRELEVANT ISSUES SURROUNDING HOMOSEXUALITY

Allow me to mention briefly some exclusions that I hope will be obvious. I am not talking about homosexual behavior that is part of a psychotic pattern of existence. For example, the male who has the delusion that he is Marie Antoinette intent on seducing every available 20th-century man would be exhibiting a pattern of sexual behavior that is best viewed as part of an unfortunate psychotic aberration. I would similarly not want to conclude that heterosexuality is sick because there are male schizophrenics who chase female nurses and try to fornicate with them in hospital dayrooms.

There is something else implicit in what I will be saying, so let me make it explicit at this juncture. Though I will often be referring to "homosexuals," I am in agreement with investigators such as Kinsey, Pomeroy, and Martin (1948) and Churchill (1967), who construe sexual preference as a continuum on which people can be placed according to the relative frequencies of their homosexual-heterosexual fantasies, feelings, and behavior. Clearly the available survey data strongly indicate that a significant number of human beings lie between the extremes of exclusive homosexuality and exclusive heterosexuality.

In any discussion of homosexuality in therapy, the question of the normality of homosexual preference has often been raised. Many studies have failed to find differences between heterosexuals and homosexuals (see Evans, 1970; Gagnon & Simon, 1973; and Chapter 8 in this volume). However, some point out the oft-cited data of Bieber et al. (1962) and to a conceptual replication by Evans (1969) as evidence supporting a pathology view of homosexuality. There are a number of serious flaws in the Bieber study, not the least of which is that the male homosexuals were all in therapy. However, there is also a major *logical* error in reasoning, namely, that one has demonstrated pathology of homosexuality by showing that male homosexuals have childhood experiences that are *different* from those of male heterosexuals. The fact is that one cannot attach a pathogenic label to a pattern of child-rearing unless one a priori labels the adult behavior pattern as pathological. For example, Bieber et al. (1962) found that what they call a "close-binding intimate mother" was present much more often in the life of the analytic male homosexual patients than among the heterosexual controls. But what is wrong with such a mother unless you happen to find her in the background of people whose current behavior you judge *beforehand* to be pathological? Moreover, even when an emotional disorder is identified in a homosexual, it could be argued that the problem is due to the extreme duress under which the person has to live in a society that asserts that homosexuals are "queer" and that actively oppresses them.

There is another issue worth discussing. Many people point to problems in homosexual relationships, prompting the conclusion that homosexuality could not possibly be normal. To such objections I would reply that homosexuals who suffer in poor relationships do not have a monopoly on stormy interpersonal functioning. Simply because there is so much marital discord in this country, one seldom hears people concluding that *hetero*sexuality is inherently bad. What I am suggesting is that clinicians might perhaps pay more attention to the *quality of human relationships* rather than to the particular gender of the adult partners (see Chapter 12 in this volume for elaboration). If one follows this further, we might consider a shift in focus in therapy with homosexuals that pays little attention to the fact that the partners are the same sex and more attention to the kind of relationship a person is in and how that relationship might be improved. Naturally, when therapeutic efforts are aimed in this direction, I believe one inevitably ends up having to deal with the considerable legal and social oppression of these groups of people.

NO CURE WITHOUT A DISEASE

I believe that clinicians spend time developing and analyzing procedures only if they are concerned about a problem. It seems very much the case with homosexuality. And yet, consider the rhetoric that typically speaks of social labeling of behavior rather than viewing a given behavior as intrinsically normal or abnormal. Consider also the huge literature on helping homosexuals (at least males) change their sexual preference (reviewed and critiqued in this volume by Haldeman) and the paucity of literature aimed at helping the labelers change their prejudicial biases and encouraging the homosexual to develop as a person without changing orientation. How can therapists honestly speak of nonprejudice when they participate in therapy regimens that by their very existence—and regardless of their efficacy—would seem to condone the current societal prejudice and perhaps also impede social change?

This point was enunciated independently by Begelman (1975) in a critique of behavior therapy, but his argument applies to any intervention:

> [The efforts of behavior therapists to reorient homosexuals to heterosexuality] *by their very existence constitute a significant causal element in reinforcing the social doctrine that homosexuality is bad.* Indeed, the point of the activist protest is that behavior therapists contribute significantly to preventing the exercise of any *real* option in decision making about sexual identity, by further strengthening the prejudices that homosexuality is a "problem

> behavior," since treatment may be offered for it. As a consequence of this therapeutic stance, as well as a wider system of social and attitudinal pressures, homosexuals tend to seek treatment *for being homosexuals.* Heterosexuals, on the other hand, can scarcely be expected to seek voluntary treatment for being "heterosexual," especially since all the social forces arrayed—including the unavailability of behavior therapy for heterosexuality—attest to the acknowledgment of the idea that whatever "problems" heterosexuals experience are not due to their sexual orientation. The upshot of this is that contrary to the disclaimer that behavioral therapy is "not a system of ethics" (Bandura, 1969, p. 87), the very act of providing therapeutic services for homosexual "problems" indicates otherwise. (p. 180)

I suggest further that the availability of a technique encourages its use. For example, many behavior therapists who have good clinical success with systematic desensitization and who are also persuaded by the experimental literature that it is useful for reducing anxiety try to conceptualize client problems in terms of this technique. Thus, social isolation might be viewed at least in part as a consequence of unnecessary sensitivities that themselves could be translated into an anxiety hierarchy. By the same token, I would suggest that the extensive clinical and experimental work in aversion therapy (for example, Feldman & MacCulloch, 1971), or "Playboy therapy" (see Davison, 1968), or heterosocial-heterosexual skills training channel the assessment and problem-solving activities of behavioral clinicians into working to change sexual orientation and to persuade homosexual clients that this is a worthwhile goal. Why else would they be spending so much time working on the techniques?

CLINICAL PROBLEMS AS CLINICIANS' CONSTRUCTIONS

This issue can be usefully placed in the context of clinical assessment. As I have argued elsewhere (e.g., Davison & Neale, 1990; Goldfried & Davison, 1976), clients seldom come to mental health clinicians with problems as clearly delineated and independently verifiable as what a patient brings to a physician. The latter practitioner/scientist has better data on which to make a diagnosis (and yet even here reliability is far from perfect). In contrast, a client usually goes to a psychologist or psychiatrist in the way described below by Halleck (1971). That is, the client is unhappy; his life is going badly; nothing seems to be meaningful; she's depressed more than her life circumstances would seem to warrant; his mind wanders when he tries to concentrate; unwanted images intrude on her consciousness or in her dreams. The clinician *transforms* these often vague and complex complaints into a diagnosis or assessment, a set of ideas about what is wrong and, usually, what might be done to alleviate what is wrong. I would argue, then, that psychological problems are for the most part *constructions* of the clinician: our clients come to us in pain, and they leave with more clearly defined problems that we assign to them.

My argument has been that when homosexuals go to a therapist, whatever psychological or physical woe they may have has all too often been construed as being caused entirely or primarily by their sexual orientation. Further, I have suggested that this happens because (a) their sexual orientation is usually the most salient part of their personhood, and/because (b) it is regarded as abnormal—regardless of whatever "liberal" stance the clinician takes overtly. This is not to say that a homosexual orientation may not sometimes cause people distress! Rather, it is to say that this salient feature of their personality—because it is negatively sanctioned, still, even with the advances made in DSM-IIIR and elsewhere in the professional literature—colors the clinician's perceptions and guides his or her data-gathering activities in a direction that implicates homosexuality and implies the desirability of a change in sexual orientation.

This is of course a very difficult proposition to verify, and it causes an empirical, cognitive-behavioral clinician like myself not a little discomfort, but I believe there is a body of data on clinician bias that presumptively supports my contention. In an analogue study conducted some years ago (Davison and Friedman, 1981), we found that descriptions of a hypothetical anxious client elicited judgments of more serious psychopathology when it was mentioned (in passing) that the client was homosexual than when he was described as heterosexual. Related findings come from the research of Lopez (Lopez, 1989; Lopez and Hernandez, 1986; Lopez and Nunez, 1987), showing that the stereotypes clinicians have about Hispanics affect their understanding of clinical complaints. The role of subjective factors in perception and problem solving has been acknowledged and demonstrated in experimental psychology since the work of Wundt more than one hundred years ago and confirmed time and again in cognitive psychology, from the "new look" in perception of the 1940s and 1950s (e.g., Bruner & Goodman, 1947) to the schema-oriented work of today in cognitive science (e.g., Neisser, 1976). And in epistemological writings such as Kuhn (1962), paradigms in science are explicitly compared to perceptual biases that affect profoundly the way data are collected and even defined. A generation of thoughtful scientists has been sensitized to the nontrivial influences our often unspoken assumptions have on our organization of the world.

A PROPOSAL ON THERAPY WITH HOMOSEXUALS

These several considerations led me in 1974 to make a proposal that surprised no one more than myself, an idea present for several years in some of the gay activist literature (see especially Silverstein, 1977b): therapists should stop engaging in change-of-orientation therapy programs, whether it was the client requesting it or someone else insisting on it. As Silverstein put it at the 1972 Association for Advancement of Behavior Therapy convention in a discussion of male homosexuality:

> To suggest that a person comes voluntarily to change his sexual orientation is to ignore the powerful environmental stress, oppression if you will, that has been telling him for years that he should change. To grow up in a family where the word "homosexual" was whispered, to play in a playground and hear the words "faggot" and "queer," to go to church and hear of "sin" and then to college and hear of "illness," and finally to the counseling center that promises to "cure," is hardly to create an environment of freedom and voluntary choice. The homosexual is expected to want to be changed and his application for treatment is implicitly praised as the first step toward "normal" behavior. What brings them into the counseling center is guilt, shame, and the loneliness that comes from their secret. If you really wish to help them freely choose, I suggest you first desensitize them to their guilt. Allow them to dissolve the shame about their desires and actions and to feel comfortable with their sexuality. After that, let them choose, but not before. I don't know any more than you what would happen, but I think their choice would be more voluntary and free than it is at present. (Silverstein, 1972, p. 4)

In other words, Silverstein suggested that therapists inquire into the determinants of the client asserting that he or she wants to change. He proposed that these determinants may be based on prejudice and ignorance and therefore *should not be* catered to or even strengthened by an establishment of therapists who offer their services to those clients who "express the wish to change."

But what should be the consequences of this? Does this not limit the choices available to the person troubled by his sexual orientation? Who is the behavior therapist or psychotherapist to decide for potential clients which options would be available in therapy? To my mind the frankest answer—but one that seems unpalatable to many—has been elaborated by Halleck (1971). Therapists already have made these decisions, perhaps not fully aware of their larger implications. By having worked so diligently and, until recently, exclusively on change techniques, has the mental health establishment not been affirming that the prejudices and laws against certain sexual acts are in fact well founded? What are therapists really saying to clients when, on the one hand, they assure them that they are not abnormal and, on the other hand, present them with an array of techniques, some of them painful, that are aimed at eliminating that set of feelings and behavior that have just been pronounced normal? What is the real range of "free choice" available to homosexually oriented people who are racked with guilt, self-hate, and discrimination? What of the anxieties arising from this discrimination—how have therapists helped them with *these* problems?

London (1969) suggested that an unappreciated danger in behavior control technology is our increasing ability to engineer what we have regarded as free will. Thus therapists seem to be capable of making people want what is available and what they feel clients should want. Moreover, just because therapists can assert that they are not doing something against the will of their clients does not free them from the responsibility of examining those factors that determine what is considered free expression of intent and desire on the part of our clients.

In a related vein—and this should be familiar not only to therapists but to those who have been clients themselves—Halleck (1971) says:

> At first glance, a model of psychiatric practice based on the contention that people should just be helped to learn to do the things they want to do seems uncomplicated and desirable. But it is an unobtainable model. Unlike a technician, a psychiatrist cannot avoid communicating and at times imposing his own values upon his patients. The patient usually has considerable difficulty in finding the way in which he would wish to change his behavior, but as he talks to the psychiatrist his wants and needs become clearer. In the very process of defining his needs in the presence of a figure who is viewed as wise and authoritarian, the patient is profoundly influenced. He ends up wanting some of the things the psychiatrist thinks he should want. (p. 19)

One might add to Halleck's caution the fact that clients seldom see a therapist when they are confident of their judgments! The social influence that a therapist wields is all the stronger, given the persuasible, even gullible state most clients would seem to be in.

But is it not harsh and unfeeling to propose that therapists deny a particular client the possibility of loosing himself or herself from his or her homosexual attraction and turning him or her on to the other half of the adult population? What about the homosexual client who could conceivably want to switch, not out of societal pressures but out of a sincere desire for those things that in our culture are usually part of the heterosexual package—a spouse and children? Why deny such a person—rare though he or she may be—the opportunity to fulfill such desires? Is not the scheme I am proposing a kind of "coercive liberalism," to use London's (1969) phrase? Coercive liberalism goes something like this: I will help you be happier, freer, more fulfilled, etc.—and you will have no choice but to be so according to my standards. By proposing that preference change programs with homosexuals be terminated, I am obviously running this risk. One solution would be simply to accept the risk; this would seem to be consistent with Halleck's views. But another way out of this dilemma is to propose that a concerted program of clinical research be encouraged for the development of maximally effective procedures to help heterosexually oriented people become homosexuality oriented if they *really want to.* That is, therapists might consider the possibility that many heterosexuals may wish to change, or at least *expand,* their sexual activities, as some homosexuals may wish to do. Are mental health professionals prepared to devote themselves to this kind of sexual enhancement enterprise? I doubt it.

NOT CAN BUT OUGHT

When trying to garner support for my proposal that we should stop trying to change homosexual orientations, I was interested for some time in documenting the failure of various behavior change regimens in eliminating homosexual inclinations. Of particular interest was the question of whether aversion therapy of various kinds has proved effective in stamping out homosexual behavior and inclinations. And indeed, I tend to believe that there is precious little evidence for a suppression of homosexual behavior and inclinations. Nonetheless, even if one were to demonstrate that a particular sexual preference *could* be modified, there remains the question of how relevant these data are to the ethical question of whether one *should* engage in such behavior change regimens. The simple truth is that data on efficacy are quite irrelevant. Even if we could effect certain changes, there is still the more important question of whether we *should.* I believe we should not.[1]

PSYCHOTHERAPY, POLITICS, AND MORALITY

The arguments put forth here should be viewed at what Rappaport (1977) calls the institutional level, not the level of the individual. An institutional analysis of human problems is concerned with those values and ideologies that guide the basic decision making of a particular society. This is the domain of workers who typically identify themselves as community psychologists or psychiatrists. In contrast, most therapists are accustomed to focusing on the individual, assuming that society is basically benign and that psychological suffering can best be alleviated by helping the client adjust to prevailing values and conditions. My underlying assumption is that issues surrounding therapy for homosexuality should be addressed at an institutional level.

The thrust of this chapter, then, is sociopolitical and ethical. While it may be interesting to present data suggesting that sexual preferences *can* be altered (for example, Sturgis & Adams, 1978), such efforts are irrelevant and, worse, misleading. It seems preferable to acknowledge candidly that therapists are purveyors of ethics, that they are contemporary society's secular priests (London, 1964, 1986), and that this heavy moral responsibility is inherent to the conduct of psychotherapy.

Indeed, although this chapter has focused on homosexuals in therapy, I have come to believe that *all* decisions on goals are made ultimately by the therapist. This thesis bothers colleagues of mine—and it should, for the responsibilities of therapists become very onerous indeed if one accepts this argument. Perry London (1964, 1986) suggested some time ago that issues of morality are part of the fabric of the technology of psychotherapeutic change. Contemporary therapists are, as I have just said, society's secular priests. We risk much by not confronting the overwhelmingly lopsided power relationships in any therapeutic alliance and the fact that psychological interventions inevitably entail a judgment by the therapist of how, in a moral sense, a given client should shape his or her existence. Even therapies that view themselves as hands-off (for example, the humanistic-existential group) set parameters for intervention. And if one refrains from suggesting a change, lest he impose his values on the client, is one not willy-nilly sanctioning the status quo, and is that not in itself a therapist decision about the goals of therapy?

It has been suggested that therapists have some kind of abstract responsibility to satisfy a client's expressed need (Sturgis & Adams, 1978). Would that it were so simple. Therapists constrain themselves in many ways when clients ask for assistance, and clients make certain requests of some therapists and will not do so with others. Requests alone have never been a sufficient justification for providing a particular form of therapy.

Finally, there is nothing in the above that advocates not dealing with homosexuals in therapy. It is one thing to say that one should not treat homosexuality; it is quite another to suggest that one should not treat homosexuals. Indeed, what I am suggesting is that therapists finally consider seriously the problems in living experienced by homosexuals. Such problems are perhaps especially severe, given the prejudice against their sexual orientation. It would be nice if an alcoholic homosexual, for example, could be helped to reduce his or her drinking without having his or her sexual orientation questioned. It would be nice if a homosexual with a sexual dysfunction could be helped as a heterosexual would be rather than guiding his or her wishes to a change of orientation. Implicit in this chapter is the hope that therapists will concentrate their efforts on such *human* problems rather than focus on the most obvious "maladjustment"—preferring as sexual and love partners members of one's own sex.

CONCLUSIONS

I have argued that change-of-orientation therapy programs are ethically improper and should be eliminated. Their availability only confirms professional and societal biases against homosexuality, despite seemingly progressive rhetoric about its normality. Forsaking the reorientation option will encourage therapists to examine the life problems of some homosexuals, rather than focus on the so-called problem of homosexuality. Viewing therapists as contemporary society's secular priests rather than as value-neutral technicians will sensitize professionals and lay people alike to large-scale social, political, and moral influences in human behavior.

NOTE

1. There may be one sense in which efficacy relates to the ethical issue. If an ineffective reorientation therapy is undertaken, the patient is going to be disappointed and likely therefore to feel even worse about his predicament—he has not only failed to achieve the reorientation goal but comes away continuing to believe that his homosexuality is bad and sick and perhaps feeling even worse about being gay.

10

Sexual Orientation Conversion Therapy for Gay Men and Lesbians: A Scientific Examination

Douglas C. Haldeman

The American Psychiatric Association's 1973 decision to remove homosexuality from its Diagnostic and Statistical Manual of Mental Disorders marked the official passing of the illness model of homosexuality. The American Psychological Association followed suit with a resolution affirming this anti-illness perspective stating, in part: "the APA urges all mental health professionals to take the lead in removing the stigma of mental illness that has long been associated with homosexual orientations" (American Psychological Association, 1975).

Homosexuality was replaced with the confusing "ego-dystonic homosexuality" diagnosis, which itself was dropped in 1988. Despite this now complete official depathologizing of homosexuality, efforts by both mental health professionals and paraprofessionals (e.g., pastoral care providers) to convert lesbians and gay men to heterosexuality have persisted. In fact, such efforts seem to be increasing at present. They span a variety of treatment modalities and are referred to as conversion therapy.

There are two major concerns about the "rehabilitation" of homosexual men and women. First, conversion therapies have long been questioned as to professional ethical standards (see Davison, this volume). These ethical concerns involve the extent to which conversion treatments are in keeping with the American Psychological Association's affirmative policies on homosexuality, as well as larger issues of therapist responsibility and consumer welfare, which are applicable to all areas of mental health practice. Second, empirical studies fail to show any evidence that conversion therapies do what they purport to do: change sexual orientation. The methodological problems with such studies will be shown to be considerable. These examples of poor science have engendered conflict among those emotionally fragile gay men and lesbians who are typical targets of conversion attempts. Many of these individuals are vulnerable to the idea of repairing in themselves what is actually society's problem: a history of rejection and discrimination based upon socially instituted homophobia. As Bryant Welch (1990), APA's executive director for professional practice, recently stated: "[these] research findings suggest that efforts to 'repair' homosexuals are nothing more than social prejudice garbed in psychological accoutrements."

Davison (1976, 1978, 1982) has detailed many of the ethical objections to conversion therapies. Silverstein (1977b) and Begelman (1975, 1977) have noted that the issues for gay people seeking sexual orientation change are social in nature, not intrinsic to homosexuality. Other relevant discussion is contained in the *Symposium on Homosexuality and the Ethics of Behavioral Intervention* (1977). This chapter, however, will focus on the scientific validity of conversion methodologies.

An examination of the literature shows that not only are conversion therapies unethical and professionally irresponsible, as Davison describes in this volume, but they additionally constitute inadequate and questionable science. Silverstein, in this volume, details similar concerns with biomedical attempts at conversion. Both the ethical and scientific perspectives offer ample and sound justification for abandoning conversion techniques.

A REVIEW OF CONVERSION METHODOLOGIES

Prior to its declassification as a mental illness, a variety of modalities were commonly employed for treating homosexuality. Psychoanalytic tradition posited that homosexual orientation represented an arrest in normal psychosexual development, most often in the context of a particular dysfunctional family constellation. Such a family typically featured a close-binding mother and an absent or distant father. This theory has never been empirically validated, but is based solely upon clinical speculation. Subsequent studies have indicated that etiologic factors in the development of sexual orientation are unclear, but that the traditional psychoanalytic formulations about family dynamics are not viable (Bell, Weinberg, & Hammersmith, 1981).

Psychoanalytic treatment of homosexuality is exemplified by the work of Bieber et al. (1962), who advocate intensive long-term therapy aimed at resolving the unconscious childhood conflicts responsible for homosexuality. Bieber's methodology has been widely criticized on numerous grounds. First, his sample is entirely a clinical one. Second, all outcomes are based upon subjective therapist impression, not externally validated data or even self-report. Last, follow-up data have been poorly presented and not at all empirical in nature. Nevertheless, Bieber et al. (1962) report a meager 27% success rate in heterosexual shift after long-term therapy. Of these, however, only 18% were exclusively homosexual in the first place; 50% were bisexual. This blending of "apples and oranges" is quite common in conversion studies, and renders misleading these claims of success, which are, in this study, not impressive in the first place.

Other analysts have "treated" homosexuality. One study reported virtually no increase in heterosexual behavior in a group of homosexual males (Curran & Parr, 1957). Other studies report greater success rates: for instance, Mayerson and Lief (1965) indicate that half of 19 subjects reported exclusive heterosexual behavior four and a half years after treatment. However, as in Bieber's study, those subjects reporting such change were bisexual to begin with; exclusively homosexual subjects reported little change. Further, all outcomes were based on patient self-report, with no external validation. Last, the authors incorrectly interpret an expansion of the sexual repertoire toward heterosexuality as equivalent to a shift of sexual orientation.

Group therapies aimed at changing sexual orientation have provided similar contradictory results. One study of 32 subjects reports a 37% shift to heterosexuality (Hadden, 1966), but the results must be viewed with some skepticism, due to the entirely self-report nature of the outcome measures. Persons involved in such group treatments are especially susceptible to social demand influence in their own reporting of "treatment success." Similarly, a study of 10 male homosexuals resulted in therapist impressionistic claims that homosexual patients were able to "increase contact" with heterosexuals (Mintz, 1966). Birk (1980) describes a combination insight-oriented/social learning group format for treating homosexuality. He claims that overall, 38% of his patients achieved "solid heterosexual shifts"; nonetheless, he states:

> It is my belief that these represent shifts in a person's salient sexual adaptation to life, not a metamorphosis. Most, if not all, people who have been homosexual continue to have some homosexual feelings, fantasies and interests. More often than not, they also have occasional, or more than occasional, homosexual outlets, even while being "happily married." (Birk, 1980)

What, then, is the intended goal of treatment? If a "solid heterosexual shift" is defined as one in which a "happily married" person may engage in "more than occasional" homosexual encounters, what does a "soft" heterosexual shift look like? This reiterates one of the major objections to conversion studies: these interventions do not shift sexual orientation at all. Rather, they instruct or coerce heterosexual activity in a minority of subjects which is not the same as reversing sexual orientation.

Eager to construe heterosexual competence as orientation change, these researchers ignore the complex question of how sexual orientation is assessed in the first place. The chapter by Gonsiorek and Weinrich in this volume discusses the complexities of defining sexual orientation. The studies discussed in this review do not display any such complexity or thoughtfulness. While they claim to change orientation, the outcomes are nearly always defined in terms of heterosexual performance.

Early behavioral work in conversion therapy operated on the rationale that if certain predetermined (homosexual) behaviors could be extinguished, and if "adaptive" (heterosexual) behaviors could be substituted, the individual's sexual orientation would change. Such early behavioral studies primarily employed aversive conditioning techniques, usually involving electric shock or nausea-inducing drugs during presentation of same-sex erotic visual stimuli. Typically, the cessation of the aversive stimuli would be accompanied by the presentation of opposite-sex erotic visual stimuli, to supposedly strengthen heterosexual feelings in the sexual response hierarchy. Some programs attempted to augment aversive conditioning techniques with a social learning component—assertiveness training, how to ask women out on dates, and so on (Feldman & McCulloch, 1965). Later, the same investigators modified their approach, calling it "anticipatory avoidance conditioning," which enabled subjects to avoid electrical shock when viewing slides of same-sex nudes (Feldman, 1966). One wonders how such a stressful situation would permit feelings of sexual responsiveness in any direction; nevertheless, a 58% "cure" rate was claimed. Again, however, the outcome criteria were defined as suppression of homosexuality, and an increased capacity for heterosexual behavior. It is not uncommon for homosexuals who have undergone aversive treatments to notice a temporary sharp decline in their homosexual responsiveness.

As with aversive techniques, the "covert sensitization" method calls for the use of noxious stimuli paired with same-sex erotic imagery. In this procedure, however, the subject does not actually experience the electric shock or induced vomiting, but is instructed to imagine such stimuli (Cautela, 1967). Outcomes here are limited to single-case studies, and are not generalizable.

More recent studies suggest that aversive interventions might extinguish homosexual responsiveness, but do little to promote alternative orientation. One investigator suggests that the poor outcomes of conversion treatments is due to the fact that they "disregard the complex learned repertoire and topography of homosexual behavior" (Faustman, 1976). Other recent studies echo the finding that "aversive therapies in homosexuality do not alter subjects' sexual orientation, but serve only to reduce sexual arousal" (McConaghy, 1981). This pattern is reflected in yet another study suggesting that behavioral conditioning decreases homosexual orientation, but does not elevate heterosexual interest (Rangaswami, 1982). In fact, such methods applied to anyone else might be called by another name: torture. Individuals undergoing such treatments do not emerge heterosexually inclined; rather, they become shamed, conflicted, and fearful about their homosexual feelings.

Throughout all the claims of sexual orientation change, not one investigator has ever raised the possibility that such treatment may harm some participants, even in a field where a 30% "success" rate is seen as high. Many conversion investigators ascribe the treatment "failures" to lack of patient motivation or the resistance of sexual orientation to change. While the latter is certainly true, it is unethical practice for researchers not to concern themselves with the potentially harmful effects of their methods.

Gay men and lesbians who are coming out are at particular risk for the harmful effects of conversion treatments. Such individuals are often tempted to hope for sexual orientation change as a panacea during a difficult period; this makes them vulnerable targets for conversionists. One study on gay and lesbian adolescents points to the dangers of identification with the dominant (heterosexual) group as a strategy for coping with homosexuality (Hetrick & Martin, 1987a, 1987b). They state: "Denial of group membership is intimately intertwined with identification with the dominant group and, thus, with self-hatred . . . which can lead, in turn, to aggression against one's own group."

The stages of coming out and gay identity formation have been well described (Malyon, 1982a, and the chapter by Gonsiorek and Rudolph in this volume). It is important, during this process, for the individual to have affirmative support for the natural evolution of her or his identity, and to be encouraged toward self-acceptance, rather than toward a conversion procedure that is likely to fail as well as confuse.

Not all behaviorally based conversion approaches use aversive techniques. Fantasy modification studies seemed initially to yield heterosexual shift in single-case designs and small group studies. However, when more rigorous experimental procedures were applied, physiological measures of sexual arousal remained unchanged (Conrad & Wincze, 1976). And though these results do not suggest conversion, at least these investigators included external, physiological measures in their outcome measures; few conversionists do this, opting instead for less rigorous self-report and subjective impression.

The work of Masters and Johnson on sexual orientation change was published in 1979, in *Homosexuality in Perspective.* Like previous volumes, it addresses, through a behavioral sex therapy format, the resolution of sexual concerns for men and women. However, this volume also includes a study of 54 "dissatisfied" homosexual males. This was unprecedented for the authors, as their previous works on heterosexual dysfunction did not include treatment for dissatisfied heterosexuals. Homosexuality is conceptualized here as the result of blocks in "normal" learning that facilitate heterosexual responsiveness. Masters and Johnson's theoretical basis is a variation on the illness theme of homosexuality: that people become homosexual because of failed or ridiculed attempts at heterosexuality. The researchers do not consider the obvious: that heterosexual "failures" among homosexual people are to be expected, since the behavior in question is outside the individual's normal sexual response pattern. At one point, the authors suggest that male ignorance of women's inherently strong sexual capacity potentiates lesbianism; despite their comments to the contrary, the study is founded upon heterosexist bias.

Gonsiorek (1981) raises a variety of concerns with the Masters and Johnson study. Beginning with selection criteria for inclusion in the sample, the authors indicate that subjects were screened for "major psychopathology or severe neurosis," though they do not explain how such screening was performed. Also missing was an explanation of how "motivation to change" was assessed, since this dimension is considered crucial by the researchers. Nevertheless, 19 of the 54 subjects were described as uncooperative during therapy, and refused to participate in a follow-up assessment. Even so, these 19 were assumed, without justification, to be among the "nonfailure" group.

The presentation of treatment methodology is avoided in the work itself; a description of therapeutic methods was published five years later (Schwartz & Masters, 1984). Still, it would be tremendously difficult to replicate this study; this is important, since the ability of independent researchers to utilize the same procedures in different experiments is fundamental to scientific research. It is of particular concern here, since these authors claim a success rate nearly twice that which is reported elsewhere, and all in two weeks' treatment time!

The confusing manner in which the Masters and Johnson data were reported makes it difficult to determine their actual procedures. They distinguish between "conversion" (leading previously nonheterosexually experienced homosexual men into newfound heterosexual competence) and "reversion" (directing homosexually identified men with a heterosexual history, even if marginal, back to heterosexual activity). The problems with this distinction are obvious, given that history of heterosexual behavior may have nothing to do with actual sexual orientation, and much to do with fulfillment of social expectations, or with a priori nonhomosexual status.

Masters and Johnson's "homosexual" sample, in fact, may not be "homosexual" in orientation at all. Of 54 subjects, only 9 (17%) identified themselves as Kinsey 5 or 6 (exclusively homosexual). The other 45 subjects (83%) ranged from 2 to 4 on the Kinsey scale (predominantly heterosexual to bisexual). Furthermore, since 30% of the sample was lost to follow-up, it is conceivable that the outcome sample does not include any homosexuals at all. Perhaps this is why such a high success rate is reported after two weeks' treatment. It is likely that rather than "converting" or "reverting" homosexuals to heterosexuality, Masters and Johnson were really strengthening heterosexual responsiveness in people with already established bisexual repertoires.

Masters and Johnson defined their results in terms of "nonfailures," which they distinguished from "successes." In long-term posttreatment follow-up, some 73% of (presumably) homosexual subjects were considered to be "nonfailures" in sexual orientation conversion or reversion. It is not clear what assessment measures were used to establish this. Moreover, the use of heterosexual competence as sole criterion for orientation shift has been criticized (Krajeski, 1984).

The general inconsistencies in this research are significant. This supposedly scientific study has left unclear who is being measured, what is being measured, and how it is being measured. Indeed, its credibility in the eyes of many is simply due to the reputation of the investigators.

The studies reviewed here have one thing in common, in addition to their purported claims to reverse sexual orientation: namely, that they represent inadequate and misleading scientific practice. They are consistently flawed by poor or nonexistent follow-up data, improper classification of subjects ("converting" bisexuals who are not primarily homosexual in the first place), and confusion of heterosexual competence with sexual orientation shift. Pervading all of this is an atmosphere of homophobic researcher bias: that homosexual behaviors are identified as "maladaptive" in the most openly prejudicial cases, and merely "troublesome to the individual" in the most covert. Most "troublesome" to the individual is the social prejudice facing her or him; but either way, such theoretical positions are in direct opposition to the diagnostic nomenclature decisions of both psychiatry and psychology, and the empirical evidence on the lack of inherent psychopathology in homosexuality, as reviewed by Gonsiorek in this volume. California psychologist Joseph Nicolosi, a specialist in "reparative therapy" with what he refers to as "nongay" homosexuals, is reported to have acknowledged that he has never had a client who left his office "cured" of homosexuality and that one of his most "successful" clients, married and the father of three, still reported "homosexual fantasies that lingered 'like a gnat buzzing around your ear'" (Buie, 1990). To promote conversion programs for something that is even acknowledged by its proponents as nearly impossible is hardly in the best interest of the consumer of psychological services.

RELIGION-BASED CONVERSION PROGRAMS

Apart from the efforts of the scientific community, the primary proponents of sexual orientation change have been pastors and religiously-oriented lay persons. This is of concern to psychology because of the unprofessional and unethical nature of some of these "spiritual" treatments. Further, an increasing number of mental health professionals are serving as referral sources to fundamentalist Christian groups promising to change the sexual orientation of many unhappy lesbians and gay men.

The professionalism and ethics of this practice are highly questionable. It has been shown that those gay men most likely to be inclined toward doctrinaire religious practice are also likely to have lower self-concepts, to see homosexuality as more "sinful," to feel a greater sense of apprehension about negative responses from others, and to be more depressed in general (Weinberg & Williams, 1974). Such individuals make vulnerable targets for the "ex-gay" ministries, as they are known. Their testimonials, therefore, are the most suspect relative to the efficacy of the pastoral conversion programs in which they enroll; nevertheless, it is such testimonials that form the basis of most claims for "successful conversion" via religious means.

Fundamentalist Christian groups, such as Homosexuals Anonymous, Metanoia Ministries, Love In Action, Exodus International, and EXIT of Melodyland are the most visible purveyors of conversion therapy. The workings of these groups are well documented by Blair (1982). In this work, agents of sexual orientation change are characterized as nonprofessional individuals, many of whom are themselves intensely troubled by conflicts regarding their own homosexuality. Their programs are understandably reluctant to provide outcome data, simply stating that they have received numerous testimonials from satisfied counselees. Blair states that although many of these practitioners publicly promise "change," they privately acknowledge that celibacy is the realistic goal to which homosexuals must aspire. Furthermore, more than one religious group leader has "fallen from grace" for having sex with clients who are themselves in treatment for conversion of sexual orientation.

Perhaps the most notorious of these is Colin Cook. Cook is a pastor whose counseling program, Quest, led to the development of Homosexuals Anonymous, the largest antigay fundamentalist counseling organization in the world. The work of Cook, his ultimate demise, and the subsequent cover-up by the Seventh Day Adventist church, are described by sociologist Ronald Lawson (1987). Lawson characterizes Cook as a troubled homosexual man who had lost a highly visible pastorate in Manhattan as a result of promiscuous homosexual behavior. Celebrating his lack of professional counseling credentials, he discovered a market for ministering to self-doubting, conflicted, homosexual men. This led to his rapprochement with the Seventh Day Adventist church, and the founding of his Quest Ministries in Reading, Pennsylvania. Through the seven years' operation of his organization, approximately 200 people received "reorientation counseling" from Cook, his wife, and an associate. From this organization sprang Homosexuals Anonymous, a 14-step program based on Alcoholics Anonymous.

Lawson (1987), in attempting to research the efficacy of Cook's program, was denied access to counselees on the basis of confidentiality. Nonetheless, he managed to interview 14 clients, none of whom reported any change in sexual orientation. All but two reported that Cook had had sex with them during "treatment," in the form of nude massage and mutual masturbation. The two clients excluded from this pattern of exploitation were an older male and a man who received only telephone counseling. Even the telephone counselee, however, reported that Cook had masturbated during a telephone counseling session.

When Lawson brought these facts to light, Cook resigned his ministry; the church, however, refused to acknowledge the abuses of Cook's "pastoral care," or to make restitution for the damage done. Now, after what he describes as a period of his own "successful rehabilitation," Cook is attempting to rejuvenate his ministry to homosexuals.

The tradition of conflicted homosexual pastors using their ministries to gain sexual access to vulnerable gay people is as long-standing as the conversion movement itself. Ralph Blair, in his 1982 monograph *Ex-gay*, reports on one of the first "Ex-Gay" programs, Liberation in Jesus Christ. This program was founded by Guy Charles, who had claimed a heterosexual conversion subsequent to his acceptance of Christ; he was assisted in his ministry by a charismatic Episcopal church in Virginia. Charles was promoted through the evangelical world as no longer gay, and that God had removed "the lusts, the desires, and the act" (Blair, 1982, p. 6). Charles's claim that homosexuality is a choice, and his plan to "divest . . . homosexual desires" were called into question, however, when several who had sought the "ex-gay" experience through Liberation in Jesus Christ complained that Charles was having sex with them in the context of the conversion "treatments." Blair states:

> He [Charles] was telling these seekers that the homosexual experiences they were having with him were not "homosexual" but "Jonathan and David" relationships. The seekers, many of whom were "seeking" against their own will because they had been sent to Charles by a church or their parents, were quite cooperative in such "Jonathan and David" relationships. The Episcopal Church, which housed Liberation in Jesus Christ, kicked Charles out, convinced he was a fraud. (Blair, 1982, p. 7)

One of the of the most notable claims for the spiritual "cure" of homosexuality was advanced by Dr. E. Mansell Pattison, a psychiatrist, and his wife Myrna Loy (credentials not specified) (Pattison & Pattison, 1980). They reported that within a "supernatural framework," utilizing "generic methods of change common to folk therapy," some 11 male subjects changed from homosexual to heterosexual. As with almost all other conversion studies, successful outcome was defined as capacity for heterosexual intercourse. This is not equivalent to the Pattisons' claim of "complete orientation reversal."

Nonetheless, the Pattisons have continued to advertise their "method" as a cure for homosexuality, despite the numerous methodological problems with their study. Foremost, the sample of 11 subjects was culled from a group of 30 "ex-gays" who had sought treatment from the charismatic self-help group, EXIT of Melodyland. The 30, however, are but 10% of the 300 total "dissatisfied" homosexuals who had initially requested treatment. The Pattisons do not explain the basis upon which 270 subjects were excluded from the study, but the presumption is that this 90% were not successfully treated. Nor do they explain why 19 others of the 30 presumable "treatment successes" declined interviews. The inherent sampling bias of 11 of 30 (preselected according to indeterminate criteria from 300) renders highly questionable any resulting data. The Pattisons' therapeutic method is inadequately explained; only vague references to spiritual issues and group support describe how their "conversions" took place.

The Pattisons defined "successful treatment" as an exclusive shift in sexual orientation. Nevertheless, despite their own criteria, their data indicate that only 3 of the 11 (of 300) subjects report no current homosexual desires, fantasies, or impulses, and that one of the three is listed as still being "incidentally homosexual." Of the other 8, several indicate ongoing "neurotic conflict" about their homosexual impulses. Though six of these men have married heterosexually, two admit to more than incidental homosexual ideation as an ongoing issue. Blair reports that, when confronted with the apparent inconsistency of claiming exclusive heterosexual shift yet having ongoing homosexual fantasies, Pattison indicated that he thought such fantasies were normal, especially after a fight with one's wife! (Blair, 1982, p. 34). Heterosexual marriage is not equivalent to sexual orientation change, since it has been reported that some 20% of gay men marry at least once (Bell and Weinberg, 1978). From a religious perspective, Blair (1982) cites other Christian theologians, such as evangelistic psychiatrist Ruth Tiffany Barnhouse, who is skeptical about converting homosexuals. Those who can function heterosexually, according to Barnhouse, simply are demonstrating that "the physiology of their sexual apparatus is in good working order," and that the fundamentalist demand for celibacy in homosexuals is an "unreasonable and cruel" demand. The Pattison data present an unconvincing picture of heterosexual conversion following a treatment program that is poorly described to begin with, and founded upon ill-defined constructs.

Recently, founders of yet another prominent "ex-gay" ministry, Exodus International, denounced their conversion therapy procedures as ineffective. Michael Busse and Gary Cooper, cofounders of Exodus and lovers for 13 years, were involved with the organization from 1976 to 1979. The program was described by these men as "ineffective . . . not one person was healed." They stated that the program often exacerbated already prominent feelings of guilt and personal failure among the counselees; many were driven to suicidal thoughts as a result of the failed "reparative therapy" (*Newswatch Briefs*, 1990).

The fundamentalist Christian approaches to conversion treatments have been characterized by a host of problems, ranging from lack of empirical support to the sexually predatory behavior of some counselors, such as Cook and Charles. To exacerbate the potential harm done to naive, shame-ridden counselees, many of these programs operate under the formidable auspices of the Christian church, and outside the jurisdiction of any professional organization that might impose ethical standards of practice and accountability on them.

CONCLUSION

Psychological ethics mandate that mental health professionals subscribe to methods that support human dignity and are effective in their stated purpose. Conversion therapy qualifies as neither. It reinforces the social stigma associated with homosexuality, and there is no evidence from any of the studies reviewed here to suggest that sexual orientation can be changed. Perhaps conversion therapy seemed viable when homosexuality was still thought to be an illness; at this point, it is an idea whose time has come and gone. At no point has there been empirical support for the idea of conversion; indeed, the methodological flaws in these studies are enormous. It now makes sense to discontinue focusing on conversion attempts and focus instead on healing and educating an intolerant social context. Some will say that an individual has the "right to choose" conversion treatment. Such a choice, however, is almost always based on the internalized effects of a hostile family and an intolerant society.

As long as we focus on homosexuality itself as the problem, we miss the point. Martin (1984, p. 46) states:

> A clinician's implicit acceptance of the homosexual orientation as the cause of ego-dystonic reactions, and the concomitant agreement to attempt sexual orientation change, exacerbates the ego-dystonic reactions and reinforces and confirms the internalized homophobia that lies at their root.

To view self-negating homosexuals seeking change otherwise is to deny the significant impact of negative social stigma that confronts the gay person at every step. If we attempt to conjure a "cure" for homosexuality, we only reinforce bigotry.

Conversionists skip this issue altogether and promote change methods assuming the pathology of homosexuality because their reasoning is based upon such bigotry, or a certain biblical interpretation. They do not attempt to prove the conceptual underpinnings of their efforts because they cannot, since their theories are entirely nonscientific. Therapy is not value-fee; nor, certainly, is religion. Both do gay people harm by trumpeting false promises of "cure," when it is the caregivers themselves—and society as a whole—that are in need of a "cure."

Mental health and paraprofessional practitioners who engage in conversion therapies may be likely to harm such clients, and in addition may also commit consumer fraud, as this damaging practice simply does not work. Professionals merely "referring" clients for such services also bear responsibility. The violation of client welfare and standards of professional conduct inherent in these practices warrants a response from professional organizations to mandate ethical and professional practice.

The American Psychological Association's "Fact Sheet on Reparative Therapy" opens with the following statement: "No scientific evidence exists to support the effectiveness of any of the conversion therapies that try to change sexual orientation." Bryant Welch (1990), in an APA statement on conversion therapy, said: "The real issue confronting our society today is not why people seek love and understanding as they do, but why some seem so unable to love and understand at all." We do gay men and lesbians, and society as a whole, a disservice by perpetuating the myth that sexual orientation can be changed.

11

Homosexual Identity: Coming Out and Other Developmental Events

John C. Gonsiorek
James R. Rudolph

The chapter on the demise of the illness model of homosexuality in this volume concluded with a puzzle. While empirical evidence overwhelmingly suggests that homosexuality is not intrinsically psychopathological, there are consistent findings suggesting a subgroup of gay men and lesbians who, at least at some point in their lives, experience significant psychological distress. High rates of alcohol and drug abuse, suicide attempts, utilization of mental health services, and greater psychological turmoil during adolescence are suggested. This chapter attempts to integrate these findings within a general framework of identity development that views homosexuality as a nonpathological variation in human behavior. We will also address whether gay and lesbian people experience unique psychological processes in developing a sense of self as gay or lesbian.

Note this is not the same as saying there is a gay or lesbian personality. As discussed in the earlier chapter, there are no consistent differences between homosexual and heterosexual populations that would warrant the concept of distinctly gay or lesbian personality features. Instead, we conceptualize gay and lesbian people as a diverse group of individuals who experience some similarity in the external pressures they face. As a result, some similarity in psychological processes they experience ensues. These events, however, are filtered through a diversity of personality structures and personal and family histories. Later in the chapter we will discuss how this theoretical explication has many implications for any group of individuals who cope with a disparaging or oppressive society.

THE BEGINNINGS OF A DEVELOPMENTAL PERSPECTIVE

Much theorizing about personality structure assumes that personal characteristics are laid down relatively early in life, and that events in later childhood, adolescence, and adulthood more or less represent an unfolding of these characteristics over time. Such approaches, however, tend to be static.They have difficulty incorporating the process of ongoing development, such as Erikson's (1980) theory about personality development occurring into and through adulthood. They also have trouble accommodating events that may occur later in life but powerfully influence psychological functioning, such as the concept of post-traumatic stress disorder.

More importantly, most personality theories operate at a "micro" level, i.e., the family as the most important influence. They do not easily incorporate "macro" effects, i.e., larger sociopolitical forces such as poverty, racism, sexism, homophobia, and similar kinds of oppression—especially as these forces may have their impact over the lifespan, not just in early childhood. Those theories that can accommodate important influences and change over the lifespan, and incorporate the effects of "macro" forces upon the individual, we label *developmental* to signify an ongoing identity development process, instead of a relatively static identity structure that merely manifests over time. Finally, developmental perspectives implicitly or explicitly utilize *the individual in context,* not simply *the individual,* as their basic unit of analysis.

Perhaps the first individual to apply a developmental perspective to the experience of oppressed groups was Allport (1954), who examined the nature and effects of stereotyping and prejudice. Allport theorized about the personality characteristics that develop in individuals who are targets of prejudice. He described these characteristics as coping mechanisms that people may develop in response to prejudice, but that may eventually become relatively stable personality traits. These he termed *traits due to victimization* and believed they were common in most persecuted groups. These traits include excessive concern and preoccupation with minority or deviant group membership, feelings of insecurity, denial of membership in the group, withdrawal and passivity, self-derision, strong in-group ties coupled with prejudice against out-groups, slyness and cunning, self-hate, aggression against one's own group, militancy, enhanced striving, neuroticism, and acting out self-fulfilling prophecies about one's own inferiority.

Allport developed his ideas by observing the effects of prejudice against blacks and Jews. His analysis did not include homosexuals. Yet, the personality traits and coping mechanisms he describes parallel closely descriptions of personality characteristics that certain psychoanalytic writers (Bergler, 1956; Bieber et al., 1962; Hatterer, 1970; Socarides, 1968) describe as inherent and pathological features of homosexuals and "evidence" that homosexuality per se is a neurotic illness. This is a clear example of the same phenomena being viewed as intrinsic by one school of thought and as reactive to an external situation by another school of thought. Allport's work is different from the theories on stereotyping described by Herek in this volume in that Allport places greater emphasis on how social situations shape and alter *personality characteristics* of stereotyped individuals. The material described by Herek places greater emphasis on how the processes of stereotyping affect target individuals' *behavior* in given situations.

The Weinberg and Williams study (1974), described earlier in regard to base rates of mental health problems, also collected other data on their subjects. They examined factors that facilitate general adjustment to homosexuality and found that individuals who were well adjusted as homosexuals had rejected the idea that homosexuality was an illness, had close and supportive associations with other homosexuals, and were not interested in changing their homosexuality. It is noteworthy that writers who advocate an illness model of homosexuality and attempt to "cure" homosexuals say many things in common. These theorists (Bergler, 1956; Bieber, et al. 1962; Caprio, 1954; Hatterer, 1970; Socarides, 1968) agree that in order to "cure" a homosexual, he or she must be convinced that such behavior is disturbed, be motivated to change, avoid homosexual relationships, and avoid social contacts with other homosexuals. These are precisely the attitudes that Weinberg and Williams (1974) found related to poor psychological adjustment in homosexuals. The question arises whether theorists who advocate "curing" homosexuals are creating or exacerbating maladjustment in their homosexual patients, or as Silverstein notes his chapter, psychiatry teaches patients to suffer.

Later research has supported and amplified the findings of Weinberg and Williams. Hammersmith and Weinberg (1973) found that positive commitment to homosexuality was related to psychological adjustment and the existence of significant others who support that identity. Farrell and Morrione (1974) found that membership in a homosexual group had positive psychological effects in a lower socioeconomic status subject group. Jacobs and Tedford (1980) found that membership in a homosexual group was positively related to self-esteem. Schmitt and Kurdek (1987) found that gay men living with a partner had a more positive self-concept, and that gay men involved in long-term relationships had less depression and anxiety, and a greater internal locus of control. The work of D'Augelli (D'Augelli, 1987; D'Augelli & Hart, 1987) describes the beneficial effects of supportive lesbian and gay male communities in rural areas.

These discussions share the ideas that a gay or lesbian person's response to the external oppression he or she faces has significant effects on psychological functioning. They set the stage for the idea that some of the problems gay and lesbian people do experience can be best understood from a *developmental* perspective.

THE COMING OUT PROCESS

If you will recall from our earlier discussion, there are suggestions that in adolescence and young adulthood, some gay and lesbian individuals experience a great deal of psychological turmoil. In the 1970s, clinicians working with gay men and lesbians began to notice patterning to these struggles and to describe a developmental process of coming to terms with homosexuality, labeled the "coming out" process. The earliest known reference to this concept is found, however, in the work of the Dutch psychiatrist Sengers (1969), who labeled the concept "self-acceptance."

These theorists and observers, who include Cass (1979), Coleman (1982), Dank (1971), Grace (1979), Hencken and O'Dowd (1977), Lee (1977), Plummer (1975), and Troiden (1979, 1988a, 1988b), suggested that gay individuals progress through a series of stages typically occurring in adolescence or young adulthood. While varying in the number and description of the stages, they generally run as follows. There is an initial stage where individuals block recognition of same-sex feelings through a variety of defensive strategies that may exact a high psychological price for their maintenance. Some individuals maintain these defensive strategies indefinitely and constrict their same-sex feelings. Usually, they consume in the process much psychological energy and incur constriction in general functioning style and damage to self-esteem. For many individuals, however, a gradual recognition of same-sex interests emerges. The individual, by stages, begins to gradually tolerate that significant same-sex feelings are present.

This is usually followed by a period of emotional and behavioral experimentation with homosexuality and often an increasing sense of normalcy about same-sex feelings. Some models postulate a second crisis after the dissolution of a first relationship in which a reemergence of negative feelings about being gay or lesbian occurs. As the individual again begins to accept his or her same-sex feelings, a sense of identity as gay or lesbian is successfully integrated and accepted as a positive aspect of the self. The models vary somewhat on the particulars of these later stages. Most writers note that while this process is described in discrete stages, it is generally unpredictable, with stops, starts, and backtracking. In particular, denial of same-sex feelings may weave in and out, periodically halting development.

This coming out process represents a shift in the person's core sexual identity and may be accompanied by dramatic levels of emotional distress. Individuals may temporarily display virtually any psychiatric symptom, especially if they are without support or adequate information about sexuality. In general, the best predictor of an individual's long-term adjustment during this phase is his or her level of functioning prior to this process, rather than the presenting symptomatology. Most gay and lesbian individuals weather these crises and emerge several years later with minimal or no symptomatology and improved functioning. A more detailed description of these events, particularly for adolescents, is described by Gonsiorek (1988).

There appear to be differences between gay men and lesbians during this process. As some have noted (see Gonsiorek, 1988), this process for males appears more abrupt and more likely to be associated with psychiatric symptoms, whereas the process for women appears characterized by greater fluidity and ambiguity. It may well be the case that differences in the pacing of identity development are influenced by sex role socialization. Because women are allowed a broader range of behavioral and emotional interactions with other women, they may experience emerging sexual and emotional intimacy as "mere friendship." Because men are confined to more narrow patterns of expression, longing for emotional and physical contact with other males is apt to be perceived as clearly "homosexual." Consistent with traditional sex role socialization, males are more prone to sexualizing distress during the coming out process and women are more likely to respond with reflection and self-absorption.

Sears (1989, p. 437) noted in his research that "important differences among males and females in the meanings constructed around these sexual feelings and experiences were evident. Lesbian participants, more often than gay men, attached emotional-romantic meaning to same-sex relationships prior to engaging in homosexual behavior, defined the term *homosexual* in an emotional romantic context, and denied the legitimacy of their own sexual feelings. . . . Some scholars have concluded that lesbians have more in common with heterosexual women than they do with gay men." Cotton (1975), Gramick (1984), Ponse (1980), and Simon and Gagnon (1967) have made similar observations. Schippers (1990, p. 14) summarizes this idea in the following way: "The psychological discourse on lesbian sexuality differs from the one about gay male sexuality . . . it is of a more exploratory nature. . . ."

These generalizations are more or less true of any single individual depending on the flexibility of his or her sex role, and other aspects of personality structure and personal history.

The coming out models are an important theoretical development. They essentially describe an *additional* developmental effort unique to the lives of lesbians and gay men. This developmental event occurs in addition to, not instead of, the psychological processes and other aspects of identity development throughout adolescence and adulthood. In other words, this additional developmental event is filtered through other aspects of the personality structure and personal and family history. The coming out models themselves vary in how sensitive they are to this variation. For example, Cass's model contains a well-developed explication of the psychological processes involved, whereas other, such as Coleman's, are relatively unelaborated.

Probably the most psychologically rich model to date was articulated by Malyon (1981, 1982a, 1982b). Malyon theorized as follows. Gay and lesbian persons, like heterosexuals, are raised with culturally sanctioned antihomosexual biases. Such biases mobilize other psychological processes that extend beyond the development of prejudice. Children who will eventually be bisexual or homosexual often develop an awareness of being different at an early age. They may not understand the sexual nature or precise meaning of their differentness, but they soon learn it is negatively regarded. As these individuals develop and mature, they reach a fuller understanding of the nature of this difference and the considerable negative societal reaction to it. These negative feelings may be incorporated into the self-image resulting in varying degrees of *internalized homophobia.* Negative feelings about one's sexual orientation may be overgeneralized to encompass the entire self. Effects of this may range from a mild tendency toward self-doubt in the face of prejudice to overt self-hatred and self-destructive behavior.

Others have theorized about different aspects and outcomes during these processes. Grace (1977) theorized that gay and lesbian adolescents generally do not partake of typical adolescent social and romantic experimentation. This creates a sense of loss that predisposes some individuals to depression, despair, and self-esteem problems in adulthood. Gonsiorek (1982c) described how certain developmental routes can result in an overlay of other symptomatology that with time becomes a more pronounced part of the personality structure. For example, he described how married or closeted men who covertly engage in anonymous same-sex sexual behavior can develop an overlay of maladaptive coping mechanisms. Daher (1981) has explicated how the sense of differentness in gay male adolescents can lead to development of feelings of inferiority.

Indeed, this area represents one of the most productive in terms of theory development about gay men and lesbians. These models, however, have been developed mainly on middle-class, white, non-Hispanic samples from the English-speaking world. One would expect that developmental events like these would be highly sensitive to cultural, class, socioeconomic, racial, and ethnic variation. Therefore, the developmental sequence described in these models should not be assumed to hold true for other populations. The application of this identity/developmental perspective to more diverse populations is one of the most important and illuminating of current research efforts.

For example, Icard (1985-1986, 1986) has applied similar ideas to U.S. black males; Loiacano (1989) to black lesbians and gay men; Greene (1986) to U.S. black lesbians and gay men; Gock (1985) to Asian/Pacific gay men; Allen (1984) to native American lesbians; Wooden, Kawasaki, and Mayeda (1983) to Japanese-American males; Hidalgo (1984) and Hidalgo and Christensen (1976-1977) to Puerto Rican lesbians in the United States; and Espin (1987) to Latina lesbians. Morales (1983) attempted a model general to Third World gay men and lesbians.

Comparable work in a variety of populations is currently in progress. While the specifics of this identity/developmental perspective change between populations, the general perspective appears to be broadly useful. Since this perspective stresses the relationship between the individual, social forces, and sense of self, these differing cultural perspectives are not variations on a theme epitomized by the white, middle-class, North American, English-speaking world. Rather, the entire developmental process and outcomes within the sense of self can vary greatly as the social forces that shape them vary. For example, both the nature of homophobia and concepts of "maleness" and "femaleness" can be significantly different in U.S. black communities; the relationship between individual and family is less rigidly drawn in the more cohesive multigenerational Hispanic family than in the relatively atomized, one-generational Anglo family; and pressures on gay and lesbian members of Asian families to prevent dishonor and loss of face for the family are especially high. An identity development perspective can accommodate cultural and other sources of variation, and differing effects upon identity development and sense of self would be predicted.

These writers generally agree that there is commonality in the psychological processes experienced by lesbian and gay members of racial and ethnic minorities. Many writers speak of double, in the case of lesbians, triple, minority statuses. For example, Gock (1985) described the perceived choice of having to identify with the homosexual community (and so address expression of intimacy) versus the ethnic minority community (and so retain cultural groundedness). Morales (1983) terms this a "conflict of allegiance" and offers a four-stage model on how ethnic lesbians and gay men resolve such conflicts of multiple identities.

Icard (Icard, 1986; Icard & Traunstein, 1987) describes how gay black men are subject to an unusually harsh triple prejudice, coming not only from the white heterosexual majority, but also from the white gay male and black heterosexual minorities. The strong pressures for social sex role conformity in black communities further exacerbate these stresses. Sears (1989), in a study of growing up lesbian in the U.S. South, describes "fragmentation of identity in the attempt to integrate multiple identities." He also notes that ethnic identity acquisition occurs first, and therefore the later lesbian identity can create a sense of betrayal to one's ethnic group.

Espin (1987) applied the Minority Identity Development Model (Atkinson, Morten, & Sue, 1979) to understand identity development among Latina lesbians. This model shares many features with the lesbian/gay developmental models described earlier. Espin suggests that the psychological processes may be similar in the integration of various disparaged identities. The task at hand, however, is somewhat different for ethnic/racial minority lesbians and gay men; namely, the integration of all minority identities in a context where all are disparaged and in which one minority group typically disparages the others. The picture is more complicated yet: One researcher found sex differences in the relative strength of which minority status is most disparaged. In her study on Asian-American lesbians and gay men, Chan (1989) found that lesbians experienced more discrimination because of being Asian, while gay men experienced more discrimination because of being homosexual. The final outcomes are complex: "The development of homosexual identity is shaped by the racial and gendered contexts in which the person is situated" (Sears, 1989, p. 447).

Sex differences between gay men and lesbians in this process have been explicated by DeMonteflores and Schultz (1978), Henderson (1984), and Lewis (1984). Cass (1984) measured aspects of the different stages and compared similarities and differences between men and women. Chapman and Brannock (1987) and Gramick (1984) researched models of lesbian identity awareness, and Sophie (1987) has detailed aspects of identity development and internalized homophobia in gay women. Browning (1987) attempts to differentiate coming out issues from other developmental events for lesbians, Groves (1985) described therapeutic strategies for lesbians in the coming out process, and Sophie (1985) has reviewed theories of coming out and identity development for lesbian women. Specific attention to relationships with family during the coming out process have been explicated by Berg-Cross (1988) for women and Cramer and Roach (1988) for men. Kimmel (1978) noted that the existing information on lesbian and gay identity formation is cross-sectional (different people, at different stages, at one point in time), and that longitudinal studies (the same people, followed across time) are needed to fully understand identity development.

Wasserman and Storms (1984) critiqued various theories about coming out and identity formation. MacDonald (1982) researched various milestone events during the coming out process, finding evidence for many of the events described in the models. Troiden and Goode (1980) also found support for gay identity development occurring over time, and related to distinct behavioral events. In Holland, the work of Deenen (Deenen, 1986; Deenen & Naerssen, 1988) also provides empirical work for aspects of these theories.

This identity/developmental perspective has reached sufficient maturity that one commentator (Schippers, 1989, 1990) has reviewed the meaning of the concept and proposed a renaming as the "acceptance and appreciation process." Schippers makes the legitimate point that this term is more accurate psychologically. The term *coming out* "really is a political term" (Schippers, 1990, p. 8). There are other problems with the term *coming out*. It can be seen as trivializing in that it connotes a single point in time and a deliberate choice. Further, the term is most specific to a particular juncture of social and political events in the mid and late 20th century Western world. "Coming out" may also be subtly sexist in that it implies a linear "male" process that is reasonably descriptive for some men, but ignores the fluidity described by many women (see the research by Golden, 1990).

This concept appears to be viable in different cultures within the Western world. While many of these theoreticians are North American, Deenen and Schippers are Dutch; it should also be noted that one of the earliest theoreticians is Australian (Cass) and another, British (Plummer). The theoretical and empirical work on this concept includes both clinical and nonclinical samples. These developmental perspectives are being applied in a variety of cultures and subcultures including Brazil (Parker, 1989), Eastern Europe (Brzek & Hubalek, 1988), England (Plummer, 1989), France (Le Bitoux, 1989), Mexico (Carrier, 1976, 1989), the U.S. South (Sears, 1989), and others. A number of cross-cultural or multicultural perspectives have appeared (Ross, 1989; Ross, Paulsen, & Stalstrom, 1988; and Tremble, Schneider, & Appathurai, 1989).

These developments in theory and research have been important. Many of the ideas about the coming out process, identity development, and internalized homophobia, however, stand apart as theoretical conceptions not tied into the main body of psychological theory. This constricts the ability of these ideas to develop further and also risks underutilization by clinicians.

What we will attempt in the remainder of this chapter is a unification of ideas pertaining to internalized homophobia, gay and lesbian identity formation, and the coming out process with an established and emerging theory about personality development, Kohut's self-psychology. This theory focuses on the effects upon the sense of self caused by traumatizing, disappointing, or disparaging events. Thus, we believe it can serve as a bridge between theories of identity development based upon the experience of disparaged minorities and more established theories of personality development. It is also an *example*—but in no sense the final word—of how the emerging ideas of gay and lesbian affirmative theory can incorporate select portions of mainstream psychological knowledge. But first, however, some background is needed to effect this bridge. We have decided to retain self-psychology terminology in an attempt to bring the models together.

A SELF-PSYCHOLOGY PERSPECTIVE

Most simply put, a *narcissistic injury* is a profound blow to one's self-esteem. For the majority of gay and lesbian youth, the point of awareness of their differentness, and eventually, homosexuality (and for sometime thereafter) is an experience in narcissistic injury. As Moses and Hawkins (1982) observed, those who encounter few problems in accepting their homosexuality, or having it accepted, are "probably fairly rare" (p. 84).

Becoming aware of one's homosexuality is a wounding both by commission and omission. The gay or lesbian youth, upon discovering that his or her sexuality is devalued and rejected by society generally, and more personally by parents, peers, and teachers, suffers a clear and explicit narcissistic injury. Equally powerfully wounding, if less obvious, is having one's sexuality, a fundamental aspect of the self (the self being defined as "the core of personality," Greene, 1984, p. 40), left unresponded to and unadmired by parents and others (see Kohut, 1977, p. 26, about the importance of responding to the "whole child"). That is, the heterosexual child's heterosexuality is anticipated, embraced, and cultivated; the homosexual child's homosexuality is not. Woodman and Lenna (1982) remarked that "[a coming out crisis] occurs when the person encounters inner conflict between what he or she feels about self and what has been learned about acceptable social and sexual behavior. Fear and anxiety arise not only from internal stress but also from perceptions that external support systems are either absent or hostile" (p. 25).

The result of this neglect and devaluation of a basic part of the personality of the gay or lesbian youth is a loss, in many cases a drastic loss, of self-esteem, initiative, and legitimate entitlement. The self is prone to fragmentation, enfeeblement, and disharmony. The coming out process can serve to heal this narcissistic injury and restore integrity and functioning to the damaged self.

Provided the gay or lesbian youth arrives at the coming out stage not otherwise psychologically crippled or severely traumatized (e.g., from prolonged involvement with pathological parents, or other toxic childhood experiences), the narcissistic injury is a temporary, albeit nontrivial, wound; a developmental challenge to be mastered. Since this wounding occurs relatively later in childhood compared with other critical developmental events, its effects are likely to be less damaging. The gay or lesbian youth who have been *chronically* narcissistically injured throughout childhood by events prior to and separate from those described here, however, reach the coming out stage in a different and highly vulnerable state. For them, the narcissistic injury of disparaged sexuality is not met as a developmental challenge to be surmounted, but rather as another danger that threatens to shatter an already tenuous psychological constitution. It is suggested these fragile gay and lesbian youth comprise a majority of the casualties of the coming out period, those for whom a resilient homosexual identity is beyond their personal resources to achieve, and for whom the narcissistic injury of their disparaged homosexuality is a coup de grâce leaving them emotionally debilitated. We theorize that it is these individuals who comprise the bulk of those whose histories are characterized by suicide attempts, alcohol and drug abuse, and increased utilization of mental health services, as noted earlier.

Heinz Kohut wrote extensively on narcissistic injury and developed an analytical psychotherapy for the healing of narcissistic injuries, or self-deficits (e.g., 1971, 1977, 1984). Although he wrote generically of the narcissistic injuries in children as a function of unresponsive, unempathic, and unavailable parents, his theoretical model can be applied, if not exactly, then heuristically, to the narcissistic injuries of gay and lesbian youth as a function of their disparaged sexuality. His model can now be briefly summarized.

HEINZ KOHUT'S SELF-PSYCHOLOGY

Kohut proposed three sectors or constituents of the self, the maturation of all, during childhood, defining optimal psychological development. Each sector matures through the laying down of psychological structure in the developing self. The three sectors he titled: (a) the grandiose-exhibitionistic sector; (b) the idealizing sector; and (c) the twinship or alterego sector. The maturation of the grandiose-exhibitionistic sector of the self is dependent upon the parent mirroring, echoing, and admiring the child's self-centered activities (e.g., walking, talking, exploring, asserting). In time, the external approval of the parent is internalized by the child as self-esteem and self-acceptance, and the reflected grandiosity and exhibitionism are internalized as feelings of vitality and the pursuit of ambitions.

The maturation of the idealizing sector is dependent upon the child being allowed to idealize the parent and merge with the parent's perceived omnipotence, thereby sharing in the parent's power and perceived perfection, and in the process receiving responses that soothe and calm the child's fears and anxieties. In time, the child develops his or her own sense of personal efficacy and the capacity for self-stabilization, and internalizes the values of the parent that serve as the ideals that guide the child's raw ambitions throughout life.

Maturation of the twinship or alterego sector is dependent upon the parent being simply, yet profoundly, a benign human presence with whom the child can identify and affiliate; the child can be with another of essential likeness, a "human among humans" (Kohut, 1984, p. 200). In time, the child develops needed life skills and talents from this important association that employs the ambitions in service to fulfilling the ideals. That is, an "uninterrupted tension arc [is established] from basic ambitions, via basic talents and skills, toward basic ideals. The tension arc is the dynamic essence of the complete nondefective self; it is a conceptualization of the structure whose establishment makes possible a creative-productive, fulfilling life" (Kohut, 1984, pp. 4-5).

The child incorporates structure for the development of the self by a process Kohut called *transmuting internalization,* and is described as follows. The parent is responsive to the child's needs by maintaining a relationship of *consistent empathic intuneness.* As a result, the child is able to use the parent as a functional part of his or her self; the parent as *selfobject* shores up the child's maturing, but as yet incomplete, self. From time to time, however, there is an unavoidable breach of empathy, or the parent is simply unavailable, and he or she fails to meet the child's needs. Provided the failure is nontraumatic (e.g., the response is only briefly delayed, or is a mild deviation from an empathic response), the child is *optimally* frustrated, and he or she takes over a fraction of the functions that the parent, as selfobject, had previously performed for him or her. Through countless optimal frustrations during childhood, psychological structure is incrementally laid down, and thereby the child's self gradually matures.

If the parent's responses are chronically unempathic, however, (e.g., absent, flat, capricious, or bizarre), the child's needs are not met and the development of the self is faulty, or arrested altogether, i.e., the child is narcissistically injured. The injury may be healed later in psychotherapy where the child develops selfobject transferences with the therapist in all three sectors of the self, the traumatic empathy failures of childhood are revived and worked through in the transferences, and delayed structuralization of the self occurs. That is, the therapist as selfobject established a relationship of consistent empathic intuneness with the client (i.e., mirrors and responds with self-confirming joy to the client's grandiose-exhibitionistic activities, allows himself or herself to be idealized and provides soothing-calming responses for the client, and serves as a benign human presence of essential likeness with whom the client can affiliate). Through occasional, unavoidable lapses in empathy, the client is optimally frustrated, transmuting internalization occurs, and delayed or compensatory structuralization of the client's self results, healing over the narcissistic injuries of early childhood. In addition, the therapist optimally frustrates the client by understanding and acknowledging, but not acting on, the client's unfulfilled needs. That is, "through the [therapist's] more or less accurate understanding, an empathic bond is established . . . between [therapist] and [client] that substitutes for the de facto fulfillment of the [client's] need" (Kohut, 1984, p. 103).

SELF-PSYCHOLOGY AND THE COMING OUT PROCESS

The process of healing the narcissistic injury of disparaged sexuality of otherwise healthy gay or lesbian youth is analogous to the process involved in the healing of the narcissistic injuries of early childhood (i.e., a process analogous to psychotherapy). The gay or lesbian youth who successfully works through his or her internalized homophobia and adopts an affirmative homosexual identity frequently does so in the context of a positive, ongoing gay/lesbian social support network. This support network, through its individual members and collectively as a group, serves the gay or lesbian youth as a selfobject, paralleling the role of the psychotherapist as selfobject to a client narcissistically injured in early childhood, or, more radically, serves as the good or wholesome parent by accepting and admiring, stabilizing and inspiring, and being a companion to the youth coming out. That is, the support network helps to heal the narcissistically injured gay or lesbian youth in all three sectors of the self. The research data on the positive relationships between self-esteem, involvement in community, and acceptance of self in lesbians and gay men, cited earlier in this chapter, is in line with this self-psychology perspective. Simply stated, a positive affirming community heals the wounds of external oppression.

Grandiose-exhibitionistic sector. The support network mirrors and admires the nascent homosexual, and homoerotic, behaviors of the gay or lesbian youth who is coming out. For example, encouragement and approval are offered as the youth begins to flirt, date, and become sexually active with same-sex others, and as the youth just generally identifies himself or herself, in various and meaningful ways, as a homosexual person. In time, the youth internalizes the approval of the support network, representing the larger homosexual community, as pride in his or her sexual orientation, as self-esteem, assertiveness, and self-acceptance. And also in time, the grandiosity and exhibitionism reflecting the youth's evolving homosexual identity are internalized as feelings of vitality and motivation for homosexual activities and concerns, and beyond.

Idealizing sector. The inexperienced youth coming out perceives the established, already-out support network as wiser and more powerful than himself or herself. In identifying with the support network, and through it with the larger homosexual community, the youth derives feelings of empowerment and greater certainty, replacing those of fear, confusion, and powerlessness. He or she receives guidance and comfort from the support network, and in time, the youth finds it less necessary to rely as heavily upon the strength and stabilizing influence of the support network as he or she develops greater internal resources. The values and ideals of the larger homosexual community (most importantly those of self-determination) are gradually incorporated into the personality structure of the coming-out youth, whose self is healing and maturing.

Twinship/alterego sector. Associating with other gay and lesbian persons in the support network both humanizes and universalizes the youth's sexuality. For the first time, the youth can be among others of essential likeness; he or she can be a "homosexual among homosexuals." In time, this benign affiliation results in the youth's acquiring skills and talents needed to succeed socially, sexually, politically, and otherwise in the larger homosexual community.

The support network establishes a somewhat less precise but analogous relationship of consistent empathic intuneness with the gay or lesbian youth. The support network is experienced by the youth as benevolent, and willing and able to meet his or her needs. Unavoidably, from time to time, the support network fails to meet the needs of the youth, who is then thrown back on his or her own resources. Provided the frustration is optimal (i.e., nontraumatic), the youth takes on a small portion of the functions previously performed for him or her by the support network. And although the support network cannot or does not always gratify the youth's needs, it provides understanding and empathy that maintain the self-selfobject relationship and substitutes for the actual fulfillment of need. Each time an optimal frustration occurs, structure is laid down in the self, and the youth's narcissistic injury, as a function of his or her disparaged and neglected sexuality, is partially healed.

Kohut (1977) argues that although we become "independent centers of initiative" (p. 99) through the acquisition of a naturally healthy or reconstituted self, we never "out grow" our need for selfobjects, but rather we replace archaic with maturely chosen selfobjects, as in "a strong self enables us to experience love and desire more intensely" (Kohut, 1984, p. 53). We still need to be admired, uplifted, and shared to feel good about ourselves. Thus, following the healing over of the narcissistic injury of disparaged homosexuality, the gay or lesbian youth chooses more developmentally mature selfobjects, those with whom he or she can experience relationships of deeper empathic resonance. Examples of behavior indicating a healing, or healed over, narcissistic injury might include a young gay male who is able without self-derision to walk away from, or object to, the telling of a homophobic joke; a young lesbian who is able to compose herself following the negative reaction of a long-time acquaintance to the disclosure of her homosexuality; or a young gay or lesbian youth who is able, despite parental disapproval, to volunteer in the campaign of a self-identified homosexual candidate, or who, for the first time, is able to go to a same-sex social club and ask someone attractive to dance. Through a multitude of such experiences during the coming out period (optimal frustrations followed by transmuting internalization), the selves of gay and lesbian youth, narcissistically injured by the disparagement of their sexuality by society and significant others, are restored to wholeness, vigor, and harmony.

The preceding discussion simplifies Kohut's theory of self-psychology, and its application to the narcissistic injuries and coming out period of gay and lesbian youth is inexact. In particular, we apply his concepts to a later developmental period than that upon which he developed his theory. Nonetheless, we believe these ideas can help create a better understanding of the dynamics of homosexual youth mediating between a self that is "different" and a society that disparages that differentness. These ideas also have clear implications for clinical practice, consistent with available research, suggesting that affirmation of a gay or lesbian identity, involvement in community, and services for gay and lesbian adolescents are likely to be important in the primary prevention and remediation of mental health problems. Finally, nothing in the above discussion alters the conclusion of Chapter 8 that sexual orientation is unrelated to psychopathology. This discussion describes the *psychological experience of the homosexual individual in an oppressive environment—not psychopathology in a homosexual person.*

SUMMARY

Recent theoretical developments supported by a small but growing amount of research suggests that gay men and lesbians experience unique and particular stresses and developmental variations in identity formation. It is clear that a supportive environment, self-acceptance, and good role models in the gay and lesbian community facilitate positive mental health. Gay men and lesbians experience additional developmental events as they negotiate the emergence of positive identity in a context of external oppression. These are in addition to, not instead of, other aspects of child, adolescent, and adult development.

We believe the model that has been outlined here is useful in a number of ways. It may serve as a framework for articulating the psychological experience and identity formation of any group of individuals who are oppressed by the majority culture and suggest ways that the wounds of oppression can be healed. This model also helps explicate differences and similarities within gay and lesbian people and offers an explanation of why there are some consistencies against a backdrop of considerable psychological variation. The concept of internalized homophobia and analogous forms that may be developed for other minority groups may be useful in explaining the tendency of minority groups to discharge their frustration primarily against each other instead of the majority culture.

The ideas described in this chapter can help form the basis of future psychological theory development and research pertaining to gay men and lesbians. As has been outlined earlier, the lack of inherent psychopathology among gay men and lesbians is a settled issue scientifically. The next tasks involve developing a fuller psychological understanding of the lives of lesbians and gay men.

12

Lesbian and Gay Relationships

Letitia Anne Peplau

Public awareness of lesbian and gay couples is growing; attention to homosexuality in the popular media is increasing. Social scientists have also begun to describe and analyze the nature of gay and lesbian relationships. The new scholarship on homosexual relationships is important both to the scientific community and to the general public.

For the emerging science of close relationships (Kelley et al., 1983), research on homosexual couples broadens the existing knowledge base by increasing the diversity of types of relationships studied to include same-sex partnerships. In the past, virtually all research on adult love relationships has focused on heterosexual dating and marriage. New studies of homosexual couples expand the range and generality of scientific knowledge about intimate relationships.

For the growing research literature on homosexuality, studies of gay and lesbian relationships also represent a new direction. Until recently, scholarship on homosexuality focused primarily on questions of pathology, individual psychological adjustment, and etiology. For example, a recent annotated bibliography included close to 5,000 citations from the social sciences, humanities, and popular press (Dynes, 1987). Only 36 of these entries were classified as dealing with gay or lesbian "couples." In contrast, there were 207 entries on psychiatry, psychotherapy, "cures," and related topics, and another 155 entries on the experiences of lesbians and gay men in prison or with the police.

For the general public, accurate information about gay and lesbian relationships is also useful. Scientific research can replace biased stereotypes with factual descriptions of the nature and diversity of homosexual couples. Research can also inform the discussion of new legal and

AUTHOR'S NOTE: An earlier version of this chapter was presented at the Fourth International Conference on Personal Relationships held at the University of British Columbia, July 3-8, 1988. I gratefully acknowledge the valuable assistance of Amanda Munoz and Steven L. Gordon in the preparation of this chapter.

public policy issues that arise as gay men and lesbians become a more visible and vocal part of society. This point is illustrated in the following case descriptions, based on recent legal cases. (For a detailed review of the legal status of lesbian and gay couples, see the chapter by Rivera in this volume.)

Case One: Emotional pain and suffering. A man in a long-term gay relationship was killed by a reckless driver. The surviving partner sued the driver for damages resulting from the grief and psychological distress of losing a spouse-equivalent. The driver's lawyer countered that gay men's relationships bear little resemblance to marriage, and that it would be ridiculous to provide such payment. This case hinges on fundamental questions about the nature of gay men's relationships. How similar are long-term gay partnerships to heterosexual marriage? What is the intensity of love and attachment experienced in enduring gay relationships, and what is the depth of grief that accompanies bereavement?

Case Two: A lesbian mother. A young woman married her college sweetheart, had two daughters, divorced her husband, and retained custody of the children. Some time later, she began a lesbian relationship and set up a joint household with her female partner. At this point, her former husband sued to gain custody of the children, claiming that the mother was an "unfit" parent. It was proposed that she might retain custody if she promised to end her lesbian relationship. At issue here are basic questions about the ability of a lesbian mother to provide a healthy family life, the role models provided by partners in a lesbian relationship, and the impact of a lesbian couple on children in the household.

Case Three: The crime of passion defense. During a heated argument, a young man bludgeoned his lover to death with a fire iron. The defense acknowledged that the man had committed the murder, but pleaded that the act was committed in a moment of passion—a defense that could potentially lead to a lesser charge than premeditated homicide. The defendant's case rested on showing that gay relationships are as emotionally intense as heterosexual ones, perhaps even more so. The lawyer argued that a threat to a relationship could send a gay man "over the edge" psychologically. In addition, since both partners were recent immigrants from a culture that is highly intolerant of homosexuality, the defense attorney argued that his client was denied the kinds of social support that might have enabled him to cope more effectively with the crisis in his relationship. The case raises questions about the nature of love, passion and jealousy in gay relationships, and the social support experienced by homosexuals.

Although existing research does not definitively resolve the questions raised by these cases, it does provide beginning answers. This chapter reviews social science research on gay and lesbian relationships. It begins by summarizing major research findings relevant to four common stereotypes about gay and lesbian relationships in America. Then, theoretical issues raised by the study of lesbian and gay couples are considered. The chapter concludes with a discussion of the variation and diversity that exists among same-sex relationships.

It is important to emphasize at the outset that most of the available studies of homosexual relationships are based on samples of younger, urban, primarily white individuals. Occasionally, studies have involved fairly large samples (e.g., Blumstein & Schwartz, 1983) or have included ethnic samples (e.g., Bell & Weinberg, 1978, surveyed both black and white respondents), but none has been completely representative of either lesbians or gay men. So it is essential to acknowledge this limitation in our newly accumulating body of research.

DEBUNKING STEREOTYPES ABOUT LESBIAN AND GAY RELATIONSHIPS

Empirical social science research on gay and lesbian relationships dates mainly from the mid-1970s. To date, the work has been largely descriptive—seeking to test the accuracy of prevailing social stereotypes about gay and lesbian relationships and to provide more reliable information. (For other reviews, see De Cecco, 1988; Harry, 1983c; Larson, 1982; Peplau & Amaro, 1982; Peplau & Cochran, 1990; Peplau & Gordon, 1983; Risman & Schwartz, 1988.)

Myth #1: Homosexuals don't want enduring relationships—and can't achieve them anyway.

Homosexuals are often depicted in the media as unhappy individuals who are unsuccessful in developing enduring same-sex ties. Drifting from one sexual liaison to another, they end up old and alone. Existing data sharply counter this stereotype.

Studies of homosexuals' attitudes about relationships find that most lesbians and gay men say they very much want to have enduring close relationships (e.g., Bell & Weinberg, 1978). Other studies have investigated the extent to which lesbians and gay men are successful in establishing intimate relationships. In surveys of gay men, between 40% and 60% of the men questioned were currently involved in a steady relationship (e.g., Bell & Weinberg, 1978; Harry, 1983c; Jay & Young, 1977;

Peplau & Cochran, 1981; Spada, 1979). These figures may actually *under*represent the true frequency of enduring relationships because men in long-term relationships tend to be somewhat older and less likely to go to bars—both factors that would reduce the chances of these men being included in current studies (Harry, 1983c). In studies of lesbians, between 45% and 80% of women surveyed were currently in a steady relationship (e.g., Bell & Weinberg, 1978; Jay & Young, 1977; Peplau, Cochran, Rook & Padesky, 1978; Raphael & Robinson, 1980; Schafer, 1977). In most studies, the proportion of lesbians in an ongoing relationship was close to 75%.

These estimates are not completely representative of all lesbians and gay men in the United States. They do indicate, however, that a large proportion of homosexuals have stable close relationships. Research also suggests that a slightly higher proportion of lesbians than gay men may be in steady relationships.

Given that substantial proportions of lesbians and gay men are involved in intimate relationships, a next question concerns the longevity of these partnerships. Lacking marriage records and representative samples, it is hard to make judgments about how long "typical" homosexual relationships last. Most studies have been of younger adults, whose relationships have lasted for a few years—as would be true for heterosexuals in their 20s. The few studies that have included older gay men and lesbians have found that relationships lasting 20 years or more are not uncommon (e.g., McWhirter & Mattison, 1984; Raphael & Robinson, 1980; Silverstein, 1981).

In a short longitudinal study, Blumstein and Schwartz (1983) followed a large sample of lesbian, gay male, cohabiting heterosexual, and married couples over an 18-month period. At the time of initial testing, lesbians, gay men, and heterosexuals were about equal in predicting that their current relationship would continue, although both lesbians and gay men speculated that gay men usually have less stable relationships than lesbians. At the 18-month follow-up, most couples were still together. Breakups were rare among couples who had already been together for more than ten years: 6% for lesbians, 4% for gay men, 4% for married couples. (None of the heterosexual cohabiting couples had been together for more than 10 years.) Among couples who had been together for 2 years or less, the breakup rate was also fairly low—less than one relationship in five ended during the 18 month period. Minor differences were found in rates of breakup among the different types of couples: 22% for lesbian couples, 16% for gay male couples, 17% for cohabiting couples, and 4% for married couples. Although these group differences are quite small, they do run counter to the suggestion that lesbians are more likely to have enduring partnerships. More important, however, is the general pattern of relationship continuity found for all groups.

The basic point to draw from these studies is that gay and lesbian relationships are very much a reality in contemporary life.

Myth #2: Gay relationships are unhappy, abnormal, dysfunctional, and deviant.

It is often believed that gay and lesbian relationships are inferior to those of heterosexuals. For example, a study of heterosexual college students found that they expected gay and lesbian relationships to be less satisfying, more prone to discord, and "less in love" than heterosexual relationships (Testa, Kinder, & Ironson, 1987). To investigate this stereotype scientifically, researchers have assessed the psychological adjustment of homosexual dyads, and have often used a research strategy of comparing the relationship functioning of matched samples of homosexual and heterosexual couples. The central question has been how well gay and lesbian relationships fare on standard measures of relationship satisfaction, dyadic adjustment, or love.

Illustrative of this research is a study that Susan Cochran and I conducted (Peplau & Cochran, 1980). We selected matched samples of 50 lesbians, 50 gay men, 50 heterosexual women, and 50 heterosexual men—all currently involved in "romantic/sexual relationships." Participants were matched on age, education, ethnicity, and length of relationship, and all completed a detailed questionnaire about their current relationship.

Among this sample of young adults, about 60% said they were "in love" with their partner; most of the rest indicated they were "uncertain." On Rubin's standardized Love and Liking Scales, lesbians and gay men generally reported very positive feelings for their partners. Lesbians and gay men also rated their current relationships as highly satisfying and very close. No significant differences were found among lesbians, gay men, and heterosexuals on any of these measures of relationship satisfaction.

We also asked lesbians, gay men, and heterosexuals to describe in their own words the "best things" and "worst things" about their relationships. Responses included such comments as these: "The best thing is having someone to be with when you wake up," or "We like each other. We both seem to be getting what we want and need. We have wonderful sex together." Worst things included "My partner is too dependent emotionally," or "Her aunt lives with us!" Systematic content analyses (Cochran, 1978) found no significant differences in the responses of lesbians, gay men, and heterosexuals—all of whom reported a similar range of joys and problems. To search for more subtle differences among groups that may not have been captured by the coding scheme, the "best things" and "worst things" statements were typed on cards in a standard format, with information about gender and sexual orientation removed. Panels of judges were asked to sort the cards, separating men and women, or separating heterosexuals and homosexuals. The judges were not able to identify correctly the responses of lesbians, gay men, or heterosexual women and men. (Indeed, judges may have been misled by their own preconceptions; they tended, for instance, to assume incorrectly that statements involving jealousy were more likely to be made by homosexuals than heterosexuals.)

Other studies have portrayed similar findings, and have extended the range of relationship measures used. In general, most gay men and lesbians perceive their relationships as satisfying. Homosexual and heterosexual couples who are matched on age and other relevant background characteristics do not usually differ in levels of love and satisfaction, nor in their scores on standardized measures such as the Locke-Wallace Scale or Spanier's Dyadic Adjustment Scale. (See Cardell, Finn, & Marecek, 1981; Dailey, 1979; Duffy & Rusbult, 1986; Kurdek & Schmitt, 1986a, 1986b, 1987a; Peplau, Cochran, & Mays, 1986; Peplau, Padesky, & Hamilton, 1982.)

None of this is to say that *all* gay and lesbian couples are happy and problem-free. Rather the point is that homosexual couples are not necessarily any more prone to relationship dissatisfactions and difficulties than are heterosexuals. However, although the likelihood of relationship problems may be similar regardless of sexual orientation, there may nonetheless be differences in the types of problems most commonly faced by gay, lesbian, and heterosexual couples. For example, therapists have suggested that issues of dependency and individuation may be especially salient in lesbian relationships (e.g., Roth, 1985; Sang, 1985; Smalley, 1987). Recently, psychotherapists have begun to develop new programs of couples counseling geared specifically for gay or lesbian couples (e.g., Berzon, 1988; Boston Lesbian Psychologies Collective, 1987; Gonsiorek, 1985; Stein & Cohen, 1986).

In summary, research findings indicate that it is no longer useful or appropriate to describe homosexual relationships in the value-laden language of "abnormal relationships" or "deviance." There is growing recognition of the wide diversity of "families" today—single parent families, "recombinant families" incorporating children from two previous marriages, and so on. Lesbian and gay partnerships should be included among this diverse array of family types.

There is also increasing evidence from historians (e.g., Boswell, 1980) and anthropologists (e.g., Herdt, 1981) that our own culture's negative evaluation of homosexual couples has not been shared universally. In other times and places, human culture has recognized and approved of gay partnerships. Interesting, too, are recent efforts by sociobiologists to consider ways in which homosexual relationships might be functional rather than dysfunctional for individuals, in the sense of enhancing their reproductive success and causing their genes to influence the direction of evolutionary change. A detailed discussion of this perspective is presented by Weinrich (1987b).

Myth #3: "Husband" and "wife" roles are universal in intimate relationships.

C. A. Tripp notes that "when people who are not familiar with homosexual relationships try to picture one, they almost invariably resort to a heterosexual frame of reference, raising questions about which partner is 'the man' and which 'the woman'" (1975, p. 152). This issue has generated a good deal of empirical research (see reviews by Harry, 1983c; Peplau & Gordon, 1983; Risman & Schwartz, 1988).

Historical accounts of gay life in the United States suggest that masculine-feminine roles have sometimes been important. For example, Wolf (1979) described lesbian experiences in the 1950s in these terms:

> The old gay world divided up into "butch" and "femmes." . . . Butches were tough, presented themselves as being as masculine as possible . . . and they assumed the traditional male role of taking care of their partners, even fighting over them if necessary. . . . Femmes, by contrast, were protected, ladylike. . . . They cooked, cleaned house, and took care of their "butch." (p. 40)

More recently, there has been a sharp decline in the occurrence of gender-linked roles in gay and lesbian relationships. Some have attributed this change to the effects of the feminist and gay rights movements and to the general loosening of traditional gender norms in American society (Marecek, Finn, & Cardell, 1982; Risman & Schwartz, 1988; Ross, 1983).

Today, however, research shows that most lesbians and gay men actively reject traditional husband-wife or masculine-feminine roles as a model for enduring relationships. (See Blumstein & Schwartz, 1983; Harry, 1983c, 1984; Jay & Young, 1977; Lynch & Reilly, 1986; Marecek, Finn, & Cardell, 1982; McWhirter & Mattison, 1984; Peplau & Amaro, 1982; Saghir & Robins, 1973.) Currently, most lesbians and gay men are in "dual-worker" relationships, so that neither partner is the exclusive "breadwinner" and each partner has some measure of economic independence. Further, examination of the division of household tasks, sexual behavior, and decision making in homosexual couples finds that clear-cut and consistent husband-wife roles are uncommon. In many relationships, there is some specialization of activities with one partner doing more of some jobs and less of others. But it is rare for one partner to perform most of the "feminine" activities and the other to perform most of the "masculine" tasks. That is, the partner who usually does the cooking does not necessarily also perform other feminine tasks such as shopping or cleaning. Specialization seems to be based on more individualistic factors such as skills or interests.

Nonetheless, a small minority of lesbians and gay men do incorporate elements of husband-wife roles into their relationships. This may affect the division of labor, the dominance structure, sexual interactions, the way partners dress, and other aspects of their relationship. In some cases, these role patterns seemed to be linked to temporary situations, such as one partner's unemployment or illness. For other couples, however, masculine-feminine roles may provide a model of choice.

Given that traditional husband-wife roles are not the template for most contemporary homosexual couples, researchers have sought to identify other models or relationship patterns. One model might be based on differences in *age*, with an older partner acting in part as a mentor or leader. In his studies of gay male relationships, Harry (1982, 1984) found that the age-difference pattern characterized only a minority of gay male couples. When it did occur, the actual differences in age tended to be relatively small, perhaps five to ten years. Harry also found that in these couples, the older partner often had more power in decision making. McWhirter and Mattison (1984) also observed age differences among some of the male couples they studied, and reported that age differences of five years or more were characteristic of couples who had been together for 30 years or more.

Finally, another pattern is based on *friendship* or peer relations, with partners being similar in age and emphasizing companionship, sharing, and equality in the relationship (e.g., Harry, 1982, 1983c; Peplau, et al., 1978; Peplau & Cochran, 1981). A friendship script typically fosters equality in relationships. In contrast to marriage, the norms for friendship assume that partners are relatively equal in status and power. Friends also tend to be similar in interests, resources, and skills. Available evidence suggests that most American lesbians and gay men have a relationship script that most closely approximates best friendship.

In summary, contemporary homosexual relationships follow a variety of patterns or models. Most common are relationships patterned after friendship. Among both lesbians and gay men, a minority of couples may incorporate elements of traditional masculine-feminine roles into their relationships. For others, age differences may be central to role patterns. We currently know little about the causal factors responsible for these different patterns. The fact that many lesbians and gay men are able to create satisfying love relationships that are not based on complementary, gender-linked role differentiation challenges the popular view that such masculine-feminine differences are essential to adult love relationships.

Myth #4: Gays and lesbians have impoverished social support networks.

Although there is growing public awareness of the existence of gay and lesbian communities, stereotypes continue to depict homosexuals as socially isolated and lacking in social support. It is certainly true that in a homophobic society, gays and lesbians may suffer from social alienation and estrangement. We should not minimize the psychological stress that results from social rejection and stigma. What is noteworthy, however, is the extent to which contemporary lesbians and gay men seem able to overcome these obstacles and to create satisfying social networks. This is especially important because of growing evidence that emotional support, guidance, assistance, and other forms of social support contribute to mental and physical health.

Illustrative of research on social support is a comparative study of lesbian and heterosexual women conducted by Aura (1985). She compared the social support experiences of 50 lesbians and 50 heterosexual women. All women were currently in a primary relationship and were matched for age, education, and length of their relationship. None had children in their household. Women filled out detailed questionnaires about many specific types of social support. Results showed that both groups of women held very similar values about the importance of social support. In addition, women reported receiving similar total amounts of support from their personal relationships. However, lesbians and heterosexuals often received support from *different sources.* In particular, many lesbians depended somewhat less on relatives and more on their partner or friends than did heterosexuals. For example, lesbians and heterosexuals reported receiving similar amounts of material assistance such as help in moving or getting a ride to the airport, but lesbians relied more on friends and heterosexuals relied more on family.

Research by Lewin investigated the social support experiences of lesbian and heterosexual divorced mothers raising children (Lewin, 1981; Lewin & Lyons, 1982). Lewin found that both lesbian and heterosexual mothers were equally likely to turn to their parents or other family members for support. About 84% of the lesbian mothers said that most or all of their relatives were aware of their homosexuality. Although this initially created stress for many lesbians and their families, over time the families seemed to come to terms with the situation. One woman who had been estranged from her family reported that she now sees her mother daily because her son stays with his grandmother after school. For both lesbian and heterosexual mothers, kinship ties were often of central importance for child care and "to offer a sense of stability, an opportunity to continue family tradition, and emotional comfort" (in Lewin & Lyons, 1982, p. 262). Results suggest that the presence of children may increase the similarity in social support experiences of lesbian and heterosexual women.

Kurdek (1988) studied social support among gay men and lesbians in couples. When asked who provided social support, virtually everyone listed not only their partner but also other friends. In addition, 81% of the gay men and 86% of the lesbians cited a family member as a source of support—most often their mother or a sister. Using the standardized Social Support Questionnaire developed by Sarason and his associates (1983), Kurdek found no differences between gay men and lesbians in the source of support or in satisfaction with support. Overall levels of support received by gays and lesbians were similar to and slightly higher than those reported by Sarason for a college student sample. (See also D'Augelli, 1987; D'Augelli & Hart, 1987; Kurdek & Schmitt, 1987b).

In summary, despite potential obstacles to the establishment of meaningful social relations, many lesbians and gay men are able to create supportive social networks.

THEORETICAL ISSUES IN THE STUDY OF GAY AND LESBIAN RELATIONSHIPS

To date, much of the work on gay and lesbian relationships has been descriptive, designed to fill gaps in the existing data base. But newer research has had a stronger theoretical or conceptual focus. Three approaches can be distinguished: (1) work that seeks to test the general applicability of relationship theories initially developed with heterosexuals, (2) work that uses comparative studies of gay, lesbian, and heterosexual relationships to test ideas about the impact of gender on interaction, and (3) work that seeks to create new theories about same-sex relationships.

The General Applicability of Theory: Social Exchange Theory

Most social science concepts, models, and theories of relationships have been based explicitly or implicitly on heterosexual experiences. Efforts to investigate the applicability of such theories to new populations of lesbians and gay men are important to the development of a science of relationships. Evidence that existing theories can usefully be applied to homosexual relationships would also have practical significance, suggesting that work on same-sex couples can build on the existing literature rather than start anew.

Social exchange theory (Burgess & Huston, 1979; Kelley & Thibaut, 1978) has been one of the most influential theoretical perspectives on relationships. Several studies have now tested predictions derived from exchange theory among lesbian and gay male couples. In general, research has confirmed the generalizability of exchange theory to this new population and has shown the usefulness of exchange concepts in understanding relationship processes.

For example, Mayta Caldwell and I (1984) investigated the balance of power in lesbian relationships. In our sample of young adults, 61% of lesbians said that their current relationship was equal in power. We explored two factors that might tip the balance of power away from equality. First, we considered the "principle of least interest"—the prediction that when one person is more dependent, involved, or interested in continuing a relationship, that person is at a power disadvantage. We found strong support for this prediction.

We also investigated the impact of personal resources on power. The prediction here is that when a person has substantially more resources than the partner, he or she will have a power advantage. In our sample, differences in both income and education were significantly related to imbalances of power, with greater power accruing to the lesbian partner who was relatively better educated or earned more money. Studies of gay male relationships by Harry (1984) have also shown that a power advantage can accrue to the partner who has a higher income and who is older. However, work by Blumstein and Schwartz (1983) raises the possibility that the importance of specific resources such as money may differ across groups. In their large-scale study, Blumstein and Schwartz found that money was related to power in heterosexual relationships and was "an extremely important force" in determining dominance in gay male relationships. But for lesbians, income was *unrelated* to power. This is a good illustration of the notion that personal resources are not universal, but rather depend on the values of the partners in a relationship.

Another way in which research has drawn on exchange principles concerns commitment in gay and lesbian relationships. The question here is whether the forces affecting commitment might be different in homosexual versus heterosexual relationships. As Levinger (1979) and others have pointed out, commitment and permanence in a relationship are affected by two separate types of factors. The first concerns the strength of the positive attractions that make us want to stay in a relationship. Although stereotypes depict gays and lesbians as having weaker attractions to their partners than do heterosexuals, we have already seen that research does not support this view. In general, homosexuals do not appear to differ from heterosexuals in the level of satisfaction and love they feel for their primary partner.

The second factor maintaining the stability of relationships are barriers that make the ending of the relationship costly, in either psychological or material terms. For heterosexuals, marriage usually creates many barriers to dissolution including the cost of divorce, the wife's financial dependence on her husband, joint investments in property, concerns about children, and so on. Such factors may encourage married couples to "work" to improve a declining relationship, rather than end it. In contrast, gay and lesbian couples may be less likely to experience comparable barriers to the ending of a relationship—they cannot marry legally, their relatives may prefer that they end their relationship, they are less likely to have children in common, and so on. Another barrier to ending a relationship might be the lack of alternative partners or resources. To the extent that a current partner is the "best available," we are less likely to leave.

This exchange theory analysis suggests that for all types of relationships, the level of commitment should be related to attractions, barriers, and alternatives. Because of differences in the social context of homosexual and heterosexual relationships, lesbian and gay male couples may tend to have fewer barriers than heterosexuals. As a result, possible differences in commitment between heterosexual and homosexual couples may result from barriers to dissolution rather than from attractions to the partner.

Empirical research has investigated these predictions. Kurdek and Schmitt (1986a) compared self-reported attractions, barriers, and alternatives in gay, lesbian, heterosexual cohabiting, and married couples. They found no differences across the groups in attractions. All groups were equally likely to report feelings of love and satisfaction. However, barriers—assessed by statements such as "many things would prevent me from leaving my partner even if I were unhappy"—did differ. Married couples reported significantly more barriers than either gays or lesbians, and cohabiting heterosexual couples reported the fewest barriers of all. In answering questions about available alternatives to the current relationship, lesbians and married couples reported the fewest alternatives; gay men and heterosexual cohabitors reported the most alternatives. For all groups, love for the partner was significantly related to perceiving many barriers to leaving, few alternatives, and many attractions. In summary, differences between gay, lesbian, and heterosexual couples were found in the barriers they perceived to ending a relationship, not in the quality of the relationship itself. Kurdek and Schmitt did not relate these factors to commitment.

Rusbult (1988) investigated the dynamics of commitment more directly, testing what she calls an "investment model" of commitment based on social exchange principles. After initial tests of her model with heterosexuals, Duffy and Rusbult (1986) conducted a comparative study of homosexual and heterosexual relationships to test the generalizability of her findings. This research found that lesbians, gay men, and heterosexuals all generally described their relationships in quite similar ways. All groups reported strong attraction to their partner (that is, high rewards and low costs from the relationship and high satisfaction), moderately high investments in the relationship, and moderately poor alternatives. All types of couples also reported strong commitment. Consistent with exchange theory principles, commitment was predicted by satisfaction, investments, and alternatives for lesbians, gay men, and heterosexuals.

These studies found somewhat different patterns of results, with Kurdek and Schmitt reporting that sexual orientation was related to differences in barriers and alternatives, and Duffy and Rusbult finding no effects of sexual orientation. Further research will be needed to explore these issues more fully. Nonetheless, available evidence does clearly suggest the usefulness of applying principles from social exchange theory to homosexual relationships. This is an important demonstration of the generalizability of the theory. Equally important, it suggests that those interested in understanding the dynamics of gay and lesbian relationships can at least sometimes take existing theory as a starting point.

The Impact of Gender on Relationships: Contrasting Gender Versus Power Interpretations

Comparative studies of same-sex and cross-sex couples provide a new approach to investigating how gender affects close relationships. For example, by comparing how women behave with male versus female partners, we can begin to disentangle the effects on social interaction of an individual's own sex and the sex of their partner. This comparative research strategy is not identical to an experiment in which participants are randomly assigned to interact with a male or female partner. In real life, individuals are obviously not randomly assigned to have heterosexual or homosexual relationships. Nonetheless, strategically planned comparisons can be informative. This point is illustrated by studies investigating gender versus power interpretations of social interaction patterns.

It has been observed that when trying to influence a partner, women and men tend to use somewhat different tactics. Women may be more likely to use tears and less likely to use logical arguments. Why? One interpretation views this sex difference as resulting from differential gender socialization—women have learned to express emotion, men to use logic. But a second interpretation is also plausible: in male-female relationships, men often have the upper hand in power. Influence tactics may stem from the partner's relative dominance in the relationship, not from male-female differences in dispositions to use particular influence tactics. Several studies have used comparisons of gay, lesbian, and heterosexual relationships to investigate these compelling interpretations.

In a study of influence strategies in intimate relationships, Toni Falbo and I (1980) compared the tactics that lesbians, gay men, and heterosexuals reported using to influence a romantic partner. We also asked questions about the balance of power in the relationship. Our results led to two major conclusions. First, gender affected power tactics, but only among heterosexuals. Whereas heterosexual women were more likely to withdraw or express negative emotions, heterosexual men were more likely to use bargaining or reasoning. But this sex difference did *not* emerge in comparisons of lesbians and gay men influencing their same-sex partner. Second, consistent with the dominance interpretation, regardless of gender or sexual orientation, individuals who perceived themselves as relatively more powerful in the relationship tended to use persuasion and bargaining. In contrast, partners low in power tended to use withdrawal and emotion.

Howard, Blumstein, and Schwartz (1986) also compared influence tactics in the intimate relationships of homosexuals and heterosexuals. They found that dependent (lower-power) partners in all three types of couples used different influence tactics than did the more powerful. Regardless of sexual orientation, a partner with relatively less power tended to use "weak" strategies such as supplication and manipulation. Those in positions of strength were more likely to use autocratic and bullying tactics, both "strong strategies." Further, individuals with male partners (i.e., heterosexual women and homosexual men) were more likely to use supplication and manipulation. Similarly, Kollock, Blumstein, and Schwartz (1985) found that signs of conversational dominance, such as interrupting a partner in the middle of a conversation, were linked to the balance of power. Although interruption has sometimes been viewed as a "male" behavior, it was in fact more often engaged in by the more powerful person in the relationship, regardless of gender. Taken together, the results of these studies provide considerable support for the dominance interpretation of sex differences in male-female interaction.

These studies demonstrate the potential benefits of using strategic comparisons of same-sex and cross-sex couples to help understand the causes of sex differences in personal relationships. (For an illustration of using comparisons of homosexual and heterosexual couples to test social versus evolutionary theories of partner selection, see Howard, Blumstein, and Schwartz, 1987.)

New Theories: Stage Models of the Development of Gay Relationships

There have been several attempts to create models of stages in the development of relationships among gay men (e.g., Harry & Lovely, 1979; McWhirter & Mattison, 1984) and lesbians (e.g., Clunis & Green, 1988). These models have typically been empirically based efforts to generate theory from clinical observations or from research studies of same-sex couples. The goal has been to capture patterns unique to gay or lesbian relationships.

For example, an early model of gay male relationships was proposed by Harry and Lovely (1979), well before the current AIDS epidemic. Observing that sexual exclusivity was uncommon in the relationships of gay men, Harry and Lovely proposed a two-stage model of gay male relationship development. Initially, they hypothesized, there is a relatively brief "honeymoon" phase of sexual monogamy. Over time, there is a "transformation of relationships from sexually closed to open ones" (pp. 193-194). Indeed, they suggested that sexual openness may be necessary for the survival of gay relationships over time.

In 1980, David Blasband and I tested this two-stage model with a sample of 40 gay male couples (Blasband & Peplau, 1985). Our data provided little support for the generality of this model. Of the 40 couples, only 20% indicated that their relationship was initially closed and later became sexually open. The rest reported other patterns. Roughly 20% indicated that their relationship had always been sexually open, 30% said it had always been closed, and the rest followed other patterns. Two couples said that they had once had a sexually open relationship but decided to become closed because of problems they were experiencing.

We were not surprised to find such a wide variety of patterns. As research on heterosexual courtship and couple development has shown (Levinger, 1983), it is exceedingly difficult to find universal, invariant stages in the development of relationships. Efforts to identify fixed and invariant stages are probably only successful when cultural scripts are rigid and widely accepted. Left to their own devices, humans are more creative in the range of relationship patterns they construct.

More recently, detailed stage models of gay and lesbian relationships have been presented. Based on a study of 156 male couples, McWhirter and Mattison (1984) proposed a six-stage model of development. Their stages, roughly linked to the length of the relationship, are: blending, nesting, maintaining, building, releasing, and renewing. Partly building on the McWhirter and Mattison work, Clunis and Green (1988) proposed a six-stage model for the development of lesbian relationships including these stages: prerelationship, romance, conflict, acceptance, commitment, and collaboration. These stage theorists have acknowledged variation among couples. As Clunis and Green comment, "Not every couple starts with the first stage. Some couples never go through all the stages, and certainly not in the order they are presented" (p. 10). Similarly, McWhirter and Mattison caution that "characteristics from one stage also are present in other stages, and they overlap. Remember, too, that not all male couples fit this model" (p. 16). These stage models represent innovative attempts to characterize the unique relationship progression of contemporary gay and lesbian relationships. Further research will be needed to assess how well these models apply to other samples of lesbian and gay male couples (e.g., Kurdek & Schmitt, 1986c).

In summary, a good deal has been learned about gay and lesbian couples during the past decade. The field has begun to move beyond basic descriptive studies in the direction of theory development and testing. The use of strategic comparisons of same-sex and cross-sex dyads appears to be a useful way to shed light on the impact of sexual orientation and gender on couples. New concepts and models based on lesbian and gay experiences need to be tested and refined, and their possible contribution to more general analyses of human relationships should be explored.

DIVERSITY AMONG GAY AND LESBIAN RELATIONSHIPS

Having debunked old stereotypes about homosexual relationships, we must continue to avoid the tendency to characterize the "typical lesbian couple" or the "typical gay male relationship." There are enormous variations among lesbian couples, as there are among gay male couples. To understand this diversity, two goals are important: First, we need to describe major ways in which homosexual couples differ from each other, for instance in dominance, or patterns of communication, or modes of conflict resolution, or degree of commitment (cf. Bell & Weinberg, 1978). Second, we need to identify factors that produce these variations or, more technically, to identify the causal conditions affecting interaction patterns.

Variation Based on Gender

A major source of variation in same-sex relationships appears to be gender. In the 1950s and 1960s, discussions of homosexuality often assumed that there were many commonalities among the experiences of gay men and lesbians—based on their "deviant" status or "abnormal" sexual orientation. Empirical research has seriously challenged this notion. Gagnon and Simon (1973) first articulated the opposite view, that it is one's socialization as male or female that most profoundly structures one's life experiences. Gagnon and Simon contended that the "female homosexual follows conventional feminine patterns in developing her commitment to sexuality and in conducting not only her sexual career but her nonsexual career as well" (p. 180). Focusing on sexuality, they suggested that lesbian sexuality would tend "to resemble closely" that of heterosexual women, and to differ radically from the sexual activity patterns of both heterosexual men and gay men. Current research clearly supports this assertion.

Although gender differences are evident in many aspects of gay and lesbian relationships, they are perhaps seen most easily in the area of sexuality (cf. Schafer, 1977). Results of comparative studies of lesbians, gay male, and heterosexual relationships—including our own work at UCLA and the large-scale study of Blumstein and Schwartz (1983)—converge on three trends.

First, in all three types of relationships, *sexual frequency* declines with the duration of the relationship. In relationships of comparable duration, the frequency of sex with the primary partner is greatest among gay men, intermediate among heterosexuals, and lowest among lesbians.

Second, *sexual exclusivity versus openness* is an issue for all couples. In general, heterosexuals and lesbians are more supportive of sexual monogamy in relationships than are gay men. Their behavior corresponds. Sexual exclusivity in relationships is least common among gay men at all stages in their relationship. For example, Blumstein and Schwartz reported that among couples together for two to ten years or more, 79% of gay men have had sex with another partner in the previous year, compared with only 11% of husbands and 9% of wives. For lesbians, the comparable figure was 19%.

Third, levels of *sexual satisfaction* are similar across lesbian, gay male, and heterosexual couples, suggesting that couples in each group find their sexual relations equally gratifying on average (e.g., Masters & Johnson, 1979).

The gender differences in these data are large and support the view that men want sex more often than women do and that men more highly value sexual novelty. Heterosexual relationships are, on some measure, a compromise between the preferences of the man and the woman (cf. Symons, 1979). In contrast, same-sex partnerships are more extreme—men with male partners have sex more often and are less inclined toward sexual exclusivity. Women with female partners have sex least often, and differ sharply from gay men in their rates of nonmonogamy. Further explorations of the way in which gender affects the relationship experiences of gay and lesbian couples would be useful. (These generalizations are based on research conducted before the AIDS crisis. It remains to be seen how AIDS may alter patterns of sexual behavior.)

Variation Based on Personal Values

Another source of differences among same-sex couples concerns the personal values about intimacy that individuals bring to their relationship. We have begun to explore individual differences in values about the nature of love relationships (Peplau, Cochran, Rook, & Padesky, 1978; Peplau & Cochran, 1980, 1981). Consistent with discussions in the relationship literature, we have found two basic value dimensions for relationships. These dimensions have sometimes been called intimacy and independence, attachment and autonomy, or closeness and separation. We have conceptualized these distinctions as value orientations and have developed two independent scales, one to assess each orientation.

We have called the first of these orientations *dyadic attachment*. It concerns the value placed on having an emotionally close and relatively secure love relationship. As one gay man described what he wants in a love relationship: "The most important thing . . . is the knowledge that someone loves and needs me. . . . It would be a stabilizing force in my life, and give me a sense of security" (cited in Spada, 1979, p. 198). On our measure, a person who scores high on attachment strongly values permanence, security, shared activities, sexual exclusivity, and "togetherness."

The second theme we have called *personal autonomy,* and it concerns the boundaries that exist between an individual and his or her partner. While some individuals wish to immerse themselves entirely in a relationship to the exclusion of outside interests and activities, others prefer to maintain personal independence. On our measure, a person who scores high on personal autonomy emphasizes the importance of having separate interests and friendships apart from a primary relationship and preserving independence within the relationship by dividing finances equally and making decisions in an egalitarian manner.

Our research has shown that these same two value themes are relevant to the experiences of lesbians, gay men, and heterosexuals. In all samples, the two measures are independent—not polar opposites. Some individuals may want to combine a high degree of togetherness with a high level of independence, others prefer a high degree of togetherness and low independence, and so on. These relationship values are predictive of variations among relationships in such factors as love and satisfaction, perceived commitment, types of problems experienced, and sexual behavior, although these linkages are not always very strong.

An important direction for future research will be to identify other sources of diversity among lesbian and gay male relationships. Other factors worth exploring include the impact of age (or cohort), ethnicity (e.g., Peplau, Cochran, & Mays, 1980), length of a relationship, or degree of integration in a lesbian or gay community. Ultimately, we will want to develop a fuller picture of how interaction in gay and lesbian couples is affected by characteristics of the individual partners, by features of the dyad itself, and by social and cultural conditions.

CONCLUSIONS

This chapter has reviewed a growing body of scientific research on gay and lesbian relationships. Research has shown that most lesbians and gay men want intimate relationships and are successful in creating them. Homosexual partnerships appear no more vulnerable to problems and dissatisfactions than their heterosexual counterparts, although the specific problems encountered may differ for same-sex and cross-sex couples. Characterizations of gay and lesbian relationships as "abnormal" or "dysfunctional" are not justifiable. Another myth that has been disconfirmed is the belief that most homosexual couples adopt "husband" and "wife" roles. Finally, new work has found that gay men and lesbians do not typically have impoverished social support networks. It is important that mental health practitioners, educators, and the general public become more informed about the realities of same-sex relationships, so that misconception can be replaced with up-to-date scientific knowledge.

Scholars are increasingly emphasizing the rich diversity that exists among gay and lesbian couples. Much needed research remains to be done to describe the varieties of same-sex partnerships, and to understand how such factors as ethnicity, social class, openness about one's sexual orientation, and participation in gay or lesbian communities influence the experiences of lesbian and gay male couples. The debunking of derogatory social stereotypes about homosexual relationships should also clear the way for an open discussion of the special problems that do affect contemporary gay and lesbian couples. The enormous impact of the AIDS epidemic on homosexual relationships is just beginning to receive the attention it deserves (e.g., Carl, 1986; Risman & Schwartz, 1988). New research investigating the effects on relationships of alcohol abuse (e.g., Weinberg, 1986) and physical violence (Leeder, 1988; Renzetti, 1988; Waterman, Dawson, & Bologna, 1989) is also important, and illustrates some of the many useful new directions for future research.

Studies of lesbian and gay couples can contribute to the emerging science of close relationships. The applicability of general theories, such as social exchange theory, to homosexual couples has now been demonstrated in several studies, and further research of this sort would be useful. This work suggests the possibility of developing general theories capable of explaining a wide variety of relationship types. Studies of same-sex partnerships can also provide a new perspective on the impact of gender on close relationships. Comparisons of same-sex and cross-sex couples provide a new research strategy for testing competing interpretations of sex differences in interaction. New theories based on the distinctive experiences of gay and lesbian couples are an important new direction for future work.

13

Lesbian Mothers and Gay Fathers

G. Dorsey Green
Frederick W. Bozett

This chapter looks at lesbian and gay parenting with two agendas in mind. The first is to educate the reader about the scientific research on gay and lesbian parents and their children. The studies are grouped together to address the most common questions raised by the media, the legal system, and people who have little or no contact with gay and lesbian parents. The second agenda is to challenge some of the current public policy pertaining to gay and lesbian parents and their children and to propose some different policies that reflect the findings in the scientific research.

INTRODUCTION

In the past, gay men and lesbians thought that because they were gay, parenthood was out of the question. Children were simply not a part of gay or lesbian persons' worlds. However, more recently there has been a consciousness-raising by both gay men and lesbians regarding family life, and what can constitute a family. Many lesbians and gay men now include the notion of children as possible "family." While there have always been gay men and lesbians in committed relationships, there seems to be more conscious attention currently being paid to the quality of those relationships, as evidenced by the recent release of new books on this topic (Marcus, 1988; Clunis & Green, 1988; Berzon, 1988; Tessina, 1989). One of us (Bozett) believes that for gay men this phenomenon has been spurred on by the AIDS epidemic in which the absence of commitment, concurrent with multiple sexual partners, unduly exposes one to the virus thought to cause AIDS, a risk that could be deadly. As a result gay men are reexamining the idea of commitment and family, and many of them now express the desire to be parents.

Most lesbian and gay parents have acquired children through a heterosexual marriage. Reasons for marrying range from love for the spouse to a "cure" of one's homosexuality. They may marry to have children, or some may think of themselves as bisexual, which then justifies a heterosexual alliance (Bozett, 1985; Ross, 1983; Wyers, 1987). The authors believe that for various reasons, heterosexual marriage will continue to be the most common means by which lesbians and gay men acquire children. Lesbians will continue to use sperm from gay and heterosexual, known and unknown, donors (as from sperm banks). There will also be an increase in gay men's use of surrogate mothers; they will continue to donate sperm to lesbians and nonlesbians who desire alternative fertilization (some of these men will participate actively in the rearing of these children); and gay men and lesbians as adoptive and foster parents will increase in number.

Because homosexuals are an invisible population, accurate statistics on the number of gay fathers and lesbian mothers are impossible to obtain. However, based on the belief that 10% of the male population is gay (Kinsey, Pomeroy, & Martin, 1948), and that 20% of the gay male population has married at least once (Bell & Weinberg, 1978; Jay & Young, 1977; Spada, 1979), and that 25% to 50% of this 20% have had children (Bell & Weinberg, 1978; Miller, 1979a), the number of gay fathers in this country is likely more than two million. Add to this estimate that 6% to 7% of the female population is lesbian (Kinsey, Pomeroy, & Martin, 1948), and that between 1.5 and 3.3 million of them are mothers (Hunter & Polikoff, 1976; Mannion, 1976) the current estimates of children of gay fathers and lesbian mothers range between 6 million (Schulenberg, 1985) and 14 million (Peterson, 1984).

RESEARCH

That sexual orientation of children or their parents is even an issue is indicative of the homophobia and heterosexism present in our culture. Most research in this area has been done to refute the charges and assumptions put forth by the courts and mainstream culture about homosexuality. In spite of this culturewide bias, the research is extraordinarily clear in its findings about lesbian and gay parents and their children: they look remarkably like their heterosexual counterparts and their children. Although most studies have found far more similarities than differences between heterosexual and gay and lesbian parents and their children, there are some differences. Steckel (1987) is the most notable in encouraging us to look at the differences from a nondefensive, more curious approach. The reader is encouraged to look at these differences and similarities with the goal in mind of how we, as a society, can learn more about the strengths and limitations of all variations of family structure.

The research on lesbian and gay parents has serious limitations in that most studies are based on nonrandom, small samples with subjects who are Caucasian, well educated, and from urban areas, who had their children within heterosexual marriages, and who are relatively accepting of their homosexuality. Thus, the data generated needs to be viewed with caution when looking at populations other than those studied. At the same time clinicians, researchers, and the court system need to address whether the absence of these populations in the research implies an additional conscious or unconscious bias against these unresearched groups as parents. Anne Peplau's chapter on gay and lesbian couples in this volume summarizes scientific research on that topic, and is a logical companion piece to this chapter.

The research review will be divided into three main sections. The section on gay fathers begins with a brief outline of two studies that focused solely on the fathers. There is also a discussion of selected findings from studies of gay fathers as parents, most of which compare them with lesbian mothers and/or nongay fathers. The section about lesbian mothers includes a review of selected studies in the empirical research on these women. This section ends with mention of some of the more comprehensive literature reviews on these topics. The third section reviews the scientific research about children of lesbian and gay parents.

Studies That Focus on Gay Fathers

While the media is full of sensational information about gay men, the general public knows little about these men as real-life people, let alone as fathers. The section on gay fathers first looks briefly at two studies that were designed to understand and explain gay father identity development. Other studies cited explore the fathers' attitudes about parenting, their actual parenting behavior, and the effects on their parenting of their being out or closeted as a gay man. These are all pieces of the bigger picture of concern that gay men are unfit fathers. It is quite clear from these studies that these gay men are, indeed, good fathers.

Bozett (1979, 1981a, 1981b, 1985, 1987, 1988, 1989) and Miller (1978, 1979b, 1983, 1986) conducted qualitative, sociological studies in which 18 and 50 fathers, respectively, were interviewed. Bozett found that gay fathers proceed through a relatively predictable set of life events from dating, marriage, becoming fathers, separation and usually divorce, to commencement of a gay life-style. Concurrent with these more public events are subjective changes in which the man's self-concept is reformulated from heterosexual or bisexual to homosexual. This change occurs over time, maybe several years, and is brought about by two primary mechanisms: (1) participation in the gay world that becomes increasingly acceptable, and (2) gradual disclosure of the gay identity to an expanded number of nongay people, and disclosure of the father identity to gays. The vast majority of people are approving. As the man begins to hear other people's approval of his two identities he begins to believe it and feels approval of himself as well. Bozett refers to this process as integrative sanctioning. Integration is defined as a state whereby the gay and father identities are congruent, are appropriately expressed overtly, with the two identities being accepted as compatible by both the father and others in his social world. Integration does not necessarily occur with all fathers. It may be complete, partial, or absent depending upon the extent to which the father accepts his homosexuality, to whom he discloses it, and how important each identity is to him.

Miller describes four typical steps in gay fathers' normal "careers," from covert behavior, to marginal involvement, to transformed participation, to open endorsement. Miller's continuum is an ideal-type model that describes the key characteristics that occur in the sequential development of gay fathers' status passage. Gay fathers proceed through the various stages from being covert about their homosexuality and homosexual identity, to being relatively accepting and public. Miller cautions, however, that the continuum should not be construed as reifying transient states into types, and that movement out of marriage into an openly gay identity is not unilateral; that there are many negotiations back and forth, in and out of the closet. He stresses that there are numerous gradations without a finite number of states. Miller remarks that it is more accurate to talk about career paths, or sets of careers, rather than a single path. The research of Bozett and Miller is complementary. Both help to explain the evolution of the gay father identity, or what Miller (1978) refers to as "adult sexual resocialization."

Studies of Gay Fathers as Parents

Turner, Scadden, and Harris (1985) interviewed 10 gay fathers and 11 lesbian mothers to identify similarities and differences in parental behaviors. Half of the fathers and somewhat more than half of the mothers did not encourage gender-typed toys. Most of the subjects reported efforts to provide an opposite-sex role model, with fathers making more of an effort than mothers. Almost all parents reported that their children seemed to be developing "normal" gender-role identification, and they thought their children were similar to other children of the same age and gender.

In a study by Wyers (1987) of 32 gay fathers and 34 lesbian mothers, 11 of the fathers reported that their children did not know of their homosexuality, whereas all except two of the children in the Turner, Scadden, and Harris study knew. Wyer's subjects gave a variety of reasons for not telling, including fear that the knowledge would damage the children, that they would not understand, and that they would be rejected. Most children of gay fathers found out from the fathers themselves, but some also found out from their mother, or overheard their parents discussing it, or figured it out for themselves. Parents reported that children's initial reactions ranged from positive to angry and confused. More untoward reactions were reported by gay fathers than by lesbian mothers. Younger children had fewer difficulties than older ones. Wyers (1987) also reported that about 21% of gay fathers' children and 58% of lesbian mothers' children experienced relationship problems because of others' knowledge of their parents' homosexuality, although most of the problems were not considered to be serious. Turner et al. (1985) generalized that: parents' homosexuality seems to create few long-term problems for children (who seem to accept it better than parents anticipate); most homosexual parents have positive relationships with their children; parental sexual orientation is of little importance in the overall parent-child relationship; and homosexual parents try harder to create stable home lives and positive relationships with their children than one would expect from traditional heterosexual parents. The reason for this last finding is most likely due to the gay and lesbian parents' fear of loss of custody or visitation rights; therefore, they make efforts to achieve as positive a home and parenting environment as possible.

Harris and Turner (1985-1986) compared gay and nongay mothers and fathers. The major differences reflected their gender or residence, not their sexual orientation. The only difference between the homosexual and heterosexual parents was the latter's tendency to make a greater effort to provide an opposite-sex role model for their children. Comparing gay fathers and lesbian mothers, gay fathers were more likely to live with lovers or male friends, felt more satisfaction with their first child, had fewer disagreements with their partner over discipline, and were more likely to encourage play with gender-typed toys. They were less likely to realize benefits of their homosexuality such as increased empathy and tolerance for others. Similar to all parents, both lesbian mothers and gay fathers admitted to having some difficulties in child rearing and getting along with their children. Harris and Turner stated that being gay is compatible with effective parenting, and that parents' sexual orientation is not the major issue in these parents' relationships with their children.

Scallen's (1981) doctoral dissertation was a study of the relationship between sexual orientation and fathers' child-rearing attitudes and behaviors. There were 20 fathers in the homosexual and 20 in the heterosexual group. Subjects in both groups appeared to endorse an active, caretaking stance regarding the paternal role. However, in spite of the overall similarities between the two groups, the findings suggest that sexual orientation does have a relationship to espoused paternal attitudes. Gay fathers were more endorsing of paternal nurturance, less endorsing of economic providing as the principal role for a father, and somewhat less traditional in their overall paternal attitudes than were heterosexual fathers. Gay fathers also seemed to have a notable psychological investment in the paternal role, and they demonstrated a significantly more positive self-assessment of their performance in the paternal role than did the heterosexual fathers.

Bigner and Jacobsen (1989a) also compared gay and nongay fathers to identify differences in parenting behavior. They found that gay fathers tend to be more strict by consistently emphasizing the importance of setting and enforcing limits, they go to greater lengths than nongay fathers in promoting their children's cognitive skills by explaining rules and regulations, they tend to be more responsive to the perceived needs of their children, they were inclined to act more as a resource for activities with children, and they were less willing than nongay fathers to be demonstrative with their partners in the children's presence. Bigner and Jacobsen (1989b) also found that homosexual parents may be less conventional and more androgynous than nongay parents, and gay fathers may incorporate a greater degree of expressive role functions into the parenting role than do more traditionally gender-role oriented nongay fathers.

According to Miller (1979b), fathers who are more publicly identified as gay, as contrasted with those who are closeted, tend to be less authoritative, use less corporal punishment, and experience stronger desires to rear children with nonsexist, egalitarian standards. Miller (1979a) suggests that the fathering of closeted men who remain married is of lower quality: They spend less time with their children since looking for or maintaining homosexual liaisons takes time away from the family; they may assuage their guilt by excessively showering their children with expensive gifts; father-child interaction seems to be tension filled and rushed; and workaholism is not uncommon.

Research on Lesbian Mothers

A question often addressed in the literature is whether lesbian mothers are somehow different from heterosexual mothers because of their sexual orientation. Historically, courts and mainstream media have assumed that differences do exist and further that these differences mean that lesbian mothers cannot be good parents. The most common assumptions seem to have been that lesbians do not care for children in maternal ways, that lesbians hate men and therefore deny their children access to positive male role models, and that their lesbianism renders them unfit for motherhood because it implies an underlying pathology. The following studies examined some aspect of lesbian mothers' functioning and whether they were different from their heterosexual counterparts. Most research purported to look at single mothers, both heterosexual and lesbian, and did not take into account that while a woman is legally single she may have a live-in lover who may take an active parenting role with the children. This was particularly true for the lesbians studied; their partners often were not noted. Kirkpatrick, Smith, and Roy (1981) admitted that they began their research with this bias and subsequently discovered a potentially richer home environment when they took this issue into account.

Mothers' Attitudes and Behavior

Kweskin and Cook (1982) examined 22 lesbian and 22 heterosexual mothers' self-described gender-role behavior and their ideal gender-role behavior in children. The mothers' self-described gender-role behavior was a better indicator of what the mothers valued in gender-role behavior in children than was the mothers' sexual orientation. There were no significant differences between groups in either their descriptions of their own behavior or in their vision of what children's ideal gender-role behavior should be.

Mucklow and Phelan (1979) examined 34 lesbian and 47 traditional mothers to determine if there were any significant differences between the two groups on measures of maternal attitude and self-concept. Traditional mother was defined as a member of the PTA, "married, heterosexual, and performing a traditional feminine role within the family" (p. 881). Maternal attitudes were measured by the women's responses to slides depicting children's behavior. The participants could respond in one of three possible ways: adult-centered, child-centered, and task-centered. They found that the two groups of mothers did not differ in maternal attitude or self-concept. This study was unusual in that they included in their definition of lesbian mother a lesbian who parented her partner's biological child.

Miller, Jacobsen, and Bigner (1981) obtained somewhat different results in their study of 34 lesbian and 47 heterosexual mothers. Like Mucklow and Phelan (1979), they looked at the caregiving behavior as measured by the mother's responses to slides of children's behavior.

They also looked at whether the two groups differed in respect to occupation, education, income, and legal marital status. The Miller et al. study found that the lesbian mothers were more likely to be child centered in their responses to the situations than were their heterosexual counterparts. The authors found no differences overall in education. They did find that the lesbian mothers were more likely to be skilled or unskilled workers and that 53% of the heterosexual mothers self-identified as housewives while none of the lesbians did. The heterosexual participants had significantly higher incomes than the lesbians. The authors surmised that this difference was due to the heterosexual women's using their husband's income as the comparison figures. The difference in the two groups' life-styles may be great enough that it raises questions about the findings of this study.

Kirkpatrick, Smith, and Roy (1981), in a study that primarily looked at 20 children with lesbian mothers and 20 children with heterosexual mothers, found that there was no difference between the mothers in marital and maternal interests, current life-styles, and child-rearing practices. Kirkpatrick et al. (1981) found that the lesbian mothers tended to be more concerned with providing male figures for their children than did the heterosexual mother group. They also found differences in that the lesbian mothers' divorces were more likely to be due to lack of intimate feelings between the spouses while the heterosexual mothers' divorces were more likely due to abuse, husbands' affairs, or psychological problems. The lesbian mothers were more likely to share living arrangements and child care with a lover.

Mothers' Coping and General Functioning

Pagelow (1980) interviewed and compared 23 heterosexual and 20 lesbian mothers in the areas of perceived problems, coping styles, and solutions to the problems they had. All the mothers saw themselves as oppressed in one or more areas. The lesbians had an additional pressure due to their fear of reprisal because of their sexual orientation. The women differed in several areas. The lesbian mothers tended to share housing with other adults, to own their own homes, and operate their own businesses more often than the heterosexual mothers. Pagelow hypothesized that these differences might have been due to the lesbians' finding positive ways of coping that helped them avoid censure from mainstream society and deal with the additional pressures of being single mothers and lesbians.

Lewin and Lyons (1982) looked at 43 lesbian and 37 heterosexual mothers. Half of each group had coresidential partners. They found that both groups had adapted as (legally) single mothers, that motherhood was the central theme of their lives, and that both groups experienced some conflict between the maternal and other aspects of their lives. The women in general had a network of friends who were central in their lives. The authors concluded that the lesbian mothers' lesbianism and the heterosexual mothers' heterosexuality were overshadowed by their identities as mothers. Lewin (1981) looked at social support systems of lesbian and heterosexual mothers and found as did Lewin and Lyons (1982) that the two groups were quite similar in coping mechanisms. Both sets of mothers relied on relatives and ex-spouses for support and help with family responsibilities.

Rand, Graham, and Rawlings (1982) studied 25 lesbian mothers by interview and psychological instruments and found that they fell within the normal range of psychological functioning. They also found that lesbians who were more open about their lesbianism had higher levels of psychological well-being.

Literature Reviews

Because of space constraints and a focus on empirical research, we were unable to include every study and article that has been done on lesbian mothers. Since a number of reviews have broader and slightly different emphases, a brief description of some of them are included as an additional resource for the reader.

Steckel's review (1987) focused on the psychosocial development of the children of lesbian mothers. Gibbs (1988), in her review of the psychological health of children of lesbian mothers, urged us to consider the role of the nonbiological or stepparent in lesbian-headed families. Knight (1983) noted that courts believe that a child will be influenced toward becoming homosexual and will be stigmatized by their mother's lesbianism. He found, however, that there is no evidence that a lesbian mother is more likely to negatively influence her child's development or that the child is more likely to become gay or lesbian.

Kirkpatrick (1987) gave case examples to illustrate the research she cited. She noted that when lesbian mothers were compared with single heterosexual mothers, "Motherhood, not sexual orientation, is the most salient factor in both groups' identity" (p. 201). Kirkpatrick concluded her review with the observation that no comparative studies have shown differences between children of single heterosexual mothers and children of lesbian mothers in gender identity and sexual development. She also added that the presence of a responsive and stable partner in the home often enriched the children's home life.

Cramer's (1986) review seemed designed both to answer the questions raised by the legal system during custody cases and to help counselors and therapists gain enough information to assist their clients. He addressed concerns about children's development, the assumption that sexual abuse is more prevalent in lesbian/gay headed families, and whether there are negative effects on children from peer pressure about parents' sexual orientation. He also found no reasons to discriminate against lesbian and gay parents.

Perhaps the most thorough review was by Falk (1989), who looked at the assumptions made about lesbian mothers in family law. She discussed the assumptions she perceived the legal system has made about lesbian mothers, for example, that lesbian women are less maternal than heterosexual women. She included both the psychological and the legal literature as she addressed these questions. She then reviewed the social science research, looking first at the mothers and then at their children. She also discussed whether social stigma due to their mother's sexual orientation affected the children. Like all the researchers on these topics, Falk (1989) found no significant differences between children of lesbian mothers and their counterparts with heterosexual mothers.

Research on Children of Lesbian Mothers and Gay Fathers

Courts, parents, and others who are concerned about the welfare of children of lesbian and gay parents have worried about whether having such a parent will affect a child's psychological and gender identity development. Again, the scientific literature remains consistent: the children in those studies who have lesbian or gay parents are comparable to the children of heterosexual parents. Their parents' sexual orientation is not the determining factor in their health and well-being.

Children of Gay Fathers

The vast majority of the studies about children of lesbian and gay parents have focused on the children of lesbian mothers. Two studies included here look specifically at the children of gay fathers. The study by Miller (1979a) on gay fathers, which was discussed above, also included 14 of their children. He reported that the children were generally accepting of their father as gay, that one son and one daughter were also gay, and that several of the children had had problems of sexual acting out.

The one major study in this area is by Bozett (1988), who interviewed children, ages 14 to 35, of 14 gay fathers. The major finding was that children were concerned that they not be thought of as gay, and thus they controlled presentation of themselves by controlling when and where they would be seen with their father. However, the use of controlling strategies was determined primarily by two things. The first was how discernible they believed their father's homosexuality to be and the second was the extent to which they identified with their father's differentness. For example, if the child had been stigmatized and made to feel different because of a weight problem, then the child was less likely to use controlling mechanisms. Likewise, controlling mechanisms were used less if the child thought the father's homosexuality was not outwardly evident to others.

Children of Lesbian Mothers

Children's gender identity and sexual orientation development. Green (1978) looked at 37 children of transsexual and lesbian mothers. Of these, 21 had lesbian mothers. Green found that 20 out of 21 children had no gender identity problems and all showed typical gender-role preferences. Of the adolescent children all appeared to be heterosexually oriented. This was consistent with Golumbok, Spencer, and Rutter's finding in their study (1983) of children of lesbian and heterosexual mothers.

In a later study Green (1982) reported on interviews with 21 children who had lived with their lesbian mothers for more than three years. He found no evidence that the children were having gender identity problems. Again, he found that of those children who had had sexual experiences, all reported heterosexual orientation. Green, Mandel, Hotvedt, Gray, and Smith (1986) found no differences between comparison groups of heterosexual and lesbian mothers or their children on personality measures including measures of peer group relationships and popularity and social adjustment.

Kirkpatrick, Smith, and Roy (1981) looked at 20 children with lesbian mothers versus a comparison group of 20 children with heterosexual mothers. The research team found no difference in gender identity development between the two groups of children. There was no difference in the amount of pathological problems between the two groups of children. As mentioned above, the lesbian mothers were more likely to share living arrangements and child care with a lover than were the heterosexual mothers. Kirkpatrick et al. found that the presence of another caring adult was perceived by the children as positive and that lesbians in couples "were the most likely to include men in planned activities and as regular visitors to the household" (Kirkpatrick, 1987, p. 204). Huggins (1989) also found that the addition of a mother's partner (male or female) in the home increased the likelihood that adolescent girls and boys would have high self-esteem.

Harris and Turner (1985-1986) found that the heterosexual parents made a greater attempt to provide opposite-sex role models for their children. This appears different from the Kirkpatrick et al. (1981) finding that their sample of lesbian mothers were more concerned than the heterosexual mothers with providing male role models. Another piece of information comes from Golumbok et al. (1983), who found that the children of the lesbian mothers saw their fathers more often than did the children of the heterosexual mothers. Turner, Scadden, and Harris (1985) found that the gay fathers made more of an effort to provide opposite-sex role models than did the lesbian mothers. Obviously, one cannot generalize that one group of parents is more likely then others to provide opposite-sex role models; clearly more research needs to be done in this area.

Children's gender-role behaviors. Hoeffer (1981) looked at children's acquisition of gender-role behaviors using 20 lesbian mothers with a comparison group of 20 single heterosexual mothers. She found no differences between the groups based on the mothers' sexual orientation. She did find some differences based on an interaction between gender of the children and gender-typed toy preference. She reported that boys in both groups showed a stronger preference for masculine toys and less preference for feminine toys than girls did for feminine toys. She also found that the heterosexual mothers preferred more gender-typed toys than did the lesbian mothers. The lesbian mothers preferred a more equal mix of gender-typed toys. Ostrow (1977), in an unpublished study, also found that sexual orientation of the parent did not appear to be a main factor in children's gender-typed play choices.

Golombok et al. (1983) found no gender-identity problems in any of the children in a study comparing 27 families headed by lesbian mothers with 27 families headed by heterosexual mothers. The children's gender-typed behavior was appropriate for their ages and genders. The research team found no differences between groups on measures of psychological health. While, in general, there was a low level of psychiatric problems among all children as determined in psychiatric interviews, more children in the heterosexual group had psychiatric difficulties and had been referred for psychiatric help than in the lesbian sample.

Peer relationships. In *Homosexuality: Social, psychological, and biological issues,* edited by Paul, Weinrich, Gonsiorek, and Hotvedt (1982), Hotvedt and Mandel reported on their previous study. They looked at 50 lesbian mothers with 58 children and 20 heterosexual mothers with 25 children. They found no significant differences in gender identity issues or in the gender of the children's best friend. In general the boys were more similar to each other than the girls, who had a wider range of scores. The daughters of lesbians tended to pick potential careers that were more nontraditional for women and to engage in a somewhat wider variety of play than the daughters of the heterosexual mothers. They also rated themselves as more popular with other girls and with boys than did the daughters of the heterosexual women. There was no evidence of gender-identity conflict, poor peer relationships, or neglect in either group. Gramlich, Nicholson, Price, Wilson, and Belcastro's (1989) work also supported these findings.

Separation and individuation. Steckel (1985) studied 11 children from heterosexual couples and 11 from lesbian couples. The children were three or four years old. Steckel examined ego functions, object relations, and independence by using a variety of psychological assessments. There were many more similarities than differences, with neither group showing more psychopathology or problems with separation-individuation. There were some differences between the two groups, which Steckel cited in her 1987 article. Children of heterosexuals had a more aggressively tinged separation process, seeing themselves as more aggressive and being seen by parents and teachers as more bossy and domineering, more active in asserting themselves, more negativistic, and more involved in power struggles. In contrast, children of lesbians demonstrated a more lovable self-image, expressed by more helplessness, and were seen by parents and teachers as more affectionate and responsive, more verbal and more protective toward younger children (p. 81).

Children's self-esteem. Huggins (1989) interviewed and tested 36 adolescent children to determine their self-esteem levels. Their mothers were heterosexual women and lesbians who had been divorced from their husbands. She found that there were no statistical differences between the two groups of adolescents in the self-esteem scores. However, the data suggested that the father's attitude toward his exwife's lesbianism was a significant factor in his child's self-esteem level.

Lewis (1980) interviewed 21 children of newly declared lesbians. She found that the mother's lesbianism became another problem around which the children had difficulty discussing their feelings. This was particularly true when there were earlier problems in the family. However, almost all the children expressed pride in their mothers' standing up for what they believed and said that this experience had given them permission to consider roles in life that were not necessarily traditional. In other words, they had permission to figure out what was right for them, and not follow convention as a matter of course.

PUBLIC POLICY CONCERNS

Many myths about gay and lesbian parents and their children are still cited as facts in spite of the scientific evidence to the contrary. Lesbians and gay men as parents are important in a variety of public policy domains: contested child custody suits, adoption and foster care regulations, domestic partnership legislation, and artificial insemination guidelines, to name a few. It is crucial that people in the position to design, pass, and implement public policy be accurately informed about the topics with which they work.

In the past, writing and research has focused almost solely on the sexuality of gays and lesbians to the neglect of all other aspects of their psychological and sociocultural functioning. This overfocusing on sex has contributed to a distorted picture of lesbians and gay men and makes them appear to be incomplete, abnormal beings. Because of society's fixation, and because homophobia is so rampant in the United States (Altman, 1982), the idea of homosexuality seems antiethical to parenting, since parents are supposed to be healthy, normal, and certainly not obsessed with sex. Much public policy reflects this bias and it has interfered with the review and updating of policies in line with current scientific research.

Parental Rights

The courts as well as social service agencies frequently oppose homosexuals' assuming the parental role, whether for biological or nonbiological (adoptive, foster) children. State statutes and regulations that have the effect of law often militate against homosexuals serving in parental roles, and in some states—for example, Florida—legislation has been enacted that forbids lesbians and gays from adopting children or becoming foster parents. There are also guidelines in some places that prohibit lesbians (and other "single" women) from utilizing sperm banks in order to get pregnant. There is no such regulation of heterosexual couples who may even have histories of being abusive to or exploitive of children. Courts have removed children from their gay/lesbian parents solely because of parental homosexuality, not because of any deficiency on the part of the parents or the household. These laws, derived from stereotypes and prejudice, are based on the belief that children in these homes will be reared in what is perceived as an immoral environment, that they will have confused gender identities, that they will grow up to be lesbian or gay themselves (and that this is negative), that they will be stigmatized, that they may contract AIDS, and that they will be molested. (Rivera, in this volume, reviews the legal status of gay men and lesbians as parents.)

Although the research is limited in some of these areas, there is none to support these allegations. The home environments of lesbian and gay persons have been found to be as moral and as physically and psychologically healthy as those of nongays. The research cited above makes it clear that lesbian and gay parents' attitudes and behaviors are very like those of other parents studied and that they facilitate their children's growing up in healthy, productive ways. Some studies even suggest that lesbian and gay parents have developed some useful coping mechanisms that would be of use to heterosexual parents.

Most gay and lesbian parents were reared by heterosexual parents whose heterosexuality did not guarantee heterosexual children. Neither homosexuality nor heterosexuality is contagious, and neither can be deliberately caused or manipulated. According to the research available, children in gay- or lesbian-headed households are lesbian or gay in roughly the same proportions reported in the general population—10%. (Miller, 1979a, reported 2 of 14 children self-identified as gay; other studies showed 10% or less.) Moreover, concern regarding the sexual orientation of children makes the assumption that heterosexual children are "better," or "superior," or are to be preferred. These are value judgments, not facts.

Adoption and Foster Parent Regulations

In addition, children who themselves are gay or lesbian (whether biological or those who need adoption or foster care) may benefit from being reared by a lesbian or gay parent or couple. Homosexual parents would serve as positive gay and lesbian role models. They could facilitate the children's socialization into both gay and nongay society, promoting the development of positive self-esteem, thus helping them avoid the guilt and pain that such children often experience in growing up (see Chapter 11 for a discussion of this). Public policy that prohibits placing these children with supportive families may inadvertently be contributing to the numbers of gay and lesbian youth who revert to living in the streets when their unsupportive, heterosexual parents throw them out of their homes. Policies that keep lesbian, gay, and heterosexual children from being placed in good homes just because the adults are gay or lesbian is a mockery of the stated value for family life. When prejudice and lack of scientific knowledge keep children from good homes, something is wrong.

Stigmatization

While the research does not show that most children feel stigmatized by having a lesbian or gay parent, it is true that some children with lesbian or gay parents may be stigmatized by their peers, and may on occasion be embarrassed by having nontraditional parents. However, these kinds of problems are similar to those experienced by children in other minority groups. Like other minority parents, lesbian mothers and gay fathers can help their children to deal with these difficult situations as they arise, while at the same time teaching them that they are as moral, ethical, and good as other people. These parents may help prevent problems by, for example, explaining to their children why, with their friends, it may be best to refer to the parent's lover as aunt or uncle, or as a "housemate" (Bozett, 1980). Or they may help their children solve problems like how to confront a friend about how that friend's prejudice has upset them. The research shows that children are often proud of their parents' standing up for themselves and that it may give them support for speaking up for themselves as well.

Discrimination Based on Fear of AIDS and Molestation

Concern that the children may contract AIDS need not be a concern, since the HIV virus is transmitted only through blood or intimate sexual contact. This concern is just another fraudulent screen behind which some people express their homophobia.

Child molestation is likely less of a problem in households with homosexual parents since, according to Rivera (1987), "child molestation is unrelated to adult (mature) sexual orientation and results from a fixation on childishness as a sexual object. In fact, the gender of the child is unimportant" (p. 211). The comprehensive text by Finkelhor (1986) concludes that most childhood sexual abuse is perpetrated by male adults who are not homosexually oriented, but rather heterosexually oriented or oriented to children (i.e., pedophiles) (see especially Chapter 3). This conclusion was also reached by Groth and Birnbaum (1978) in their literature review. These two facts should assuage concerns regarding the molestation of children who live with their homosexual parent (for further detail, see Herek's discussion in this volume).

Couple and Family Rights

Laws and regulations that discriminate against gay and lesbian families, limiting their full and equal participation in American life, need to be combated.

> Social hostility is probably greater toward homosexuals than toward any other form of family. Gay and lesbian families are suppressed by legal, social, religious, and economic forces. . . .[for example] homosexual cou-

> ples may not marry, and because of this are denied social security and insurance benefits, inheritance rights, and major medical care for live-in lovers. Gay men and lesbians are not protected under Title VII of the Civil Rights Act of 1964 because it does not include sexual orientation, and home ownership by unrelated individuals is illegal in some communities. (Bozett, 1989, p. 193)

It appears that one of the most viable ways to achieve equivalence with heterosexual family households is through domestic partner legislation. Such legislation needs to be promoted nationwide in large and small communities alike.

Another way to recognize and support gay- and lesbian-headed families is through legislation that permits lesbian and gay male couples to become parents jointly. Generally, only one member of a lesbian or gay male couple may become the legal parent. Thus, if the couple separates, or if the legal parent dies or become incapacitated, the other parent has no legal claim over the child. This can threaten the continued stability of the family.

There is precedent for joint and second-parent adoptions (Ricketts & Achtenberg, 1987); Washington State has recently seen three cases where the nonbiological mother has been granted the right to adopt the couple's child, thus making both women legal parents. This clearly contributes to the stability of the family, something all parents want for their children. It is essential that such or similar legal arrangements be promoted to ensure the best interests of both the children and the family unit.

CONCLUSION

The most striking feature of the research on lesbian mothers, gay fathers, and their children is the absence of pathological findings. The second most striking feature is how similar the groups of gay and lesbian parents and their children are to the heterosexual parents and their children that were included in the studies. It is evident that homosexuality is compatible with effective parenting: that both lesbians and gay men who are parents are as sufficient in the roles as heterosexuals, and that the home life they provide is at least of equal quality. Children do not seem in any way to be at risk or harmed because of parental homosexuality. Gay and lesbian parents are highly committed as parents, and they have a high emotional investment in the parent-child relationship; they are often highly creative in designing environments that take care of themselves and their children. Moreover, the parent-child bond may be closer than is found in more traditional families.

Since having two caring adults present in a household enriches a child's home environment, it is better for children to be reared with their gay or lesbian parent and his or her lover, rather than the two living separately as some courts have mandated.

Admittedly, however, research is limited. As has previously been pointed out, sample sizes are small, and there is almost no research on subjects from the working class, from communities of color, from smaller communities in more rural areas, or on those who have less formal education. Since suggestions for research have already been made elsewhere (Bozett, 1987), we will say here that one of the most pressing needs is longitudinal study of entire family units to determine the effect of being reared in a homosexual household on the growth and development of children over time and into their adulthood. There may be some characteristics about gay and lesbian families that could be useful to heterosexual parents as they rear their children. There may be some information from heterosexual-headed families that can help lesbian and gay parents. Until we begin to value healthy difference we miss the opportunities for growth and knowledge that having different family structures gives us. Harry and DeVall (1978) have remarked that as preoccupation with the sex lives of gays and lesbians has diminished, interest in other aspects of their lives has expanded. It is now time to get on with the task of conducting the much-needed research on the gay and lesbian family form.

14

Partner Notification as an Instrument for HIV Control

Edmund F. Dejowski
Lidia Dengelegi
Stephen Crystal
Pearl Beck

PUBLIC HEALTH: SCIENCE *AND* POLITICS

Partner notification or "contact tracing" has been one of the most controversial and emotion-laden issues in AIDS prevention policy, second perhaps only to quarantine in its evocative power. It has important implications for the human rights and security of people who are infected with the human immunodeficiency virus (HIV), and for the entire gay community. Groups representing persons with AIDS demonstrated their concern over the issue by assembling large demonstrations against Stephen Joseph, then commissioner of the City of New York Department of Health, when he endorsed a variation of partner notification. These protests resurfaced once again following news that Joseph's successor, Woodrow Myers, had supported the concept (Woodard, 1990). In another example of the intensity surrounding the discussion of partner notification, the policy director of the Gay Men's Health Crisis has charged popular newspaper columnist Nat Hentoff with using the issue to drive a specious wedge between gay men and heterosexual women of color (Sweeney, 1990).

This chapter seeks to use available social science and public health data to explore the place of partner notification as an instrument of public policy for reducing HIV transmission. Public health policy evolves not only in response to scientific knowledge about disease and prevention, but also in response to a political and social climate. Public health officials are appointed, confirmed, and retained at the will of elected executives or legislatures, and the amount and nature of public health appropriations define the limits of the possible for health authorities. In this framework public health policies that bear on issues such as HIV can become clouded by emotion and politics and should be subject to the closest professional scrutiny to assure that they are grounded in the best scientific knowledge. We seek to present here the available information on partner notification and to draw inferences that respond to the array of policy considerations involved—public health, community mental health, economics, ethics, and justice.

While respectful of the position of the many and varied individuals who see partner notification as an unacceptable threat to civil liberties, we write from a different point of view—specifically, that notification services can play a useful role as a voluntary and cooperative effort, and need not necessarily infringe on individual liberties or civil rights. Simultaneously, however, we seek to examine partner notification critically from our viewpoint that the final word is not in on all questions of outcome, efficacy, cost-benefit, and ethics.

Definition

Partner notification in this context has come to mean the process of identifying and locating sexual and needle-sharing partners of persons who have tested positive for the human immunodeficiency virus and informing them of their exposure. The rationale is that sexual and needle-sharing partners of those testing positive are at risk themselves and should receive educational messages to (1) learn that they may be at high risk for HIV infection (2) be offered immediate counseling in risk reduction (3) be encouraged to seek testing or medical services (4) be encouraged to avoid placing others at risk; that is, to suspend high-risk activities, unless or until their own serostatus is known and (5) for females of childbearing capacity, learn the potential for communicability of the virus from mother to child in time to make a fully informed decision concerning procreation.

Federal legislation and Centers for Disease Control (CDC) regulations routinely employ the term, *partner notification* in preference to *contact tracing,* which is the term historically used in connection with sexually transmitted disease (STD) prevention programs. An advocate of the term *partner notification* explains, "We prefer the term 'partner notification' to the term 'contact tracing' because it more comprehensively describes a process in which the infected person or that person's physician may provide information to an at-risk partner, not just a process in which a public health worker traces the partners" (Vernon & Hoffman, 1988). *Partner notification* also sounds more benign than *contact tracing,* a fact that undoubtedly influenced the naming of the program.

We use the term *partner notification* here in recognition of the fact that success in such programs depends on much more than just "tracing" and locating contacts. We use the term *STD* to distinguish the common venereal diseases such as syphilis and gonorrhea from HIV. HIV can itself be transmitted sexually, of course.

ANALOGY WITH STDS

Contact tracing has been reported to be useful in the preventive treatment of syphilis, which can lie dormant and thus undetected for long periods of time. It has been estimated that, in 1987, contact tracing has led to the identification and preventive treatment of 37,000 sex partners of patients with a diagnosis of primary, secondary, and early latent syphilis (U.S. Public Health Service, 1987). Contact tracing and notification has also helped control local epidemics of antibiotic-resistant gonorrhea (Handsfield, Sandstrum, Knapp, et al., 1982) and reduce gonorrhea within endemically infected core groups in specific high-risk populations (Rothenberg, 1983). But even though contact tracing has been effective in controlling local outbreaks of STDs and it can be shown that certain numbers of infected persons were notified and treated, it has not been a panacea in controlling infection nationwide. Even in the presence of effective treatments and with the work of contact tracing programs, the prevalence of syphilis has actually been on the rise in the past few years.

Health authorities disagree on the extent to which partner notification in the context of AIDS is analogous to STD contact notification. Some of its proponents say it is no different (Vernon & Hoffman, 1988); but the American Public Health Association Special Initiative on AIDS (APHA, 1988) identified and described a range of differences. It indicated that contact notification was effective in containing local outbreaks of STD; but that in this context, effectiveness was based on curing the victim, thus eliminating the source of contagion. It noted that this is not currently possible for HIV seropositivity, since no cure is known to exist. It noted other differences as well: the danger of discrimination is higher in the case of AIDS, while confidentiality is difficult to assure; the widespread prevalence of infection in certain geographic areas indicates that public education campaigns in such places might reach more persons at risk at a lower cost; for gonorrhea, male contacts within the 14 days prior to symptoms are considered relevant, while HIV's uniquely long latency period means that partners should be traced back for many years; HIV counseling, including facilitation of permanent behavior change, requires particular skills and attitudes that may be foreign to persons trained in STD contact tracing; and the cost per contact located is high, a factor that must be considered in allocating resources among competing needs (APHA, 1988).

ARGUMENTS FOR AND AGAINST PARTNER NOTIFICATION

New Reasons for Notification

Despite the differences between AIDS and STDs with respect to contact notification, the arguments for tracing contacts of persons with AIDS may be increasing with advances in treatment opportunities. Until recently, the reasons for being tested included relieving uncertainty and learning whether it was advisable to procreate or to settle one's affairs. Some would add, "learning whether it was necessary to take precautions to protect others from contagion." But for those who had already adopted safe sex practices, knowledge of serostatus would have had no bearing on this issue. In that context, many persons at risk deliberately chose not to be tested, feeling that they would not be able to, or did not wish to, deal with the knowledge of being infected. Now, however, there are medications—pentamidine and trimethoprim-sulfamethoxazole (Bactrim)—that can be used as prophylaxis against *Pneumocystis carinii* pneumonia (PCP), the most common mortal sequel of AIDS. The CDC has now issued recommendations (CDC, 1989) that all persons at risk should be tested for HIV antibody, and those found to be positive should have the status of their immune system monitored every six months; when the infected person's CD4 level drops below 200, prophylaxis for PCP becomes appropriate. Further, clinical trials of AZT (azydothymidine or ziduvidine) have shown that the drug is effective in delaying the onset of AIDS in persons with 500 or fewer CD4 cells. Many other drugs are being evaluated, and seropositive persons have the option of enrolling in clinical trials of these. It has also become an accepted medical tenet that HIV-positive persons who take steps to improve their immune system may be able to delay the onset of AIDS.

But Can Knowing Cause Harm?

Knowledge about one's seropositive status may now be used to lengthen one's life expectation, one would hope to the time when more efficacious treatments become available. However, facing the fact that one is seropositive remains a potentially traumatic life event, with unpredictable emotional and behavioral sequelae.

For some, the benefits of knowing their serostatus may be outweighed by the consequences of that knowledge. Overwhelming anxiety and disabling depression, a retreat into substance abuse, and even suicide are possible consequences (Marzuk et al., 1988). While many of these effects may be ameliorated by providing the assistance of skilled mental health professionals and specially designed programs of behavior modification, the extensive and long-term assistance often required is not offered by partner notification programs nor by AIDS counseling and testing programs, which are oriented toward very short-term counseling, mostly by case workers not qualified to provide mental health services.

While several states have reported successful outcomes from their partner notification program, none have as yet published good evidence of the effects of notification on those notified. Without weighing any harmful effects the program may have on the short- and long-term emotional well-being and behavior of those notified, it is not possible to accurately determine a program's benefit.

Can Sexual Behavior Be Modified?

Unlike the case of those STDs for which medical treatment could ensure that the infection would not be spread further, partner notification regarding HIV must lead to long-term and substantial changes in behavior to be effective. But behaviors related to sexuality and drug addiction are extremely difficult to alter, even for high-functioning mentally healthy individuals, and the catastrophic news of an HIV-positive status could impair the ability to make well-reasoned choices.

The strongest scientific evidence that individuals can make the substantial health behavior changes that would be required to prevent HIV transmission comes from the "health promotion and disease prevention" literature (see, e.g., Leventhal, Prohaska, & Hirshman, 1985). The methods shown to be effective employ techniques such as building the self-worth of individuals and rehearsing healthy behavioral repertoires. As applied to AIDS prevention, many of the most effective techniques would be seen by some as "promoting homosexual behavior," which is prohibited by amendments to federal AIDS funding laws. Because of the ruinous penalties imposed by the law, and uncertainty as to its sweep, programs tend to keep far away from any activities that might be interpreted as violating it. Thus assistance of the kind shown to be effective in altering health behaviors is seldom available (Dejowski, 1989). The arguments in favor of partner notification programs would be strengthened if scientifically sound behavior change programs were available to those notified.

Confidentiality and Discrimination

The stigma associated with being the carrier of a sexually transmitted disease is greatly intensified in the case of the HIV virus. Fear of contagion and death cause many people to ignore assurances from medical authorities that HIV cannot be transmitted through casual contact and to distance themselves even from those they only suspect of being infected. Aside from being shunned by many, persons who are HIV-infected face serious practical problems such as housing and job discrimination and the denial of health insurance at a time they need it most. It is very difficult to assure confidentiality. In Albany, New York, for example, it was revealed that the police and fire departments had compiled a surreptitious list of persons believed to have AIDS, which was to be made available for personnel responding to emergencies (Dunne & Serio, 1988). Between 1983 and 1988 more than a thousand complaints of discrimination and disclosure were brought before New York City's Human Rights Commission (Dunne & Serio, 1988). Fear of such real discrimination and breach of confidentiality affects the likelihood that persons will test for HIV; whether they will be willing to reveal their names to their counselor, that is, be tested confidentially rather than anonymously; and whether they would notify their sexual or needle-sharing partners, or reveal their partners' names to professional partner notifiers.

POLITICIZING PARTNER NOTIFICATION

The debate among health professionals over whether and under which circumstances partner notification is appropriate in the context of AIDS has produced a certain consensus, described below, even in the absence of strong empirical evidence of outcome or effectiveness. However, the issue has not been left in the arena of public health experts. It has occasionally become politicized, and this politicization has sometimes heated the issue to the point where public health expert opinion and empiricism itself have become overwhelmed by politics and passions of the moment.

Examples of this politicization include the so-called "Dannemeyer Initiative," California Proposition 102 (1988). The initiative, had it passed, would have required: "Every person who is informed that he or she has tested positive for any test indicating infection by any probable causative agent for AIDS shall, within seven days, report to the local health official the name and address of any person from whom the disease may have been contracted and to whom the disease may have been transmitted" (§14.199.27). Violators would have been guilty of a misdemeanor. Each health officer would thereupon have been required to investigate the "sources and possible transmittal," and to "take all measures reasonably necessary to prevent the transmission of the infection." The measures were to include notification of the subject's spouse, other known sex partners, and any other person the health officer had reasonable cause to believe was exposed (§12.199.26.a). Early voter polls indicated that the initiative would pass with overwhelming voter support (The Field Institute, 1988). "Mainstream" associations representing medical, nursing, and health professionals, together with advocates for persons with AIDS and members of the gay community, managed to change voter opinion by election day through a costly education effort, and the initiative was defeated.

The issue is kept alive by the introduction into federal AIDS bills each year of amendments that would mandate extreme and impracticable forms of partner notification. Recently attempting to explain the way one of these amendments would work, Representative Dannemeyer stated: "Under the law, if you choose not to reveal your sexual contacts, we will come and arrest you and take you into custody until the message gets through that you are required for the sake of preventing the transmissibility of this disease to other people so that we can contact these sexual contacts and advise them as to the status. If you do not choose to do that voluntarily, we will keep you in custody" (135 Congressional Record H 6163).

As with Proposition 102, such proposals typically call for mandatory reporting of identities of HIV-seropositive individuals in addition to contact notification, since they rely on criminal sanctions, which would be ineffective if individuals can continue to be tested anonymously or use pseudonyms. Representative Dannemeyer explains: "You cannot have it both ways. You would have to pursue reportability to pursue contact tracing" (135 Congressional Record H 7988).

It is important to point out that these extreme proposals are inconsistent with the entire direction and approach of the public health community. The CDC and state public health authorities, even in those states with the most vigorous partner notification programs, support voluntariness and cooperation rather than the use of criminal sanctions in their partner notification programs. The campaigns described above, however, repeatedly cited the programs of states such as Colorado, South Carolina, and Indiana as examples to show the value and workability of their own extreme proposals. Unfortunately, some proponents of vigorous CDC-style partner notification efforts were not as vigorous as they could have been in making differences between their own programs and these proposals clear to the public. In fact, public health officials sometimes continue to contribute unnecessarily to the political polarization of the issue. For example, one important journal recently published an article by several county and state health officials from Colorado, in which they asserted that those who oppose notification are either homosexuals or members of other "stigmatized groups." They went on to summarily dismiss the possibility that there may be some differences between contact notification for HIV seropositivity and for such illnesses as syphilis and gonorrhea: "It is true that in the past, stigmatized groups, especially gay men, have pressured the political and public health establishments to treat this disease as an exception and to discourage use of time-honored approaches. . . . " (Potterat, Spencer, et al., 1989). Many persons concerned with human rights issues, some who may be members of "stigmatized groups," and many others who are not, have questions about the value and appropriateness of partner notification for HIV seropositive persons. Also, as indicated above, there is wide professional disagreement concerning the appropriateness of the analogy to STD contact tracing. Injudicious statements by professionals are used as support for proposals such as the Dannemeyer Initiative, and may lead more moderate persons to fear partner notification as a potential rallying point for extremists, ideologues, and demagogues.

SOURCES OF PARTNER NOTIFICATION

Partner Notification by Physicians

Considerable debate has taken place concerning the duty and authority of health practitioners, particularly physicians, to notify contacts of their patients who are seropositive (Dejowski, 1988). Concern over potential harm to the public from the uneven, unmonitored, and uncoordinated system that would ensue has led to a strong policy preference in most places for a publicly run program to which health professionals could turn when faced with situations where notification appears indicated. All states that receive federal AIDS prevention and surveillance funds through cooperative agreements are required to establish standards and implement procedures for confidential notification of sex and needle-sharing partners of persons with AIDS and HIV infections (CDC, n.d.)

Brief History of Testing and Counseling Services

One of the largest line items in federal and state budgets for preventing the spread of AIDS is voluntary HIV antibody testing and counseling. Partner notification cannot be understood without being viewed in the context of these programs, since they are the primary source of contact identification. The most common form of partner notification, patient referral (see below), depends entirely on the testing and counseling program for its efficacy and outcome. In turn, a major purpose of notification is to convince the notified to seek testing and counseling services.

Testing and counseling services, perhaps the centerpiece of federal AIDS prevention efforts, began in a roundabout way. It was feared that some individuals at high risk of AIDS would donate blood as a way of finding out if they were seropositive. Since the early blood tests had significant false negative rates, it was determined to establish "alternative testing sites" where high-risk individuals could receive free HIV testing without potentially endangering the blood supply. The programs developed a life of their own. The Health Omnibus Extension Act of 1988 (P.L. 100-607) authorized $100 million each for 1989 and 1990 for these services. In 1989 the funds were distributed among 63 state, local, or territorial health departments through cooperative agreements (United States General Accounting Office, 1989). In 1989, 5,013 counseling and testing sites operated. Of these, 1,297 were freestanding and 877 were operated through STD clinics. Other sites were located in family planning, prenatal, and obstetric clinics, private physicians' offices, drug treatment programs, prisons and colleges. Between January 1988 and September 1989, these sites provided testing to 1,400,000 persons. Of these, 159,140 identified themselves as homosexual or bisexual; and of that cohort, 26,366 tested positive (CDC, 1990). The core services include at a minimum pretest counseling; drawing of blood; testing; post-test counseling; and partner notification assistance. Programs, at state discretion, may be "confidential" or "anonymous." "Confidential" means that the client must provide a name, and that the state's law will determine the rules for confidentiality of the information provided (many of those who informally learn that they will not be required to produce identification give pseudonyms). "Anonymous" means that clients are told they have the option of giving no name, and code numbers are used as identifiers. This issue has important consequences for partner notification programs, since anonymity reduces the range and extent of coercion that can be brought to bear on the index person to participate. There is evidence that confidential testing is a deterrent for many persons considering being tested. Following a change from confidential to anonymous testing in Oregon, the demand for services increased 125% for gay men, 56% for female prostitutes, 17% for intravenous drug users, and 32% for other clients (Fehrs et al., 1988). Conversely, when mandatory name reporting of those who test HIV-positive was enacted in South Carolina, the number of gay men seeking to be tested declined by 51% and the overall number of those testing positive fell by 43%, suggesting that high-risk persons were being discouraged from counseling and testing (Johnson, Sy, & Jackson, 1988). Thus the appeal of being able to access complete information about those infected with HIV must be balanced by the reality that containment of the AIDS epidemic requires the consent and cooperation of the persons at risk.

Linkage of Partner Notification to Testing

A fundamental element in partner notification efforts is the encouragement of those notified to receive testing and counseling. It is hoped that those who test positive will behave responsibly by protecting others from infection and themselves from reinfection, but this may or may not happen. Some fear that those who are tested pursuant to notification rather than at a time they choose when they feel capable of handling the situation might be prone to nonconstructive, antisocial reactions. These concerns raise questions about the desirability of procedures such as Colorado's, whereby blood may be drawn "in the field" during the partner notification process, when individuals may be so overwhelmed by the circumstances that they are unable to make a well-reasoned choice whether to accept testing.

Even negative results could have untoward consequences. Since the majority of those who test for HIV are virus-free, it is important to know of the effects of a negative result: does it encourage people to "turn over a new leaf" and discontinue risky behavior? Or does it cause risky behavior to persist by giving a sense of invulnerability to the virus? The implication for public health policy is that counseling and support should be made available on an ongoing basis for all persons tested, particularly when knowledge of their risk status has been thrust upon them.

"Patient Referral"

The CDC has issued guidelines for partner notification. These depend on the voluntary cooperation of persons with HIV infections. The guidelines set notification by the seropositive individual as the central point in the strategy. That is, they recommend that such persons receive instruction in how to notify their sexual and needle-sharing partners, and to refer them for testing and counseling. This is called "patient referral." If the seropositive individual is unwilling, or "if it cannot be assured that their partners will seek counseling," they recommend that physicians or health department personnel assure the partners are notified, using confidential procedures. This is "provider referral." Such notification by third parties depends on the index person voluntarily providing names, addresses, and descriptions of contacts. The guidelines indicate that the identity of the index person is never revealed to the identified contact. By June 1989 all states and four other jurisdictions receiving funds had established patient referral services, and all made health department services available to patients who requested referral by a third party for certain partners, while 23 provided referral by health department staff for all partners when requested by the index person (CDC, 1989).

Adaptation to Local Circumstances

An exploratory case study of the development and implementation of AIDS partner notification programs in five places—Colorado, Virginia, Florida, San Francisco, and Seattle—was conducted for the Public Health Service. The authors concluded that currently, "state and local realities determine both the mix of methodologies being used in HIV prevention/education programs and also the particular approach being taken to partner notification. Further, the choices appeared to be made with some concern for cost effectiveness balanced by a concern for public health" (Macro Systems, Inc., 1988).

Some programs target provider referral efforts to specific subpopulations. The San Francisco program targets female sex partners of childbearing age, under the presumption that the benefits of notification are likely to be highest for unsuspecting sexual partners, such as women unaware of their sexual partner's intravenous drug habit or bisexuality. By contrast, programs in low-prevalence areas may be more likely to target homosexual and bisexual male partners (see Wykoff et al., 1988).

Provider notification occurs relatively infrequently with needle-sharing, nonsexual partners of intravenous drug users, or with homosexual contacts for persons with a history of multiple sexual partners who live in a high-prevalence area. Many health officials believe that locating such persons would be a formidable if not impossible task, and that those located are already likely to know of their risk. Crystal et al. (1990) found that a large proportion of contacted intravenous drug users in New Jersey were already aware of their risk, or have been tested for HIV previously. But those who view partner notification as an opportunity to target educational efforts and to connect persons at risk with support services nevertheless consider notification worthwhile for those already aware of their risk status. However, sufficient information is not yet available to know the relationship between notification and subsequent risky behaviors, nor the range of reaction to the stressful information that is imparted.

WILL PATIENTS SELF-NOTIFY?

There is a certain mutual distrust between populations at risk and state health workers. Partner notifiers prefer not to rely on self-notification when they cannot verify it, and seropositive persons are reluctant to disclose information that may be held against them or their partners. The two groups hardest hit by the AIDS epidemic—gay men and intravenous drug users—already experience stigmatization and are wary of an added penalty for being identified as HIV carriers. In addition, intravenous drug users engage in activities for which they can be prosecuted, as do homosexuals in the 25 states that still purport to criminalize certain consensual homosexual acts (*Bowers v. Hardwick*, 478 U.S. 186; 106 S. Ct. 2841). Many in each group will refuse to disclose information about their cohorts. Unwilling to risk exposing their friends to trouble with the state, sometimes fearful that contacts will deduce who "turned them in," many HIV-positive persons assure their counselor that they prefer to self-notify. Many who would benefit might opt not to get tested if they learn on the street that they will be pressured into revealing the names of their sexual or needle-sharing partners at the testing sites. This distrust of state officials is seen even among some HIV counselors who sometimes identify more with their clients than with what they may perceive to be ill-conceived "state directives" to identify contacts.

With these limitations, can we ensure that those who promise to self-notify will do so? If this cannot be ensured, should states take it upon themselves to notify all contacts at risk? The presumption that underlies reliance on self-notification is the same as that which underlies the entire partner notification effort—that people will take responsible steps to protect themselves and others if they are informed of the risks. Partner notification would appear to lack a compelling rationale without this presumption about human nature.

OUTCOMES OF PARTNER NOTIFICATION PROGRAMS

Colorado, Idaho, South Carolina, and Virginia have collected and reported data from their partner notification programs. These provide information such as the number of contact names elicited, number of contacts located and counseled, and possibly whether the contacts were tested for HIV following notification. Life-style changes following notification are more difficult to measure, because they require a follow-up interview with the notified person. But it is difficult to draw responsible conclusions about these programs in the absence of well-designed outcome research. It is important to know the effects of notification both in cases where the partner at risk tests HIV positive and when he or she tests HIV negative.

One evaluation is suggestive. Wykoff et al. (1988) reported on South Carolina's partner notification program. Starting with one seropositive man and his 19 contacts, they identified a total of 83 sexual contacts of seropositive men. Of the 64 contacts who were county residents, 63 agreed to be tested for HIV, and 11 tested HIV positive. Comparing reported numbers of sexual contacts for the 6-month periods before and after notification, the mean number of sexual contacts decreased by 82% for HIV-positive men, and by 54% for HIV-negative men. While none of the men reported using condoms at the time of notification, at a six-month follow-up 4 (80%) of the 5 seropositive men and 25 (69%) of the seronegative men reported using condoms at least some of the time.

The results reported by Wykoff et al. are indeed interesting; it would appear that from only one seropositive index person, a large number of seropositives were identified, and notification and testing had an effect in reducing self-reports of risky sexual behavior in both seropositive and seronegative partners. However, professional contact notification may be especially effective in a case such as this where, in a low-prevalence community, multiple sexual partners are involved, and the index person is not likely to be able to self-notify all past partners. Unfortunately, this is only an anecdotal example of what can happen in the process of attempting to notify partners at risk.

We have performed an evaluation of aspects of New Jersey's newly established partner notification program (Crystal, Dengelegi, Beck, & Dejowski, 1990). That program consists of a team of notifiers who are state Health Department employees, unaffiliated with local testing sites. While initially there was friction between the notifiers and the HIV counselors, the evaluators concluded that one year after its inception, New Jersey's Notification Assistance Program had been successful in creating an effective working relationship with counselors at testing sites and clinics. In the course of a year counselors and notifiers were able to see the situation from each others' point of view—protecting privacy and promoting public health—and were able to work together in the service of both goals. This change was reflected in an increase in the number of clients who provided contact names, presumably because partner notification was presented to them in a more positive manner by the counselors. However, the numbers of contact names provided were still not very large, with only a little more than 1 out of 10 seropositive persons using the services of the notification program. An unknown portion of the remaining seropositive persons notify their own partners. Persons in long-standing sexual relationships were most likely to indicate a preference for self-notification. It is probably the case that a majority of sexual and needle-sharing contacts are not notified, particularly those with whom the index case is no longer in contact. The counselors reported that most clients, especially intravenous drug users, distrust the provider notification program and fear harm coming to themselves or to the contacts they would name. Surprisingly, very few of the partners contacted showed animosity or distrust of the notifiers. Rather, they were usually appreciative of their efforts. It is likely that these persons, being members of the same risk groups as the indexes who named them, also tend to distrust official agencies. But in face-to-face interaction with a supportive counselor, preconceived ideas about "the State" may have been dispelled, and the counseling may have helped them feel benefited from the service.

CONCLUSIONS

Partner notification, as an activity coordinated with the public health authority, and relying on the voluntary participation of index persons, appears to have become an accepted part of AIDS prevention and control efforts.

A consensus is developing that coercion with the threat of criminal or other sanctions is not an effective adjunct to HIV partner notification. Cooperation from infected individuals is essential. Understanding and support must be used to help infected persons do what is in the final analysis best for themselves and for the rest of society. It is appropriate that representatives of high-risk groups, such as homosexuals and intravenous drug users, should engage in continuous dialogue with policymakers, to assure that policies that are developed optimize outcomes for the infected as well as the uninfected.

The central element of partner notification programs is "patient referral," which refers to the process of educating and training seropositive individuals to notify their own contacts and refer them for testing and counseling. The HIV counselor's role is to coach such clients in how to approach their partners and how best to discuss this information. Alternatively, the counselor could participate in this discussion when requested by the client. For persons with a history of multiple sexual or needle-sharing partners, it is less likely that the seropositive person will be able to reach all of them, even if motivated to do so. "Provider referral," that is, confidential notification by public health personnel, might be appropriate under such circumstances.

Appropriate timing of notification is essential. People asked to think about notifying partners immediately after being told of their seropositive status are often not responsive, because they must first come to absorb and accept their own situation. Rather than use pressure to obtain information about contacts, it would be useful to schedule follow-up visits with HIV-positive persons.

Partner notification services of the kind described above can operate without compromising individual liberties if conducted in accordance with the recommendations presented above, and such services appear to have some impact. However, since many other educational and outreach efforts are available, effective, and less costly, we recommend that professional partner notification should be used to complement these other methods of public education by focusing notification efforts on those least likely to have been reached by other efforts, or least likely to have categorized themselves as being at risk for HIV infection.

Research on the outcome of partner notification programs is insufficient at this point to draw conclusions concerning efficacy, cost, or outcome. Such evaluations, conducted by persons who are fully independent of the programs they are evaluating, should be a high priority for AIDS prevention research. Evaluation should examine the effects of notification on behavior and on mental health, including suicidal potential; it should compare different models of notification including patient referral and provider referral; examine the relation of cost to benefit; compare efficacy and cost of notification with other methods of prevention and education; and examine the effects of such programs on driving infected or at-risk individuals to or from counseling, health care, or other kinds of assistance. Finally, it should examine the impact on civil liberties and fundamental human rights.

We do not believe that partner notification should halt in the absence of adequate research. Common sense, small-scale research, and anecdotal reports offer probable cause to believe the programs can save some lives. But those advocating and operating such programs should retain appropriate modesty in the claims they make and in the expectations they raise for these programs in the face of the limited empirical evidence that exists concerning their outcome. Health professionals should be especially sensitive to the possible harm that could be caused by notification programs, and until more information is available about the effects of notification, they should go to great lengths to assure that notified individuals receive all the counseling and support they require to deal with the impact of the notification.

15

AIDS Prevention and Public Policy: The Experience of Gay Males

John C. Gonsiorek
Michael Shernoff

Although the percentage of HIV-infected individuals who are gay and bisexual men has dropped about 20% in recent years, the AIDS epidemic has been and remains a crisis of unmitigated proportions for the gay male community in the United States. Figures vary according to geographical location and population characteristics, but it is likely that 20% to 60% of homosexual men who are not in monogamous relationships are infected with HIV (Anderson & Levy, 1985; Jaffe et al., 1985). The intense concentration of the AIDS epidemic in the gay male community has exacerbated and complicated a variety of public policy issues related both to gay men and to the AIDS epidemic.

This chapter will focus on behavior change in response to the AIDS epidemic, and intervention techniques to prevent the spread of HIV primarily as these relate to gay males. This area is but a small part of the public policy issues that AIDS has raised. Historical perspectives have been articulated by Brandt (1987, 1988); health policy issues by Brandt (1985); social consequences by Cassens (1985); and legal and ethical issues by Bayer, Levine and Wolff (1986), Lamb, Clark, Drumheller, Frazzell, and Suney (1989), Melton and Gray (1988), and Melton (1988). In this volume Herek discusses social stigma and violence related to those infected with HIV and Dejowski and his colleagues have articulated the complexities of contact notification, historically the preferred tool of public health departments in dealing with sexually transmitted diseases. The psychosocial problems generated by the AIDS epidemic have been amply described (Bouknight & Bouknight, 1988; Carballo-

AUTHORS' NOTE: We would like to thank the following colleagues whose comments on earlier drafts were most helpful: Ed Dejowski, Ph.D; Rob Fulton, M.Ed., Ramsey County Public Health Dept., Minnesota; Alan Roberts, Ph.D., Scripps Institute Behavioral Medicine Clinic, California; and David Swarthout, Hennepin County Red Door Clinic, Minnesota.

Dieguez, 1989; Christ, Wiener, & Moynihan, 1986; Dilley, Pies, & Helquist, 1989; Gonsiorek, 1986; Morin, Charles, & Malyon, 1984; and Shernoff, 1990).

Valisseri (1989, p. 147) suggests that the AIDS epidemic is unique because prior to AIDS, behavioral interventions were not needed, as medical responses sufficed. This is not entirely accurate. Brandt (1987) has described the history of social and behavioral interventions regarding sexually transmitted diseases in the preantibiotic era. He documents that much of the current controversy about appropriate AIDS prevention strategies mirrors debates in the first half of the century pertaining to syphilis and gonorrhea. Unfortunately, current debates do not seem to have been informed or elucidated by errors in the past. We have focused this chapter on prevention because as Shernoff and Palacios-Jimenez (1988) have noted, prevention is currently "the only vaccine available."

A BEHAVIORAL PERSPECTIVE AND ITS IMPLICATIONS

Behavioral approaches to health behavior problems have developed in recent decades and have been successful in a number of areas previously thought unamenable to behavioral intervention (Fordyce, 1966; Fordyce, Fowler, & De Lateur, 1968; Ince, 1976; Roberts, Dinsdale, Matthews, & Cole, 1969; Ullman & Krasner, 1965). From a behavioral perspective, programs attempting to modify health behavior should share a number of features:

1. The goals should be as simple as possible to achieve the desired change. Increasing the complexity of goals reduces the likelihood of success. Goals should be specific and concrete. Goals that are vague or global reduce the likelihood of success.

2. Behavior change should be accomplished in a gradual step-by-step fashion. This allows for fine tuning of the program and, more importantly, allows for rewards and a sense of accomplishment throughout the process.

3. While *mild* fear-based messages can motivate target groups for behavior change, programs themselves should be reinforcement based, not punishment or fear based. The overwhelming superiority of reinforcement-based programs is without question. The only real application of punishment or fear-based behavior change programs is when there is substantial difficulty in finding reinforcements.

4. Behavioral intervention, in order to be effective in the long term, should have an ongoing follow-up component to address problems of

relapse and recurrence of problem behaviors or new contingencies that may arise.

5. Behavioral programs should be carefully planned and individually tailored to the individuals for whom the program is intended. Different populations usually require programmatic changes.

Applying this perspective to HIV infection prevention programs, one would argue that the programs most likely to succeed are those that have the most minimal goals possible to prevent infection; that are highly concrete and specific; that involve a gradual step-by-step process; that are based on reward and reinforcement; that have the capacity for follow-up to address the problems of relapse; and that are highly specific to the target population. Programs with the features suggested here have been implemented and initial data suggest substantial behavior change (Kelly, St. Lawrence, Hood, & Brasfield, 1989; Swarthout, Gonsiorek, Simpson, & Henry, 1989).

THE INTRUSION OF GOALS UNRELATED TO PUBLIC HEALTH

As has been the case throughout the history of prevention efforts for sexually transmitted diseases, issues unrelated to infection prevention hinder the ability to develop effective programs. Since AIDS is most typically transmitted either through sexual or blood exposure (from sharing intravenous drug paraphernalia), issues of morality pertaining to sexual behavior or drug use confound public health goals and effectiveness of infection prevention interventions.

At various points during the AIDS epidemic, health professionals have taken a role in this confusion. For example, Crenshaw (1987), an original member of the Presidential AIDS Commission, publicly stated that the only ways to stop the spread of AIDS were "monogamy, masturbation and abstinence." This information is simply untrue, given the facts of HIV transmission. It also violates the behavioral principles noted above. Not surprisingly, Catania et al. (1989) have documented that men in San Francisco who attempted monogamy or celibacy frequently discontinued these practices. Gochros (1988) reported that during periods of sexual abstinence, men became depressed and anxious and increased alcohol and drug use. A behaviorist would say that such strategies are not sufficiently reinforcement based, or are more global than necessary, and therefore likely to fail.

Another example is the mistaken belief that quantity of partners is a primary risk factor for HIV. While many studies of HIV infection among gay men reflect that the number of sexual partners appears to have statistical significance as a risk factor, three recent studies found no correlation between multiple sexual partners and seroconversion for women who were sexual partners of men seropositive for HIV (Cohen et al., 1987; Fischl et al., 1987; Padian et al., 1987). The majority of women who became infected did so after engaging in high-risk behaviors with *one* partner who was seropositive. Thus, women who believe that having fewer sexual partners reduces their risk of contracting HIV may be falsely reassured about their risk status, particularly if those few partners happen to share drug-using paraphernalia, have sex with men, or are already seropositive. Studies on gay men reflect number of partners as a risk factor only as an artifact, since research has repeatedly shown that it is specific *behaviors* that directly place an individual at risk for HIV infection. The number of partners may or may not be a risk depending on the specific behaviors in which the individual engages.

Brandt (1987) documents the failure of abstinence and monogamy strategies in reducing rates of sexually transmitted diseases during World War II. Current similar campaigns focused on adolescent sexual behavior are failures in reducing the sharply rising rates of teenage pregnancy and new cases of sexually transmitted diseases among adolescents. In general, HIV infection prevention programs have been hampered by the inclusion of moralistic, social policy, or other goals that bear no necessary relationship to HIV infection prevention: for example, the elimination of IV drug use, the elimination of same-sex behavior or adolescent sexual behavior, the encouragement of monogamy or sexual abstinence, or the attempt to alter the living habits of the urban poor.

Examples of interference from political goals unrelated to HIV abound. Perhaps the most egregious is the Helms amendment, which denies federal funding to any agency that promotes or encourages homosexuality. Only three U.S. senators voted against the amendment. Another example is Senator Helms's attack on AIDS education materials developed specifically for gay men, as "smut" and likely to corrupt children. More recently, the Centers for Disease Control appear to be operating more to avoid offending right-wing political constituencies than to control disease. These are clear examples of bias or political agendas interfering with HIV infection prevention, in a way that will worsen the AIDS epidemic.

SOME COMPLEX EXAMPLES

Sometimes, however, these misguided efforts take a more complex guise. An instructive case is the confusion that has surrounded the relative risk of HIV transmission through fellatio. On a theoretical level, it would appear that fellatio is a reasonable method of transmitting HIV, as there are a variety of opportunities for semen and blood interaction. A number of studies (McCusker et al., 1988; Melbye et al., 1984; Scheckter et al., 1986; Winkelsteen et al., 1987) suggest, however, that transmission by fellatio appears to be trivial or nonexistent. The situation is further confused because other studies (Darrow et al., 1987; Melbye et al., 1986) suggest that fellatio can be a transmission route for HIV. The current state of scientific thought is that fellatio is a possible but unlikely and inefficient route of HIV transmission, especially when compared with receptive unprotected anal intercourse, which is an extremely efficient route of HIV infection, and receptive unprotected vaginal intercourse, which is an efficient route but less so than anal intercourse. Ingestion of semen increases risk; noningestion decreases it. Condom use in fellatio also decreases risk.

The response of the scientific community to this information has been peculiar. A scientist interested only in behavior change designed to reduce the likelihood of HIV infection would look at fellatio with its markedly lower risk, compare it with receptive anal intercourse with its drastically higher risk, and conclude that substituting other behaviors for receptive anal intercourse is a very high priority, whereas substituting other behaviors for fellatio is a lower priority. In attempting to balance simplicity of the goal and maintenance of a reinforcing pattern of sexual behavior with the most effective HIV infection prevention, the recommendations regarding fellatio become complex. One runs the risk of reducing the efficiency of attempts to reduce receptive anal intercourse by focusing on the less important goal of reducing fellatio. In addition, there is a risk of making the entire behavioral program less reinforcing by restricting more and more sexual behaviors. Yet unprotected fellatio is *not* a safe behavior, and it does have a low but apparently possible risk of HIV transmission. Although a solution to this problem for the behaviorist is not simple, principles are clear. One behavior is highly dangerous. The other behavior is mildly dangerous. A continuum or hierarchy of the risk behavior is apparent. The most appropriate response involves an individualized risk management program that includes optimal reinforcement strategies and containment of behavioral vulnerabilities.

Instead, however, the response of most public health officials in the United States has been to place the risk of fellatio as very close to receptive anal intercourse. In exaggerating its risk, efficiency of all behavioral change and credibility of programs is reduced. It is noteworthy that public health authorities in Canada view fellatio as much less risky than do those in the United States (Canadian AIDS Society, 1988).

It is also curious that there is so little research to ascertain why fellatio, which ought to be a reasonably vigorous transmission route, is a weak one. It is likely that a political fear of "promoting" fellatio is interfering with legitimate scientific inquiry that is germane to HIV prevention efforts.

The scientific disinterest in fellatio has a parallel in the lack of scientific interest in women's sexuality. For years, there has been ample evidence that unprotected vaginal intercourse is an effective method of transmitting HIV. Yet there has been little research on how and where HIV enters a woman's bloodstream as a result of vaginal intercourse. The federal government began a multicenter cohort study of HIV transmission in gay men in 1983; the comparable study on heterosexual transmission did not begin until 1987. Current funding to customize AIDS prevention programs that have proven successful for gay men into relevant programs for heterosexual women is almost nonexistent. These are consistent with the historical lack of importance afforded to women's health issues. As noted by a former women's education coordinator at AIDS Action Committee of Massachusetts: "There is very little importance attached to the fact that women themselves are becoming infected in increasing numbers. The concern is simply there for women's alleged role as vectors of transmission to either infants or men in the 'general population'" (Irvine, personal communication, November 30, 1989). Women and gay men share a societal stigma in that their sexuality is viewed as unimportant and expendable. This stigma inappropriately distorts public policy decisions and even basic scientific research.

GOALS OF HIV INFECTION PREVENTION IN GAY MEN

A behavioral perspective is helpful in targeting the most appropriate goals for HIV infection prevention. For example, it would suggest that eroticizing safe, noninsertive sex (i.e., mutual masturbation, frottage, massage, etc.) is the core behavioral goal with gay men. Such behaviors are virtually without risk of HIV transmission. They are inherently reinforcing, simple, and concrete, and can be mastered by a step-by-step learning process. Implementation problems, such as lack of social assertiveness, are also amenable to behavioral interventions.

By contrast, condom usage is a problematic and therefore lower priority goal, and best serves as a "backup" skill when an individual is unsuccessful at implementing other noninsertive safe behaviors. Proper condom use requires numerous behavioral tasks such as appropriate storage, careful selection of lubricant type, proper fitting, careful removal, and attention during sexual activity to signs of tearing. This is a complex behavioral sequence, with numerous potential anxiety cues (e.g., to be alert for signs of condom tearing in the midst of sexual activity) that can attenuate the inherent reinforcing power of insertive sex with condoms. There are also more opportunities for interpersonal events to adversely intervene; for example, the receptive partner must initiate a series of assertive requests, and continue monitoring the process, as opposed to the fewer and simpler assertions needed to initiate and monitor mutual masturbation, for example. Finally, condom usage is a less successful HIV prevention strategy even when both parties follow the "correct" behavioral sequence, because condoms still tear or rupture. Withdrawal before ejaculation during insertive sex with a condom reduces these transmission problems, but creates other problems as it may reduce the reinforcing value of the act.

Ironically, both governmental agencies and many segments of gay male communities share a heavy reliance on condom usage as primary in HIV infection prevention. It is our observation that the usually vague public health messages regarding condom usage exemplify exactly the lack of behavioral specificity we find so problematic. We suspect that part of the message's appeal is its vagueness. One can remain erotophobic, yet still be doing "something" (albeit ineffectual) to stop the spread of AIDS with such messages; a tenuous balance not possible with the more explicitly prosexual stance required to make noninsertive safe sex maximally erotic and reinforcing.

Alcohol and other drug use is another example of the usefulness of a behavioral perspective. Research indicates that alcohol and other drug consumption increases, at times drastically, the rate of unsafe sexual behavior (Research and Decisions Corporation, 1985; Stall, Coates, & Hoff, 1988). A goal of diminishing or, even more radically, eliminating alcohol and drug abuse is at times suggested. As desirable a goal as elimination of substance abuse is, success in achieving it has been mixed to poor. More importantly, it adds numerous goals unrelated to the task of HIV infection prevention, and the added goals themselves are vague, behaviorally complex, and difficult. The simplest—and therefore most preferable—behavioral goal is the separation *in time* of sexual behavior from alcohol or other drug consumption (i.e., sexual behavior and alcohol or drug consumption should be *at separate times,* with no overlap).

Both behaviorally and in terms of HIV transmission reduction, we propose that the two primary goals for gay men are the maximal eroticization of safe, noninsertive sexual behavior and the separation in time of sexual behavior from any alcohol/drug consumption (because the latter so clearly interferes with the former). Secondary goals include insertive sex with condoms and fellatio without exposure to semen. The secondary goals are advisable only as "backup" techniques should primary goals fail, and/or when insertive behaviors are the only reinforcing behaviors in the individual's sexual repertoire. It is important with secondary goals that individuals recognize that some HIV transmission risk exists with them. Finally, gay men should have complete and accurate information about a continuum of HIV transmission risk behaviors, so that if there is a failure of both primary and secondary goals, then the least risky behaviors can be chosen (e.g., unprotected fellatio with semen exposure instead of unprotected anal intercourse).

Yet the official public health agenda is often almost the inverse of this. Gay men are urged to change sexual orientation, abstain, or masturbate alone, strategies known to fail; or grudgingly urged to use condoms. The most effective strategy behaviorally and in terms of HIV infection prevention, i.e., eroticization of safe sex, is difficult for many policymakers to endorse because it involves the exploration, affirmation, encouragement, and eroticization of a vigorous but safe gay male sexuality.

It is clear that what is occurring is the intrusion of unrelated moral agendas into HIV infection prevention. We maintain that *any* deviation from the most direct attempts to single-mindedly reduce HIV transmission attenuates program effectiveness, increases program expense (as money is wasted on ineffective programs), and directly contributes to the worsening of the AIDS epidemic.

HIV INFECTION PREVENTION EFFORTS IN GAY MEN

As Weinrich (1989) has noted, the idea that hundreds of thousands of men, particularly gay men, would be capable of reducing numbers of sexual partners, using condoms, and making substantive changes in sexual practices would have been absurd 15 years ago to public health specialists in sexually transmitted diseases. Yet, that is precisely what has occurred. Gay males have changed their behavior on an unprecedented scale. Becker and Joseph (1988), in their review of the literature on AIDS and behavior change, state, "Indeed in some populations of homosexual/bisexual man this may be the most rapid and profound response to a health threat which has ever been documented." Similarly, Stall, Coates, and Hoff, in their review (1988), described the behavior changes reducing risk for HIV infection among bisexual and gay men as "the most profound modifications of personal health related behaviors ever recorded."

These changes, however, are far from evenly distributed or stable. For example, Becker and Joseph, while describing the behavior change as rapid and profound, also note that it is incomplete and point to a number of longitudinal studies suggesting that the behavior change is unstable over time or that there are relapse problems. Stall, Coates, and Hoff amplify these cautions and suggest that these studies on gay men are not necessarily generalizable to nongay, nonurban, and nonwhite populations and specifically recommend further research to understand the role that alcohol and other drugs play in interfering with HIV risk reduction behavior changes. These reviewers note that even despite such optimistic changes, there remains a core group, albeit a minority, of gay men who have not made significant behavior changes. Relapse problems are documented and troublesome (Bartolomeo, 1990; Stall & Ekstrand, 1989).

From the broader perspective of health behavior change, comparing the HIV epidemic to other behavior change efforts in smoking cessation, cardiac risk management, weight reduction, and so forth, these findings are not unusual. Indeed, what is unusual is that the first wave of change efforts have been so successful. One would expect in a major health behavior change effort that an initial group of individuals for whom the first behavior change techniques are best tailored will be identified and make the most dramatic changes. There will be other groups, however, for whom change is negligible or nonexistent. From a behavioral perspective, this may mean that the programs have not been sufficiently tailored to such individuals or that other technical aspects of the program such as the reinforcement or other components have been inadequately understood. Relapse, while troublesome, is also not a sign of failure. Behavior change has to be stable enough for relapse to occur. Relapse, then, is a sign that initial desirable behavior change has occurred enough that the deviation from the desired goal, not its acquisition, is most noteworthy. The most appropriate response to relapse is to design increasingly effective follow-up programs to understand and address the factors that cause relapse.

In general, then, the form that health behavior change programs are likely to take is that the first wave of programs will be successful with a segment of the target population but that a portion of this segment will have relapse problems. The second wave of programs must target relapse prevention as well as become increasingly creative and individualized in developing successful programs for the groups the first wave of programs have failed. As different kinds of programs are identified as successful for different kinds of people and as more and more sophisticated relapse prevention programs become identified, desired behavior change becomes possible for a greater number of individuals.

It appears likely that with regard to white urban adult gay men, we are completing the first phase of such a process. It is instructive to pose the question of why this successful change occurred in gay male communities. We would suggest at least two factors. The first is that gay male communities have developed behavior change programs from within. The decade of the 1980s saw a concentrated effort within gay male communities to develop a variety of education and prevention programs. These programs coming from *within* the affected community were viewed positively. Second, the gay male community approximated those behavioral principles noted above. Despite lack of funding or underfunding, political criticism, governmental interference, bigotry, and scientific scorn, numerous programs were developed within the gay male community. For example, the program developed by Palacios-Jiminez and Shernoff (1986) has been particularly well suited to the social and sexual mores of the gay male community.

It is also important to note that the problem with populations who are nongay, nonurban, nonadult, and nonwhite is a technical one in terms of the particulars of the programs and not a characteristic of the population. In other words, behavioral scientists have not yet determined the most effective methods to reach other populations. There is no reason to believe that these populations are inherently more difficult to reach. Keep in mind the pessimism with which public health officials viewed sexual behavior change in gay men 15 years ago. The core problem is that racial/ethnic minorities, the uneducated, and the poor have been virtually ignored by basic health care and behavioral science research. Not surprisingly, successful health behavior change programs in these populations are almost nonexistent. For example, the dramatic decrease in adult cigarette smoking has been almost entirely confined to educated or middle-class and above segments of the population—the poor and poorly educated smoke as much as before. No one yet knows how to do health behavior change with nonwhite, nonadult, and non-middle class populations because almost no one has tried.

Despite this neglect, and a comparable neglect of women's health care, a literature on AIDS prevention for communities of color and women is emerging. It is again noteworthy that this literature tends to come from *within* the affected communities, not from the health care and public health establishments.

Since its inception, the AIDS epidemic has disproportionately affected black and Hispanic communities (Bakeman et al., 1987). Strategies for AIDS prevention have been described for Hispanic gay men (Caraballo-Dieguez, 1989); Mexican-American IV drug users (Mata & Jorquez, 1989); black communities in general (Mays, 1989); black males in general (Bouknight & Bouknight, 1988); black and Hispanic males (Peterson &

Marin, 1988); native American groups (Tafoya, 1989); Asian-American populations (Aoki et al, 1989); Hispanic women (Amaro, 1989); black and Hispanic women (Mays & Cochran, 1988); women in general (Cochran, 1989), and others.

It would be a serious error to view these efforts as "addenda" to HIV infection prevention strategies developed for gay white males. Rather, it is important to recall that successful efforts for changing gay male risk behaviors derived from an understanding of the social, political, and cultural context of gay males, followed by an analysis of appropriate goals, optimal reinforcers, and specific relapse vulnerabilities within this context. Comparable analyses will be required with each target population, and no particular set of strategies is superior a priori. The only reasonable criterion for program superiority is effectiveness in reducing HIV transmission in the target populations.

Yet, a double standard in public health departments persists to this day. For example, Valiserri (1989), in his discussion of traditional public health partner notification programs, is quite forgiving of the lack of strong empirical follow-up data to justify them: "While there are limited data as yet on the efficacy of voluntary partner notification, the process . . . has potential benefits" (p. 224). Later in the same volume (p. 263), he states, "when testing the use of controversial prevention modalities . . . only a clear cut demonstration of improved efficacy and outcome can enable policy makers and legislators to support the promotion of such approaches." If this latter standard had been applied to traditional partner notification procedures, it is likely they would have been abandoned during their consistent failures in the first half of this century. It is clear that many in traditional governmental public health agencies are more interested in the *acceptability* of public health approaches to the general public and politicians than their *efficacy* with target populations; a most peculiar—and negligent—definition of public health, indeed.

SOME BROADER ISSUES

There is a suggestion in the literature that a positive self-image with regard to homosexuality is a foundation upon which gay men successfully participate in and implement HIV infection prevention strategies (Prieur, 1989; Shernoff & Bloom, in press; see also the chapter by Gonsiorek and Rudolph in this volume). It is likely that those gay men with the highest self-esteem and the most positive sense of gay identity are the most likely to make effective behavioral changes. To the extent that a positive gay-affirming sense of identity for homosexual individuals is unacceptable to society, the most efficacious behavior change programs run the risk of being compromised.

Altman (1986) noted that the AIDS epidemic lays bare institutional structural weaknesses, even when not directly related to AIDS. We would like to suggest an area of institutional weakness that is not often clearly articulated—the uneasy and paradoxical status of public health departments in the United States.

We are not alone in this concern. The Institute of Medicine (1988), in their report *The Future of Public Health,* stated:

> Tension between professional expertise and politics can be observed throughout the nation's public health system. Public health professionals rely on expert knowledge. . . . A central tenet of their professional ethic is the commitment to use this knowledge to fulfill the public interest in reducing human suffering and enhancing the quality of life. . . . The dynamics of American politics, however, make it difficult to fulfill this commitment. . . . Decisions are made largely on the basis of competition, bargaining and influence rather than comprehensive analysis. The idea that politics can be restricted to the legislative arena while the work of public agencies remains neutral has been discredited. (p. xvi)

Historically, public health departments in the United States have been instruments of political policy. Those in charge of public health agencies, usually politically appointed administrators, have functioned more like political operatives than health care professionals. This is in contrast to the rank and file staff of public health agencies who are typically more aligned with the values of science and professionalism typical of health care professionals, and of the ethical standards of the American Public Health Association. Indeed, health department "front line" staff have at times been remarkable in their ability to resist ill-conceived political initiatives through their unions, professional associations, and at times even sabotage. Nevertheless, politically appointed administrators and their managers set the agenda.

One of the hallmarks of an *independent profession,* be it public health, medicine, social work, psychology, nursing, or other, is that its members are held to a code of ethical and professional conduct that supersedes the requirements and demands of any particular employer. For example, health care professionals must and do take a strong interest in confidentiality, even if it means opposing inappropriate government initiatives to reduce confidentiality. We maintain that the history of public health departments in the United States has been first and foremost articulating the political agendas of governmental administration, by far the primary employer of those in public health, and only secondarily promoting public health. Until administrators of public health departments are freed of political control, public health will not emerge as a truly independent profession. More work needs to be done to develop and enforce a code of conduct that addresses the differentiation between governmental expediency versus the highest standards of public health practice, and the obligation to operate via the latter. Until then, public health departments will continue to be an impediment in the fight against AIDS and, for that matter, any disease to which political agendas are attached.

Further, it is crucial that public health department administrators and appointees be drawn solely from the ranks of health professionals. Finally, we question the wisdom of government in having public health staff politically appointed at all. Until such changes occur, we fear that public health departments will continue to occupy an incongruous, ineffective, and untenable middle ground between political operative and health care profession.

SUMMARY

Despite the enormous toll the AIDS epidemic has taken on gay male communities, gay men in the United States have developed, with virtually no outside support, creative, successful, and innovative programs for HIV infection prevention that are community based and somewhat surprisingly also based on reasonably sound behavioral principles. The initial success rate of these programs has been promising. Nevertheless, significant problems remain. Some segments of the gay male population have not yet adequately changed risk behavior, and a second generation of problems related to relapse is emerging. An ongoing program to extend the depth and breadth of such behavior change efforts is required. While what works best for adult, white, middle-class gay men will probably not be specifically applicable to other populations, the principles of program development articulated here are likely to be helpful.

Despite discomfort in some segments of the public with such procedures, the most effective HIV infection prevention behavior change programs for gay men rest upon a foundation of valuing, supporting, and affirming gay men and their sexuality. The most effective program goals involve encouraging and eroticizing noninsertive gay male sexual behavior, and separating in time the use of mind-altering substances, as primary goals. Secondary goals are those that are less efficacious from behavioral and transmission reduction perspectives, such as condom use, and middle-level risk behaviors, such as fellatio, to substitute for the highest-risk behaviors (receptive unprotected anal intercourse) when the primary goal fails.

Throughout the AIDS epidemic, traditional public health measures have been minimally effective. A historical view of public health departments would suggest that they have not been able to develop behavioral strategies to reduce epidemics but rather have served a muddled social/political agenda until such time as medicine successfully intervened. Because of the particular characteristics of HIV, a medical *deus ex machina* is not likely soon. A major restructuring of the nature of professional conduct within an independent profession of public health and a depoliticization of public health departments are needed.

Conclusion

John C. Gonsiorek

This chapter summarizes the most salient scientific and public policy findings of each contribution. It is important to note that these complete conclusions may or may not be endorsed by every author; each chapter has its own conclusions. There are some overall themes that are striking.

The first is that many of science's attempts to understand homosexuality were frankly biased, despite the less prejudiced work of some of the earliest contributors, such as Havelock Ellis and Sigmund Freud. Most scientific theory and research on homosexuality earlier than the last 30 years, and some more recent as well, is an abuse of scientific information to reinforce societal prejudices. Sexual orientation can join the list of topics in which science has served at best as a dupe, or at worst as an enforcer, for bigotry. Other examples abound. Earlier "scientific" understanding of women, racial and ethnic minorities, the poor, other cultures and societies, and those who are different have suffered from a comparable level of distortion. Like these other examples, the change in scientific information about homosexuality, once bias has been reduced, is breathtaking. Science is moving from being the enforcer and apologist for prevailing values, to performing its proper function of investigation in as unbiased a manner as is humanly possible.

This contrast reminds us that science is undertaken by all too human scientists. The process of eliminating bias from the scientific enterprise is an ongoing one. It will be the mark of "true" science if, 50 years from now, scientists can point to other varieties of prejudice and bias that have been reduced, to join the list of racism, sexism, homophobia, classism, ageism, and ethnocentrism. We all, scientists included, see the world through filters containing degrees of distortion. It is the professional and ethical responsibility of scientists and scholars to maintain an ongoing process of recognizing and reducing such distortions (for a thorough discussion of these issues, see Regal, 1990). There is little question that this is an exceptionally difficult undertaking. There is also little question that scientists and scholars are obliged to undertake it.

A second general theme is the striking degree to which homosexuals and heterosexuals are alike. This is not to say that differences do not exist. This volume has described differences in identity development, relationship patterns, and most certainly the social psychological forces and legal environment that impinge upon gay and lesbian individuals. Despite these, there is little that distinguishes homosexual from heterosexual people, particularly once the distortions of external oppression and its psychological aftermath are remedied. Relationship patterns, ability to rear children, psychological adjustment, functioning in the everyday world, and other areas suggest a level of difference between homosexual and heterosexual individuals that is unremarkable. A purely rational observer of our culture—like a Mr. Spock of *Star Trek*—might conclude that there has been much ado about almost nothing. But for those who study, document, or experience homophobic or any other bias, it can at times be the most central experience in the world.

Whatever exacerbates the divisions between the homosexual, bisexual, and heterosexual portions of humanity and further polarizes and stigmatizes these differences has no rational or scientific justification. Attempts to legitimize this divisiveness with a veneer of scientific respectability should be seen for the fraud they are. These rationalizations are not science but hatred dressed up to look respectable.

Cross-cultural research can lay bare and elucidate assumptions we did not know we were making and inform us about a more basic range of human behavior. In a similar manner, the study of sexual orientation lays bare what was not earlier articulated. Anne Peplau has documented how the study of gay, lesbian, and heterosexual couples challenges basic concepts of couples research. The attempts to develop a biological understanding of sexual identity shows similar promise. The process of identity development that gay men and lesbians experience as they attempt to form a stable and affirming psychological identity in an unpredictably oppressive world provides a model of how the individual and society interface, similar to innovative work in progress on the development of identity in racial/ethnic minority communities.

Finally, the value of multidisciplinary research and understandings is also apparent. A number of authors in this volume have documented the unprofessional, unscientific, and unethical behavior of illness model theoreticians and practitioners, whether from biology, psychiatry, psychology, or the religious right. Just as no one discipline has been free from prejudice regarding homosexuality, all the disciplines have positive contributions to offer. In this volume, authors from a diversity of perspectives have been true to their disciplines; both in understanding sexual orientation through that particular discipline's limited but uniquely informative framework, and in demonstrating the best of which it is capable. Should a volume like this be undertaken again in the future, I am confident that all the disciplines will have important and different things to say about sexual orientation, just as all will struggle with reducing bias in the exercise of that discipline.

Important conclusions can be drawn from the individual chapters in this volume.

Defining and measuring sexual orientation is a complex process, and becomes more so as understanding about sexual identity deepens. Such problems are common in the behavioral sciences. There is no doubt that there are large numbers of homosexual and bisexual persons in the population. Depending on the estimate used, gay and lesbian people are the first, second, or third largest minority group in the United States. While the prevalence of different sexual orientations is a legitimate scientific question, it is irrelevant in its public policy implications. The numerical size of a minority group does not form a legitimate basis for determining its rights.

Homosexuality is as biologically natural as heterosexuality, and homosexuality is not a biological error or aberration. There are few, if any, differences between homosexual and heterosexual people in adult hormones; the evidence is inconclusive regarding prenatal hormone levels, cognitive abilities, and observable physical and behavioral characteristics. Gay men and, to a lesser researched extent, lesbians respond on certain measures of psychological interest in ways that are intermediate between the modal patterns of heterosexual men and women. Sexual orientations are probably diverse within themselves, and are not likely due to a simple or single cause. These variations, however, do not constitute any handicap, anomaly, or deficit. Different societies, cultures, and historical periods have conceptualized and structured sexual orientation in radically different ways. Yet there are consistencies across geography and time to suggest that sexual orientation, or some factor like it, is not merely a culturally constructed artifact but an enduring aspect of humanity.

Sexual orientation is not related to mental illness or psychopathology; neither is there a gay or lesbian personality structure. The evidence to support this is substantial. Theories alleging that homosexuality is a mental illness are scientifically fraudulent. Homosexual people do, however, experience unique psychological stresses and appear to have an additional event in their psychological development as they integrate same-sex orientation into their identity within the context of a hostile and disparaging society. Some individuals experience temporary psychological disruption during this process. A few, typically those whose psychological problems predate sexual identity concerns, are overwhelmed by this challenge and develop self-destructive behaviors; but most emerge psychologically sound and function well. The challenge of integrating multiple disparaged identities renders this process especially complicated for racial/ethnic minority individuals.

Attempts to change sexual orientation are of questionable ethics and are clearly demonstrated as unsuccessful. Either is an adequate reason to discontinue such attempts; both together are impelling. Earlier change attempts were based on ignorance and bias; more recent attempts are part of ongoing political harassment in religious or scientific guise, preying on the most vulnerable gay and lesbian individuals. The mental health disciplines have an inglorious history of betraying their professions' ethical responsibilities in the service of enforcing societal prejudices, and continue to remain vulnerable to such unprofessional conduct.

There is significant violence and prejudice directed toward lesbians and gay men. These are mediated by psychological processes that distort information and create stereotypes. Like comparable myths, the stereotype that homosexual persons are prone to child abuse is without foundation. Legally, gay men and lesbians continue to be treated as second class citizens and are systematically denied justice. Attempts to remedy this have had some limited success. The formulation for this institutionalized bias is based not on sound legal principle but on quasi-religious and moralistic arguments.

Gay men and lesbians function in a parenting role as well as heterosexuals, and their children show no signs of adverse effects. Same-sex couples desire intimate relationships, and are as successful in creating them as opposite sex couples. Heterosexual and homosexual partnerships do not differ in degree of problems experienced, although types of problems encountered may differ across various dyads. There is no justification for viewing gay and lesbian couples as abnormal, nor do such couples adopt stereotyped roles.

The AIDS epidemic has exacerbated prejudice and violence. Gay men have been successful at initial behavior change attempts to reduce HIV transmission. However, many challenges remain in expanding the depth, breadth, longevity, and populations responsive to these changes. The most serious impediments to HIV infection prevention are political, not technical, although the legacy of sexist, racist, and classist based neglect in health care also seriously impedes efforts. The AIDS epidemic illustrates a chronic need to restructure the public health system in the United States. Research on partner notification programs is insufficient to determine efficacy, but such programs probably have a useful place in a network of public health efforts, provided that civil liberties, protection from intimidation and coercion, attention to timing, and sensitivity to psychosocial issues are observed.

I would like to conclude that the world will listen to our weighing of evidence concerning homosexuality and its public policy implications, take what we have said seriously, and make significant changes. A more realistic outcome may be that hatemongers of any persuasion will have a more difficult time distorting scientific information about sexual orientation to divide people from each other and nurture hatred.

As Rhonda Rivera notes in this volume, the *Bowers v. Hardwick* decision by the U.S. Supreme Court supported legitimized harassment of gay and lesbian citizens by allowing criminalization of same-sex sexual behavior to continue. The American Psychological Association filed an *amicus curiae* brief in this case (American Psychological Association, 1986) that drew extensively from the 1982 edition of this book. While the U.S. Supreme Court was not persuaded by the APA's brief or others that were submitted in support of the rights of gay and lesbian citizens, an important change did occur. The Supreme Court justices made their decision purely on religious and moralistic principles (see Rivera's discussion for detail). They did not, because they could not, support their position claiming that homosexuality is an illness. In so doing, the bigotry of their position was made more transparent. This book is offered to the readers by its authors in the hopes that similar gains will be realized.

References

Aaronson, B. S., & Grumpelt, H. R. (1961). Homosexuality and some MMPI measures of masculinity-femininity. *Journal of Clinical Psychology, 17,* 245-247.

Adam, B. D. (1978). *The survival of domination: Inferiorization and everyday life.* New York: Elsevier.

Adam, B. D. (1987). *The rise of a gay and lesbian movement.* Boston: Twayne.

Adelman, M. R. (1977). A comparison of professionally employed lesbians and heterosexual women on the MMPI. *Archives of Sexual Behavior, 6,* 193-201.

Adorno, T., Frenkel-Brunswik, E., Levinson, D. J., & Sanford, R. N. (1950). *The authoritarian personality.* New York: Harper & Row.

Akers, J. S., & Conaway, C. H. (1979). Female homosexual behavior in *Macaca mulatta. Archives of Sexual Behavior, 8,* 63-80.

Allen, P. G. (1984). Beloved women: The lesbian in American Indian culture. In T. Darty & S. Potter (Eds.), *Women-identified women* (pp. 83-96). Palo Alto, CA: Mayfield.

Allport, G. W. (1954). *The nature of prejudice.* Reading, MA: Addison-Wesley.

Altemeyer, B. (1988). *Enemies of freedom: Understanding right-wing authoritarianism.* San Francisco: Jossey-Bass.

Altman, D. (1982). *The homosexualization of America, the Americanization of the homosexual.* New York: St. Martin's.

Altman, D. (1986). *AIDS in the mind of America.* New York: Anchor/Doubleday.

Amaro, H. (1989). Considerations for prevention of HIV infection among Hispanic women. *Psychology of Women Quarterly, 12,* 429-444.

American Medical Association, Council on Ethical and Judicial Affairs. (1987). *Ethical issues involved in the growing AIDS crisis.* Chicago: American Medical Association.

American Psychiatric Association. (1942). *Statistical manual for the use of hospitals for mental diseases* (10th ed.). Committee on Statistics, American Psychiatric Association, in collaboration with the National Committee for Mental Hygiene. Utica: State Hospitals Press.

American Psychiatric Association. (1980). *Diagnostic and statistical manual of mental disorders* (3rd ed.) (rev. ed., 1987) Washington, DC: American Psychiatric Association.

American Psychological Association. (1975). Minutes of the Council of Representatives. *American Psychologist, 30,* 633.

American Psychological Association. (1986). *Amicus curiae* brief filed in U.S. Supreme Court case *Bowers v. Hardwick,* 478 U.S. 186.

American Psychological Association. (1990, July). Sullivan is criticized by APA over report. *APA Monitor,* p. 40.

American Public Health Association Special Initiative on AIDS. (1988). *Report number 2: Contact tracing and partner notification.* Washington, DC: American Public Health Association.

Amir, Y. (1969). Contact hypothesis in ethnic relations. *Psychological Bulletin, 71*(5), 319-342.

Anderson, C. L. (1981). The effect of a workshop on attitudes of female nursing students toward homosexuality. *Journal of Homosexuality, 7*(1), 57-69.

Anderson, C. L. (1982). Males as sexual assault victims: Multiple levels of trauma. *Journal of Homosexuality, 7,* 145-162.

Anderson, R. E., & Levy, J. A. (1985). Prevalence of antibodies to AIDS-associated retrovirus in single men in San Francisco. *Lancet, 1,* 217.

Anderson, S. C., & Henderson, D. C. (1985). Working with lesbian alcoholics. *Social Work, 31,* 518-525.

Aoki, B., Ngin, C. P., Mo, B., & Ja, D. Y. (1989). AIDS prevention models in Asian-American communities. In V. M. Mays, G. W. Albee, & S. F. Schneider (Eds.), *Primary prevention of AIDS: Psychological Approaches* (pp. 290-308). Newbury Park, CA: Sage.

Ashmore, R. D., & DelBoca, F. K. (1981). Conceptual approaches to stereotypes and stereotyping. In D. L. Hamilton (Ed.), *Cognitive processes in stereotyping and intergroup behavior* (pp. 1-35). Hillsdale, NJ: Lawrence Erlbaum.

Association of Medical Superintendents of American Institutions for the Insane. (1871). *Statistical Tables.* Harrisburg: T. F. Scheffer, printer.

Association of State and Territorial Health Officials, National Association of County Health Officials, and U.S. Conference of Local Health Officers. (1988). *Guide to public health practice: HIV partner notification strategies.* Washington, DC: Public Health Foundation.

Atkinson, D. R., Morten, G., & Sue, D. W. (1979). *Counseling American minorities.* Dubuque, IA: Brown.

Aura, J. (1985). *Women's social support: A comparison of lesbians and heterosexuals.* Unpublished doctoral dissertation, University of California, Los Angeles.

Bakeman, R., McCray, E., Lumb, J. R., Jackson, R. E., & Whitley, P. N. (1987). The incidence of AIDS among blacks and Hispanics. *Journal of the National Medical Association, 79,* 921-928.

Baker v. Wade, 106 Federal Rules Decisions 526 (N.D. Texas, 1985).

Baker, S. W., & Ehrhardt, A. A. (1974). Prenatal androgen, intelligence, and cognitive sex differences. In R. C. Friedman, R. M. Richart, & R. L. Vande Weile (Eds.), *Sex differences in behavior* (Chap. 4). New York: John Wiley & Sons.

Bakwin, H. (1968). Deviant gender-role behavior in children: Relation to homosexuality. *Pediatrics, 41,* 620-629.

Bandura, A. (1969). *Principles of behavior modification.* New York: Holt, Rinehart, & Winston.

Bard, M., & Sangrey, D. (1979). *The crime victim's book.* New York: Basic Books.

Barker-Benfield, B. (1975). Sexual surgery in nineteenth century America. *International Journal of Health Sciences, 2,* 279-298.

Barlow, D. H., Leitenberg, H., & Agras, W. S. (1969). Experimental control of sexual deviations through manipulation of the noxious scene in covert sensitization. *Journal of Abnormal Psychology, 74,* 596-601.

Barr, R. F., & Catts, S. V. (1974). Psychiatry opinion and homosexuality: A short report. *Journal of Homosexuality, 1,* 213-215.

Bartolomeo, N. (1990, April 6). Study: One in five gay men sometimes "slip" into unsafe sex. *Washington Blade, 21*(14), p. 6.

Baum, M. J., Carroll, R. S., Erskine, M. S., & Tobet, S. A. (1985). Neuroendocrine response to estrogen and sexual orientation. *Science, 230,* 960-961.

Bayer, R. (1981). *Homosexuality and American psychiatry.* New York: Basic Books.

Bayer, R. (1987). *Homosexuality and American psychiatry: The politics of diagnosis* (2nd ed.). Princeton, NJ: Princeton University Press.

Bayer, R., Levine, C., & Wolff, S. M. (1986). HIV antibody screening: An ethical framework for evaluating proposed programs. *Journal of the American Medical Association, 256,* 1768-1774.

Becker, M. H., & Joseph, J. G. (1988). AIDS and behavioral change to reduce risk: A review. *American Journal of Public Health, 78,* 394-409.

Begelman, D. A. (1975). Ethical and legal issues of behavior modification. In M. Hersen, R. Eisler, & P. M. Miller (Eds.), *Progress in behavior modification.* New York: Academic Press.

Begelman, D. A. (1977). Homosexuality and the ethics of behavioral intervention. *Journal of Homosexuality, 2*(3), 213-219.

Bell, A. (1972). Human sexuality—A response. *International Journal of Psychiatry, 10*, 99-102.

Bell, A. P., & Weinberg, M. S. (1978). *Homosexualities: A study of diversity among men and women.* New York: Simon & Schuster.

Bell, A. P., Weinberg, M. S., & Hammersmith, S. K. (1981). *Sexual preference: Its development in men and women.* Bloomington: Indiana University Press.

Bem, S. L. (1974). The measurement of psychological androgyny. *Journal of Consulting and Clinical Psychology, 42*, 155-162.

Bem, S. L. (1978). Beyond androgyny: Some presumptuous prescriptions for a liberated sexual identity. In J. A. Sherman & F. L. Denmark (Eds.), *The psychology of women: Future directions in research.* New York: Psychological Dimensions.

Bem, S. L. (1979). Theory and measurement of androgyny: A reply to the Pedhazur-Tetenbaum and Locksley-Colten critiques. *Journal of Personality and Social Psychology, 37*, 1047-1054.

Bem, S. L. (1981). The Bem sex role inventory. Palo Alto, CA: Consulting Psychologists Press.

Berdie, R. F. (1959). A femininity adjective check list. *Journal of Applied Psychology, 43*, 327-333.

Berg-Cross, L. (1988). Lesbians, family process and individuation. *Journal of College Student Psychotherapy, 3*, 97-112.

Bergler, E. (1956). *Homosexuality: Disease or way of life?* New York: Collier.

Berkey, B. R., Perelman-Hall, T., & Kurdek, L. A. (1990). The multidimensional scale of sexuality. *Journal of Homosexuality, 19*, 67-87.

Bernard, L. C., & Epstein, D. J. (1978a). Sex role conformity in homosexual and heterosexual males. *Journal of Personality Assessment, 42*, 505-511.

Bernard, L. C., & Epstein, D. J. (1978b). Androgyny scores of matched homosexual and heterosexual males. *Journal of Homosexuality, 4*, 169-178.

Berrill, K. T. (1989). *Anti-gay violence, victimization, and defamation in 1988.* Washington, DC: National Gay and Lesbian Task Force. [Available from NGLTF, 1517 U Street, NW, Washington, DC 20009]

Berrill, K. T. (1990). Anti-gay violence and victimization in the United States: An overview. *Journal of Interpersonal Violence, 5*(3), 274-294.

Berrill, K. T., & Herek, G. M. (1990). Primary and secondary victimization in anti-gay hate crimes: Official response and public policy. *Journal of Interpersonal Violence, 5*(3), 401-413.

Bérubé, A. (1990). *Coming out under fire: The history of gay men and women in World War II.* New York: Free Press.

Berzon, B. (1988). *Permanent partners: Building gay and lesbian relationships that last.* New York: Dutton.

Bieber, I., Dain, H. J., Dince, P. R., Drellich, M. G., Grand, H. G., Gundlach, R. H., Kremer, M. W., Rifkin, A. H., Wilbur, C. B., & Bieber, T. B. (1962). *Homosexuality: A psychoanalytic study.* New York: Basic Books.

Bierly, M. M. (1985). Prejudice toward contemporary outgroups as a generalized attitude. *Journal of Applied Social Psychology, 15*(2), 189-199.

Bigner, J. J., & Jacobsen, R. B. (1989a). Parenting behaviors of homosexual and heterosexual fathers. *Journal of Homosexuality, 18*(1, 2), 173-186.

Bigner, J. J., & Jacobsen, R. B. (1989b). The value of children to gay and straight fathers. *Journal of Homosexuality, 18*(1, 2), 163-172.

Birk, L. (1980). The myth of classical homosexuality: Views of a behavioral psychotherapist. In J. Marmor (Ed.), *Homosexual behavior: A modern reappraisal.* New York: Basic Books.

Birt, C. M., & Dion, K. L. (1987). Relative deprivation theory and responses to discrimination in a gay male and lesbian sample. *British Journal of Social Psychology, 26,* 139-145.

Blair, R. (1982). *Ex-Gay.* New York: Homosexual Counseling Center.

Blanchard, R., & Freund, K. (1983). Measuring masculine gender identity in females. *Journal of Consulting and Clinical Psychology, 51,* 205-214.

Blasband, D., & Peplau, L. A. (1985). Sexual exclusivity versus openness in gay male couples. *Archives of Sexual Behavior, 14*(5), 395-412.

Blendon, R. J., & Donelan, K. (1988). Discrimination against people with AIDS: The public's perspective. *New England Journal of Medicine, 319*(15), 1022-1026.

Blumstein, P., & Schwartz, P. (1983). *American couples: Money, work, sex.* New York: Morrow.

Bogoras, W. (1904-1909). The Chukchee. *Memoirs of the American Museum of Natural History, 11,* 1-732.

Boston Lesbian Psychologies Collective (Eds.). (1987). *Lesbian psychologies: Explorations and challenges.* Urbana: University of Illinois Press.

Boswell, J. E. (1980). *Christianity, social tolerance, and homosexuality: Gay people in Western Europe from the beginning of the Christian era to the fourteenth century.* Chicago: University of Chicago Press.

Boswell, J. (1982). Revolutions, universals, and sexual categories. *Salmagundi, 58-59,* 89-113.

Bouknight, R., & Bouknight, L. (1988). Acquired immunodeficiency syndrome in the black community: Focusing on education and the black male. *New York State Journal of Medicine, 88,* 638-641.

Bowers v. Hardwick, 106 S. Ct. 2841 (1986).

Bozett, F. W. (1979). Gay fathers: The convergence of a dichotemized identity through integrative sanctioning. *Dissertation Abstracts International, 40,* 2608-2609B. (University Microfilms No. 79-26,643).

Bozett, F. W. (1980). Gay fathers: How and why they disclose their homosexuality to their children. *Family Relations, 29*(2), 173-179.

Bozett, F. W. (1981a). Gay fathers: Evolution of the gay-father identity. *American Journal of Orthopsychiatry, 52*(3), 552-559.

Bozett, F. W. (1981b). Gay fathers: Identity conflict resolution through integrative sanctioning. *Alternative Lifestyles, 4*(1), 90-107.

Bozett, F. W. (1985). Gay men as fathers. In S. M. H. Hanson & F. W. Bozett (Eds.), *Dimensions of fatherhood* (pp. 327-352). Beverly Hills, CA: Sage.

Bozett, F. W. (1987). Gay fathers. In F. W. Bozett (Ed.), *Gay and lesbian parents* (pp. 3-22). New York: Praeger.

Bozett, F. W. (1988). Gay fatherhood. In P. Bronstein & C. P. Cowan (Eds.), *Fatherhood today: Men's changing role in the family* (pp. 214-235). New York: John Wiley.

Bozett, F. W. (1989). Fathers who are gay. In R. Kus (Ed.), *Helping your gay and lesbian client: A psychosocial approach from gay and lesbian perspectives.* Boston: Alyson.

Braaten, L. J., & Darling, C. D. (1965). Overt and covert homosexual problems among male college students. *Genetic Psychology Monographs, 71,* 269-270.

Brandt, A. M. (1985). *No magic bullet: A social history of venereal disease in the United States since 1880.* Oxford, UK: Oxford University Press.

Brandt, A. M. (1987). *No magic bullet: A social history of venereal disease in the United States since 1980* (rev. ed.). New York: Oxford University Press.

Brandt, A. M. (1988). AIDS in historical perspective: Four lessons from the history of sexually transmitted diseases. *American Journal of Public Health, 78,* 367-371.

Brewer, M. B., & Kramer, R. M. (1985). The psychology of intergroup attitudes and behavior. *Annual Review of Psychology, 36,* 219-243.

Brown, H. (1976). *Familiar faces, hidden lives.* New York: Harcourt Brace Jovanovich.

Brown, R. D., & Cole, J. K. (1985). Letter to the editor. *Nebraska Medical Journal, 70,* 410-414.

Brown, W. J., Donohue, J. F., Axnick, N. W., Blount, J. H., Ewen, N. H., & Jones, O. G. (1970). *Syphilis and other venereal disease.* Cambridge, MA: Harvard University Press.

Browning, C. (1987). Therapeutic issues and intervention strategies with young adult lesbian clients: A developmental approach. *Journal of Homosexuality, 14*(1, 2), 45-52.

Bruner, J. S., & Goodman, C. C. (1947). Value and need as organizing factors in perception. *Journal of Personality, 16,* 69-77.

Bryant, A. (1977). *The Anita Bryant story: The survival of our nation's families and the threat of militant homosexuality.* Old Tappan, NJ: Fleming H. Revell.

Brzek, A., & Hubalek, S. (1988). Homosexuals in Eastern Europe: Mental health and psychotherapy issues. *Journal of Homosexuality, 15*(1, 2), 153-162.

Buhrich, N., & Loke, C. (1988). Homosexuality, suicide and parasuicide in Australia. *Journal of Homosexuality, 15*(1, 2), 113-129.

Buhrich, N., & McConaghy, N. (1979). Tests of gender feelings and behavior in homosexuality, transvestism and transsexualism. *Journal of Clinical Psychology, 35,* 187-191.

Buie, J. (1990, March). "Heterosexual ethic" mentality is decried. *APA Monitor,* p. 20.

Bullough, V. L. (1974). Homosexuality and the medical model. *Journal of Homosexuality, 1,* 99-110.

Bullough, V. L. (1976). *Sexual variance in society and history.* Chicago: University of Chicago Press.

Burch, B. (1986). Psychotherapy and the dynamics of merger in lesbian couples. In T. Stein & C. Cohen (Eds.), *Contemporary perspectives on psychotherapy with lesbians and gay men* (pp. 57-73). New York: Plenum.

Burdick, J., & Stewart, D. (1974). Differences between "show" and "no-show" volunteers in a homosexual population. *Journal of Social Psychology, 92,* 159-160.

Burgess, R. L., & Huston, T. L. (Eds.). (1979). *Social exchange in developing relationships.* New York: Academic Press.

Burton, A. (1947). The use of the masculinity femininity scale of Minnesota Multiphasic Personality Inventory as an aid in the diagnosis of sexual inversion. *Journal of Psychology, 24,* 161-164.

Caldwell, M. A., & Peplau, L. A. (1984). The balance of power in lesbian relationships. *Sex Roles, 10,* 587-600.

Callender, C., & Kochems, L. M. (1983). The North American berdache. *Current Anthropology, 24,* 443-456.

Cameron, P. (1981). Social psychological aspects of the Judeo-Christian stance toward homosexuality. *Journal of Psychology and Theology, 9,* 40-57.

Cameron, P. (1985). Homosexual molestation of children / sexual interaction of teacher and pupil. *Psychological Reports, 57,* 1227-1236.

Cameron, P. (1986). AIDS in haemophiliacs and homosexuals. *Lancet, 1,* 36.

Cameron, P. (1988). Kinsey sex surveys. *Science, 240,* 867.

Cameron, P., Proctor, K., Coburn, W., Jr., & Forde, N. (1985). Sexual orientation and sexually transmitted disease. *Nebraska Medical Journal, 70,* 292-299.

Cameron, P., Proctor, K., Coburn, W., Jr., Forde, N., Larson, H., & Cameron, K. (1986). Child molestation and homosexuality. *Psychological Reports, 58,* 327-337.

Canadian AIDS Society. (1988, December). *Safer sex guidelines: A resource document for educators and counselors.* (Available from Canadian AIDS Society, Box 55, Station F, Toronto, Canada, M4Y 2L4.)

Caprio, F. S. (1954). *Female homosexuality: A modern study of lesbianism.* New York: Grove.

Caraballo-Diguez, A. (1989). Hispanic culture, gay male culture, and AIDS: Counseling implications. *Journal of Counseling and Development, 68,* 26-30.

Cardell, M., Finn, S., & Marecek, J. (1981). Sex-role identity, sex-role behavior, and satisfaction in heterosexual, lesbian, and gay male couples. *Psychology of Women Quarterly, 5*(3), 488-494.

Carl, D. (1986). Acquired immune deficiency syndrome: A preliminary examination of the effects on gay couples and coupling. *Journal of Marital and Family Therapy, 12*(3), 241-247.

Carlson, H. M., & Baxter, L. A. (1984). Androgyny, depression and self-esteem in Irish homosexual and heterosexual males and females. *Sex Roles, 10,* 457-467.

Carlson, H. M., & Steuer, J. (1985). Age, sex-role categorization and psychological health in American homosexual and heterosexual men and women. *Journal of Social Psychology, 125,* 203-211.

Carnes, P. (1983). *Out of the shadows: Understanding sexual addiction.* Minneapolis: CompCare Publications.

Carrier, J. M. (1976). Cultural factors affecting urban Mexican male homosexual behavior. *Archives of Sexual Behavior, 5,* 103-124.

Carrier, J. M. (1980). Homosexual behavior in cross-cultural perspective. In J. Marmor (Ed.), *Homosexual behavior: A modern reappraisal* (pp. 100-122). New York: Basic Books.

Carrier, J. M. (1986). Childhood cross-gender bahavior and adult homosexuality. *Archives of Sexual Behavior, 15,* 89-93.

Carrier, J. M. (1989). Gay liberation and coming out in Mexico. *Journal of Homosexuality, 17*(3, 4), 225-252.

Carson, G. (1957). Cornflake crusade. *American Heritage, 8,* 65-85.

Cass, V. C. (1979). Homosexual identity formation: A theoretical model. *Journal of Homosexuality, 4,* 219-236.

Cass, V. C. (1983-1984). Homosexual identity: A concept in need of a definition. *Journal of Homosexuality, 9,* 105-126.

Cass, V. C. (1984). Homosexual identity formation: Testing a theoretical model. *Journal of Sex Research, 20,* 143-167.

Cassens, B. J. (1985). Social consequences of the acquired immunodeficiency syndrome. *Annals of Internal Medicine, 103,* 768-771.

Catania, J. A., Coates, T. J., Kegeles, S. M., Edstrand, W., Guydisk, J. R., & Bye, L. L. (1989). Implications of the AIDS risk reduction model for the gay community: The importance of perceived sexual enjoyment and help seeking behaviors. In V. M. Mays, G. W. Albee, & S. F. Schneider (Eds.), *Primary prevention of AIDS: Psychological approaches* (pp. 242-261). Newbury Park, CA: Sage.

Cattell, R. B., & Morony, J. H. (1962). The use of the 16PF in distinguishing homosexuals, normals, and general criminals. *Journal of Consulting Psychology, 26,* 531-540.

Cautela, J. (1967). Covert sensitization. *Psychological Reports, 20,* 459-468.

Centers for Disease Control. (n.d.). *Announcement number 002, fiscal year 1990 HIV cooperative agreements.* Atlanta: Author.

Centers for Disease Control. (1988). Definition and model for partner notification, 1988. *Mortality and Morbidity Weekly Report, 37,* 393-396.

Centers for Disease Control. (1989). Guidelines for prophylaxis against *pneumocystis carinii* pneumonia for persons infected with human immunodeficiency virus. *Mortality and Morbidity Weekly Report, 38,* 1-9.

Centers for Disease Control. (1990). Publicly funded HIV counseling and testing—United States, 1985-1989. *Journal of the American Medical Association, 263*(14), 1901.

Cerny, J. A., & Polyson, J. (1984). Changing homonegative attitudes. *Journal of Social and Clinical Psychology, 2*(4), 366-371.

Chan, C. S. (1989). Issues of identity development among Asian-American lesbians and gay men. *Journal of Counseling and Development, 68,* 16-20.

Chang, J., & Block, J. (1960). A study of identification in male homosexuals. *Journal of Consulting Psychology, 24,* 307-310.

Chapman, B. E., & Brannock, J. C. (1987). A proposed model of lesbian identity development: An empirical investigation. *Journal of Homosexuality, 14*(3, 4), 69-80.

Chapman, L. J., & Chapman, J. P. (1969). Illusory correlation as an obstacle to the use of valid psychodiagnostic signs. *Journal of Abnormal Psychology, 74,* 271-280.

Chevalier-Skolnikoff, S. (1974). Male-female, female-female, and male-male sexual behavior in the stumptail monkey, with special attention to female orgasm. *Archives of Sexual Behavior, 3,* 95-116.

Chevalier-Skolnikoff, S. (1976). Homosexual behavior in a laboratory group of stumptail monkeys (*Macaca arctiodes*): Forms, contexts, and possible social functions. *Archives of Sexual Behavior, 5,* 511-527.

Christ, G., Wiener, L., & Moynihan, R. (1986). Psychological issues for AIDS patients. *Psychiatric Annals, 16,* 173-179.

Christie, D., & Young, M. (1986). Self-concept of lesbian and heterosexual women. *Psychological Reports, 59,* 1279-1282.

Churchill, W. (1967). *Homosexual behavior among males: A cross-cultural and cross-species investigation.* New York: Hawthorn.

Clark, T. R. (1975). Homosexuality and psychopathology in non-patient males. *American Journal of Psychoanalysis, 35,* 163-168.

Clarke, A. C. (1958, April). Standing room ONLY. *Harper's,* pp. 54-57.

Clarke, R. V. G. (1965). The Slater Selective Vocabulary Test and male homosexuality. *British Journal of Medical Psychology, 38,* 339-340.

Clingman, J., & Fowler, M. G. (1976). Gender roles and human sexuality. *Journal of Personality Assessment, 40,* 276-284.

Clunis, D. M., & Green, G. D. (1988). *Lesbian couples.* Seattle, WA: Seal Press.

Cochran, S. D. (1978, April). *Romantic relationships: For better or for worse.* Paper presented at the Western Psychological Association meeting, San Francisco.

Cochran, S. D. (1989). Women and HIV infection: Issues in prevention and behavior change. In V. M. Mays, G. W. Albee, & S. F. Schneider (Eds.), *Primary prevention of AIDS: Psychological approaches* (pp. 309-327). Newbury Park, CA: Sage.

Cochran, S. D., & Mays, V. M. (1988). Epidemiologic and sociocultural factors in the transmission of HIV infection in black gay and bisexual men. In M. Shernoff & W. Scott (Eds.), *The sourcebook on gay and lesbian health care* (2nd ed.) (pp. 202-211). Washington, DC: National Lesbian and Gay Health Foundation.

Cohen, G. (1989, October 31). Hate crimes bill stalled by Helms' opposition. *San Francisco Chronicle,* p. A10.

Cohen, J., Haver, L., Poole, L., & Wofsky, C. (1987, June). *Sexual and other practices and risk of HIV infection in a cohort of 450 sexually active women in San Francisco.* Paper presented at the Third International Conference on AIDS, Washington, DC.

Colasanto, D. (1989, October 25). Gay rights support has grown since 1982, Gallup poll finds. *San Francisco Chronicle,* p. A21.

Coleman, E. (1978). Toward a new model of treatment of homosexuality: A review. *Journal of Homosexuality, 3,* 345-359.

Coleman, E. (1982). Developmental stages of the coming-out process. In J. Gonsiorek (Ed.), *Homosexuality and psychotherapy: A practitioner's handbook of affirmative models* (pp. 31-44). New York: Haworth.

Coleman, E. (1987). *Psychotherapy with homosexual men and women: Integrated identity approaches for clinical practice.* New York: Haworth.

Congregation for the Doctrine of the Faith. (1986). *Letter to the bishops of the Catholic Church on the pastoral care of homosexual persons.* Vatican City: Author.

Conover, M. R., Miller, D. E., & Hunt, G. L., Jr. (1979). Female-female pairs and other unusual reproductive associations in ring-billed and California gulls. *The Auk, 96,* 6-9.

Conrad, S., & Wincze, J. (1976). Orgasmic reconditioning: A controlled study of its effects upon the sexual arousal and behavior of male homosexuals. *Behavior Therapy, 7,* 155-166.

Coppen, A. J. (1959). Body-build of male homosexuals. *British Medical Journal, 2,* 1443-1445.
Cory, D. W. (1951). *The homosexual in America.* New York: Greenberg.
Cotton, W. (1975). Social and sexual relationships of lesbians. *Journal of Sex Research, 11,* 148.
Craig, R. J. (1987). MMPI-derived prevalence estimates of homosexuality among drug-dependent patients. *International Journal of the Addictions, 22,* 1139-1145.
Cramer, D. (1986). Gay parents and their children: A review of research and practical implications. *Journal of Counseling and Development, 64,* 504-507.
Cramer, D. W., & Roach, A. S. (1988). Coming out to mom and dad: A study of gay males and their relationships with their parents. *Journal of Homosexuality, 15*(3, 4), 79-91.
Crenshaw, T. (1987, April). AIDS update: Condoms are not enough. *American Association of Sex Educators, Counselors and Therapists Newsletter,* pp. 20-22.
Cronbach, L. J., & Meehl, P. E. (1955). Construct validity in psychological tests. *Psychological Bulletin, 52,* 281-302.
Crosby, F., Bromley, S., & Saxe, L. (1980). Recent unobtrusive studies of black and white discrimination and prejudice: A literature review. *Psychological Bulletin, 87* 546-563.
Crystal, S. (1988, August). Contact notification and alternative policy options—practical, ethical and cost/benefit considerations. In E. Dejowski (Chair), AIDS, contact notification and public policy: A multi-disciplinary symposium. Symposium conducted at the annual convention of the American Psychological Association, Atlanta.
Crystal, S., Dengelegi, L., Back, P., & Dejowski, E. (1990). Aids contact notification: Initial program results in New Jersey. *Journal of AIDS Education and Prevention, 2,* 284-295.
Cubitt, G. H., & Gendreau, P. (1972). Assessing the diagnostic utility of MMPI and 16 PF indexes of homosexuality in a prison sample. *Journal of Consulting and Clinical Psychology, 39,* 342.
Curran, D., & Parr, D. (1957). Homosexuality: An analysis of 100 male cases. *British Medical Journal, 1,* 797-801.
Daher, D. (1981). The loss and search for the puer: A consideration of inferiority feelings in certain male adolescents. *Adolescence, 16,* 145-158.
Dahlstrom, W. G., Welsh, G. S., & Dahlstrom, L. E. (1973). *MMPI handbook: Vol. 1* (rev. ed.). Minneapolis: University of Minnesota Press.
Dailey, D. M. (1979). Adjustment of heterosexual and homosexual couples in pairing relationships: An exploratory study. *Journal of Sex Research, 15*(2), 143-157.
Dalton, K. (1979). Intelligence and prenatal progesterone: A reappraisal. *Royal Society of Medicine, 72,* 397-399.
Dank, B. M. (1971). Coming out in the gay world. *Psychiatry, 34,* 180-197.
Darke, R. A., & Geil, G. A. (1948). Homosexual activity: Relation of degree and role to the Goodenough Test and to the Cornell Selectee Index. *Journal of Nervous and Mental Disease, 108,* 217-240.
Darrow, W. W., Echenberg, D. F., Jaffe, H. W., O'Malley, P., Byers, R. H., Gebhard, S. P., & Curran, J. W. (1987). Risk factors for human immunodeficiency virus infection in homosexual men. *American Journal of Public Health, 77,* 479-483.
Darwin, C. R. (1975). *Charles Darwin's natural selection* (R. C. Stauffer, Ed.). Cambridge, UK: Cambridge University Press.
D'Augelli, A. R. (1987). Social support patterns of lesbian women in a rural helping network. *Journal of Rural Community Psychology, 8*(1), 12-21.
D'Augelli, A. R., & Hart, M. M. (1987). Gay women, men, and families in rural settings: Toward the development of helping communities. *American Journal of Community Psychology, 15*(1), 79-93.
Davison, G. C. (1968). Elimination of a sadistic fantasy by a client-controlled counterconditioning technique: A case study. *Journal of Abnormal Psychology, 73,* 84-90.
Davison, G. C. (1974). Homosexuality: The ethical challenge. Presidential address to the annual convention of the Association for Advancement of Behavior Therapy, Chicago.

Davison, G. C. (1976). Homosexuality: The ethical challenge. *Journal of Consulting and Clinical Psychology, 44*, 157-162.

Davison, G. C. (1978). Not "can" but "ought:" The treatment of homosexuality. *Journal of Consulting and Clinical Psychology, 46*(1), 170-172.

Davison, G. C. (1982). Politics, ethics, and therapy for homosexuality. *American Behavioral Scientist, 25*(4), 423-434.

Davison, G. C., & Friedman, S. (1981). Sexual orientation stereotypy in the distortion of clinical judgment. *Journal of Homosexuality, 6*, 37-44.

Davison, G. C., & Neale, J. M. (1990). *Abnormal psychology* (5th ed.). New York: John Wiley.

Dawkins, R. (1976). *The selfish gene.* New York: Oxford University Press.

De Cecco, J. P. (1981). Definition and meaning of sexual orientation. *Journal of Homosexuality, 6*(4), 51-67.

De Cecco, J. P. (1987). Homosexuality's brief recovery: From sickness to health and back again. *Journal of Sex Research, 23*, 106-114.

De Cecco, J. P. (Ed.). (1988). *Gay relationships* Binghamton, NY: Haworth.

De Cecco, J. P., & Shively, M. G. (1983/1984). From sexual identity to sexual relationships: A contextual shift. *Journal of Homosexuality, 9*(2, 3), 1-26.

Dean, R. B., & Richardson, H. (1964). Analysis of MMPI profiles of forty college-educated overt male homosexuals. *Journal of Consulting Psychology, 28*, 483-486.

Dean, R. B., & Richardson, H. (1966). On MMPI high-point codes of homosexual versus heterosexual males. *Journal of Consulting Psychology, 30*, 558-560.

Deaux, K., & Lewis, L. L. (1984). Structure of gender stereotypes: Interrelationships among components and gender label. *Journal of Personality and Social Psychology, 46*, 991-1004.

Deenen, A. (1986). *Homoseksuele identiteit in ontwikkeling* [The developing homosexual identity]. Unpublished doctoral dissertation, Catholic University of Nijmegen, The Netherlands.

Deenan, A., & Naerssen, A. X. van. (1988). Een onderzoek naar enkele aspecten van de homoseksuele identiteitsontwikkeling [An investigation into some aspects of the development of homosexual identity]. *Tijdschrift voor Seksuologie, 12*, 105-116.

Dejowski, E. F. (1989). Federal restrictions on AIDS prevention efforts for gay men. *St. Louis University Public Law Review, 8*, 275-298.

Dejowski, E. F. (1988, August). AIDS, contact notification, and public policy. In E. Dejowski, (Chair), AIDS, contact notification, and public policy: A multi-disciplinary symposium. Symposium conducted at the annual convention of the American Psychological Association, Atlanta.

D'Emilio, J. (1983). *Sexual politics, sexual communities: The making of a homosexual minority in the United States, 1940-1970.* Chicago: University of Chicago Press.

DeMonteflores, C., & Schultz, S. (1978). Coming out: Similarities and differences for lesbians and gay men. *Journal of Social Issues, 34*, 59-72.

Denniston, R. H. (1980). Ambisexuality in animals. In J. Marmor (Ed.), *Homosexual behavior: A modern reappraisal.* New York: Basic Books.

Devereux, G. (1937). Institutionalized homosexuality of the Mohave Indians. *Human Biology, 9*, 498-527. Reprinted in H. M. Ruitenbeek (Ed.), *The problem of homosexuality in modern society* (1963, pp. 183-226). New York: Dutton.

Devlin, P. K., & Cowan, G. A. (1985). Homophobia, perceived fathering, and male intimate relationships. *Journal of Personality Assessment, 49*, 467-473.

Dilley, J., Pies, S., & Helquist, M. (1989). *Face to face: A guide to AIDS counseling.* San Francisco: University of California AIDS Health Project.

Dion, K. L. (1986). Responses to perceived discrimination and relative deprivation. In J. M. Olson, C. P. Herman, & M. P. Zanna (Eds.), *Relative deprivation and social comparison: The Ontario Symposium, Vol. 4* (pp. 159-179). Hillsdale, NJ: Lawrence Erlbaum.

Dizick, M., & Bly, M. (1985). *Dogs are better than cats.* New York: Dolphin/Doubleday.

Doidge, W., & Holtzman, W. (1960). *Implications of homosexuality among Air Force trainees. Journal of Consulting Psychology, 24*, 9-13.

Dörner, G. (1976). *Hormones and brain differentiation.* Amsterdam: Elsevier.

Dörner, G. (1980). Sexual differentiation of the brain. *Vitamins and Hormones, 38*, 325-381.

Dörner, G. (1983). Letter to the editor. *Archives of Sexual Behavior, 12*, 577-582.

Dörner, G., Geirer, T., Ahrens, L., Krell, L., Munx, G., Kittner, E., & Muller, H. (1980). Prenatal stress as possible aetiogenic factor of homosexuality in human males. *Endokrinologie, 75*, 365-368.

Dörner, G., Gotz, F., Rohde, W., Stahl, F., & Tonjes, R. (1987). Sexual differentiation of gonadotrophin secretion, sexual orientation, and gender role behavior. *Journal of Steroid Biochemistry, 27*, 1081-1087.

Dörner, G., Rohde, W., Stahl, F., Krell, L., & Masius, W.-G. (1975). A neuroendocrine predisposition for homosexuality in men. *Archives of Sexual Behavior, 4*, 1-8.

Dörner, G., Schenk, B., Schmiedel, B., & Ahrens, L. (1983). Stressful events in prenatal life of bi- and homosexual men. *Experimental Clinical Endocrinology, 81*, 83-87.

Downey, J., Becker, J. V., Ehrhardt, A. A., Schiffman, M., Abel, G. G., & Dyrenfurth, I. (1982). Behavioral, psychophysiological, and hormonal correlates in lesbian and heterosexual women. In *Abstracts, International Academy of Sex Research,* Eighth annual meeting, Copenhagen, Denmark, August 21-26, p. 9.

Duffy, S. M., & Rusbult, C. E. (1986). Satisfaction and commitment in homosexual and heterosexual relationships. *Journal of Homosexuality, 12*(2), 1-24.

Dunne, J. R., and Serio, G. V. (1988). Confidentiality: An integral component of AIDS public policy. *St. Louis University Public Law Review, 7*, 25-34.

Dynes, W. R. (1987). *Homosexuality: A research guide.* New York: Garland.

Ehrhardt, A. A., Meyer-Bahlburg, H. F. L., Rosen, L. R., Feldman, J. F., Veridiano, N. P., Zimmerman, I., & McEwen, B. S. (1985). Sexual orientation after prenatal exposure to exogenous estrogen. *Archives of Sexual Behavior, 14*, 57-77.

Eisinger, A. (1972). Female homosexuality. *Nature, 238*, 106.

Ellis, H. (1922). *Studies in the psychology of sex: Vol. 2* (3rd ed.). Philadelphia: F. A. Davis.

Epstein, S. (1987). Gay politics, ethnic identity: The limits of social constructionism. *Socialist Review, 17*, 9-54.

Erikson, E. H. (1963). *Childhood and society* (2nd ed.). New York: Norton.

Erikson, E. H. (1980). *Identity and the life cycle.* New York: Norton.

Espin, O. M. (1987). Issues of identity in the psychology of Latina lesbians. In Boston Lesbian Psychologies Collective (Eds.), *Lesbian psychologies: Explorations and challenges* (pp. 35-51). Urbana: University of Illinois Press.

Ettore, E. M. (1980). *Lesbians, women, and society.* London: Routledge & Kegan Paul.

Evans, R. B. (1969). Childhood parental relationships of homosexual men. *Journal of Consulting and Clinical Psychology, 33*, 128-135.

Evans, R. B. (1970). Sixteen personality factor questionnaire scores of homosexual men. *Journal of Consulting and Clinical Psychology, 34*, 212-215.

Evans, R. B. (1971). Adjective check list scores of homosexual men. *Journal of Personality Assessment, 35*, 344-349.

Evans, R. B. (1972). Physical and biochemical characteristics of homosexual men. *Journal of Consulting and Clinical Psychology, 39*, 140-147.

Falbo, T., & Peplau, L. A. (1980). Power strategies in intimate relationships. *Journal of Personality and Social Psychology, 38*(4), 618-628.

Falk, P. (1989). Lesbian mothers: Psychosocial assumptions in family law. *American Psychologist, 44*, 941-947.

Fallows, J. (1980, February). The tests and the "brightest." *Atlantic,* pp. 37-48.

Family Research (1988, October-December). Newsletter of the Family Research Institute Inc. Washington, DC, 8 pp.

Farrell, R. A., & Morrione, T. J. (1974). Social interaction and stereotypic responses to homosexuals. *Archives of Sexual Behavior, 3*, 425-442.

Faustman, W. (1976). Aversive control of maladaptive sexual behavior: Past developments and future trends. *Psychology, 13*(4), 53-60.

Fay, R. E., Turner, C. F., Klassen, A. D., & Gagnon, J. H. (1989). Prevalence and patterns of same-gender sexual contact among men. *Science, 243*, 338-348.

Fehrs, L. J., Fleming, D., Foster, L. R., McAlister, R. O., Fox, V., Modesitt, S., & Conrad, R. (1988). Trial of anonymous versus confidential human immunodeficiency virus testing. *Lancet, 2*, 379-381.

Feldman, M. (1966). Aversion therapy for sexual deviation: A critical review. *Psychological Bulletin, 65*, 65-69.

Feldman, M., & MacCulloch, M. (1965). The application of anticipatory avoidance learning to the treatment of homosexuality: Theory, technique, and preliminary, results. *Behavior Research and Therapy, 2*, 165-183.

Feldman, M., & MacCulloch, M. J. (1971). *Homosexual behavior: Therapy and assessment.* New York: Pergamon.

Feldman, P. (1977). Helping homosexuals with problems: A commentary and a personal view. *Journal of Homosexuality, 2*, 241-250.

Fettner, A. G. (1985, September 23). The evil that men do. *New York Native*, pp. 23-24.

Field Institute, The. (1988, August 16). The California poll. Release Number 1459. San Francisco: Author.

Finegan, J.-A.K., Zucker, K. J., Bradley, S. J., & Doering, R. W. (1982). Patterns of intellectual functioning and spatial ability in boys with gender identity disorders. *Canadian Journal of Psychiatry, 27*, 135-139.

Finkelhor, D, (1986). *A sourcebook on child sexual abuse.* Newbury Park, CA: Sage.

Fischl, M. A., Dickinson, G. M., Scott, G. B., Klimas, N., Fletcher, M. A., & Parks, W. (1987). Evaluation of heterosexual partners, children, and household contacts of adults with AIDS. *Journal of the American Medical Association, 257*, 640-644.

Ford, C. S., & Beach, F. A. (1951). *Patterns of sexual behavior.* New York: Harper & Row.

Fordyce, W. E. (1966). *Behavior methods for chronic pain and illness.* St. Louis: C.V. Mosby.

Fordyce, W. E., Fowler, R. S., & DeLateur, B. J. (1968). An application of behavior modification technique to a problem of chronic pain. *Behavior Research and Therapy, 6*, 105-107.

Forstein, M. (1988). Homophobia: An overview. *Psychiatric Annals, 18*, 33-36.

Freedman, M. (1971). *Homosexuality and psychological functioning.* Belmont, CA: Brooks/Cole.

Freedman, M. (1975). Homosexuals may be healthier than straights. *Psychology Today, 8*(10), 28-32.

Freud, S. (1922). Some neurotic mechanisms in jealousy, paranoia and homosexuality. *Standard Edition, 18*, 223-232.

Freud, S. (1923). The ego and the id. *S.E., 19*, 3-66.

Freund, K. W. (1974). Male homosexuality: An analysis of the pattern. In J.A. Loraine (Ed.), *Understanding homosexuality: Its biological and psychological bases* (pp. 25-81). New York: Elsevier.

Freund, K. W. (1977). Should homosexuality arouse therapeutic concern? *Journal of Homosexuality, 2*, 235-240.

Freund, K. W., Langevin, R., Chamberlayne, R., Deosoran, A., Zajac, Y. (1974). The phobic theory of male homosexuality. *Archives of General Psychiatry, 31*, 495-499.

Freund, K., Langevin, R., Satterberg, J., & Steiner, B. (1977). Extension of the Gender Identity Scale for males. *Archives of Sexual Behavior, 6*, 507-519.

Freund, K., Nagler, E., Langevin, R., Zajac, A., & Steiner, B. (1974). Measuring feminine gender identity in homosexual males. *Archives of Sexual Behavior, 3*, 249-260.

Freund, K., Steiner, B. W., & Chan, S. (1982). Two types of cross-gender identity. *Archives of Sexual Behavior, 11,* 49-63.

Friberg, R. (1967). Measures of homosexuality: Cross-validation of 2 MMPI scales and implications for usage. *Journal of Consulting Psychology, 31,* 88-91.

Friedman, R. C. (1988). *Male homosexuality: A contemporary psychoanalytic perspective.* New Haven, CT: Yale University Press.

Friedman, R. C., & Stern, L. O. (1980). Juvenile aggressivity and sissiness in homosexual and heterosexual males. *Journal of the American Academy of Psychoanalysis, 8,* 427-440.

Frieze, I. H., Hymer, S., & Greenberg, M. S. (1984). Describing the victims of crimes and violence. In A. Kahn (Ed.), *Victims of crime and violence: Final report of the APA Task Force on the Victims of Crime and Violence* (pp. 19-78). Washington, DC: American Psychological Association.

Fromhart, M. V. (1971). Characteristics of male homosexual college students. *Journal of the American College Health Association, 19,* 247-252.

Fyfe, B. (1983). "Homophobia" or homosexual bias reconsidered. *Archives of Sexual Behavior, 12,* 549-554.

Gadpaille, W. J. (1972). Research into the physiology of maleness and femaleness: Its contributions to the etiology and psychodynamics of homosexuality. *Archives of General Psychiatry, 26,* 193-206.

Gagnon, J. H. (1987). Science and the politics of pathology. *Journal of Sex Research, 23,* 120-122.

Gagnon, J. H., & Simon, W. (1973). A conformity greater than deviance: The lesbian. In J. H. Gagnon & W. Simon (Eds.), *Sexual conduct: The social sources of human sexuality.* Chicago: Aldine.

Garnets, L., Herek, G. M., & Levy, B. (1990). Violence and victimization of lesbians and gay men: Mental health consequences. *Journal of Interpersonal Violence, 5*(3), 366-383.

Gay Law Students Association v. Pacific Telephone and Telegraph Company, Sup., 156 Cal. Rptr. 14 (1979).

Gebhard, P. H. (1972). Incidence of overt homosexuality in the United States and Western Europe. In J. J. Livingood (Ed.), *NIMH Task Force on Homosexuality: Final report and background papers* (DHEW publication No. (HSM) 72-9116). Rockville, MD: National Institute of Mental Health.

Gebhard, P. H., & Johnson, A. B. (1979). *The Kinsey data: Marginal tabulations of the 1938-1963 interviews conducted by the Institute for Sex Research.* Philadelphia: W. B. Saunders.

Geist, V. (1975). *Mountain sheep and man in the northern wilds.* Ithaca, NY: Cornell University Press.

Gentry, C. S. (1987). Social distance regarding male and female homosexuals. *Journal of Social Psychology, 127,* 199-208.

Gergen, K. J., & Gergen, M. M. (1981). *Social psychology.* New York: Harcourt Brace Jovanovich.

Gibbs, E. D. (1988). Psychosocial development of children raised by lesbian mothers: A review of research. *Women and Therapy, 8*(1, 2), 65-75.

Gibson, P. (1986, June). *Gay and lesbian youth suicide.* Paper presented at the American Educational Research Association, Oakland, CA.

Gilman, S. L. (1985). *Difference and pathology: Stereotypes of sexuality, race, and madness.* Ithaca, NY: Cornell University Press.

Gladue, B. A., Beatty, W. W., Larson, J., & Staton, R. D. (1990). Sexual orientation and spatial ability in men and women. *Psychobiology, 18,* 101-108.

Gladue, B. A., Green, R., & Hellmann, R. E. (1984). Neuroendocrine response to estrogen and sexual orientation. *Science, 225,* 1496-1499.

Glantz, K., & Pearce, J. K. (1989). *Exiles from Eden: Psychotherapy from an evolutionary perspective.* New York: Norton.

Gochros, H. (1988). Risk or abstinence: Sexual decision making in the AIDS era. *Social Work, 33*, 254-256.
Gock, T. S. (1985, August). *Psychotherapy with Asian/Pacific gay men: Psychological issues, treatment approach and therapeutic guidelines.* Paper presented at Asian American Psychological Association, Los Angeles, CA.
Goddard, H. H. (1917). Mental tests and the immigrant. *Journal of Delinquency, 2*, 243-277.
Goffman, E. (1963). *Stigma: Notes on the management of spoiled identity.* Englewood Cliffs, NJ: Prentice-Hall.
Goldberg, R. (1982). Attitude change among college students toward homosexuality. *Journal of American College Health, 30*(6), 260-268.
Golden, C. (1990, August). *Our politics and our choices: The feminist movement and sexual orientation.* Paper presented at the American Psychological Association, Boston.
Goldfoot, D. A., Westerborg-van Loon, H., Groeneveld, W., & Slob, A. K. (1980). Behavioral and physiological evidence of sexual climax in the female stump-tailed macaque (*Macaca arctoides*). *Science, 208*, 1477-1479.
Goldfried, M. R., & Davison, G. C. (1976). *Clinical behavior therapy.* New York: Holt, Rinehart & Winston.
Goldfried, M. R., Stricker, G., & Weiner, I. (1971). *Rorschach handbook of clinical and research applications.* Englewood Cliffs, NJ: Prentice-Hall.
Golumbok, S., Spencer, A., & Rutter, M. (1983). Children in lesbian and single-parent households: Psychosexual and psychiatric appraisal. *Journal of Child Psychology and Psychiatry, 24*, 551.
Gonsiorek, J. C. (1977). *Psychological adjustment and homosexuality.* Social and Behavioral Sciences Documents, MS 1478. San Raphael, CA: Select Press.
Gonsiorek, J. C. (1981). [Review of *Homosexuality in Perspective*]. *Journal of Homosexuality, 6*(3), 81-88.
Gonsiorek, J. C. (Ed.). (1982a). *Homosexuality and psychotherapy: A practitioner's handbook of affirmative models.* New York: Haworth.
Gonsiorek, J. C. (1982b). Results of psychological testing on homosexual populations. In W. Paul, J. D. Weinrich, J. C. Gonsiorek, & M. E. Hotvedt (Eds.), *Homosexuality: Social, psychological, and biological issues* (1st ed.). Beverly Hills, CA: Sage.
Gonsiorek, J. C. (1982c). The use of diagnostic concepts in working with gay and lesbian populations. In J. C. Gonsiorek (Ed.), *Homosexuality and psychotherapy: A practitioner's handbook of affirmative models* (pp. 9-20). New York: Haworth.
Gonsiorek, J. C. (Ed.). (1985). *A guide to psychotherapy with gay and lesbian clients.* New York: Harrington Park Press.
Gonsiorek, J. C. (1986). Psychotherapeutic issues in working with clients having AIDS related illnesses. In P. A. Keller & L. G. Ritt (Eds.), *Innovations in clinical practice: A source book* (Vol. 5, pp. 221-230). Sarasota, FL: Professional Resource Exchange.
Gonsiorek, J. C. (1988). Mental health issues of gay and lesbian adolescents. *Journal of Adolescent Health Care, 9*, 114-122.
Goode, E. (1981). Comments on the homosexual role. *Journal of Sex Research, 17*, 54-65.
Gough, H. G. (1952). Identifying psychological femininity. *Educational Psychology Measurement, 12*, 427-439.
Gough, H. G. (1966). A cross-cultural analysis of the CPI Femininity Scale. *Journal of Consulting Psychology, 30*, 136-141.
Grace, J. (1977, November). *Gay despair and the loss of adolescence.* Paper presented at the fifth biennial professional symposium of the National Association of Social Workers, San Diego, CA.
Grace, J. (1979, November). *Coming out alive.* Paper presented at the sixth biennial professional symposium of the National Association of Social Workers, San Antonio, TX.

Gramick, J. (1984). Developing a lesbian identity. In T. Darty & S. Potter (Eds.), *Women identified women* (pp. 31-44). Palo Alto, CA: Mayfield.

Gramlich, T., Nicholson, T., Price, J., Wilson, R., & Belcastro, P. (1989, November). *Children raised by homosexual parents: Sexual orientation, mental and sexual health.* Paper presented at the meeting of the Society for the Scientific Study of Sex, Toronto.

Green, R. (1976). One-hundred ten feminine and masculine boys: Behavioral contrasts and demographic similarities. *Archives of Sexual Behavior, 5,* 425-446.

Green, R. (1978). Sexual identity of 37 children raised by homosexual or transsexual parents. *American Journal of Psychiatry, 135,* 692-697.

Green, R. (1979). Childhood cross-gender behavior and subsequent sexual preference. *American Journal of Psychiatry, 136,* 106-108.

Green, R. (1982). The best interests of the child with a lesbian mother. *Bulletin of the American Academy of Psychiatry and the Law, 10,* 7-15.

Green, R. (1985). Gender identity in childhood and later sexual orientation: Followup of 78 males. *American Journal of Psychiatry, 142,* 339-341.

Green, R. (1987). *The "sissy boy syndrome" and the development of homosexuality.* New Haven, CT: Yale University Press.

Green, R. (1988). The immutability of (homo)sexual orientation: Behavioral science implications for a constitutional (legal) analysis. *Journal of Psychiatry & Law, 16,* 537.

Green, R., Mandel, J. B., Hotvedt, M. E., Gray, J., & Smith, L. (1986). Lesbian mothers and their children: A comparison with solo parent heterosexual mothers and their children. *Archives of Sexual Behavior, 15,* 167-184.

Green, R., & Money, J. (Eds.). (1969). *Transsexualism and sex reassignment.* Baltimore, MD: Johns Hopkins University Press.

Green, R., Roberts, C. W., Williams, K., Goodman, M., & Mixon, A. (1987). Specific cross-gender behavior in boyhood and later homosexual orientation. *British Journal of Psychiatry, 151,* 84-88.

Greene, A. G. (1984). The self psychology of Heinz Kohut: A synopsis and critique. *Bulletin of the Menninger Clinic, 48*(11), 37-53.

Greene, B. A. (1986). When the therapist is white and the patient is black: Considerations for psychotherapy in the feminist heterosexual and lesbian communities. *Women and Therapy, 5,* 41-65.

Grellert, E. A., Newcomb, M. D., & Bentler, P. M. (1982). Childhood play activities of male and female homosexuals and heterosexuals. *Archives of Sexual Behavior, 11,* 451-478.

Griffin, D. R. (1976). *The question of animal awareness.* New York: Rockefeller University Press.

Griffiths, P. D., Merry, J., Browning, M. C. K., Eisinger, A. J., Huntsman, R. G., Lord, E. J. A., Polani, P. E., Tanner, J. M., & Whitehouse, R. H. (1974). Homosexual women: An endocrine and psychological study. *Journal of Endocrinology, 63,* 549-556.

Gross, A. E., Green, S. K., Storck, J. T., & Vanyur, J. M. (1980). Disclosure of sexual orientation and impressions of male and female homosexuals. *Personality and Social Psychology Bulletin, 6,* 307-314.

Gross, L., Aurand, S. K., & Addessa, R. (1988). *Violence and discrimination against lesbian and gay people in Philadelphia and the Commonwealth of Pennsylvania.* Philadelphia: Philadelphia Lesbian and Gay Task Force. [Available from the Task Force, 1501 Cherry Street, Philadelphia, PA 19102]

Groth, A. N., & Birnbaum, H. J. (1978). Adult sexual orientation and attraction to underage persons. *Archives of Sexual Behavior, 7*(3), 175-181.

Groves, P. (1985). Coming out: Issues for the therapist working with women in the process of lesbian identity formation. *Women and Therapy, 4,* 17-22.

Guilford, J. P., Guilford, J. S., & Zimmerman, W. S. (1978). The Guilford-Zimmerman Temperament Survey: Directions for administering, scoring, and interpreting. Orange, NJ: Sheridan Psychological Services.

Gundlach, H. (1967, July). Research project report: Descriptive data about lesbian and non-lesbian respondents. *The Ladder: A Lesbian Review*, 2-9.

Gurwitz, S. B., & Marcus, M. (1978). Effects of anticipated interaction, sex, and homosexual stereotypes on first impressions. *Journal of Applied Social Psychology, 8*, 47-56.

Hacker, H. M. (1971). Homosexuals: Deviant or minority group? In E. Sagarin (Ed.), *The other minorities* (pp. 65-92). Waltham, MA: Ginn.

Hadden, S. (1966). Treatment of male homosexuals in groups. *International Journal of Group Psychotherapy, 16*, 13-22.

Hall, M. (1987). Sex therapy with lesbian couples: A four stage approach. In E. Coleman (Ed.), *Psychotherapy with homosexual men and women: Integrated identity approaches for clinical practice* (pp. 137-156). New York: Haworth.

Halleck, S. L. (1971). *The politics of therapy.* New York: Science House.

Hamilton, D. L. (Ed.). (1981). *Cognitive processes in stereotyping and intergroup behavior.* Hillsdale, NJ: Lawrence Erlbaum.

Hamilton, W. D. (1972). Altruism and related phenomena, mainly in social insects. *Annual Review of Ecology and Systematics, 3*, 193-232.

Hammersmith, S. K., & Weinberg, M. S. (1973). Homosexual identity: Commitment, adjustment and significant others. *Sociometry, 36*, 56-79.

Handsfield, H. H., Sandstrom, E. G., Knapp, J. S., Perine, P. L., Whittington, W. H., Sayers, D. E., & Holmes, K. K. (1982). Epidemiology of penicillinase-producing *neisseria gonorrhoeae* infections: Analysis by auxotyping and serogrouping. *New England Journal of Medicine, 306*, 950-954.

Harris, M. B., & Turner, P. H. (1985-1986). Gay and lesbian parents. *Journal of Homosexuality, 12*(2), 101-113.

Harry, J. (1982). Decision making and age differences among gay male couples. *Journal of Homosexuality, 8*(2), 9-22.

Harry, J. (1983a). Defeminization and adult psychological well-being among male homosexuals. *Archives of Sexual Behavior, 12*, 1-19.

Harry, J. (1983b). Parasuicide, gender and gender deviance. *Journal of Health & Social Behavior, 24*, 350-361.

Harry, J. (1983c). Gay male and lesbian relationships. In E. Macklin & R. Rubin (Eds.), *Contemporary families and alternative lifestyles: Handbook on research and theory* (pp. 216-234). Beverly Hills, CA: Sage.

Harry, J. (1984). *Gay couples.* New York: Praeger.

Harry, J., & DeVall, W. B. (1978). *The Social Organization of Gay Males.* New York: Praeger.

Harry, J., & Lovely, R. (1979). Gay marriages and communities of sexual orientation. *Alternative Lifestyles, 2*(2), 177-200.

Hart, M., Roback, H., Tittler, B., Weitz, L., Walston, B., & McKee, E. (1978). Psychological adjustment of nonpatient homosexuals: Critical review of the research literature. *Journal of Clinical Psychiatry, 39*, 604-608.

Hartman, B. (1967). Comparison of selected experimental MMPI profiles of sexual deviates and sociopaths without sexual deviation. *Psychological Reports, 20*, 234.

Hassell, J., & Smith, E. W. (1975). Female homosexuals' concepts of self, men and women. *Journal of Personality Assessment, 39*, 154-159.

Hatfield, L. (1989, June 5). Method of polling. *San Francisco Examiner*, p. A20.

Hatterer, L. (1970). *Changing homosexuality in the male.* New York: McGraw-Hill.

Hay, H. (1980, July 5). *Towards the new frontiers of fairy vision . . . subject-subject consciousness.* Unpublished manuscript, Los Angeles, 11 pp.

Heilbrun, A. B. (1976). Measurement of masculine and feminine sex role identities as independent dimensions. *Journal of Consulting and Clinical Psychology, 44*, 183-190.

Hencken, J. D. (1982). Homosexuality and psychoanalysis: Toward a mutual understanding. In W. Paul, J. D. Weinrich, J. C. Gonsiorek, & M. E. Hotvedt (Eds.), *Homosexuality: Social, psychological and biological issues.* Beverly Hills, CA: Sage.

Hencken, J. D., & O'Dowd, W. T. (1977). Coming out as an aspect of identity formation. *Gay Academic Union Journal: Gai Saber, 1*, 18-22.

Henderson, A. I. (1984). Homosexuality in college years: Developmental differences between men and women. *Journal of American College Health, 32*, 216-219.

Henley, N. M., & Pincus, F. (1978). Interrelationships of sexist, racist, and antihomosexual attitudes. *Psychological Reports, 42*, 83-90.

Henry, G. W. (1948). *Sex variants: A study of homosexual patterns.* New York: Paul B. Hoeber.

Herdt, G. H. (1981). *Guardians of the flutes: Idioms of masculinity.* New York: McGraw-Hill.

Herek, G. M. (1984a). Beyond "homophobia": A social psychological perspective on attitudes toward lesbians and gay men. *Journal of Homosexuality, 10*, (1/2) 1-21.

Herek, G. M. (1984b). Attitudes toward lesbians and gay men: A factor analytic study. *Journal of Homosexuality, 10*, (1/2) 2-17.

Herek, G. M. (1986a). The instrumentality of attitudes: Toward a neofunctional theory. *Journal of Social Issues, 42*(2), 99-114.

Herek, G. M. (1986b). On heterosexual masculinity: Some psychical consequences of the social construction of gender and sexuality. *American Behavioral Scientist, 29*(5), 563-577.

Herek, G. M. (1986c). The social psychology of homophobia: Toward a practical theory. *NYU Review of Law & Social Change, 14*(4), 923-934.

Herek, G. M. (1987a). Religion and prejudice: A comparison of racial and sexual attitudes. *Personality and Social Psychology Bulletin, 13*(1), 56-65.

Herek, G. M. (1987b). Can functions be measured? A new perspective on the functional approach to attitudes. *Social Psychology Quarterly, 50*(4), 285-303.

Herek, G. M. (1988). Heterosexuals' attitudes toward lesbians and gay men: Correlates and gender differences. *Journal of Sex Research, 25*(4), 451-477.

Herek, G. M. (1989). Hate crimes against lesbians and gay men: Issues for research and policy. *American Psychologist, 44*(6), 948-955.

Herek, G. M. (1990a). The context of antigay violence: Notes on cultural and psychological heterosexism. *Journal of Interpersonal Violence, 5*(3), 316-333.

Herek, G. M. (1990b). Illness, stigma, and AIDS. In P. Costa, Jr., & G. R. VandenBos (Eds.), *Psychological aspects of serious illness: Chronic conditions, fatal diseases, and clinical care* (pp. 103-150). Washington, DC: American Psychological Association.

Herek, G. M. (1990c). Gay people and government security clearances: A social perspective. *American Psychologist, 45*, 1035-1042.

Herek, G. M., & Berrill, K. T. (Eds.). (1990). Violence against lesbians and gay men: Issues for research, practice, and policy [Special issue]. *Journal of Interpersonal Violence, 5*(3).

Herek, G. M., & Glunt, E. K. (1988). An epidemic of stigma: Public reactions to AIDS. *American Psychologist, 43*(11), 886-891.

Herek, G. M., & Glunt, E. K. (1990). Public reactions to AIDS in the United States. In preparation.

Hetrick, E., & Martin, A. D. (1987a). Developmental issues and their resolution for gay and lesbian adolescents. In E. Coleman (Ed.), *Psychotherapy with homosexual men and women: Integrated identity approaches for clinical practice.* (pp. 25-44). New York: Haworth.

Hetrick, E., & Martin, A. D. (1987b). Developmental issues and their resolution for gay and lesbian adolescents. *Journal of Homosexuality, 14*(1, 2), 25-43.

Hetrick, E., & Stein, T. (Eds.). (1984). *Innovations in psychotherapy with homosexuals.* Washington, DC: American Psychiatric Association Press.
Hidalgo, H. (1984). The Puerto Rican lesbian in the United States. In T. Darty & S. Potter (Eds.), *Women-identified women* (pp. 105-115). Palo Alto, CA: Mayfield.
Hidalgo, H. A., & Christensen, E. H. (1976-1977). The Puerto Rican lesbian and the Puerto Rican community. *Journal of Homosexuality, 2,* 109-121.
Hippler, M. (1989). *Matlovich: The good soldier.* Boston: Alyson.
Hirschfield, M. (1936). The homosexual as an intersex. In V. Robinson (Ed.), *Encyclopaedia Sexualis.* New York: Dingwall-Rock.
Hockenberry, S. L., & Billingham, R. E. (1987). Sexual orientation and boyhood gender conformity: Development of the Boyhood Gender Conformity Scale (BGCS). *Archives of Sexual Behavior, 16,* 475-492.
Hoeffer, B. (1981). Children's acquisition of sex-role behavior in lesbian-mother families. *American Journal of Orthopsychiatry, 51,* 536-544.
Holeman, R. E., & Winokur, G. (1965). Effeminate homosexuality: A disease of childhood. *American Journal of Orthopsychiatry, 35,* 48-56.
Hooberman, R. E. (1979). Psychological androgyny, feminine gender identity and self-esteem in homosexual and heterosexual males. *Journal of Sex Research, 15,* 306-315.
Hood, R. W., Jr. (1973). Dogmatism and opinions about mental illness. *Psychological Reports, 32,* 1283-1290.
Hooker, E. A. (1957). The adjustment of the male overt homosexual. *Journal of Projective Techniques, 21,* 17-31.
Hopkins, J. (1969). The lesbian personality. *British Journal of Psychiatry, 115,* 1433-1436.
Horstman, W. R. (1972). Homosexuality and psychopathology: A study of the MMPI responses of homosexual and heterosexual male college students. *Dissertation Abstracts International, 33,* 2347B.
Horstman, W. R. (1975). MMPI responses of homosexual and heterosexual male college students. *Homosexual Counseling Journal, 2,* 68-76.
Hotvedt, M., & Mandel, G. L. (1982). Children of lesbian mothers. In W. Paul, J. D. Weinrich, J. C. Gonsiorek, & M. E. Hotredt, (Eds.), *Homosexuality: Social, psychological and biological issues* (pp. 275-285). Beverly Hills, CA: Sage.
Howard, J. A., Blumstein, P., & Schwartz, P. (1986). Sex, power, and influence tactics in intimate relationships. *Journal of Personality and Social Psychology, 51*(1), 102-109.
Howard, J. A., Blumstein, P., & Schwartz, P. (1987). Social or evolutionary theories? Some observances on preferences in human mate selection. *Journal of Personality and Social Psychology, 53*(1), 194-200.
Hrdy, S. B. (1975). *Male and female strategies of reproduction among the langurs of Abu.* Unpublished doctoral dissertation, Harvard University, Cambridge, MA.
Hudson, W. W., & Ricketts, W. A. (1980). A strategy for the measurement of homophobia. *Journal of Homosexuality, 5*(4), 357-372.
Huggins, S. L. (1989). A comparative study of self-esteem of adolescent children of divorced lesbian mothers and divorced heterosexual mothers. *Journal of Homosexuality, 18*(1, 2), 123-136.
Humphreys, L. (1972). *Out of the closets: The sociology of homosexual liberation.* Englewood Cliffs, NJ: Prentice-Hall.
Hunt, G. L., Jr., & Hunt, M. W. (1977). Female-female pairing in western gulls (*Larus occidentalis*) in southern California. *Science, 196,* 1466-1467.
Hunt, M. (1974). *Sexual behavior in the 1970s.* Chicago: Playboy Press.
Hunter, N. D., & Polikoff, N. D. (1976). Custody rights of lesbian mothers: Legal theory and litigation strategy. *Buffalo Law Review, 25,* 691-733.
Hutchinson, G. E. (1959). A speculative consideration of certain possible forms of sexual selection in man. *American Naturalist, 93,* 81-91.

Icard, L. (1985-1986). Black gay men and conflicting social identities: Sexual orientation versus racial identity. *Journal of Social Work and Human Sexuality, 4*(1-2), 83-93.

Icard, L. (1986). Black gay men and conflicting social identities: Sexual orientation versus racial identity. In J. Gripton & M. Valentich (Eds.), *Social work practice in sexual problems* (pp. 83-93) [Special issue of the *Journal of Social Work & Human Sexuality, 4*(1-2)]. New York, London: Haworth.

Icard, L., & Traunstein, D. M. (1987). Black gay alcoholic men: Their character and treatment. *Social Casework: The Journal of Contemporary Social Work, 68*, 267-272.

Ince, L. P. (1976). *Behavior modification in rehabilitation medicine.* Springfield, IL: Charles C Thomas.

Institute of Medicine. (1988). *The future of public health.* Washington, DC: National Academy Press.

Isay, R. A. (1985). On the analytic therapy of homosexual men. In A. J. Solnit, R. S. Eissler, & P. B. Neubauer (Eds.), *The psychoanalytic study of the child* (Vol. 40, pp. 235-254). New Haven: Yale University Press.

Isay, R. A. (1987). Fathers and their homosexually inclined sons in childhood. *The Psychoanalytic Study of the Child, 42*, 275-294.

Isay, R. A. (1989). *Being homosexual: Gay men and their development.* New York: Farrar, Straus, & Giroux.

Jackson, P. A. (1989). *Male homosexuality in Thailand: An interpretation of contemporary Thai sources.* Elmhurst, NY: Global Academic Publishers.

Jacobs, J. A., & Tedford, W. H. (1980). Factors affecting self-esteem of the homosexual individual. *Journal of Homosexuality, 5*, 373-382.

Jacobs, S. (1983). Comments. *Current Anthropology, 24*, 459-460.

Jaffe, H. W., Darrow, W. W., Echenberg, D. F., O'Malley, P. M., Getchell, J. P., Kalyanaram, V. S., Byers, R. H., Drennan, D. P., Braff, E. H., Gurran, J. N., & Francis, D. P. (1985). The acquired immunodeficiency syndrome in a cohort of homosexual men. *Annals of Internal Medicine, 103*, 210-214.

Janis, I. L., & Mann, L. (1977). *Decision making.* New York: Free Press.

Janoff-Bulman, R. (1979). Characterological versus behavioral self-blame: Inquiries into depression and rape. *Journal of Personality and Social Psychology, 37*, 1798-1809.

Janoff-Bulman, R., & Frieze, I. H. (Eds.). (1983). Reactions to victimization [Special issue]. *Journal of Social Issues, 39*(2).

Jay, K., & Young, A. (1977). *The gay report: Lesbians and gay men speak out about sexual experiences and lifestyles.* New York: Summit Books.

Johnson, R. L., & Shrier, D. (1987). Past sexual victimization by females of male patients in an adolescent medicine clinic population. *American Journal of Psychiatry, 144*, 650-652.

Johnson, W. D., Sy, F. S., & Jackson, K. L. (1988, June). *The impact of mandatory reporting of HIV seropositive persons in North Carolina.* Paper presented to the Fourth International Conference on AIDS, Stockholm, Sweden.

Jones, E. E., Farina, A., Hastorf, A. H., Markus, H., Miller, D. T., & Scott, R. A. (1984). *Social stigma: The psychology of marked relationships.* New York: W. H. Freeman.

Jones, R. W., & Bates, J. E. (1978). Satisfaction in male homosexual couples. *Journal of Homosexuality, 3*(3), 217-224.

Jones, S. L., & Workman, D. E. (1989). Homosexuality: The behavioral sciences and the church. *Journal of Psychology and Theology, 17*, 213-225.

Judson, F. N., & Vernon, T. M. (1988). The impact of AIDS on state and local health departments: Issues and a few answers. *American Journal of Public Health, 78*, 387-393.

Kahneman, D., Slovic, P., & Tversky, A. (Eds.). (1982). *Judgment under uncertainty: Heuristics and biases.* Cambridge, UK: Cambridge University Press.

Kameny, F. E. (1971). Homosexuals as a minority group. In E. Sagarin (Ed.), *The other minorities* (pp. 50-65). Waltham, MA: Ginn.

Karr, R. (1978). Homosexual labeling and the male role. *Journal of Social Issues, 34*(3), 73-83.

Katchadourian, H. A. (Ed.). (1979). *Human sexuality: A comparative and developmental perspective.* Berkeley: University of California Press.

Katz, D., Sarnoff, I., & McClintock, C. (1956). Ego-defense and attitude change. *Human Relations, 9,* 27-45.

Katz, J. N. (1983). *Gay/lesbian almanac: A new documentary.* New York: Harper & Row.

Kelley, H. H., Berscheid, E., Christensen, A., Harvey, J. H., Huston, T. L., Levinger, G., McClintock, E., Peplau, L. A., & Peterson, D. R. (1983). *Close relationships.* New York: W. H. Freeman.

Kelley, H. H., & Thibaut, J. W. (1978). *Interpersonal relations: A theory of interdependence.* New York: Wiley-Interscience.

Kelley, K. (1978, May). Playboy interview: Anita Bryant. *Playboy, 25*(5), 73-250.

Kelly, J. A., St. Lawrence, J. S., Hood, H., & Brasfield, T. (1989). Behavioral intervention to reduce AIDS risk activities. *Journal of Consulting and Clinical Psychology, 57,* 60-67.

Kennedy, H. C. (1980/1981). The "third sex" theory of Karl Heinrich Ulrichs. *Journal of Homosexuality, 6,* 103-111.

Kenyon, F. E. (1968). Physique and physical health of female homosexuals. *Journal of Neurology and Neurosurgical Psychiatry, 31,* 487-489.

Kenyon, F. (1968). Studies in female homosexuality: Psychological test results. *Journal of Consulting and Clinical Psychology, 32,* 510-513.

Kiernan, J. G. (1884). Insanity: Lecture XXVI—Sexual perversion. *Detroit Lancet, 7,* 481-484.

Kimmel, D. C. (1978). Adult development and aging: A gay perspective. *Journal of Social Issues, 34,* 113-130.

Kinsey, A. C., Pomeroy, W. B., & Martin, C. E. (1948). *Sexual behavior in the human male.* Philadelphia: W. B. Saunders.

Kinsey, A. C., Pomeroy, W. B., Martin, C. E., & Gebhard, P. H. (1953). *Sexual behavior in the human female.* Philadelphia: W. B. Saunders.

Kirkpatrick, M. (1987a). Clinical implications of lesbian mother studies. In E. Coleman (Ed.), *Psychotherapy with homosexual men and women: Integrated identity approaches for clinical practice* (pp. 201-212). New York: Haworth.

Kirkpatrick, M. (1987b). Clinical implications of lesbian mother studies. *Journal of Homosexuality, 14*(1, 2), 201-212.

Kirkpatrick, M., Smith, C., & Roy, R. (1981). Lesbian mothers and their children. *American Journal of Orthopsychiatry, 51,* 545-551.

Kirsch, J.A.W., & Rodman, J. E. (1977). The natural history of homosexuality. *Yale Scientific, 51,* (3), 7-13.

Kite, M. E. (1984). Sex differences in attitudes toward homosexuals: A meta-analytic review. *Journal of Homosexuality, 10* (1/2), 69-81.

Kite, M. E., & Deaux, K. (1986). Attitudes toward homosexuality: Assessment and behavioral consequences. *Basic and Applied Social Psychology, 7*(2), 137-162.

Kite, M. E., & Deaux, K. (1987). Gender belief systems: Homosexuality and the implicit inversion theory. *Psychology of Women Quarterly, 11*(1), 83-96.

Kitzinger, C. (1987). *The social construction of lesbianism.* London: Sage.

Klassen, A. D., Williams, C. J., & Levitt, E. E. (1989). *Sex and morality in the U.S.* Middletown, CT: Wesleyan University Press.

Klein, F., Sepekoff, B., & Wolf, T. (1985). Sexual orientation: A multi-variable dynamic process. *Journal of Homosexuality, 12,* 35-49.

Knight, R. (1983). Female homosexuality and the custody of children. *New Zealand Journal of Psychology, 12*(1), 23-27.

Knutson, D. C. (Ed.) (1980). *Homosexuality and the law.* New York: Haworth.

Kohut, H. (1971). *The analysis of the self.* New York: International Universities Press.

Kohut, H. (1977). *The restoration of the self.* New York: International Universities Press.

Kohut, H. (1984). *How does analysis cure?* Chicago: University of Chicago Press.

Kollock, P., Blumstein, P., & Schwartz, P. (1985). Sex and power in interaction: Conversational privileges and duties. *American Sociological Review, 50*, 34-46.

Kourany, R. F. (1987). Suicide among homosexual adolescents. *Journal of Homosexuality, 13*(4), 111-117.

Krafft-Ebing, R. (1901). *Psychopathia sexualis* (3rd ed., translation of 10th German ed.). Chicago: W. T. Keener.

Krajeski, J. (1984). Masters and Johnsons' article "seriously flawed." *American Journal of Psychiatry, 141*(9), 1131.

Krippner, S. (1964). The identification of male homosexuality with the MMPI. *Journal of Clinical Psychology, 20*, 159-161.

Kuhn, T. S. (1962). *The structure of scientific revolutions.* Chicago: University of Chicago Press.

Kurdek, L. A. (1988). Perceived social support in gays and lesbians in cohabiting relationships. *Journal of Personality and Social Psychology, 54*(3), 504-509.

Kurdek, L. A., & Schmitt, J. P. (1986a). Relationship quality of partners in heterosexual married, heterosexual cohabiting, and gay and lesbian relationships. *Journal of Personality and Social Psychology, 51*, 711-720.

Kurdek, L. A., & Schmitt, J. P. (1986b). Relationship quality of gay men in closed or open relationships. *Journal of Homosexuality, 12*(2), 85-99.

Kurdek, L. A., & Schmitt, J. P. (1986c). Early development of relationship quality in heterosexual married, heterosexual cohabiting, gay, and lesbian couples. *Developmental Psychology, 22*, 305-309.

Kurdek, L. A., & Schmitt, J. P. (1987a). Partner homogamy in married, heterosexual cohabiting, gay, and lesbian couples. *Journal of Sex Research, 23*, 212-232.

Kurdek, L. A., & Schmitt, J. P. (1987b). Perceived emotional support from family and friends in gay, lesbian, and heterosexual cohabiting couples. *Journal of Homosexuality, 14*, 57-68.

Kus, R. J. (1988). Alcoholism and non-acceptance of gay self: The critical link. *Journal of Homosexuality, 15*(1, 2), 25-41.

Kweskin, S. L., & Cook, A. S. (1982). Heterosexual and homosexual mothers' self-described sex-role behavior and ideal sex-role behavior in children. *Sex Roles, 8*, 967-975.

LaHaye, T. (1978). *What everyone should know about homosexuality.* Wheaton, IL: Tyndale.

Lamb, D. H., Clark, C., Drumheller, P., Frazzell, K., & Suney, L. (1989). Applying Tarasoff to AIDS-related psychotherapy issues. *Professional Psychology: Research & Practice, 20*, 37-43.

Lame Deer, J. F., & Erdoes, R. (1972). *Lame Deer: Seeker of visions.* New York: Simon & Schuster.

Lance, L. M. (1987). The effects of interaction with gay persons on attitudes toward homosexuality. *Human Relations, 40*(6), 329-336.

Laner, M. R., & Laner, R. H. (1979). Personal style or sexual preference: Why gay men are disliked. *International Review of Modern Sociology, 9*, 215-228.

Langevin, R., Paitich, D., Freeman, R., et al. (1978). Personality characteristics and sexual anomalies in males. *Canadian Journal of Behavioral Science, 10*, 222-238.

Langevin, R., Paitich, D., & Steiner, B. (1977). The clinical profile of male transsexuals living as females vs. those living as males. *Archives of Sexual Behavior, 6*, 143-154.

Larsen, K. S., Reed, M., & Hoffman, S. (1980). Attitudes of heterosexuals toward homosexuality: A Likert-type scale and construct validity. *Journal of Sex Research, 16*(3), 245-257.

Larson, P. C. (1982). Gay male relationships. In W. Paul, J. D. Weinrich J. C. Gonsiorek, & M. E. Hotvedt (Eds.), *Homosexuality: Social, psychological, and biological issues* (pp. 219-232). Beverly Hills, CA: Sage.

LaTorre, R. A., & Wendenburg, K. (1983). Psychological characteristics of bisexual, heterosexual and homosexual women. *Journal of Homosexuality, 9*(1), 87-97.

Lawson, R. (1987). Scandal in the Adventist-funded program to "heal" homosexuals: Failure, sexual exploitation, official silence, and attempts to rehabilitate the exploiter and his methods. Paper given at the American Sociological Association, Chicago.

Le Bitoux, J. (1989). To be 20 and homosexual in France today. *Journal of Homosexuality, 17*(3, 4), 291-297.

Lebovitz, P. S. (1972). Feminine behavior in boys: Aspects of its outcome. *American Journal of Psychiatry, 128*, 1283-1289.

Lee, J. A. (1977). Going public: A study into the sociology of homosexual liberation. *Journal of Homosexuality, 3*(1), 49-78.

Leeder, E. (1988). Enmeshed in pain: Counseling the lesbian battering couple. *Women and Therapy, 7*(1), 81-99.

Lehne, G. K. (1976). Homophobia among men. In D. S. David & R. Brannon (Eds.), *The forty-nine percent majority: The male sex role* (pp. 66-88). Reading, MA: Addison-Wesley.

Lerner, M. J. (1970). The desire for justice and reactions to victims. In J. Macaulay & L. Berkowitz (Eds.), *Altruism and helping behavior* (pp. 205-229). New York: Academic Press.

Leventhal, H., Prohaska, T. R., & Hirshman, R. S. (1985). Preventive health behavior across the life span. In J. C. Rosen & L. J. Solomon (Eds.), *Prevention in health psychology*, Hanover, NH: University Press of New England.

Levin, J., & Karni, E. S. (1971). A comparative study of the CPI Femininity Scale: Validation in Israel. *Journal of Cross-Cultural Psychology, 2*, 387-391.

Levine, M. P. (1979a). Employment discrimination against gay men. *International Review of Modern Sociology, 9*(5-7), 151-163.

Levine, M. P. (1979b). Gay ghetto. In M. P. Levine (Ed.), *Gay men: The sociology of male homosexuality* (pp. 182-204). New York: Harper & Row.

Levine, M. P., & Leonard, R. (1984). Discrimination against lesbians in the work force. *Signs, 9*(4), 700-710.

Levine, M. P., & Troiden, R. R. (1988). The myth of sexual compulsivity. *The Journal of Sex Research, 25*, 347-364.

Levinger, G. (1979). A social psychological perspective on marital dissolution. In G. Levinger & O. C. Moles (Eds.), *Divorce and separation* (pp. 37-63). New York: Basic Books.

Levinger, G. (1983). Development and change. In H. H. Kelley et al., *Close relationships* (pp. 315-359). New York: W. H. Freeman.

Levitt, E. E., & Klassen, A. D. (1974). Public attitudes toward homosexuality: Part of the 1970 national survey by the Institute for Sex Research. *Journal of Homosexuality, 1*(1), 29-43.

Lewes, K. (1988). *The psychoanalytic theory of male homosexuality*. New York: Simon & Schuster.

Lewin, E. (1981). Lesbianism and motherhood: Implications for child custody. *Human Organization, 40*(1), 6-14.

Lewin, E., & Lyons, T. A. (1982). Everything in its place: The coexistence of lesbianism and motherhood. In W. Paul, J. D. Weinrich, J. C. Gonsiorek, & M. E. Hotvedt (Eds.), *Homosexuality: Social, psychological, and biological issues* (pp. 249-274). Beverly Hills, CA: Sage.

Lewis, K. (1980). Children of lesbians: Their point of view. *Social Work, 25*(3), 198-203.

Lewis, L. A. (1984). The coming out process for lesbians: Integrating a stable identity. *Social Work, 29*(5), 464-469.

Lockard, R. B. (1971). Reflections on the fall of comparative psychology: Is there a message for us all? *American Psychologist, 26*, 168-179.

Loiacano, D. K. (1989). Gay identity issues among black Americans: Racism, homophobia, and the need for validation. *Journal of Counseling and Development, 68,* 21-25.

London, P. (1964). *The modes and morals of psychotherapy.* New York: Holt, Rinehart, & Winston.

London, P. (1969). *Behavior control.* New York: Harper & Row.

London, P. (1986). *The modes and morals of psychotherapy* (2nd ed.). New York: Hemisphere.

Lopez, S. (1989). Patient variable biases in clinical judgment: Conceptual overview and methodological considerations. *Psychological Bulletin, 106,* 184-203.

Lopez, S., & Hernandez, P. (1986). How culture is considered in evaluations of psychopathology. *Journal of Nervous and Mental Disease, 176,* 598-606.

Lopez, S., & Nunez, J. A. (1987). Cultural factors considered in selected diagnostic criteria and interview schedules. *Journal of Abnormal Psychology, 96,* 270-272.

Loulan, J. (1986). Psychotherapy with lesbian mothers. In T. Stein & C. Cohen (Eds.), *Contemporary perspectives on psychotherapy with lesbians and gay men* (pp. 181-208). New York: Plenum.

Lynch, J. M., & Reilly, M. E. (1986). Role relationships: Lesbian perspectives. *Journal of Homosexuality, 12*(2), 53-69.

Maccoby, E. E. (1979). Gender identity and sex-role adoption. In H. A. Katchadourian (Ed.), *Human sexuality: A comparative and developmental perspective.* Berkeley: University of California Press.

MacDonald, A. P., Jr. (1983). A little bit of lavender goes a long way: A critique of research on sexual orientation. *Journal of Sex Research, 19,* 94-100.

MacDonald, A. P., Jr., & Games, R. G. (1974). Some characteristics of those who hold positive and negative attitudes towards homosexuals. *Journal of Homosexuality, 1*(1), 9-27.

MacDonald, G. J. (1982). Individual differences in the coming-out process for gay men: Implications for theoretical models. *Journal of Homosexuality, 8*(1), 47-60.

Macro Systems Inc. (1988). *Assessment of the development and implementation of state AIDS/HIV partner notification programs: Five case studies.* Author.

Malyon, A. K. (1981). The homosexual adolescent: Developmental issues and social bias. *Child Welfare, 60,* 321-330.

Malyon, A. K. (1982a). Biphasic aspects of homosexual identity formation. *Psychotherapy: Theory, Research & Practice, 19,* 335-340.

Malyon, A. K. (1982b). Psychotherapeutic implications of internalized homophobia in gay men. In J. C. Gonsiorek (Ed.), *Homosexuality and psychotherapy: A practitioner's handbook of affirmative models* (pp. 59-69). New York: Haworth.

Malyon, A. K. (1982c). Psychotherapeutic implications of internalized homophobia in gay men. *Journal of Homosexuality, 7*(2, 3), 59-69.

Mannion, K. (1976). *Female homosexuality: A comprehensive review of theory and research.* Washington, DC: American Psychological Association. (Catalogue of Selected Documents, 6:44).

Manosevitz, M. (1970a). Early sexual behavior in adult homosexual and heterosexual males. *Journal of Abnormal Psychology, 76,* 396-402.

Manosevitz, M. (1970b). Item analyses of the MMPI Mf scale using homosexual and heterosexual males. *Journal of Consulting and Clinical Psychology, 35,* 395-399.

Manosevitz, M. (1971). Education and MMPI Mf scores in homosexual and heterosexual males. *Journal of Consulting and Clinical Psychology, 36,* 395-399.

Marcus, E. (1988). *The male couple's guide to living together.* New York: Harper & Row.

Marecek, J., Finn, S. E., & Cardell, M. (1982). Gender roles in the relationships of lesbians and gay men. *Journal of Homosexuality, 8*(2), 45-50.

Maret, S. M. (1984). Attitudes of fundamentalists toward homosexuality. *Psychological Reports, 55,* 205-206.

Martin, A. (1984). The emperor's new clothes: Modern attempts to change sexual orientation. In E. S. Hetrick & T. S. Stein (Eds.), *Innovations in psychotherapy with homosexuals.* Washington, DC: American Psychiatric Association.

Martin, A. (1989). Lesbian parenting: A personal odyssey. In J. Offerman-Zuckerberg, *Gender in transition* (pp. 249-262). New York: Plenum.

Martin, A. D., & Hetrick, E. S. (1988). The stigmatization of the gay and lesbian adolescent. In M. W. Ross (Ed.), *Psychopathology and psychotherapy in homosexuality* (pp. 163-184). New York: Haworth.

Marzuk, P. M., Tierney, H., Tardiff, K., Hull, H. F., Sewell, C. M., Wilson, J., & McFeeley, P. (1988). The risk of suicide in persons with AIDS. *Journal of the American Medical Association, 260*(1), 29.

Masters, W. H., & Johnson, V. E. (1979). *Homosexuality in perspective.* Boston: Little, Brown.

Mata, A. B., Jr., & Jorquez, J. S. (1989). Mexican-American intravenous drug users' needle-sharing practices: Implications for AIDS prevention. In V. M. Mays, G. W. Albee, & S. F. Schneider (Eds.), *Primary prevention of AIDS: Psychological approaches* (pp. 329-344). Newbury Park, CA: Sage.

Mattison, A. M. (1985). *Group treatment of sexually compulsive gay and bisexual men.* Paper presented at the annual meeting of the Eastern Region of the Society for the Scientific Study of Sex, Philadelphia.

Mayer, K. D., Ayotte, D., Groopman, J. E., Stoddard, A. M., Sarngaharan, M., & Gallo, R. (1986). Association of human T-lymphotropic virus type III antibodies with sexual and other behaviors in a cohort of homosexual men from Boston with and without generalized lymphohadenopathy. *Journal of the American Medical Association, 80,* 357-363.

Mayerson, P., & Lief, H. (1965). Psychotherapy of homosexuals: A follow-up study of nineteen cases. In J. Marmor (Ed.), *Sexual inversion.* New York: Basic Books.

Mays, V. M. (1989). AIDS prevention in black populations: Methods of a safer kind. In V. M. Mays, G. W. Albee, & S. F. Schneider (Eds.), *Primary prevention of AIDS: Psychological approaches* (pp. 264-279). Newbury Park, CA: Sage.

Mays, V. M., & Cochran, S. D. (1988). Interpretation of AIDS risk and risk reduction activities by black and Hispanic women. *American Psychologist, 43,* 949-957.

McCauley, E. A., & Ehrhardt, A. A. (1977). Role expectations and definitions: A comparison of female transsexuals and lesbians. *Journal of Homosexuality, 3,* 137-147.

McClintock, C. (1958). Personality syndromes and attitude change. *Journal of Personality, 26,* 479-492.

McClosky, H., & Brill, A. (1983). *Dimensions of tolerance: What Americans believe about civil liberties.* New York: Russell Sage.

McConaghy, N. (1976). Is a homosexual orientation irreversible? *British Journal of Psychiatry, 129,* 556-563.

McConaghy, N. (1981). Controlled comparison of aversive therapy and covert sensitization in compulsive homosexuality. *Behavior Research and Therapy, 19*(5), 425-434.

McConaghy, N., Proctor, D., & Barr, R. (1972). Subjective and penile plethysmography responses to aversive therapy for homosexuality: A partial replication. *Archives of Sexual Behavior, 2,* 65-78.

McCusker, J., Stoddard, A. M., Mayer, K. H., Cowan, D. W., & Groopman, J. E. (1988). Behavioral risk factors for HIV infection among homosexual men at a Boston community health center. *American Journal of Public Health, 78,* 68-71.

McDaniel, L. A. (1989). *Preservice adjustment of homosexual and heterosexual military accessions: Implications for security clearance suitability* (PERS-TR-89-004). Monterey, CA: Defense Personnel Security Research and Education Center.

McDonald, G. J. (1981). Misrepresentation, liberalism, and heterosexual bias in introductory psychology textbooks. *Journal of Homosexuality, 6,* 45-60.

McDonald, G. J. (1982). Individual differences in the coming out process for gay men: Implications for theoretical models. *Journal of Homosexuality, 8,* 47-60.

McGuire, W. J. (1985). Attitudes and attitude change. In G. Lindzey & E. Aronson (Eds.), *Handbook of social psychology, Vol. 2* (pp. 233-346). New York: Random House.

McIntosh, M. (1968). The homosexual role. *Social Problems, 16,* 182-192.

McNeill, J. J. (1976). *The church and the homosexual.* Kansas City: Sheed Andrews & McMeel.

McNeill, W. H. (1976). *Plagues and Peoples.* Garden City, NY: Anchor.

McWhirter, D. P., & Mattison, A. M. (1984). *The male couple.* Englewood Cliffs, NJ: Prentice-Hall.

Mead, M. (1961). Cultural determinants of sexual behavior. In W. C. Young (Ed.), *Sex and internal secretions* (3rd ed., pp. 1433-1479). Baltimore, MD: Williams & Wilkins.

Melbye, M., Biggar, R. J., Ebbesen, P., Sarngadharan, M. G., Weiss, S. H., Gallo, R. C., & Blackner, W. A. (1984). Seroepidemiology of HTLV-III antibody in Danish homosexual men: Prevalence, transmission, and disease outcome. *British Medical Journal, 289,* 573-575.

Melton, G. B. (1988). Ethical and legal issues in AIDS-related practice. *American Psychologist, 43,* 941-947.

Melton, G. B. (1989). Public policy and private prejudice: Psychology and law on gay rights. *American Psychologist, 44,* 933-940.

Melton, G. B., & Gray, J. N. (1988). Ethical dilemmas in AIDS research. *American Psychologist, 43,* 60-64.

Meredith, R. L., & Reister, R. W. (1980). Psychotherapy responsibility and homosexuality: Clinical examination of socially deviant behavior. *Professional Psychology, 11,* 174-193.

Meyer, J. K. (1985). Ego-dystonic homosexuality. In H. Kaplan & B. Sadock (Eds.), *Comprehensive textbook of psychiatry IV* (pp. 1056-1065). Baltimore, MD: Williams & Wilkins.

Meyer-Bahlburg, H.F.L. (1977). Sex hormones and male homosexuality in comparative perspective. *Archives of Sexual Behavior, 6,* 297-325.

Meyer-Bahlburg, H.F.L. (1979). Sex hormones and female homosexuality: A critical examination. *Archives of Sexual Behavior, 8,* 101-119.

Meyer-Bahlburg, H.F.L. (1980). Hormones and homosexuality. *Psychiatrica Clinica North America, 3,* 349-364.

Meyer-Bahlburg, H.F.L. (1982). Hormones and psychosexual differentiation: Implications for the management of intersexuality, homosexuality, and transsexuality. *Clinical Endocrinology and Metabolism, 11,* 681-701.

Meyer-Bahlburg, H.F.L. (1984). Psychoendocrine research on sexual orientation: Current status and future options. *Progress in Brain Research, 61,* 375-398.

Meyer-Bahlberg, H.F.L., Feldman, J. F., Cohen, P., & Ehrhardt, A. A. (1988). Perinatal factors in the development of gender-related play behavior: Sex hormones versus pregnancy complications. *Psychiatry, 51,* 260-271.

Miller, B. (1978). Adult sexual resocialization. *Alternative Lifestyles, 1*(2), 207-234.

Miller, B. (1979a). Gay fathers and their children. *The Family Coordinator, 28*(4), 544-552.

Miller, B. (1979b). Unpromised paternity: The life-styles of gay fathers. In M. P. Levine (Ed.), *Gay men: The sociology of male homosexuality* (pp. 239-252). New York: Harper & Row.

Miller, B. (1983). *Identity conflict and resolution: A social psychological model of gay family men's adaptations.* Unpublished doctoral dissertation, University of Alberta, Edmonton.

Miller, B. (1986). Identity resocialization in moral careers of gay husbands and fathers. In A. Davis (Ed.), *Papers in honor of Gordon Hirabavashi* (pp. 197-216). Edmonton, Canada: University of Alberta Press.

Miller, J. A., Jacobsen, R. B., & Bigner, J. J. (1981). The child's home environment for lesbian v. heterosexual mothers: A neglected area of research. *Journal of Homosexuality, 7*(1), 49-56.

Miller, W. G. (1963). Characteristics of homosexually-involved incarcerated females. *Journal of Consulting Psychology, 27,* 277.

Mintz, E. (1966). Overt male homosexuals in combined group and individual treatment. *Journal of Consulting Psychology, 20,* 193-198.

Money, J. (1972a). Editorial comment: Strategy, ethics, behavior modification, and homosexuality. *Archives of Sexual Behavior, 2,* 79-81.

Money, J. (1972b). Pubertal hormones and homosexuality, bisexuality, and heterosexuality. In J. M. Livingood (Ed.), *NIMH task force on homosexuality: Final report and background papers.* DHEW Publication No. (HSM)72-9116. Rockville, MD: National Institute of Mental Health.

Money, J. (1980). *Love and love sickness: The science of sex, gender difference, and pair-bonding.* Baltimore, MD: Johns Hopkins University Press.

Money, J. (1988). *Gay, straight and in-between: The sexology of erotic orientation..* New York: Oxford University Press.

Money, J., Ehrhardt, A. A. (1972). *Man and woman, boy and girl: The differentiation and dimorphism of gender identity from conception to maturity.* Baltimore, MD: Johns Hopkins University Press.

Money, J., & Russo, A. J. (1979). Homosexual outcome of discordant gender identity/role in childhood: Longitudinal followup. *Journal of Pediatric Psychology, 4,* 29-41.

Money, J., Schwartz, M., & Lewis, V. G. (1984). Adult erotosexual status and fetal hormonal masculinization and demasculization: 46, XX congenital virilizing adrenal hyperplasia and 46, XX androgen-insensitivity syndrome compared. *Psychoneuroendocrinology, 9,* 405-414.

Money, J., & Wang, C. (1966). Human figure drawing. I: Sex of first choice in gender-identity anomalies, Klinefelter's syndrome and precocious puberty. *Journal of Nervous and Mental Disease, 143,* 157-162.

Morales, E. (1983, August). *Third World gays and lesbians: A process of multiple identities.* Paper presented at the American Psychological Association, Anaheim, CA.

Morin, S. F. (1974). Educational programs as a means of changing attitudes toward gay people. *Homosexual Counseling Journal, 1,* 160-165.

Morin, S. F. (1977). Heterosexual bias in psychological research on lesbianism and male homosexuality. *American Psychologist, 32,* 629-637.

Morin, S. F., & Charles, K. A. (1981). Heterosexual bias in psychotherapy. In J. Murray & P. R. Abramson (Eds.), *The handbook of bias in psychotherapy.* Los Angeles: University of California Press.

Morin, S. F., Charles, K. A., & Malyon, A. (1984). The psychological impact of AIDS on gay men. *American Psychologist, 39,* 1288-1293.

Morin, S. F., & Garfinkle, E. M. (1978). Male homophobia. *Journal of Social Issues, 34*(1), 29-47.

Mosbacher, D. (1988). Lesbian alcohol and substance abuse. *Psychiatric Annals, 18*(1), 47-50.

Moses, A. E., & Hawkins, R. D., Jr. (1982). *Counseling lesbian women and gay men.* St. Louis: C. V. Mosby.

Mosher, D. (1989). The threat to sexual freedom: Moralistic intolerance instills a spiral of fear. *Journal of Sex Research, 26,* 492-509.

Mosher, D. L. (1991). Scared straight: Homosexual threat in heterosexual therapists. In C. Silverstein (Ed.), *Gays, lesbians and their therapists: Studies in psychotherapy.* New York: Norton.

Mosher, D. L., & O'Grady, K. E. (1979). Homosexual threat, negative attitudes toward masturbation, sex guilt, and males' sexual and affective reactions to explicit sexual films. *Journal of Consulting and Clinical Psychology, 47,* 860-873.

Mucklow, B. M., & Phelan, G. K. (1979). Lesbian and traditional mothers' responses to adult response to child behavior and self-concept. *Psychological Reports,* 44, 880-882.

Myers, M. F. (1982). Counseling the parents of young homosexual male patients. In J. C. Gonsiorek (Ed.), *Homosexuality and psychotherapy: A practitioner's handbook of affirmative models* (pp. 131-144). New York: Haworth.

Nanda, S. (1984). The hijras of India: A preliminary report. *Medicine and Law, 3,* 59-75.

Nanda, S. (1990). *Neither man nor woman: The hijras of India.* Belmont, CA: Wadsworth.

Neisser, U. (1976). *Cognition and reality.* San Francisco: Freeman.

Nevid, J. S. (1983). Exposure to homoerotic stimuli: Effects on attitudes and affects of heterosexual viewers. *Journal of Social Psychology, 119,* 249-255.

Newswatch briefs. (1990, February 22). *Gay Chicago Magazine, 8,* p. 43.

Newton, D. E. (1978). Homosexual behavior and child molestation: A review of the evidence. *Adolescence, 13,* 29-43.

Nichols, S. E. (1986). Psychotherapy and AIDS. In T. Stein & C. Cohen (Eds.), *Contemporary perspectives on psychotherapy with lesbians and gay men* (pp. 209-240). New York: Plenum.

Nishiyama, T. (1975). Validation of the CPI Femininity Scale in Japan. *Journal of Cross-Cultural Psychology, 6,* 482-489.

Nungesser, L. G. (1983). *Homosexual acts, actors, and identities.* New York: Praeger.

Nurius, P. A. (1983). Mental health implications of sexual orientation. *Journal of Sex Research, 19,* 119-136.

Oberman, H. A. (1984). *The roots of anti-semitism in the age of Renaissance and Reformation* (J. I. Porter, Trans.). Philadelphia: Fortress. (Original work published 1981)

Ohlson, E. L. (1974). A preliminary investigation into the self-disclosing ability of male homosexuals. *Psychology, 11*(2), 21-25.

Ohlson, E. L., & Wilson, M. (1974). Differentiating female homosexuals from female heterosexuals by use of the MMPI. *Journal of Sex Research, 10,* 308-315.

Oldham, S., Farnill, D., & Ball, I. (1982). Sex-role identity of female homosexuals. *Journal of Homosexuality, 8,* 41-46.

Oliver, W. H., & Mosher, D. L. (1968). Psychopathology and guilt in heterosexual and subgroups of homosexual reformatory inmates. *Journal of Abnormal Psychology, 73,* 323-329.

Omark, R. C. (1978). A comment on the homosexual role. *Journal of Sex Research, 14,* 273-274.

Ostrow, D. (1977). *Gay and straight parents: What about the children?* Unpublished bachelor's thesis, Hampshire College, Amherst, MA.

Ovesey, L., & Woods, S. M. (1980). Pseudohomosexuality and homosexuality in men: Psychodynamics as a guide to treatment. In J. Marmor (Ed.), *Homosexual behavior: A modern reappraisal.* New York: Basic Books.

Padian, N., Marquis, L., Fronies, D. P., Anderson, R. E., Rutherford, G. W., O'Malley, P. M., & Winkelstein, W. (1987). Male to female transmission of HIV. *Journal of the American Medical Association, 258,* 788-790.

Pagelow, M. (1980). Heterosexual and lesbian single mothers: A comparison of problems, coping, and solutions. *Journal of Homosexuality, 5,* 189-204.

Pagtolun-An, I., & Clair, J. M. (1986). An experimental study of attitudes toward homosexuals. *Deviant Behavior, 7,* 121-135.

Palacios-Jimenez, L., & Shernoff, M. (1986). *Facilitator's guide to eroticizing safer sex.* New York: Gay Men's Health Crisis.

Panton, J. R. (1960). A new MMPI scale for the identification of homosexuality. *Journal of Clinical Psychology, 16,* 17-21.

Parker, R. (1989). Youth identity, and homosexuality: The changing shape of sexual life in contemporary Brazil. *Journal of Homosexuality, 17*(3, 4), 269-289.

Parsons, E. C. (1916). The Zuñi la'mana. *American Anthropologist, 18,* 521-528.

Pattison, E., & Pattison, M. (1980). Ex-gays: Religiously-mediated change in homosexuals. *American Journal of Psychiatry, 137*(12), 1553-1562.

Paul, W. (1982). Minority status for gay people: Majority reactions and social context. In W. Paul, J. D. Weinrich, J. C. Gonsiorek, & M. E. Hotvedt (Eds.), *Homosexuality: Social, psychological, and biological issues* (pp. 351-369). Beverly Hills, CA: Sage.

Paul, W., Weinrich, J. D., Gonsiorek, J. C., & Hotvedt, M. E. (Eds.). (1982). *Homosexuality: Social, psychological, and biological issues.* Beverly Hills, CA: Sage.

Peplau, L. A., & Amaro, H. (1982). Understanding lesbian relationships. In W. Paul, J. D. Weinrich, J. C. Gonsiorek, & M. E. Hotvedt (Eds.), *Homosexuality: Social, psychological, and biological issues* (pp. 233-248). Beverly Hills, CA: Sage.

Peplau, L. A., & Cochran, S. D. (1980, September). *Sex differences in values concerning love relationships.*Paper presented at the annual meeting of the American Psychological Association, Montreal, Canada.

Peplau, L.A., & Cochran, S. D. (1981). Value orientations in the intimate relationships of gay men. *Journal of Homosexuality, 6*(3), 1-19.

Peplau, L. A., & Cochran, S. D. (1990). A relationship perspective on homosexuality. In D. P. McWhirter, S. A. Sanders, & J. M. Reinisch (Eds.), *Homosexuality/heterosexuality: The Kinsey scale and current research.* New York: Oxford University Press.

Peplau, L. A., Cochran, S. D., & Mays, V. M. (1986, August). *Satisfaction in the intimate relationships of black lesbians.* Paper presented at the annual meeting of the American Psychological Association, Washington, DC.

Peplau, L. A., Cochran, S., Rook, K., & Padesky, C. (1978). Women in love: Attachment and autonomy in lesbian relationships. *Journal of Social Issues, 34*(3), 7-27.

Peplau, L. A., & Gordon, S. L. (1983). The intimate relationships of lesbians and gay men. In E. R. Allgeier & N. B. McCormick (Eds.), *The changing boundaries: Gender roles and sexual behavior* (pp. 226-244). Palo Alto, CA: Mayfield.

Peplau, L. A., Padesky, C., & Hamilton, M. (1982). Satisfaction in lesbian relationships. *Journal of Homosexuality, 8,* 23-35.

Perkins, M. W. (1981). Female homosexuality and body build. *Archives of Sexual Behavior, 10,* 337-345.

Peterson, J. L., & Marin, G. (1988). Issues in the prevention of AIDS among black and Hispanic men. *American Psychologist, 43,* 871-877.

Peterson, N. (1984, April 30). Coming to terms with gay parents. *USA Today,* p. 30.

Pierce, D. M. (1973). Test and non-test correlates of active and situational homosexuality. *Psychology, 10*(4), 23-26.

Pillard, R. C. (1988). Sexual orientation and mental disorder. *Psychiatric Annals, 18*(1), 51-56.

Pillard, R. C., & Weinrich, J. D. (1987). The periodic table model of the gender transpositions: Part I. A theory based on masculinization and defeminization of the brain. *Journal of Sex Research, 23,* 425-454.

Plato. (1956). The symposium. In E. H. Warmington & P. G. Rouse (Eds.) (W. H. D. Rouse, Trans.), *Great dialogs of Plato* (pp. 69-117). New York: New American Library.

Pleck, J. H. (1981). *The myth of masculinity.* Cambridge, MA: MIT Press.

Pleck, J. H., O'Donnell, L., O'Donnell, C. R., & Snarey, J. (1988). AIDS-phobia, contact with AIDS, and AIDS-related job stress in hospital workers. *Journal of Homosexuality, 15*(3, 4), 41-54.

Plummer, K. (1975). *Sexual stigma: An interactionist account.* London: Routledge & Kegan Paul.

Plummer, K. (1989). Lesbian and gay youth in England. *Journal of Homosexuality, 17*(3, 4), 195-223.

Ponse, B. (1980). Finding self in the lesbian community. In M. Kirkpatrick (Ed.), *Women's sexual development* (pp. 181-200). New York: Plenum.

Poole, K. (1972). The etiology of gender identity and the lesbian. *Journal of Social Psychology, 87,* 51-57.

Potterat, J. J., Nancy, E. S., Woodhouse, D. E., & Muth, J. B. (1989). Partner notification in the control of human immunodeficiency virus infection. *American Journal of Public Health, 79*(7), 874-876.

Potterat, J. J., Spencer, N. E., Woodhouse, D. E., & Muth, J. B. (1989). Partner notification in the control of human immunodeficiency virus infection. *American Journal of Public Health, 79,* 874-876.

Prieur, A. (1989, April). *Gay men: Reasons for continued practice of unsafe sex.* Paper presented at the Eleventh National Lesbian/Gay Health Conference, San Francisco.

Pryor, J. B., Reeder, G. D., & Vinacco, R. (1989). The instrumental and symbolic functions of attitudes toward persons with AIDS. *Journal of Applied Social Psychology, 19,* 377-404.

Prytula, R. E., Wellford, C. D., & Demonbreun, B. G. (1979). Body self-image and homosexuality. *Journal of Clinical Psychology, 35,* 567-572.

pseudo-Lucian. (1967). Affairs of the heart. In M. D. Macleod (Trans.), *Lucian* (pp. 205-207), *8,* 150-235. Cambridge, MA: Loeb Classics.

Quadland, M. C. (1985). Compulsive sexual behavior: Definition of a problem and an approach to treatment. *Journal of Sex and Marital Therapy, 11,* 121-132.

Rado, S. (1940). A critical examination of the concept of bisexuality. *Psychosomatic Medicine, 2,* 459-467.

Rado, S. (1949). An adaptational view of sexual behavior. In P. H. Hoch & J. Zubin (Eds.), *Psychosexual development in health and disease.* New York: Grune & Stratton.

Rand, C., Graham, D. L. R., & Rawlings, E. I. (1982). Psychological health and factors the court seeks to control in lesbian mother custody trials. *Journal of Homosexuality, 8*(1), 27-39.

Rangaswami, K. (1982). Difficulties in arousing and increasing heterosexual responsiveness in a homosexual: A case report. *Indian Journal of Clinical Psychology, 9*(2), 147-151.

Raphael, S. M., & Robinson, M. K. (1980). The older lesbian: Love relationships and friendship patterns. *Alternative Lifestyles, 3*(2), 207-230.

Rappaport, J. (1977). *Community psychology: Values, research and action.* New York: Holt, Reinhardt & Winston.

Rayside, D., & Bowler, S. (1988). Public opinion and gay rights. *Canadian Review of Sociology and Anthropology, 25,* 649-660.

Reece, R. (1987). Causes and treatment of sexual desire discrepancies in male couples. In E. Coleman (Ed.), *Psychotherapy with homosexual men and women: Integrated identity approaches for clinical practice* (pp. 157-172). New York: Haworth.

Regal, P. J. (1990). *The anatomy of judgment.* Minneapolis: University of Minnesota Press.

Reinisch, J. M., Sanders, J. A., & Ziemba-Davis, M. (1989). Sex research around the AIDS crisis. In B. Voller, J. M. Reinisch, & M. Gottlieb (Eds.), *AIDS and sex: An integrated biomedical approach.* New York: Oxford University Press.

Reiss, B. F. (1980). Psychological tests in homosexuality. In J. Marmor (Ed.), *Homosexual behavior: A modern reappraisal* (pp. 296-311). New York: Basic Books.

Reiss, B. F., Safer, J., & Yotive, W. (1974). Psychological test data on female homosexuality. *Journal of Homosexuality, 1,* 71-85.

Renzetti, C. M. (1988). Violence in lesbian relationships. *Journal of Interpersonal Violence, 3* (4), 381-399.

Report of the Presidential Commission on the Human Immonudeficiency Virus Epidemic (1988). Washington, DC: U.S. Government Printing Office.

Research and Decisions Corporation. (1985). *A report on designing an effective AIDS prevention campaign strategy for San Francisco: Results from the second probability sample of an urban gay male community.* Report prepared for the San Francisco AIDS Foundation.

Results of poll. (1989, June 6). *San Francisco Examiner,* p. A19.

Rich, C. L., Fowler, R. C., Young, D., & Blenkush, M. (1986). The San Diego suicide study: Comparison of gay to straight males. *Suicide and Life Threatening Behavior, 16,* 448-457.

Ricketts, W., & Achtenberg, R. (1987). The adoptive and foster gay and lesbian parent. In F. W. Bozett (Ed.), *Gay and lesbian parents* (pp. 89-111). New York: Praeger.

Rieber, I., & Sigusch, V. (1979). Guest editorial: Psychosurgery on sex offenders and sexual "deviants" in West Germany. *Archives of Sexual Behavior, 8,* 523-527.

Risman, B., & Schwartz, P. (1988). Sociological research on male and female homosexuality. *Annual Review of Sociology, 14,* 125-147.

Rivera, R. R. (1987). Legal issues in gay and lesbian parenting. In F. W. Bozett (Ed.), *Gay and lesbian parents* (pp. 199-227). New York: Praeger.

Roberts, A. H., Dinsdale, S. M., Matthews, R. E., & Cole, R. M. (1969). Modifying persistent undesirable behavior in a medical setting. *Archives of Physical Medicine and Rehabilitation, 50,* 147-153.

Roesler, T., & Deisher, R. (1972). Youthful male homosexuality: Homosexual experience and the process of developing homosexual identity in males ages 16 to 22 years. *Journal of the American Medical Association, 219,* 1018-1023.

Rosen, G. (1969). *Madness in society: Chapters in the historical sociology of mental illness.* New York: Harper & Row.

Rosen, R. C., & Beck, J. G. (1988). *Patterns of sexual arousal: Psychophysiological processes and clinical applications.* New York: Guilford.

Rosenberg, C. E. (1987). *The cholera years* (2nd ed.). Chicago: University of Chicago Press.

Ross, M. W. (1983). *The married homosexual man: A psychological study.* London: Routledge & Kegan Paul.

Ross, M. W. (1983). Femininity, masculinity, and sexual orientation: Some cross-cultural comparisons. *Journal of Homosexuality, 9* (1), 27-36.

Ross, M. W. (1985). Psychosocial factors in admitting to homosexuality in sexually transmitted disease clinics. *Sexually Transmitted Diseases, 12,* 83-87.

Ross, M. W. (Ed.). (1988). *Psychopathology and psychotherapy in homosexuality.* New York: Haworth.

Ross, M. W. (1989). Gay youth in four cultures: A comparative study. *Journal of Homosexuality, 17*(3, 4), 299-314.

Ross, M. W., Paulsen, J. A., & Stalstrom, O. W. (1989). Homosexuality and mental health: A cross-cultural review. *Journal of Homosexuality, 15,* 131-152.

Roth, S. (1985). Psychotherapy issues with lesbian couples. *Journal of Marital and Family Therapy, 11,* 273-286.

Rothenberg, R. B. (1983). The geography of gonorrhea: Empirical demonstration of core group transmission. *American Journal of Epidemiology,* 117, 688-694.

Rueda, E. T. (1982). *The homosexual network: Private lives and public policy.* Old Greenwich, CT: Devin Adair.

Rusbult, C. E. (1988). Commitment in close relationships: The investment model. In L. A. Peplau, D. O. Sears, S. E. Taylor, & J. L. Freedman (Eds.), *Readings in Social Psychology,* 2nd ed. (pp. 147-157). Englewood Cliffs, NJ: Prentice-Hall.

Ruse, M. (1984). Nature/nurture: Reflections on approaches to the study of homosexuality. *Journal of Homosexuality, 10,* 141-151.

Rutherford, G. W., & Woo, J. M. (1988). Contact tracing and the control of human immunodeficiency virus infection. *Journal of the American Medical Association, 256*(24), 3609-3610.

Ryder, J. P., & Somppi, P. L. (1979). Female-female pairing in ring-billed gulls. *The Auk, 96,* 1-5.

Saghir, M. T., & Robins, E. (1973). *Male and female homosexuality: A comprehensive investigation.* Baltimore, MD: Williams & Wilkins.

Saghir, M. T., & Robins, E. (1973). *Male and female homosexuality: A comprehensive investigation.* Baltimore, MD: Williams & Wilkins.

Saghir, M. T., Robins, E., Walbran, B., & Gentry, K. A. (1970a). Homosexuality III: Psychiatric disorders and disability in the male homosexual. *American Journal of Psychiatry, 126,* 1079-1086.

Saghir, M. T., Robins, E., Walbran, B., & Gentry, K. A. (1970b). Homosexuality IV: Psychiatric disorders and disability in the female homosexual. *American Journal of Psychiatry, 127,* 147-154.

Sanders, G., & Ross-Field, L. (1986). Sexual orientation and visuo-spatial ability. *Journal of Brain and Cognition, 5,* 280-290.

Sanders, G., & Ross-Field, L. (1987). Neuropsychological development of cognitive abilities: A new research strategy and some preliminary evidence for a sexual orientation model. *International Journal of Neuroscience, 36,* 1-16.

Sang, B. (1985) Lesbian relationships: A struggle toward partner equality. In T. Darty & S. Potter (Eds.), *Women-identified women* (pp. 51-66). Palo Alto, CA: Mayfield.

Sarason, I. G., Levine, H. M., Basham, R. B., & Sarason, B. R. (1983). Assessing social support: The Social Support Questionnaire. *Journal of Personality and Social Psychology, 44,* 127-139.

Sarbin, T. R., & Carols, K. E. (1988). *Nonconforming sexual orientation and military suitability* (PERS-TR-89-002). Monterey, CA: Defense Personnel Security Research and Education Center.

Saunders, J. M., & Valente, S. M. (1987). Suicide risk among gay men and lesbians: A review. *Death Studies, 11*(1), 1-23.

Scacco, A. M., Jr. (1982). *Male rape.* New York: AMS Press.

Scallen, R. M. (1981). An investigation of paternal attitudes and behaviors in homosexual and heterosexual fathers (Doctoral dissertation, California School of Professional Psychology, Los Angeles). *Dissertation Abstracts International, 42*(9), 3809-3813.

Schafer, S. (1977). Sociosexual behavior in male and female homosexuals: A study in sex differences. *Archives of Sexual Behavior, 6,* 355-364.

Scheckter, M. T., Bayko, W. J., Douglas, B., Willoughby, B., McLeod, A., Maynard, M., Croib, K., & O'Shaughnessey, M. (1986). The Vancouver lymphodenopathy-AIDS study: 6 HIV seroconversion in a cohort of homosexual men. *Canadian Medical Association Journal, 135,* 1355-1360.

Schippers, J. (1989). *Voorkeur voor mannen: Theorie en praktijk van de hulpverlening aan homoseksuele mannen* [A preference for men: Theory and practice of psychosocial help for gay men]. The Hague: S.D.U./Schorer.

Shippers, J. (1990, August). *Gay affirmative counseling and psychotherapy in the Netherlands.* Paper presented at meeting of the American Psychological Association, Boston, MA.

Schmidt, G. (1984). Allies and persecutors: Science and medicine in the homosexual issue. *Journal of Homosexuality, 10*(3, 4), 127-140.

Schmidt, G., Schorsch, E. (1981). Psychosurgery of sexually deviant patients: Review and analysis of new empirical findings. *Archives of Sexual Behavior, 10,* 301-323.

Schmitt, K. P., & Kurdek, L. H. (1987). Personality correlates of positive identity and relationship involvement in gay men. *Journal of Homosexuality, 13*(4), 101-109.

Schneider, B. (1986). Coming out at work: Bridging the private/public gap. *Work and Occupations, 13*(4), 463-487.

Schneider, W., & Lewis, I. A. (1984, February/March). The straight story on homosexuality and gay rights. *Public Opinion, 7,* 16-20, 59-60.

Schulenburg, J. (1985). *Gay parenting.* Garden City, NY: Anchor Books.

Schwartz, M., & Masters, W. H. (1984). The Masters and Johnson treatment program for dissatisfied homosexual men. *American Journal of Psychiatry, 141*(2), 173-181.

Sears, J. T. (1989). The impact of gender and race on growing up lesbian and gay in the South. *National Women's Studies Association Journal, 1,* 422-457.

Seeman, M. (1981). Intergroup relations. In M. Rosenberg & R. H. Turner (Eds.), *Social psychology: Sociological perspectives* (pp. 378-410). New York: Basic Books.

Seligman, M. E. P. (1970). On the generality of the laws of learning. *Psychological Review, 77,* 406-418.

Sell, R. L., Wells, J. A., Valleron, A.-J., Will, A., Cohen, M., & Umbel, K. (1990, June). *Homosexual and bisexual behavior in the United States, the United Kingdom and France.* Paper presented at the Sixth International Conference on AIDS, San Francisco, CA.

Selwyn, P. A., Feiner, C., Cox, C. P., Lipshutz, C., & Cohen, R. L. (1987). Knowledge about and high risk behavior among intravenous drug users in New York City. *AIDS, 1,* 247-254.

Sengers, W. (1969). *Homosexualiteit als Klacht Ein psychiatrische studie* [Homosexuality as a complaint: A psychiatric study]. Hilversum, The Netherlands: Brand.

Serdaheley, W. J., & Ziemba, G. J. (1984). Changing homophobic attitudes through college sexuality education. *Journal of Homosexuality, 10*(1, 2), 109-116.

Sexual survey #4: Current thinking on homosexuality. (1977). *Medical Aspects of Human Sexuality, 11,* 110-111.

Shernoff, M. (1990). Why every social worker should be challenged by AIDS. *Social Work, 35,* 5-8.

Shernoff, M., & Bloom, D. C. (in press). Designing effective AIDS prevention workshops for gay and bisexual men. *AIDS Education and Prevention.*

Shernoff, M., & Palacios-Jimenez, L. (1988). AIDS: Prevention is the only vaccine available: An AIDS prevention educational program. *Journal of Social Work and Human Sexuality, 6,* 135-150.

Shilts, R. (1982). *The mayor of Castro Street: The life and times of Harvey Milk.* New York: St. Martin's.

Shively, M. G., & De Cecco, J. P. (1977). Components of sexual identity. *Journal of Homosexuality, 3,* 41-48.

Shorter, E. (1975). *The making of the modern family.* New York: Basic Books.

Siegelman, M. (1972a). Adjustment of homosexual and heterosexual women. *British Journal of Psychiatry, 120,* 477-481.

Siegelman, M. (1972b). Adjustment of male homosexuals and heterosexuals. *Archives of Sexual Behavior, 2,* 9-25.

Sigusch, V., Schorsch, E., Dannecker, M., & Schmidt, G. (1982). Guest editorial: Official statement by the German Society for Sex Research (Deutsche Gesellschaft für Sexualforschung e. V.) on the research of Prof. Dr. Guner Doerner on the subject of homosexuality. *Archives of Sexual Behavior, 11,* 445-449.

Silverstein, C. (1972, October). *Behavior modification and the gay community.* Paper presented at the annual convention of the Association for the Advancement of Behavior Therapy, New York City.

Silverstein, C. (1977a). *A family matter: A parents' guide to homosexuality.* New York: McGraw-Hill.

Silverstein, C. (1977b). Homosexuality and the ethics of behavioral intervention: Paper 2. *Journal of Homosexuality, 2,* 205-211.

Silverstein, C. (1980). [Review of W. H. Masters & V. E. Johnson *Homosexuality in Perspective*]. *Contemporary Psychology, 25,* 357-358.

Silverstein, C. (1981). *Man to man: Gay couples in America.* New York: William Morrow.

Silverstein, C. (1988). The borderline personality disorder and gay people. *Journal of Homosexuality, 15,* 185-212.

Simon, W., & Gagnon, J. H. (1967a). Femininity in the lesbian community. *Social Problems, 15,* 212-221.

Simon, W., & Gagnon, J. H. (1967b). Homosexuality: The formulation of a sociological perspective. *Journal of Health and Social Behavior, 8,* 177-185.

Singer, M. I. (1970). Comparison of indicators of homosexuality on the MMPI. *Journal of Consulting and Clinical Psychology, 34,* 15-18.

Smalley, S. (1987). Dependency issues in lesbian relationships. *Journal of Homosexuality, 14,* 125-135.

Smith, J. (1988). Psychopathology, homosexuality, and homophobia. In M. W. Ross (Ed.), *Psychopathology and psychotherapy in homosexuality* (pp. 59-74). New York: Haworth.

Smith, K. T. (1971). Homophobia: A tentative personality profile. *Psychological Reports, 29,* 1091-1094.

Smith, M. B., Bruner, J. S., & White, R. W. (1956). *Opinions and personality.* New York: John Wiley.

Snyder, M. (1981). On the self-perpetuating nature of social stereotypes. In D. Hamilton (Ed.), *Cognitive processes in stereotyping and intergroup behavior* (pp. 183-212). Hillsdale, NJ: Lawrence Erlbaum.

Snyder, M., & Uranowitz, S. W. (1978). Reconstructing the past: Some cognitive consequences of person perception. *Journal of Personality and Social Psychology, 36,* 941-950.

Snyderman, M., & Hernstein, J. R. (1983). Intelligence tests and the immigration act of 1924. *American Psychologist, 38*(9), 986-995.

Sobel, H. J. (1976). Adolescent attitudes toward homosexuality in relation to self concept and body satisfaction. *Adolescence, 11*(43), 443-453.

Socarides, C. W. (1968). *The overt homosexual.* New York: Grune & Stratton.

Socarides, C. W. (1970). Homosexuality and medicine. *Journal of the American Medical Association, 212,* 1199-1202.

Socarides, C. W. (1975). *Beyond sexual freedom.* New York: Quadrangle.

Socarides, C. W. (1978). *Homosexuality.* New York: Jason Aronson.

Socarides, C. W. (1980). The sexual unreason. *Book Forum, 1,* 172-185.

Sociology group criticizes work of Paul Cameron. (1985, September 10). *Lincoln (NE) Star.*

Sonenschein, D. (1966). Homosexuality as a subject of anthropological inquiry. *Anthropological Quarterly, 39,* 73-82.

Sonenschein, D. (1968). The ethnography of male homosexual relationships. *Journal of Sex Research, 4,* 69-83.

Sophie, J. (1985). A critical examination of stage theories of lesbian identity development. *Journal of Homosexuality, 12*(2), 39-51.

Sophie, J. (1987). Internalized homophobia and lesbian identity. *Journal of Homosexuality, 14*(1, 2), 53-65.

Spada, J. (1979). *The Spada report.* New York: New American Library.

Spence, J. T., & Helmreich, R. L. (1978). *Masculinity and femininity: Their psychological dimensions, correlations and antecedents.* Austin: University of Texas Press.

Spencer, N.E., Hoffman, R. E., & Raevsky, C. A. (1989). *Results and benefit-cost analysis of provider-assisted HIV partner notification and referral.* Paper presented at the Fifth International Conference on AIDS, Montreal, Canada.

Srivastava, A., Borries, C., & Sommer, V. (in press). Homosexual mounting in free-ranging female Hanuman langurs (*Presbytus entellus*). *Archives of Sexual Behavior.*

Stall, R. D., Coates, T. J., & Hoff, C. (1988). Behavioral risk education for HIV infection among gay and bisexual men: A review of results from the United States. *American Psychologist, 43,* 878-885.

Stall, R. D., & Ekstrand, M. (1989). Implications of relapse from safe sex. *Focus: A Guide to AIDS Research, 4*(3), 3.

Steckel, A. (1985). *Separation-individuation in children of lesbian and heterosexual couples.* Unpublished doctoral dissertation, Wright Institute, Berkeley, CA.

Steckel, A. (1987). Psychosocial development of children of lesbian mothers. In F. W. Bozett (Ed.), *Gay and lesbian parents* (pp. 75-85). New York: Praeger.

Stein, T. S., & Cohen, C. J. (Eds.). (1986). *Contemporary perspectives on psychotherapy with lesbians and gay men.* New York: Plenum.

Stekel, W. (1933). *Bi-sexual love.* Brooklyn: Physicians and Surgeons Book Co.

Stephan, W. G. (1985). Intergroup relations. In G. Lindzey & E. Aronson (Eds.), *Handbook of social psychology: Vol. 2* (pp. 599-658). New York: Random House.

Stevenson, M. R. (1988). Promoting tolerance for homosexuality: An evaluation of intervention strategies. *Journal of Sex Research, 25*(4), 500-511.

Stipp, H., & Kerr, D. (1989). Determinants of public opinion about AIDS. *Public Opinion Quarterly, 53,* 98-106.

Stokes, K., Kilmann, P. R., & Wanlass, R. L. (1983). Sexual orientation and sex role conformity. *Archives of Sexual Behavior, 12,* 427-433.

Stoller, R. J. (1967). "It's only a phase": Femininity in boys. *Journal of the American Medical Association, 201,* 314-315.

Stoller, R. J. (1968). *Sex and gender: Volume I. The development of masculinity and femininity.* New York: Jason Aronson.

Storms, M. D. (1978). Attitudes toward homosexuality and femininity in men. *Journal of Homosexuality, 3*(3), 257-263.

Storms, M. D., Stivers, M. L., Lambers, S. M., & Hill, C. A. (1981). Sexual scripts for women. *Sex Roles, 7,* 699-707.

Stringer, P., & Grygier, T. (1976). Male homosexuality, psychiatric patient status, and psychological masculinity and femininity. *Archives of Sexual Behavior, 5,* 15-27.

Sturgis, E. T., & Adams, H. E. (1978). The right to treatment: Issues in the treatment of homosexuality. *Journal of Consulting and Clinical Psychology, 46,* 165-169.

Sulloway, F. J. (1979). *Freud, biologist of the mind.* New York: Basic Books.

Swanson, H. D. (1974). *Human reproduction: Biology and social change.* New York: Oxford University Press.

Swarthout, D., Gonsiorek, J. C., Simpson, M., & Henry, K. (1989, June). A behavioral approach to HIV prevention among seronegative or untested gay/bisexual men with a history of unsafe behavior. *Proceedings of the Fifth International Conference on AIDS,* Montreal, Canada, p. 784.

Sweeney, T. J. (1990, February 17). Contact tracing won't stop AIDS [Letter to the editor]. *Washington Post,* p. A28.

Symons, D. (1979) *The evolution of human sexuality.* New York: Oxford University Press.

Symposium on homosexuality and the ethics of behavioral intervention. (1977). *Journal of Homosexuality, 2,* 195-259.

Szasz, T. S. (1961). *The myth of mental illness.* New York: Dell.

Szasz, T. S. (1970). *The manufacture of madness: A comparative study of the Inquisition and the mental health movement.* New York: Harper & Row.

Szasz, T. S. (1977). *The myth of mental illness.* New York: Harper & Row.

Tafoya, T. (1989). Pulling coyote's tale: Native American sexuality and AIDS. In V. M. Mays, G. W. Albee, & S. F. Schneider (Eds.), *Primary prevention of AIDS: Psychological approaches* (pp. 280-289). Newbury Park, CA: Sage.

Tajfel, H. (1981). *Human groups and social categories: Studies in social psychology.* Cambridge, UK: Cambridge University Press.

Terman, L. A., & Miles, C. (1936). *Sex and personality: Studies in masculinity and femininity.* New York: McGraw-Hill.

Tessina, T. (1989). *Gay relationships.* Los Angeles: Jeremy P. Tarcher.

Testa, R. J., Kinder, B. N., & Ironson, G. (1987). *Journal of Sex Research, 23,* 163-172.

Thompson, N. L., McCandless, B. R., & Strickland, B. (1971). Personal adjustment of male and female homosexuals and heterosexuals. *Journal of Abnormal Psychology, 78,* 237-240.

Thompson, N. L., Schwartz, D. M., McCandless, B. R., & Edwards, D. (1973). Parent-child relationships and sexual identity in male and female homosexuals and heterosexuals. *Journal of Consulting and Clinical Psychology, 41*, 120-127.

Toomey, K. (1989). *Partner notification for HIV prevention: Current state programs and policies in the United States.* Paper presented at the Fifth International Conference on AIDS, Montreal, Canada.

Tremble, B., Schneider, M., & Appathurai, C. (1989). Growing up gay or lesbian in a multicultural context. *Journal of Homosexuality, 17*(3, 4), 253-267.

Tripp, C. A. (1975). *The homosexual matrix.* New York: Signet.

Trivers, R. L. (1971). The evolution of reciprocal altruism. *Quarterly Review of Biology, 46*(4), 35-57.

Trivers, R. L. (1974). Parent-offspring conflict. *American Zoologist, 14*, 249-264.

Trivers, R. L. (1976). Sexual selection and resource-accruing abilities in *Anolis garmani. Evolution, 30*, 253-269.

Trivers, R. L. (1985). *Social evolution.* Menlo Park, CA: Benjamin/Cummings.

Troiden, R. R. (1979). Becoming homosexual: A model of gay identity acquisition. *Psychiatry, 42*, 362-373.

Troiden, R. R. (1988a). Homosexual identity development. *Journal of Adolescent Health Care, 9*, 105-113.

Troiden, R. R. (1988b). *Gay and lesbian identity: A sociological analysis.* Dix Hills, NY: General Hall, Inc.

Troiden, R. R., & Goode, E. (1980). Variables related to the acquisition of a gay identity. *Journal of Homosexuality, 5*(4), 383-392.

Turner, P. H., Scadden, L., & Harris, M. B. (1985, March). *Parenting in gay and lesbian families.* Paper presented at the First Future of Parenting Symposium, Chicago.

Turner, R. K., Pielmaier, H., James, S., & Orwin, A. (1974). Personality characteristics of male homosexuals referred for aversion therapy: A comparative study. *British Journal of Psychiatry, 125*, 447-449.

Ullman, O., & Krasner, L. (1965). *Case studies in behavior modification.* New York: Holt, Rinehart, & Winston.

United States General Accounting Office. (1989, February). *AIDS education: Issues affecting counseling and testing programs.* Washington, DC: U.S. Government Printing Office.

United States Public Health Service Task Force on AIDS. (1986). Coolfont report: A PHS plan for prevention and control of AIDS and the AIDS virus. *Public Health Reports, 101*, 341-348.

United States Public Health Service. (1987). *Sexually transmitted disease statistics—1987.* Atlanta, GA: Author.

Vadiserri, R. O. (1989). *Preventing AIDS: The design of effective programs.* New Brunswick, NJ: Rutgers University Press.

Vance, C. S. (1984). *Pleasure and danger: Exploring female security.* Boston: Routledge & Kegan Paul.

Vernon, T. M., & Hoffman, R. E. (1988). Contact tracing to control the spread of HIV [Letter to the editor]. *Journal of the American Medical Association, 260* (22), 3274.

Voth, H. M. (1977). *The castrated family.* Kansas City: Sheed, Andrews, & McMeel.

Walter, D. (1985, October 29). Paul Cameron. *The Advocate*, pp. 28-33.

Ward, I. L. (1974). Sexual behavior differentiation: Parental hormonal and environmental control. In R. C. Friedman, R. M. Richart, & R. L. Vande Wiele (Eds.), *Sex Differences in Behavior.* New York: John Wiley.

Warren, C. (1980). Homosexuality and stigma. In J. Marmor (Ed.), *Homosexual behavior: A modern reappraisal* (pp. 123-141). New York: Basic Books.

Wasserman, E. B., & Storms, M. D. (1984). Factors influencing erotic orientation development in females and males. *Women and Therapy, 3*(2), 51-60.
Waterman, C. K., Dawson, L. J., & Bologna, M. J. (1989). Sexual coercion in gay male and lesbian relationships: Predictors and implications for support services. *Journal of Sex Research, 26*(1), 118-124.
Wedin, R. W. (1984). The sexual compulsive movement. *Christopher Street, 8,* 48-53.
Weeks, J. (1985). *Sexuality and its discontents.* London: Routledge & Kegan Paul.
Weeks, R. B., Derdeyn, A. P., & Langmon, M. (1975). Two cases of children of homosexuals. *Child Psychiatry and Human Development, 6,* 26-32.
Weinberg, G. (1972). *Society and the healthy homosexual.* New York: St. Martin's.
Weinberg, M. S., & Williams, C. J. (1974). *Male homosexuals: Their problems and adaptations.* New York: Oxford University Press.
Weinberg, T. S. (1983). *Gay men, gay selves: The social construction of homosexual identities.* New York: Irvington.
Weinberg, T. S. (1984). Biology, ideology, and reification of developmental stages in the study of homosexual identities. *Journal of Homosexuality, 10,* 77-84.
Weinberg, T.S. (1986). Love relationships and drinking among gay men. *Journal of Drug Issues, 16*(4), 637-648.
Weinrich, J. D. (1977). Human reproductive strategy. *Dissertation Abstracts International, 37*(10), 5339-B. (University Microfilms No. 77-8348.)
Weinrich, J. D. (1978). Nonreproduction, homosexuality, transsexualism, and intelligence: I. A systematic literature search. *Journal of Homosexuality, 3,* 275-289.
Weinrich, J. D. (1980a). Homosexual behavior in animals: A new review of observations from the wild, and their relationship to human homosexuality. In R. Forleo & W. Pasini (Eds.), *Medical sexology: The Third International Congress* (pp. 288-295). Littleton, MA: PSG Publishing.
Weinrich, J. D. (1980b). On a relationship between homosexuality and I.Q. test scores: A review and some hypotheses. In R. Forleo & W. Pasini (Eds.), *Medical Sexology: The Third International Congress* (pp. 312-317). Littleton, MA: PSG Publishing.
Weinrich, J. D. (1987a). A new sociobiological theory of homosexuality applicable to societies with universal marriage. *Ethology and Sociobiology, 8,* 37-47.
Weinrich, J. D. (1987b). *Sexual landscapes: Why we are what we are, why we love whom we love.* New York: Scribners.
Weinrich, J. D. (1988a). Sex survey. *Science, 242,* 16.
Weinrich, J. D. (1988b). The periodic-table model of the gender transpositions: Part II. Limerent and lusty sexual attractions and the nature of bisexuality. *Journal of Sex Research, 24,* 113-129.
Weinrich, J. D. (1989, August). *AIDS, sexual politics, and the sexual landscape.* Paper presented at the American Psychological Association Convention, New Orleans.
Welch, B. L. (1990, January 26). Statement of Homosexuality. [Available from American Psychological Association, 1200 17th Street, NW, Washington, DC 20036.]
Wells, J. W., & Kline, W. B. (1987). Self-disclosure of homosexual orientation. *Journal of Social Psychology, 127*(2), 191-197.
Wheeler, W. M. (1949). An analysis of Rorschach indices of male homosexuality. *Journal of Projective Techniques, 13,* 97-126.
Whitaker, L., Jr. (1961). The use of an extended Draw-A-Person Test to identify homosexual and effeminate men. *Journal of Consulting Psychology, 25,* 482-485.
Whitam, F. L. (1977a). The homosexual role: A reconsideration. *Journal of Sex Research, 13,* 1-11.
Whitam, F. L. (1977b). Childhood indicators of male homosexuality. *Archives of Sexual Behavior, 6,* 89-96.

Whitam, F. L. (1980). The prehomosexual male child in three societies: The United States, Guatemala, Brazil. *Archives of Sexual Behavior, 9*, 87-99.

Whitam, F. L. (1983). Culturally invariable properties of male homosexuality: Tentative conclusions from cross-cultural research. *Archives of Sexual Behavior, 12*, 207-226.

Whitam, F. L., & Zent, M. (1984). A cross-cultural assessment of early cross-gender behavior and familial factors in male homosexuality. *Archives of Sexual Behavior, 13*, 427-439.

Wikan, U. (1982). *Behind the veil in Arabia: Women in Oman*. Baltimore, MD: Johns Hopkins University Press.

Williams, S. G. (1981). Male homosexual responses to MMPI combined subscales Mf1 and Mf2. *Psychological Reports, 49*, 606.

Williams, W. L. (1986). *The spirit and the flesh: Sexual diversity in American Indian culture.* Boston: Beacon.

Williams, W. L. (in press). What we can learn from homosexual patterns in the third world: A review essay on gay theory, community building, and homophobia. *Journal of Homosexuality.*

Wilson, E. O. (1975a). *Sociobiology: The new synthesis.* Cambridge, MA: Harvard University Press.

Wilson, E. O. (1975b, October 12). Human decency is animal. *New York Times Magazine,* pp. 38-50.

Wilson, E. O. (1978). *On human nature.* Cambridge, MA: Harvard University Press.

Wilson, M. L., & Green, R. L. (1971). Personality characteristics of female homosexuals. *Psychological Reports, 28*, 407-412.

Winkelsteen, W., Lyman, D. M., Padian, W., Grant, R., Sammel, M., Wiley, J. A., Anderson, R. E., Long, W., Riggs, J., & Levy, J. A. (1989). Sexual practices and risk of infection by the human immunodeficiency virus. *Journal of the American Medical Association, 257*, 321-325.

Wolf, D. G. (1979). *The lesbian community.* Berkeley: University of California Press.

Wolff, C. (1986). *Magnus Hirschfield: A portrait of a pioneer in sexology.* New York: Quartet Books.

Woodard, C. (1990, January 24). Myers tells critics: Just give me time. *Newsday,* City Edition, p. 6.

Wooden, W. S., Kawasaki, H., & Mayeda, R. (1983). Lifestyles and identity maintenance among gay Japanese-American males. *Alternative Lifestyles, 5*, 236-243.

Woodman, N. J., & Lenna, H. R. (1982). *Counseling with gay men and women.* San Francisco: Jossey-Bass.

World Health Organization. (1989). Consensus statement form consultation on partner notification for preventing HIV transmission. Geneva: Author.

Wyers, N. L. (1987). Homosexuality in the family: Lesbian and gay spouses. *Social Work, 32*(2), 143-148.

Wykoff, R. F., Heath, C. W., Jr., Hollis, S. L., Leonard, S. T., Quiller, C. B., Jones, J. L., Artzrouni, M., and Parker, R. L. (1988). Contact tracing to identify human immunodeficiency virus in a rural community. *Journal of the American Medical Association, 259*(24), 3563-3566.

Yellen, J. E. (1990, April). The transformation of the Kalahari !Kung. *Scientific American,* pp. 96-105.

Zucker, K. J. (1985). Cross-gender identified children. In B. W. Steiner (ed.), *Gender dysphoria: Development, research, management* (pp. 75-147). New York: Plenum.

Zucker, R. A., & Manosevitz, M. (1966). MMPI patterns of overt male homosexuals: Reinterpretation and comment on Dean and Richardson's study. *Journal of Consulting Psychology, 30*, 555-557.

Zuger, B. (1966). Effeminate behavior present in boys from early childhood: I. The clinical syndrome and follow-up studies. *Journal of Pediatrics, 69,* 1098-1107.

Zuger, B. (1978a). A neglected source-book on homosexuality. *British Journal of Psychiatry, 133,* 87-88.

Zuger, B. (1978b). Effeminate behavior present in boys from childhood: Ten additional years of followup. *Comprehensive Psychiatry, 19,* 363-369.

Zuger, B. (1984). Early effeminate behavior in boys: Outcome and significance for homosexuality. *Journal of Nervous and Mental Disease, 172,* 90-97.

Zuger, B. (1988). Is early effeminate behavior in boys early homosexuality? *Comprehensive Psychiatry, 29,* 509-519.

Index

Abstinence and monogamy, 233
Adaptation School of Psychoanalysis, 104
Adjective check lists, 37, 130
Adolescence, 161
  psychological problems during, 133
Adoption and Foster Parent Regulations, 211
Adult sex hormones, 41-42
Affectional orientation, 7
AIDS, viii, ix, 25, 29, 215-229, 247
  behavior change in, 237-238
  prevention, 230-243
  risk reduction via behavior changes, 237-240
Alcohol abuse, 132-134, 136, 161
Alcohol and other drug use, role in HIV infection, 236, 238
Altruism, reproductive, 26-30
American Indian tribes, 49-51
American Psychiatric Association, 101-102, 105, 138
American Psychological Association, 138, 149, 150, 160
American Public Health Association, 217-218
Ancient Greece, 25, 46-48, 52-54
Androgyny, 38, 42
Anti-gay prejudice, 60, 166
  AIDS and, 75-76
  and attitude change, 73
  and authoritarianism, 10
  and contact with gay men and lesbians, 65
  and racism, 66
  and religion, 65-66
  correlates, 65
  effects on gay people, 73-75
  effects on heterosexuals, 75
  psychological motivations for, 72-73
  sex differences in heterosexuals attitudes, 65
Artificial insemination, 93
Association for Advancement of Behavior Therapy, 138, 144
Atypical gender behavior, 32-34

Balanced polymorphism, 23-26
Base rates, 119
Behavior change, 217-218
Behavioral perspective, in HIV infection prevention, 231-232
Berdache, 49-51
Bem Sex Role Inventory, 38-40
Biologically based treatment, xi
Biological sex, 1
Biology, ix, 245
Biomedical research and ethical problems, 110-111
Biomedical treatments of homosexuality, 106-111
Bisexuality, 2, 17-18, 25-26, 46, 104
Blood supply, 223
Body build, 40-41
Borderline conditions in gay people, 113
Boutilier v. Immigration and Naturalization Service, 88
Bowers v. Hardwick, 64, 83, 248
Braschi v. State Associates Co., 93

California Psychological Inventory (CPI), 37-39, 129-130
Castration, to cure homosexuality, 107
Center for Disease Control, 216, 218, 221-222, 223
Child molestation, stereotypes about, 70-72
Children
  of gay fathers, 206-207
  of lesbian mothers, 207-208
Choice, in sexual orientation, 55-56
Civil rights for gay people, heterosexuals attitudes toward, 60-62
Clinician bias, 143
"Coercive liberalism," 146
Cognitive abilities, 41, 246
Coming out, 1, 64, 74-76, 78, 153, 164-170

Commitment, 188-182
Committee on Lesbian and Gay Concerns, viii
Comparative studies, 36-40
Condom usage, 235-236
Confidentiality, 217, 220, 222, 228-229
Construct validity, 10
Contact tracing, 215-217, 220-221, 228-229
Control group, 120, 123
Conversion treatments, to change sexual orientation, xii, 137-148
Couple and family rights, 212-213
Couples, gay male and lesbian, xii, 177-196, 245, 247
Cross-cultural research, xi, 2, 30, 44-59, 246
Custody, 91-93

Decriminalizing adult private consensual sex, 82
Demographic variables, 120, 123
Density-dependent population control, 23
Depression, measures of, 130-131
Developmental models, 162
Diagnosis, xi, 115
  as social control, 102-103
Discrimination, 60, 64-65, 217, 220
  based on fear of AIDS and molestation, 212
Doe v. Commonwealth's Attorney, 82-83
Dominance, 187-191
Drapetomania, 70
DSM-III, 102, 138
DSM-IIIR, 138, 143

Economic discrimination, 93
Edwards Personal Preference Schedule (EPPS), 129-130
Ego-dystonic homosexuality 138, 149, 160
Eisenstadt v. Baird, 82
Empathetic intuneness, consistent, 172
Employment
  health benefits, 93
  laws, 88-90
Employment-at-Will Doctrine, 89
Endocrine abnormalities and homosexuality, 109
Essentialism, 10
Ethics, ix, xi-xii, 146-148
  of conversion therapy, 150
Ethnocentrism, 44, 45-46

Evolutionary biology, 20
Executive orders, 90
"Ex-gay" movement, 156-159
EXIT of Melodyland, 156, 158
Exodus International, 156, 159
External stress, 119
  on gay people, 112
Evolutionary, xi
  purpose, 22-30
  theory, 13
Eysenck Personality Inventory (EPI), 121,129

Family patterns/homosexuality, 124-127
Federal employees, 90
Feminine boys, 34
Feminine Gender Identity Scale, 37
Femininity, 32-43
Free speech rights of gay college students, 87-88

Gay family issues, 93-94
Gay Law Students Association v. Pacific Telephone and Telegraph, 64
Gay or lesbian bar samples, 122
Gay people, minority group status, 63-65
Gender identity, 1
  and sexual orientation development in children, 207-208
Gender
  mixing, 50
  role, 34
  role behaviors in children, 208
Goodenough Draw-a-Person (DAP), 37
Grandiose-exhibitionistic sector, 171-172, 174
Griswold v. Connecticut, 82
Guilford-Zimmerman Temperament Survey, 37-38

Hate Crimes Statistics Act, 63
Health behavior change, xii, 238-239
Health promotion and disease prevention, 218-219
Heterosexism, 62. *See also* Anti-gay prejudice
Heterosexist bias, ix-x
Heterosexual couples, 245
Heterozygote advantage, 24, 26

Hijra, 51-52
HIV, 215-219, 220-226, 228-229
counseling and testing, 219, 222-224, 229
infection prevention, xii, 215-229, 232-237
infection prevention goals, 231
HIV transmission, 247
through intercourse, 234, 235
eroticizing safe sex, 235-237
fellatio, 233-235
Homophobia, x, 62, 112. *See also* Anti-gay prejucice
Homosexual behavior in animals, 14-19
in captivity, 15
definitions of "natural," 15
dominance, 15-16
pair bonds, 16-17
Homosexuality, attitudes toward, public opinion polls, 60-62
as inadequate masculinity, 107
mental status of, 113-114
phobic theory of, 104, 106
Homosexuality, in other cultures, 47-52
in prison, 16, 121-122
Homosexuality, as a disease, 104-105, 115
removal of, 105-106
Homosexuality, treatments for, aversive conditioning, 152-153
aversion therapy, 142, 146
behavioral methods, 152
covert sensitization, 152
fantasy modification, 152
group therapy, 151-152
"Playboy therapy," 142
psychoanalytic methods, 150-151
Homosexuals Anonymous, 156-157
Hormones, xi, 41, 246
imbalance, 21
Human rights, 215, 219, 221, 227

Idealizing sector, 171-172, 174
Identity, development, xii, 161, 166, 245
formation, 113
gay and lesbian, 161-176, 246
Illness model of homosexuality, xi, 119, 163
Immigration, 88
Immigration Act of 1924, 102-103
Immutability of sexual orientation, 84
Incidence of homosexuality, 3-5, 18
Inclusive fitness, 28
Interactionist view, 10, 55
Internalized homophobia, 113, 166
Intravenous drug users, 222, 224-225, 226, 227-228, 229
IQ tests, 41
Islam, 51

Just cause, 89

Kathoey, 49
Kin selection, 23
Kinsey heterosexual homosexual continuum, 7, 123

Legal status, xi, 112, 81-100
Liberation of Jesus Christ (conversion program), 157-158
Lifestyles, 1-2
Lesbian mothers
attitudes and behavior, 203-204
coping styles and general functioning, 204-205
literature reviews, 205-206
Longitudinal studies, 168-169
Love in Action (conversion program), 156

Make-A-Picture Story Test (MAPSI), 131
Masculinity, 32-43
Masculinity-Femininity Scale (MF), 36-37, 127
Maternal stress and homosexuality, 108
Matlovich, L., 85-86
Mental health services, utilization of 161
Mental illness, ix, 246
Metanioa Ministries, 157
Methodological problems, 117-120
Military, U.S., 85-87
Minnesota Multi-phasic Personality Inventory (MMPI), 37-39, 124-125, 127-129
Model penal code, 82
Moral values, x

Native Americans. *See* American Indian Tribes

Naturalistic fallacy, 31
Nature, 13-31, 246
Normal range differences, 118

Objective observations, 5
Oedipus complex, and homosexuality, 113
  as cause of homosexuality, 104

Palmore v. Sudoti, 92
Parenting, gay and lesbian, ix, xii, 91, 197-214, 247
Parent-offspring conflict, 29
Parental rights, 210-211
Partner notification, xii, 215-229, 247
Patient referral, 221-222, 223, 227
Pedophilia, 91
Peer relationships in children, 208-209
Pentagon, studies of gays in military, 87
Perinatal androgen and adult homosexuality, 108
Peripheral hormone treatment to cure homosexuality, 107
Personality development, 162
Physical characteristics, 246
Plethysmograph, 5-6
Political agendas, xi
Political control, 241-242
Politics, 215, 220
Prenatal hormone, 41-42, 246
  and homosexuality, 114
  treatment to cure homosexuality, 108-111
Prisoner sample, 121-122, 124, 125-126
Private employers, 89
Projective testing, 131
Proposition 102, 220-221
Prospective studies of sex dimorphic tests, 34-35
Provider referral, 226-227
Psychiatric diagnosis, 115
  as a political act, 116
  as punishment, 101-102
Psychoanalysis and homosexuality, 111, 113
Psychological adjustment, 163
Psychological disturbance, 117
Psychological testing, 127-132
Psychopathic personality, 88
Psychopathology, 131-133
Psychotherapy, 182
  gay and lesbian affirmative, xii, 112
Public health, xii, 88, 247
  departments, 230, 240-242
Public policy, ix, xiii
  and AIDS, xii, 230-243
  concerns, 210, 215, 228-229
  debates on homosexuality, vii-viii

Quest ministries, 157
Quethos, 50

Racial/ethnic minorities, xii, 3, 239-240, 245-246
  identities, 167-168
Rational nexus, 90
Reciprocal altruism, 29-30
Relapse, to unsafe behavior, 238
Relationships, 177-196
Religious concerns, x
Religious right wing, vii-viii
Representative sample, of homosexuals, 123
Reproduction, 20
Reproductive fitness, 22
Research
  on children of lesbian mothers and gay fathers, 206
  on lesbian mothers, 202-203
  on gay fathers, 199-200
  multidisciplinary, 245
Researcher bias, in psychoanalysis, 127
Retrospective distortion, 36
Retrospective studies, 35-36
Right of privacy, 82
Rorschach test, 128

Sampling, xi
  problems in, 120-127
Science, viii, ix, xiii, 244
Scientific discourse, xi
Scientific knowledge, x
Scientific paradigms, 143
Self-disclosure, risks of, 4
Self-esteem, 163, 240
  in children, 209
  loss of, 171
  measures of, 130-131

Self-psychology, xii, 170-176
Separation and Individuation, 209
Seventh-Day Adventist Church, 157
Sex differences, 189-191, 193-194
  between gay men and lesbians, 168
Sex-dimorphic characteristics, 34
Sex role socialization, 165
Sexism, x
Sexual addiction, 104
Sexual compulsion, 104
Sexual identity, 245
  core, 165
Sexual orientation, 1-2
  change of, 149-160, 247
  choice in, 8
  defining and measuring, 1-12, 246
  gene for, 24-25
  longitudinal stability of, 8
  nature and causes, ix, xi
  over the lifespan, 8
Sexual orientation grid, 8
Sexual preference, 1-2
Sexually transmitted disease, 216-218, 219, 221, 229
Sixteen Personality Factor Questionnaire (16PF), 121, 125-126, 129
Social exchange theory, 187-189
  roles, 183-185
  sex role, 1
  support, 185-186
Social constructionism 9, 44-47, 55
Social control, 115
Socialization, 21
Society for the Psychological Study of Social Issues (SPSSI), vii
Society for the Scientific Study of Lesbian and Gay Issues, viii
Sociobiology, 183
Statistical significance, 119
Stereotypes, 170-186, 247
  about lesbians and gay men, 69-72
  nature and effects of 162
Stigmatization, 211-212
Suicide, 161
  adolescent, 133-134
  attempts at, 132-133, 136
  and homosexuals, 103
Surgical techniques to cure homosexuality, 107
  hypothalamotomies, 107
Suspect classification, 84
Systematic desensitization, 142

Task Force on Sexual Orientation, vii
Teleology, 20
Tennessee Self Concept Scale (TSCS), 130
Thematic Apperception Test (TAT), 131
Title VII, 89
Traits, independent, 38
Transmuting internalization, 172
Transsexuals, 32
Treatment of homosexuality, efficacy of, 110-111
Twinship or alterego sector, 172, 174-175
United States Armed Services, 134-135. *See also* Military, U.S.

Variation, racial and ethnic, 167
  social-economic, 167
Victimization, traits due to 162
Violence, 247
  against gay people, 61, 75

Watkins v. United States, 86-87
Winke, 49-50

Xanith, 51

About the Authors

Pearl Beck, Ph.D., is a research associate at the Rutgers University Institute for Health, Health Care Policy, and Aging Research. She is currently codirecting an evaluation of New Jersey's Respite Care Program. Previously, she directed an AIDS prevention intervention and research program and the evaluation of New Jersey's HIV Contact Notification Program. She received her doctorate in social psychology from the Graduate Center of the City University of New York. For the past 15 years, she has conducted research on a broad spectrum of public policy issues including AIDS, long-term care, and homelessness. Her major publications are in the area of aging and long-term care.

Frederick W. Bozett, RN, DNS, was a professor in the graduate program, College of Nursing, University of Oklahoma. He was editor of *Gay and Lesbian Parents* (1987), coeditor of *Dimensions of Fatherhood* (Sage, 1985), and editor of *Homosexuality and the Family* (1989). He published extensively in the area of fatherhood and gay fathers and was undertaking a longitudinal study of custodial gay father families, as well as studies of gay father-child relationships and gay grandfathers, at the time of his death in the fall of 1991.

Stephen Crystal is Associate Professor of Social Work and Sociology, and Chair of the Division on Aging at the Institute for Health, Health Care Policy, and Aging Research at Rutgers University. He is the principal investigator of several studies relating to health services utilization and health status of persons with HIV infection. He has recently received an award from the National Center for Health Services Research to conduct a three-year survey of psychosocial, health care, and behavioral aspects of the illness. Previously, he served as chief of the Division of Health Care Sciences and was an assistant professor of community and family medicine at the University of California in San Diego. He also served as director of the Bureau of Management Systems, Planning, Research, and Evaluation for the City of New York Human Resources Administration. He received a Ph.D. in sociology from Harvard University in 1981.

Gerald C. Davison is Professor of Psychology at the University of Southern California. He joined USC's psychology faculty in 1979 as director of Clinical Training and from 1984 to 1990 served as department chair. He is a Fellow of the American Psychological Association and of the American Psychological Society, and from 1973 to 1974 served as President of the Association for Advancement of Behavior Therapy. In 1988 he earned an award from the Committee on Lesbian and Gay Concerns of APA's Board of Social and Ethical Responsibility. His books include *Abnormal Psychology,* 5th ed. (1990), *Case Studies in Abnormal Psychology,* 3rd ed. (1991), *Clinical Behavior Therapy* (1976), and *Readings in Abnormal Psychology* (1989).

Edmund F. Dejowski, J.D., Ph.D., is a senior research associate with the Institute for Health, Health Care Policy, and Aging Research at Rutgers University. In that capacity he serves as co-investigator and director of a study of respite care, and is an investigator in several AIDS studies. Previously, he served at the Institute as a postdoctoral trainee through the Rutgers-Princeton Program in Mental Health Research. Before coming to the Institute, he was a research scientist for the City of New York Human Resources Administration. In that capacity, he directed and was co-investigator for a four-year multistate investigation of adult protective services. He has also served as a clinical and community psychologist in New Jersey and in Maine.

Lidia Dengelegi has an M.A. in psychology from New York University and a Ph.D. in social psychology from Temple University. She has worked at Beth Israel Medical Center in New York overseeing AIDS clinical trials and has conducted an assessment of the AIDS-related knowledge, attitudes, and behaviors of intravenous drug users in New York City. Presently she is a research associate at the Institute for Health, Health Care Policy, and Aging at Rutgers University, where she was the project director for the evaluation of New Jersey's HIV Notification Assistance Program.

John C. Gonsiorek received his Ph.D. in clinical psychology in 1978 from the University of Minnesota. He is a Diplomate in Clinical Psychology of the American Board of Professional Psychology. He is currently Associate Director of Training at the Minnesota School of Professional Psychology and also has a private practice in Minneapolis. He has published extensively in the areas of psychotherapy with gay and lesbian individuals, professional ethics and boundaries, quality assurance in mental health, and other areas.

G. Dorsey Green, Ph.D., is a psychologist in private practice in Seattle, Washington. She is the coauthor of *Lesbian Couples* (1988) and has written about and worked with lesbian and gay couples and parents over the last ten years. She also teaches and consults about gay and lesbian issues. She and four other Seattle psychologists are working on a research project that looks at social support systems of single, coupled, and parenting lesbians. She is currently involved in developing a community of 20 households to live on shared land near Seattle. The group is following the model of similar communities in Denmark and hopes to move to the new homes in early 1992.

Douglas C. Haldeman, Ph.D., is a counseling psychologist in private practice in Seattle, Washington. He is active in educating other mental health professionals and the general public on issues relevant to sexual minorities, and serves on the assistant clinical faculty of the University of Washington. His special area of interest and expertise is the ethical and psychological implications of conversion therapy for gay men and lesbians.

Gregory M. Herek, Ph.D., is an associate research psychologist at the University of California at Davis. A noted authority on the social psychology of prejudice and violence against lesbians and gay men, he has published numerous scholarly articles on these and related topics. He is past chairperson of the Committee on Lesbian and Gay Concerns of the American Psychological Association (APA), and a member of the APA Task Force on AIDS. His advocacy work has included testifying on behalf of the APA for congressional hearings on antigay violence, public speaking about prejudice against lesbians and gay men, and numerous appearances on national and local media.

John A.W. Kirsch, Ph.D., is Professor of Zoology and Director of the University of Wisconsin Zoological Museum in Madison, where he teaches a gay studies course in addition to introductory biology, taxonomy, and several graduate seminars. His chief interest is in the phylogeny of marsupials, another group of misunderstood mammals, using biochemical techniques to establish relationships—work that involves him in frequent trips to the southern hemisphere. He has published nearly 100 papers, book chapters, and reviews, including several on the biology of homosexuality.

Letitia Anne Peplau is Professor of Social Psychology and Acting Co-Director of the Center for the Study of Women at the University of California, Los Angeles. She received her doctorate in social psychology from Harvard University in 1973. Her research interests include gender, close relationships (both homosexual and heterosexual), and loneliness.

She has published, with others, numerous journal articles and several books including *Social Psychology,* 7th Ed., *Close Relationships,* and *Loneliness: A Sourcebook of Current Theory, Research, and Therapy.* She is currently a member of the Task Force on Bias in Psychotherapy with Lesbians and Gay Men of the Committee on Lesbian and Gay Concerns of the American Psychological Association.

Richard C. Pillard, M.D., is Professor of Psychiatry at Boston University School of Medicine, Medical Director of the Solomon Carter Fuller Mental Health Center, and cofounder of Boston's Homophile Community Health Service. He has done research into the psychopharmacology of psychoactive drugs, and on whether homosexuality runs in families. He was the first publicly identified gay psychiatrist in the United States.

Rhonda R. Rivera is Professor of Law, The Ohio State University College of Law. She received an M.P.A. in 1960 from Syracuse University and a J.D. from Wayne State University College of Law. She wrote the germinal work on sexual orientation law in 1979, *Our straight-laced judges: The legal position of homosexual persons in the United States,* (30 *Hastings Law Journal* 799). In the ten years following, she has updated that work with three more major law review articles. She is the cofounder of the Gay/Lesbian Legal Issues Section of the American Association of Law Schools and a practicing attorney.

James R. Rudolph received his Ph.D. in counseling psychology from Lehigh University in 1988. He is currently Clinical Director at Carver County Mental Health Center, Waconia, Minnesota. He is also an adjunct assistant professor of psychology at St. Mary's College Graduate Center in Minneapolis, where he teaches coursework on psychological assessment. He has written on counselors' attitudes toward homosexuality and is planning future writing projects integrating self-psychology and affirmative gay/lesbian psychotherapy.

Michael Shernoff, CSW, ACSW, is founder and codirector of Chelsea Psychotherapy Associates in Manhattan. He also serves as adjunct faculty to the Department of Education at Gay Men's Health Crisis. He is former cochairperson of the AIDS Task Force of the Society for the Scientific Study of Sex.

Charles Silverstein is a psychologist in private practice in New York City. He was the founding editor of the *Journal of Homosexuality* and the founding director of both Identity House and the Institute for Human Identity. He is editor of *Gays, Lesbians and Their Therapists: Studies in*

Psychotherapy. His previous published works include *A Family Matter: A Parents' Guide to Homosexuality, Man to Man: Gay Couples in America,* and, with Edmund White, *The Joy of Gay Sex.* He is a Fellow of the American Psychological Association and a consultant to the New York University AIDS project.

James D. Weinrich, Ph.D., is Assistant Research Psychobiologist in the Department of Psychiatry at the University of California, San Diego, where he is Center Manager of the HIV Neurobehavioral Research Center. Author of *Sexual Landscapes: Why We Are What We Are, Why We Love Whom We Love,* he has written and lectured extensively on matters of sex, gender, and evolutionary biology. In 1987 he and Richard C. Pillard shared an award from the Society for the Scientific Study of Sex for the best paper published that year in the *Journal of Sex Research.*

Walter L. Williams, Ph.D., is Associate Professor of Anthropology and the Study of Women and Men in Society at the University of Southern California. He has published books about interethnic relations, most notably *The Spirit and the Flesh: Sexual Diversity in American Indian Culture* (1986). In 1987-1988, he was a Fulbright Scholar in Indonesia, which resulted in his most recent book, *Javanese Lives: Women and Men in Modern Indonesian Society* (1991). He is Director of Postgraduate Studies at the Institute for the Study of Human Resources in Los Angeles.

4725